PROCESS ALGEBRA

Cambridge Tracts in Theoretical Computer Science

Managing Editor Professor C.J. van Rijsbergen, Department of Computing Science, University of Glasgow

Editorial Board

S. Abramsky, Department of Computing Science, Imperial College of Science and Technology
P.H. Aczel, Department of Computer Science, University of Manchester
J.W. de Bakker, Centrum voor Wiskunde en Informatica, Amsterdam
J.A. Goguen, Programming Research Group, University of Oxford
J.V. Tucker, Department of Mathematics and Computer Science, University College of Swansea

Titles in the series

1. G. Chaitin *Algorithmic Information Theory*
2. L.C. Paulson *Logic and Computation*
3. M. Spivey *Understanding Z*
4. G. Revesz *Lambda Calculus, Combinators and Logic Programming*
5. S. Vickers *Topology via Logic*
6. A. Ramsay *Formal Methods in Artificial Intelligence*
7. J-Y. Girard, Y. Lafont & P. Taylor *Proofs and Types*
8. J. Clifford *Formal Semantics & Pragmatics for Natural Language Querying*
9. M. Winslett *Updating Logical Databases*
10. K. McEvoy & J.V. Tucker (eds) *Theoretical Foundations of VLSI Design*
12. G. Brewka *Nonmonotonic Reasoning*
13. G. Smolka *Logic Programming over Polymorphically Order-Sorted Types*
15. S. Das Gupta *Design Theory and Computer Science*
17. J.C.M. Baeten (ed) *Applications of Process Algebra*

PROCESS ALGEBRA

J.C.M. Baeten and W.P. Weijland
Centre for Mathematics and Computer Science, Amsterdam

The right of the University of Cambridge to print and sell all manner of books was granted by Henry VIII in 1534. The University has printed and published continuously since 1584.

CAMBRIDGE UNIVERSITY PRESS

Cambridge

New York Port Chester Melbourne Sydney

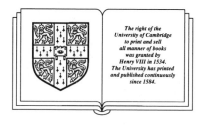

Published by the Press Syndicate of the University of Cambridge
The Pitt Building, Trumpington Street, Cambridge CB2 1RP
40 West 20th Street, New York, NY 10011, USA
10 Stamford Road, Oakleigh, Melbourne 3166, Australia

First published 1990

Printed in Great Britain at the University Press, Cambridge

Library of Congress cataloguing in publication data available

British Library cataloguing in publication data available

ISBN 0 521 40043 0

Preface

This book was written in the years 1989 and 1990 at the Centre for Mathematics and Computer Science in Amsterdam. Much of the material comes from a Dutch book (reference BAETEN [1986]), that was used in university courses at the University of Amsterdam and the University of Utrecht.

For the first time, this book brings together a lot of work in the area of algebraic process theory, as this has been developed since 1982 by a group of people in Amsterdam and Utrecht under the guidance of Jan Bergstra. Most of the research that found its way into this book was funded by European programmes, notably METEOR (ESPRIT I), SPECS (RACE), CONCUR (ESPRIT II BRA).

Many people contributed in one way or another to this book. We want to mention (in alphabetical order) Gert-Jan Akkerman, Jan Bergstra, Wiet Bouma, Jeroen Bruijning, Nicolien Drost, Rob van Glabbeek, Jan Friso Groote, Jan Willem Klop, Karst Koymans, Evangelos Kranakis, Sjouke Mauw, Kees Middelburg, Hans Mulder, Eric Nieuwland, Ernst-Rüdiger Olderog, Alban Ponse, Scott Smolka, Frits Vaandrager, Gert Veltink, Jos Vrancken, Han Zuidweg. Thanks are due to the head of the Department of Software Technology of the Centre for Mathematics and Computer Science, Jaco de Bakker, who created an excellent working atmosphere.

The first author wants to dedicate this book to his wife Jeanne, who was very important in its writing, but cannot see its completion.

Amsterdam, July 1990.

Contents

1. Preliminaries
   - 1.1 Introduction 1
   - 1.2 Terms and equations 3
   - 1.3 Algebras 6
   - 1.4 Term rewriting systems 10

2. Basic process algebra
   - 2.1 The basic system 15
   - 2.2 Deadlock and termination 21
   - 2.3 Recursion 25
   - 2.4 Projection and bounded non-determinism 29
   - 2.5 The term model 37
   - 2.6 Projective limit model 42
   - 2.7 Process graphs 45
   - 2.8 Regular processes 60
   - 2.9 Stack 62

3. Concurrent processes
   - 3.1 Interleaving 67
   - 3.2 Some theorems on PA 70
   - 3.3 Merge and termination 75
   - 3.4 Models 79
   - 3.5 Bag 83
   - 3.6 Renaming 87

4. Communication
   - 4.1 Communication function 91
   - 4.2 ACP 93
   - 4.3 Some theorems on ACP 96

4.4 Termination 100
4.5 Models 102
4.6 Examples 105
4.7 Alternating Bit Protocol (specification) 108
4.8 Queue 114

5. Abstraction
5.1 Abstraction and silent step 119
5.2 ACP^{τ} 122
5.3 Termination 126
5.4 Models 129
5.5 Recursion 145
5.6 Divergence and fairness 151
5.7 Alternating Bit Protocol (verification) 160
5.8 Observation equivalence 162

6. Features
6.1 Priorities and interrupts 169
6.2 Alphabets and conditional axioms 174
6.3 Localization, traces and restriction 179
6.4 State operator 185
6.5 Asynchronous communication 190
6.6 Asymmetric communication 193
6.7 Process creation 197
6.8 Synchronous cooperation 199
6.9 Signals and observation 205

7. Semantics
7.1 Bisimulation and trace semantics 209
7.2 Failure and ready semantics 212
7.3 Failure trace and ready trace semantics 216

8. Sources and related work
8.1 Historical remarks 221
8.2 CCS 223
8.3 CSP 224

Bibliography 227

Glossary 235

Index of names 239

Index of symbols and notation 243

Chapter 1

Preliminaries

1.1 INTRODUCTION

This book provides a systematic introduction to process algebra, suitable for teaching purposes. By the term *process algebra* we mean the study of concurrent communicating processes in an algebraic framework, following the approach of J.A. Bergstra and J.W. Klop (see section 8.1). In the present book we treat concurrency theory (the theory of concurrent communicating processes) in an *axiomatic* way, just as for instance the study of mathematical objects as groups or fields starts with an axiomatization of the intended objects. This axiomatic method is algebraic in the sense that we consider structures (also called "process algebras") as models of some set of (mostly) equational axioms. These structures are equipped with several operators, and so we use the term *algebra* in the sense of model theory. R. Milner, with his Calculus of Communicating Systems (CCS), is generally considered to be the initiator of the field of process algebra. CCS forms the basis for most of the axiom systems presented below.

There is ample motivation for such an axiomatic-algebraic approach to concurrency theory. The main reason is that there is not one definitive notion of *process*. There is a staggering amount of properties which one may or may not attribute to processes, there are dozens of views (*semantics*) which one may have on processes, and there are infinitely many models of processes. So an attempt to organize this field of process theories leads very naturally and almost unavoidably to an axiomatic methodology. A curious consequence is that one has to answer the question "What is a process?" with the seemingly circular answer "A process is something that obeys a certain set of axioms ... for processes". The axiomatic method has proven effective in mathematics and mathematical logic. In our opinion it has its merits in computer science as well, if only for its organizing and unifying power.

Next to the organizing role of this set-up with axiom systems, their models and the study of their relations, we have the obvious *computational* aspect. Even more than in mathematics and mathematical logic, in computer science it is *algebra* that counts. For instance, in a system verification the use of transition diagrams may be very illuminating. For larger systems, however, it may be desirable to have a formalized mathematical language at our disposal in which specifications, computations and proofs can be given in what is in principle a linear notation. Only then can we hope to succeed in attempts to mechanize formal dealings with the objects of interest. In our case the mathematical language is algebraic, with basic constants, operators to construct larger processes, and equations defining the nature of the processes under consideration. (The format of pure equations will not be enough, though. On occasion, we will use conditional equations and some infinitary proof rules.) To be specific: we will always insist on the use of congruences, rather than mere equivalences in the construction of process algebras, in order to preserve the purely algebraic format.

A further advantage of the use of the axiomatic-algebraic method is that the entire apparatus of mathematical logic and the theory of abstract data types is at our service. For instance, one can study extensions of axiom systems that are homomorphisms of the corresponding process algebras, and one can formulate exact statements as to the relative expressibility of some process operators (definability results).

Of course, the present axiomatizations for concurrency theory do not cover the entire spectrum of interest. Several aspects of processes are as yet not well treated in the algebraic framework. The most notable examples concern the real-time behaviour of processes, and what is called *true concurrency* (non-interleaving semantics). Algebraic theories for these aspects are under development at the moment, however.

In our view, process algebra can be seen as a worthy descendant of "classical" automata theory as it originated three or four decades ago. The crucial difference is that nowadays one is interested not merely in the execution traces (or language) of one automaton, but in the behaviour of systems of communicating automata. As Milner and also Hoare, in his Communicating Sequential Processes (CSP), have discovered, it is no longer sufficient to abstract the behaviour of a process to a language of execution traces. Instead, one has to work with more discriminating process semantics, in which also the timing of choices of a system component is taken into account. Mathematically, this difference is very sharply expressed in the equation $x \cdot (y + z) = x \cdot y + x \cdot z$, where + denotes choice and $\cdot$ is sequential composition; x,y,z are processes. If one is interested in languages of execution traces (trace semantics), this equation holds, but in process algebra it will in general not hold. Nevertheless, process algebra retains the option of adding this equation and studying its effect. In fact, one goal of process algebra is to form a uniform framework in which several different process semantics can be compared and related (see chapter 7). One can call this *comparative concurrency semantics.*

We bring structure in our theory of process algebra by *modularization,* i.e. we start from a minimal theory (containing only the operators $+,\cdot$), and then add new features one at a time. This allows us to study features in isolation, and to combine the modules of the theory in different ways.

The book contains enough material for a one-year graduate course for students of computer science or mathematics. Also, shorter courses can be given. A short course may for example consist of chapters 2,3,4, and optionally chapter 5 or chapter 7.

There are no specific prerequisites, but some exposure to mathematics, specifically algebra and logic, will come in handy.

Every section, except this one, will be concluded with a number of exercises, which the reader can use to check his understanding of the material. Also, some theory is treated in the exercises, but such theory will not be used later on, so that the exercises can be skipped without problems.

We conclude with a short overview of the contents. In the rest of this chapter, we give a review of the algebraic notions that we will use in the remaining chapters. In chapter 2 we discuss the basic theory, with alternative composition (non-deterministic choice) and sequential composition as operators. We formulate a few simple laws for these operators, and discuss subjects like recursion (processes specified by means of recursive equations). We also take a look at various models for the theory.

In chapter 3 we add parallel composition, and in chapter 4 communication. A large example of how to use the resulting theory in practical applications is a specification of the alternating bit protocol.

In chapter 5 we consider at length the difficult issue of abstraction. We look at notions like fairness, and verify the alternating bit protocol specified in chapter 4.

In chapter 6 we discuss some additional features and operators that can be used in certain applications. Chapter 7 considers different ways to give semantics for theories of concurrency, and chapter 8 looks at the relationship of the theory that is presented in this book with other concurrency theories, specifically CCS and CSP. The book concludes with a bibliography on concurrency.

1.2 TERMS AND EQUATIONS

1.2.1 DEFINITION

We begin with the concept of an **equational specification** (Σ, E). Here, E is a set of **equations** of the form $t_1 = t_2$ where t_1 and t_2 are **terms** and Σ is the **signature**, i.e. the set of constant and function symbols that may appear in the specification. Σ also gives the **arity** of each function symbol (the number of arguments). The equations are often referred to as **axioms**.

1.2.2 EXAMPLE

The equational specification E_1 in table 1 describes the natural numbers, and has a constant symbol 0 and function symbols s (successor), a (addition) and m (multiplication).

We see that signature Σ_1 has a constant symbol 0, and function symbols s, a and m of arity 1, 2 and 2 respectively. A function symbol of arity 1 is called **unary**, and of arity 2 **binary**. A function symbol is sometimes called an **operator** symbol.

$a(x, 0) = x$
$a(x, s(y)) = s(a(x, y))$
$m(x, 0) = 0$
$m(x, s(y)) = a(m(x, y), x)$

TABLE 1.

1.2.3 NOTE

We talk about function *symbols* and constant *symbols*. We do this in order to distinguish between these purely formal objects and "real" functions (or operators) and constants in "real" algebras, which we will discuss later in 1.3. For now, we play a purely formal game with sets of symbols and equations that have no meaning as yet.

1.2.4 DEFINITION

The four axioms of E_1 also contain **variables** x,y. We will always assume that every signature Σ contains as many variables as we want. We denote variables by x, y, z, ..., possibly subscripted.

1.2.5 DEFINITION

Now we can define inductively the notion of a **term**:

i. variables x, y, ... are terms;
ii. constant symbols c, c', ... are terms;
iii. if F is a function symbol of arity n, and $t_1,...,t_n$ are terms, then $F(t_1,...,t_n)$ is a term.

A term that contains a variable is called an **open** term; a term without variables is called a **closed** or **ground** term.

1.2.6 DEFINITIONS

In an equation with open terms like

$$m(x, s(y)) = a(m(x, y), x) \quad (1)$$

we may substitute terms from the signature Σ for the variables. For example, we can substitute s(s(0)) for x and 0 for y to obtain

$$m(s(s(0)), s(0)) = p(m(s(s(0)), 0), s(s(0))) \quad (2).$$

The variables x and y are *bound* to the terms s(s(0)) and 0 respectively. If a variable x is bound to a term, this term must be substituted in every occurrence of x. So separate occurrences of a variable cannot be bound to different terms.

We have just shown that equation (2) can be **derived** from E_1; in symbols

$$E_1 \vdash m(s(s(0)), s(0)) = p(m(s(s(0)), 0), s(s(0))).$$

In general, derivability of an equation either means that it is *in* E, by the rule

i. $s=t \in E$ implies $E \vdash s=t$,

or that it can be obtained from E by means of the following three rules:

ii. **substitution**:
$E \vdash t(x_1,....,x_n) = s(x_1,....,x_n)$ implies $E \vdash t(t_1,....,t_n) = s(t_1,....,t_n)$;
iii. forming **contexts**:
$E \vdash t=s$ implies $E \vdash C[t] = C[s]$,
where C[ ] is a *context*, i.e. a term containing a hole [ ] as in m(x,[ ]). In other words: if $E \vdash t=s$, then in every occurrence of t as a *subterm* in a larger term it can be replaced by s. In this formulation the rule is often referred to as the *replacement* rule.
iv. the **equivalence** properties of =, namely:
symmetry: $E \vdash t=s$ implies $E \vdash s=t$;
reflexivity: $E \vdash t=t$;

transitivity: $E \vdash t=s$ and $E \vdash s=u$ imply $E \vdash t=u$.

1.2.7 EXAMPLE

We prove that $E_1 \vdash a(s(0), s(0)) = s(s(0))$:

1. $E_1 \vdash a(x, s(y)) = s(a(x, y))$ (the second equation of E_1)
2. $E_1 \vdash a(s(0), s(0)) = s(a(s(0), 0))$ (substitution in line 1)
3. $E_1 \vdash a(x, 0) = x$ (the first equation of E_1)
4. $E_1 \vdash a(s(0), 0) = s(0)$ (substitution in line 3)
5. $E_1 \vdash s(a(s(0), 0)) = s(s(0))$ (using the context $s([\ ])$ and line 4)
6. $E_1 \vdash a(s(0), s(0)) = s(s(0))$ (transitivity of =, from 2 and 6)

(In this way, we can make $1+1=2$ difficult!)

Usually, we are not so long-winded, and will write down the proof above as follows:

$E_1 \vdash p(s(0), s(0)) = s(p(s(0), 0))$ (from the second equation)

$= s(s(0))$ (from the first equation).

1.2.8 DEFINITION

Another important notion is that of the **occurrence** of a term s in a term t. For instance, the term $s(0)$ occurs twice in the term $m(s(s(0)), s(0))$. When s occurs in t, we call s a **subterm** of t.

We use the notation $\equiv$ for **syntactical identity**, i.e. $t \equiv s$ when t,s are identical terms. Note that $\equiv$ is different from =. For instance, we have

$$E_1 \vdash p(0, 0) = 0, \text{ but not } p(0, 0) \equiv 0.$$

1.2.9 EXAMPLE

We add to the signature Σ_1 of example 1.2.2 a binary function symbol e (exponentiation). We extend the set of equations E_1 to E_2 in table 2.

$a(x, 0) = x$
$a(x, s(y)) = s(a(x, y))$
$m(x, 0) = 0$
$m(x, s(y)) = a(m(x, y), x)$
$e(x, 0) = s(0)$
$e(x, s(y)) = m(e(x, y), x)$

TABLE 2.

Using a more suggestive notation, we can write down E_2 as in table 3.

$x + 0 = x$
$x + s(y) = s(x + y)$
$x \cdot 0 = 0$
$x \cdot s(y) = x \cdot y + x$
$x^0 = s(0)$
$x^{s(y)} = x^y \cdot x$

TABLE 3.

1.2.10 CONDITIONAL EQUATIONS

Sometimes we will use implication symbols $\Rightarrow$ in our specifications, interpreted as logical implication. An axiom of the form $G \Rightarrow s=t$ (sometimes written as $\frac{G}{s=t}$), with G a set of equations, is called a **conditional equation** (or **conditional axiom**). If G is an infinite set, we talk about an **infinitary conditional equation.** A specification in which a conditional equation occurs is called a **conditional specification**. What we call a conditional specification, is called a **theory** in mathematical logic. In the literature equational specifications (thus without the symbol $\Rightarrow$) are often called **algebraic** specifications.

In the case of conditional equations, we extend the definition of derivability in 1.2.6 with the following clause:

v. If the conditional equation $G \Rightarrow s=t$ is in E, and, for a certain substitution, all substitution instances of G are derivable from E, then the substitution instance of s=t is derivable from E (using the same substitution).

1.2.11 EXERCISES

1. Show that $E_1 \vdash m(s(s(0)),s(s(0))) = a(s(s(0)),s(s(0)))$.
2. Show by an inductive argument that for every closed term t over Σ_1, either $E_1 \vdash t=0$, or there is a term t' such that $E_1 \vdash t = s(t')$.

It follows that for every closed term t over Σ_1, there is a term t' of the form $s^n(0)$ $(n \geq 0)$ such that $E_1 \vdash t = t'$. (The terms $s^n(0)$ are defined inductively: $s^0(0) \equiv 0$, and $s^{n+1}(0) \equiv s(s^n(0))$.)

3. The same as exercise 2, but now for (Σ_2,E_2).
4. Prove that (a) $E_2 \vdash x + (y + 0) = (x + y) + 0$, and (b) if for a closed term t we have $E_2 \vdash x + (y + t) = (x + y) + t$, then also $E_2 \vdash x + (y + s(t)) = (x + y) + s(t)$.

Notice that this proves the **associativity** $x + (y + z) = (x + y) + z$ for all *closed* terms z (use exercise 3).

5. Prove that $E_2 \vdash x \cdot (y + z) = x \cdot y + x \cdot z$ for all *closed* terms x,y,z. Hint: write z in the form $s^n(0)$ and use exercise 4.
6. Let $E_3 = \{F(F(F(x)))=x, F(F(F(F(F(x)))))=x\}$. Prove that $E_3 \vdash F(x) = x$.

1.3 ALGEBRAS

1.3.1 SEMANTICS

Until now, we have only talked about **syntax**: sets of equations without meaning. Now we discuss the meaning or **semantics** of specifications (Σ,E). We talk about an **algebra** or **model**: an algebra $\mathbb{A}$ consists of a set of elements, A, together with constants in A and functions f from A^n to A (where n is the arity of f). The set A is called the **universe** or **domain** of $\mathbb{A}$.

1.3.2 EXAMPLES

$(\mathbf{N},+,\cdot,s,0)$ is the algebra of the natural numbers ($\mathbf{N} = \{0,1,2,...\}$) with functions +, ·, s and constant 0. $(\mathbf{Z},+,\cdot,s,0)$ is the algebra of the integers ($\mathbf{Z} = \{..-2,-1,0,1,2,...\}$) with the same signature, but with a larger domain. $(\mathbf{Z},+,\cdot,p,s,0)$ is the algebra of integers with the predecessor operator p, and has a richer signature than (**Z**,+,·,s,0), but apart from the presence of p they are the same.

Another example is the algebra of the Booleans $\mathbb{B}$=(**B**,xor,and,not,0), where **B** = {0,1}, 0 is a constant symbol ("falsity"), and and not are the usual conjunction and negation operators and xor is the "exclusive or" operator, defined by:

xor(x, y)=1 $\Leftrightarrow$ x=1 or y=1, but not: x=1 *and* y=1.

It is important to see that (by definition) the domain of an algebra is closed with respect to function applications. For instance, if we would want to define an algebra (**N**,+,·,p,s,0) of natural numbers with predecessor then we cannot just adopt the definition of p from the larger model (**Z**,+,·,p,s,0) since in the latter we have that p(0) = -1 which is not an element in **N**. Therefore, under the same interpretation of p the algebra (**N**,+,·,p,s,0) is not well-defined.

1.3.3 DEFINITION

If Σ is a signature, then we call the algebra $\mathbb{A}$ a **Σ-algebra** when there is a correspondence between the constant symbols in Σ and the "real" constants, and between the formal function symbols in Σ and the "real" functions with the same arity in $\mathbb{A}$. Such a correspondence is called an **interpretation.**

For example, if Σ_1={a,m,s,0} like in example 1.2.2, then we can make (**N**,+,·,s,0) into a Σ_1-algebra by means of the interpretation

a — +
m — ·
s — s
0 — 0.

Notice that there is also another interpretation, viz.

a — ·
m — +
s — s
0 — 0.

1.3.4 DEFINITION

If $\mathbb{A}$ is a Σ-algebra, then the equation $t_1 = t_2$ over (Σ,E) has a meaning in $\mathbb{A}$, when we interpret the constant and function symbols in t_1, t_2 by the corresponding constants and functions in $\mathbb{A}$. Further, the variables x,y,.... in t_1,t_2 are always **universally quantified**, e.g.

a(x, s(y)) = s(a(x, y)) (*)

means in (**N**,+,·,s,0) that:

for all n,m $\in$ **N** n + s(m) = s(n + m) (**).

If this second statement (**) is actually **true** in $\mathbb{A}$, we write

$\mathbb{A} \models$ a(x, s(y)) = s(a(x, y))

and say: $\mathbb{A}$ **satisfies** (*), or (*) **holds in** $\mathbb{A}$.

For a conditional equation, this works similarly; the equation

x + s(0) = y $\Rightarrow$ y = s(x)

means in (**N**,+,·,s,0) that:

for all n,m $\in$ **N**, if n + 1 = m, then m = s(n).

If the Σ-algebra $\mathbb{A}$ satisfies all equations $t_1 = t_2$ of E, we use the abbreviation

$$\mathbb{A} \models E.$$

If this is the case, we say that $\mathbb{A}$ is an **algebra for** E, or a **model of** E. We also say that E is a **sound axiomatization** of $\mathbb{A}$.

1.3.5 EXAMPLE

We have $(\mathbf{N},+,\cdot,s,0) \models E_1$ (E_1 as in 1.2.2) under the first interpretation of 1.3.3 (*not* under the other one). One might think that $\mathbb{N} = (\mathbf{N},+,\cdot,s,0)$ is the *only* model for E_1, but that is not the case: this algebra is not uniquely determined. Another algebra that satisfies E_1 is $\mathbb{B} = (\mathbf{B}$, xor, and, not, 0) from 1.3.2, under the interpretation

a — xor
m — and
s — not
0 — 0.

$\mathbb{B}$ satisfies even more equations than $(\mathbf{N},+,\cdot,s,0)$, because $\mathbb{B} \models s(s(x)) = x$, but $\mathbb{A} \not\models s(s(x)) = x$ ($\not\models$ means: does not satisfy). Thus, in general a specification has more than one model.

1.3.6 INITIAL ALGEBRA

Let us write $Alg(\Sigma,E)$ for the set of Σ-algebras $\mathbb{A}$ with $\mathbb{A} \models E$. Then there is one special algebra in $Alg(\Sigma,E)$, the so-called **initial algebra** of (Σ,E) – denoted by $I(\Sigma,E)$ – that satisfies *only* E and nothing more. To be more precise: the domain of $I(\Sigma,E)$ consists of equivalence classes of closed terms over (Σ,E), such that two closed terms s and t are equivalent iff $E \vdash s=t$.

As a consequence, $I(\Sigma,E)$ satisfies only those equations between closed terms that are formally derivable from E, and no others, which is expressed as follows:

For all closed terms t,s
$I(\Sigma,E) \models t=s \;\Leftrightarrow\; (\Sigma,E) \vdash t=s$

One can think of the initial algebra as the *set of closed terms* (over Σ) *modulo derivability*.

There may be several algebras in $Alg(\Sigma,E)$ that satisfy the property in the box (i.e. equations between closed terms hold iff they are derivable from the theory). Such an algebra is called **complete** for the theory (Σ,E), or the theory is called a **complete axiomatization** of the algebra.

1.3.7 EXAMPLE

Let (Σ_1,E_1) be as in 1.2.2 (table 1). Then, the initial algebra $I(\Sigma_1,E_1)$ has a domain with elements as in fig. 1.

Every element is an equivalence class of closed terms, and two terms belong to the same equivalence class exactly when E_1 proves that they are equal. In fact, $I(\Sigma_1,E_1)$ is "the same" as $(\mathbf{N},+,\cdot,s,0)$. To be exact: they are *isomorphic*, meaning that there exists a one-to-one correspondence between the domain elements of both models preserving the function equalities.

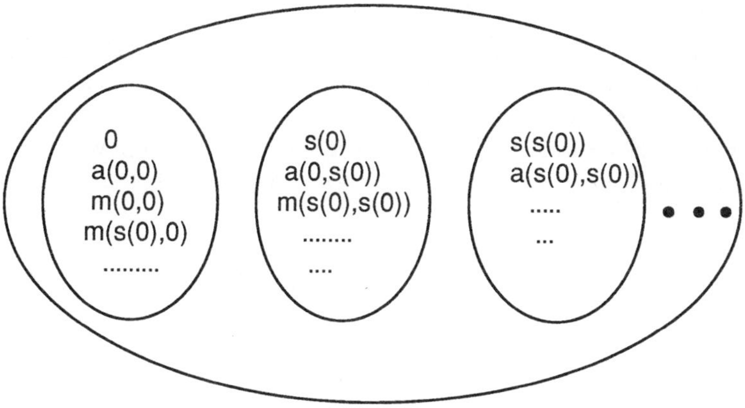

FIGURE 1.

1.3.8 DEFINITION

Suppose we want to alter a model by identifying elements from its domain by means of some equivalence relation (thus decreasing the number of its elements). Then we may wonder whether the resulting structure – with *classes* of elements in its domain, instead of the elements themselves – is again a model. As it turns out, this is not always the case: we need to make sure that in the new model the function values remain independent from the choice of the elements from its equivalence class.

Let $\mathbb{A}$ be a Σ-algebra, then a **congruence** on $\mathbb{A}$ is a binary relation R on the domain A of $\mathbb{A}$ that satisfies the following requirements:

i. R is an equivalence relation on A (i.e. reflexive, symmetric and transitive);

ii. for every n and every n-ary function f of Σ, we have for all $a_1,..,a_n$, $b_1,...b_n \in A$ the following implication:

$$R(a_1, b_1) \,\&\, ... \,\&\, R(a_n, b_n) \Rightarrow R(f(a_1,...,a_n), f(b_1,...,b_n)).$$

This second requirement states that R behaves correctly with respect to functions of Σ. The relation R can be seen as an intended equality relation between objects.

1.3.9 DEFINITION

If R is a congruence on $\mathbb{A}$, then we can obtain a new Σ-algebra by factoring R out on $\mathbb{A}$. The new algebra is called $\mathbb{A}/R$, pronounced $\mathbb{A}$ **modulo** R, and the elements of this algebra are the equivalence classes of R on $\mathbb{A}$. If we denote the equivalence class of a ($\{b \in A : R(a, b)\}$) by [a], then the interpretation of the constants and functions in $\mathbb{A}/R$ is as follows:

a is mapped to [a];

$$f([a_1], ..., [a_n]) = [f(a_1,...,a_n)].$$

In order to characterize the initial algebra exactly, we need the following important property of this factoring construction.

1.3.10 THEOREM

The intersection of a family of congruences is again a congruence.

PROOF: see exercises.

1.3.11 PROPOSITION

Now let a signature Σ be given which generates at least one closed term and let $I(\Sigma)$ denote the set of closed terms over Σ. In fact, $I(\Sigma)$ is a Σ-algebra itself, since the set of closed terms contains the constants and is closed under the functions. Now let a set of equations E be given, and define R_E to be the intersection of all congruence relations R on $I(\Sigma)$ with the property that $I(\Sigma)/R \models E$. Then $I(\Sigma)/R_E$ is exactly $I(\Sigma,E)$ (i.e. is isomorphic to it).

1.3.12 TERMINOLOGY

The initial algebra $I(\Sigma,E)$ is also called the **term model** of (Σ,E). For example, the term model of ({a,m,s,0}, E_1) (see 1.2.2) is isomorphic to the model of natural numbers (**N**,+,·,s,0).

In the literature, the expression **abstract data type** is used in many different ways. In one of them, $Alg(\Sigma,E)$ is an abstract data type, but in another it is $I(\Sigma,E)$.

1.3.13 NOTE

It is possible that there is an equation t = s between *open* terms t,s, that holds in an initial algebra $I(\Sigma,E)$, but that does not follow from E. An example of this is the equation x + y = y + x, which holds in (**N**,+,·,s,0), but is not derivable from E_1 (see exercises).

1.3.14 THEOREM

The following is the **completeness theorem** for conditional equational theories:

$$\text{for all open terms t,s:} \quad (\Sigma,E) \vdash t=s \iff \text{for all } \mathbb{A} \in Alg(\Sigma,E): \ \mathbb{A} \models t=s$$

A corollary of this theorem is that E_1 has a model in which x + y = y + x does not hold (see note 1.3.13).

1.3.15 EXERCISES

1. Show that $\mathbb{B}$ in 1.3.5 is indeed a model of (Σ_1,E_1).
2. Find a model of (Σ_1,E_1) in which x + y = y + x does not hold.
3. Verify that $\mathbb{B} \models$ s(m(x, y)) = a(a(s(x), s(y)), m(s(x),s (y))) ($\mathbb{B}$ from 1.3.5). Does this formula also hold in (**N**,+,·,s,0)?
4. Prove theorem 1.3.10.

1.4 TERM REWRITING SYSTEMS

1.4.1 MOTIVATION

Let us look again at the equational specification (Σ_1,E_1) of 1.2.2, that has the equations in table 1 (copied below).

$$\begin{aligned} &a(x,0) = x \\ &a(x,s(y)) = s(a(x,y)) \\ &m(x,0) = 0 \\ &m(x,s(y)) = a(m(x,y),x) \end{aligned}$$

Now we can "calculate" that "2 + 2 = 4":

$$
\begin{aligned}
&a(s(s(0)),s(s(0))) = \\
&s(a(s(s(0)),s(0))) = \\
&s(s(a(s(s(0)),0))) = \\
&s(s(s(s(0)))).
\end{aligned}
$$

The equations in table 1 have a certain *direction* when applied in this derivation: when read from left to right they simplify terms, they *reduce* them. Therefore, we write $\rightarrow$ instead of =, as in table 4.

$a(x,0) \rightarrow x$
$a(x,s(y)) \rightarrow s(a(x,y))$
$m(x,0) \rightarrow 0$
$m(x,s(y)) \rightarrow a(m(x,y),x)$

TABLE 4.

This is an example of a term rewriting system or term reduction system (TRS).

1.4.2 DEFINITION
A **term rewriting system** (Σ,R) consists of a signature Σ and a set of **(rewrite) rules** R. The rules have the form $t_1 \rightarrow t_2$, where t_1 and t_2 are terms over Σ (as defined in 1.2.5). Moreover, we must have:
i. t_1 is not just a variable;
ii. every variable that occurs in t_2, must already occur in t_1 (a rewrite rule may not introduce any variables).

1.4.3 DEFINITION
Just like in 1.2.6, we can *derive* reductions from a TRS. We define a relation $\rightarrow$ on terms (**one step reduction**) as follows: $t_1 \rightarrow t_2$ holds when this is derivable from the rewrite rules R by means of:
i. substitution;
ii. forming contexts.

Thus, the rewrite steps in example 1.4.1 (where we reduced 2+2 to 4) are all one step reductions.

Then, we define the relation $\twoheadrightarrow$ (**reduction relation**) on terms as follows:

$t_1 \twoheadrightarrow t_2$ holds when there are a number of one-step reductions that lead from t_1 to t_2 (this number may also be 0). To be somewhat more formal: $t_1 \twoheadrightarrow t_2$ holds when this is derivable from the relation $\rightarrow$ by:
iii. $t_1 \twoheadrightarrow t_2$ if $t_1 \rightarrow t_2$;
iv. (reflexivity) $t \twoheadrightarrow t$;
v. (transitivity) if $t_1 \twoheadrightarrow t_2$ and $t_2 \twoheadrightarrow t_3$ then also $t_1 \twoheadrightarrow t_3$;

So in example 1.4.1 we have $a(s(s(0)),s(s(0))) \twoheadrightarrow s(s(s(s(0))))$.

1.4.4 DEFINITION
Let (Σ,R) be a TRS.
i. A term t is a **normal form**, or is a term **in normal form**, if there is no term s with $t \rightarrow s$.
ii. A term t **has a normal form** if there is a term s *in* normal form such that $t \twoheadrightarrow s$.

1.4.5 PROPERTIES OF A TRS

It is very desirable for a TRS that every (closed) term has a ***unique normal form.*** For example, for the TRS in table 4 (in 1.4.1) we can prove (not without difficulty!) that every closed term has a unique normal form of the form $s^n(0)$ (with $n \geq 0$).

Often, such a proof consists of proving that the following two properties are satisfied by a TRS:

i. **strong normalization**: there is no infinite sequence of reductions

$$t_0 \rightarrow t_1 \rightarrow t_2 \rightarrow ....$$

ii. **confluence** (also called the *Church-Rosser* or *diamond* property): if we have for terms t, t_1, t_2 that $t \twoheadrightarrow t_1$ and $t \twoheadrightarrow t_2$, then we can find a term t_3 such that $t_1 \twoheadrightarrow t_3$ and $t_2 \twoheadrightarrow t_3$ (i.e. we can complete the diamond in fig. 2).

Usually, we are only interested in these properties for closed (or ground) terms, and then we talk about **ground normalization** and **ground confluence.**

In order to prove confluence for a TRS, we need to look at all so-called *critical pairs,* i.e. the left-hand sides of two reduction rules that have overlap and thus can be applied to the same term.

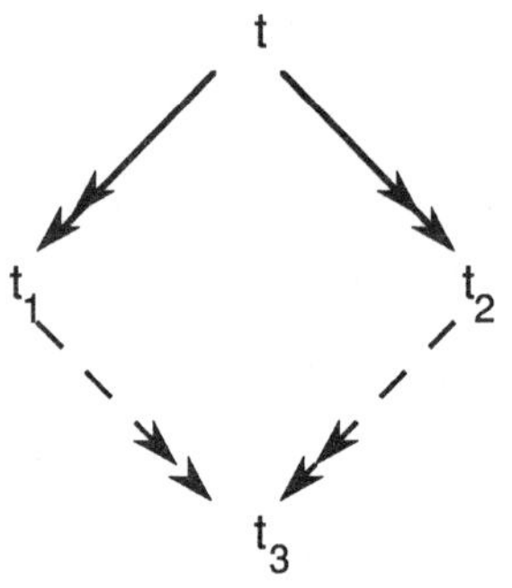

FIGURE 2.

1.4.6 THEOREM

Let (Σ, R) be a TRS. If (Σ, R) is strongly normalizing and confluent, then every term has a unique normal form. If (Σ, R) is ground normalizing and ground confluent, then every closed term has a unique normal form.

1.4.7 NOTE

We can always turn a TRS into an equational specification, by replacing every $\rightarrow$ in the reduction rules by the symbol =. If the TRS is strongly normalizing and confluent, that gives us a decision procedure to find out if two terms are equal in the resulting specification: reduce both terms to normal form; if they are identical, then the terms are equal, if they are not, then the terms are not equal. In this way we obtain an operational (i.e. executable) notion of derivability in a specification. Unfortunately, we cannot give such an operational notion for every specification, since equality is not always decidable.

1.4.8 EXERCISES

1. Prove for the TRS in table 4 that

$$m(a(s(s(0)),s(0)),s(s(0))) \twoheadrightarrow s(s(s(s(s(s(0))))))).$$

2. Prove that the closed normal forms for the TRS in table 4 are the terms of the form $s^n(0)$ (with $n \geq 0$).

3. We consider a TRS with a unary function $\neg$, and binary functions $\wedge$, $\vee$. The reduction rules are given in table 5 (in infix notation, leaving out many brackets).

$\neg\neg x \to x$
$\neg(x \vee y) \to \neg x \wedge \neg y$
$\neg(x \wedge y) \to \neg x \vee \neg y$
$x \vee (y \wedge z) \to (x \vee y) \wedge (x \vee z)$
$(x \wedge y) \vee z \to (x \vee z) \wedge (y \vee z)$

TABLE 5.

Reduce the term $\neg(x \wedge \neg y) \wedge z$ to normal form. (Note: the normal forms of this TRS are known in propositional logic as *conjunctive normal forms*.)

4. Prove that the TRS with the one rule

$$f(f(x)) \to f(g(f(x)))$$

is strongly normalizing.

5. Is the TRS with the one rule

$$f(g(x,y)) \to g(g(f(f(x)),y),y)$$

strongly normalizing?

Chapter 2

Basic Process Algebra

2.1 THE BASIC SYSTEM

In this chapter we will introduce some basic concepts of process algebra. We will do this in a *modular* way: first we will consider the theory BPA (**Basic Process Algebra**) as the kernel of all other theories that are given later. In the following sections we will show how to add some features such as deadlock, termination, projection and recursion to this theory in order to make it more powerful in its theoretical and practical applications. Each additional feature yields a *conservative extension* of the theories, so that we may consider the additional equations as a modular extension. Whether or not such a module should be added to the theory depends on what we want to use the theory for.

Starting in section 2.5, we consider various models for the algebraic theories that we found up to that point. Finding these models is important for more than one reason. First of all, it guarantees that the theories are *consistent* in the sense that the equations do not force undesirable identities to hold. Also, the models can help the intuition, they can help to visualize processes. Our models will in all cases be complete for the given theory, so the equality of two terms is true in the model exactly when it is derivable from the theory.

2.1.1 SYNTAX

We begin immediately with the equational specification BPA = (Σ_{BPA}, E_{BPA}).

Σ_{BPA} has two binary operators, + and ·, and a number of constants, denoted by a, b, c, ... Exactly how many constants we have, will depend on the particular application, and is not important here. We denote the set of constants by A. The set A can be considered a *parameter* of our theory, and will be (partly) specified, when discussing applications of the theory.

E_{BPA} consists of the five equations in table 6.

In this table, we use the following notational conventions:

i. The operator · is often omitted. Thus, xy means x·y.

$x + y = y + x$	A1
$(x + y) + z = x + (y + z)$	A2
$x + x = x$	A3
$(x + y)z = xz + yz$	A4
$(xy)z = x(yz)$	A5

TABLE 6. BPA.

ii. Also many brackets are omitted. In general, we will have that $\cdot$ binds stronger than all other operators, and + binds weaker. Thus, $xy + z$ means $(xy) + z$, and the brackets in $x(y + z)$ cannot be omitted.

These conventions coincide with the conventions for the "normal" +, $\cdot$.

Equations such as in table 6, contain variables x, y, z,... which are universally quantified. That is, the equations are assumed to be valid for every instance of the variables. If $\mathbb{M}$ is a model for BPA, the elements of its domain are called **processes**. So the variables stand for processes from some arbitrary model for BPA.

2.1.2 SEMANTICS

We provide the specification BPA with the following intuitive meaning. The constants a,b,c,... are called **atomic actions** or **steps**, and we consider them as indivisible actions or events.

$\cdot$ is product or **sequential composition**; $x{\cdot}y$ is the process that first executes x, and upon completion of x starts y;

+ is sum or **alternative composition**; $x + y$ is the process that either executes x, or executes y (but not both).

In the term $x + y$ a *choice* is made between x and y, and this explains the first three axioms of BPA:

- A1 (the **commutativity of** +) says that a choice between x and y is the same as a choice between y and x;
- A2 (the **associativity of** +) says that a choice between x and choosing between y and z is the same as a choice between z and choosing between x and y; in each case a choice will be made from three alternatives;
- A3 (the **idempotency of** +) says that a choice between x and x amounts to a choice for x. Together, these axioms say that at every moment, we have a choice from a *set* of alternatives.
- A4 (the **right distributivity of $\cdot$ over** +) says that a choice between x and y, followed by z, is the same as a choice between x followed by z and y followed by z.
- A5 (the **associativity of** $\cdot$) is evident.

2.1.3 NON-DETERMINISM

An axiom that does *not* appear in BPA is

$$x(y + z) = xy + xz,$$

that would give full distributivity. We have not included this axiom on intuitive grounds. For in $x(y + z)$ *first* x must be executed, and *then* a choice is made between y and z, while on the other hand in $xy + xz$ *first* a choice is made, and *then* the chosen term is executed. We see that the moment of choice in these terms is different.

The difference between processes that differ in the moment of choice such as in the example above, is in the literature often referred to as a difference in **branching structure**, as we will explain later when considering models of BPA. Roughly speaking, the choice operator indicates that a process has two ways to proceed, which can be represented by two branches in a state transition diagram. Obviously, $xy + xz$ has two branches right at the beginning, whereas $x(y + z)$ has subprocesses y and z branching off only deeper down in its structure. It is not always necessary to distinguish between processes that only differ in branching structure, but by not adding the other distributive law to our basic system, we retain the freedom of adding it when we want it.

If y and z are different processes, a choice as in $xy + xz$ between alternatives that are initially identical is called a **non-deterministic** choice, and such choices are the subject of many investigations in the theory of concurrency. In the literature, there is no uniformity in the use of the term non-determinism; other writers give it a different meaning than we do.

2.1.4 EXAMPLE

We want to illustrate the difference between $x(y + z)$ and $xy + xz$ with the following example.

Suppose you find yourself in a building with two elevators. One of them is perfectly safe, but the other one definitely is not. In the hall you find two elevator doors, but unfortunately you cannot tell which one leads to the safe elevator. Now you call for the elevator by pushing the "up"-button and after a while a door opens...

We can describe this situation by use of the following atomic actions:

door = the elevator doors open,
risk = the offered elevator is highly dangerous,
safe = the offered elevator is perfectly safe.

Then we are dealing with the following process:

$$door\cdot risk + door\cdot safe,$$

we find that after one of the two doors is opened, we are no longer capable of chosing between the risky or safe elevator: we are forced to take the elevator as it is and just wait and see what happens. This is very different from the process:

$$door\cdot(risk + safe),$$

where *after* the doors open, the choice is made between the risky and safe elevator, implying that they can be distinguished, for example by an alarm signal inside.

2.1.5 BASIC TERMS

Inductively, we define a set of terms that we will call **basic terms**:

i. every atomic action a is a basic term;
ii. if t is a basic term, and a an atomic action, then $a\cdot t$ is a basic term;
iii. if t,s are basic terms, then $t + s$ is a basic term.

If we consider terms that only differ in the order of the summands to be identical (i.e. we work *modulo* axioms A1 and A2), we see that the basic terms are exactly the terms of the form

$$t = a_0t_0 + ... + a_{n-1}t_{n-1} + b_0 + ... + b_{k-1},$$

for certain atomic actions a_i, b_j and basic terms t_i (where $i<n$, $j<k$, $n+k>0$).

In basic terms, we have a restricted format of multiplication: in each subterm of the form $t\cdot s$, t will be an atomic action. We call this restricted form of multiplication **prefix multiplication** (we can, in this case, delete the binary operator $\cdot$ in favour of *unary* operators $a\cdot$, for each $a\in A$).

2.1.6 PROPOSITION

For every closed BPA term t, there is a basic term s such that BPA $\vdash$ t=s.

PROOF: We consider a term rewriting system with rules corresponding to the BPA axioms A4 and A5:

$$(x + y)z \to xz + yz$$
$$(xy)z \to x(yz).$$

It is not hard to see that this term rewrite system is confluent and strongly normalizing, and that a normal form of a closed term must be a basic term. Therefore, given a closed term t, we can find s by reducing t until a normal form is reached.

Because of proposition 2.1.6, basic terms are useful for technical purposes in proofs. If we want to prove some statement valid for all closed terms, it is sufficient to prove it valid for all *basic* terms, defined inductively in 2.1.5. This means we can use structural induction as a proof method.

2.1.7 ACTION RELATIONS

A useful visualization of BPA terms can be obtained if we use so-called **action relations.** To give an **operational semantics** for process expressions we say which actions a process can perform.

On the set of BPA terms we define binary relations $\xrightarrow{a}$, and unary relations $\xrightarrow{a} \surd$, for each $a \in A$. The intuitive idea of these relations is as follows:

- $t \xrightarrow{a} s$ denotes that t can execute a and thereby turn into s; i.e. in state t, doing a step a can lead us into state s;
- $t \xrightarrow{a} \surd$ denotes that t can terminate by executing a.

The symbol $\surd$ (pronounced as **tick**) stands for successful termination.

An inductive definition is given in table 7. We will say that $t \xrightarrow{a} s$ holds if and only if it can be derived using the rules in this table.

$a \xrightarrow{a} \surd$		
$x \xrightarrow{a} x'$	$\Rightarrow$	$x+y \xrightarrow{a} x'$ and $y+x \xrightarrow{a} x'$
$x \xrightarrow{a} \surd$	$\Rightarrow$	$x+y \xrightarrow{a} \surd$ and $y+x \xrightarrow{a} \surd$
$x \xrightarrow{a} x'$	$\Rightarrow$	$xy \xrightarrow{a} x'y$
$x \xrightarrow{a} \surd$	$\Rightarrow$	$xy \xrightarrow{a} y$

TABLE 7. Action relations for BPA.

If σ is a non-empty sequence of symbols from A ($\sigma \in A^+$), then we also use the following notations:

- $t \overset{\sigma}{\twoheadrightarrow} s$: t can evolve into s via the sequence of actions σ;
- $t \overset{\sigma}{\twoheadrightarrow} \surd$: t can terminate after performing the sequence of actions σ.

Any sequence σ such that either $t \overset{\sigma}{\twoheadrightarrow} s$ for some s or $t \overset{\sigma}{\twoheadrightarrow} \surd$ is called a **trace** of t.

The inductive definition of the generalized action relations is easy to write down:

$t \xrightarrow{a} s \Rightarrow t \overset{a}{\twoheadrightarrow} s$
$t \overset{\sigma}{\twoheadrightarrow} s$ and $s \overset{\rho}{\twoheadrightarrow} r \Rightarrow t \overset{\sigma\rho}{\twoheadrightarrow} r$
$t \xrightarrow{a} \surd \Rightarrow t \overset{a}{\twoheadrightarrow} \surd$
$t \overset{\sigma}{\twoheadrightarrow} s$ and $s \overset{\rho}{\twoheadrightarrow} \surd \Rightarrow t \overset{\sigma\rho}{\twoheadrightarrow} \surd$

TABLE 8. Generalized action relations.

2.1.8 EXAMPLES

1. $ab \xrightarrow{a} b \xrightarrow{b} \surd$, so $ab \overset{ab}{\twoheadrightarrow} \surd$.
2. $(a + b)c \xrightarrow{a} c$ and $(a + b)c \xrightarrow{b} c$.
3. $ac + bc \xrightarrow{a} c$ and $ac + bc \xrightarrow{b} c$.
4. Given a closed term, we can draw a graph that gives all possible successive action relations, starting at this term. In fig. 3 below, we draw this graph for term $(a + bb)c$.

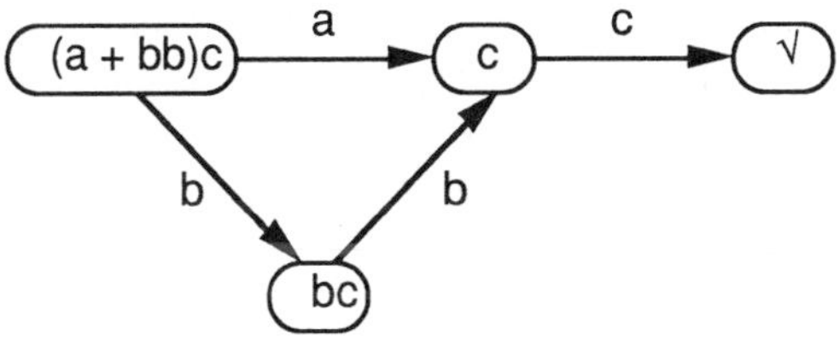

FIGURE 3.

2.1.9 DEFINITION

i. We say a term s is a **summand** of term t if there is a term r such that A1, A2 $\vdash t = s + r$, or A1, A2 $\vdash t = s$.

ii. We call a term s a **BPA-summand** of term t, notation $s \leq t$, if BPA $\vdash t = s + t$.

Note that $\leq$ is a partial ordering on processes (see exercise 7 below).

2.1.10 LEMMA

Let t be a basic term. Then:

i. $t \xrightarrow{a} s \Leftrightarrow t$ has a summand as;

ii. $t \xrightarrow{a} \surd \Leftrightarrow t$ has a summand a.

Let t,t' be a general closed terms, and BPA $\vdash t = t'$. Then:

iii. $t \xrightarrow{a} s \Rightarrow$ there is a closed term s' such that BPA $\vdash s = s'$ and $t' \xrightarrow{a} s'$,

iv. $t \xrightarrow{a} \surd \Leftrightarrow t' \xrightarrow{a} \surd$.

PROOF: (i) and (ii) follow easily from definitions 2.1.5 and 2.1.7. (iii) and (iv) follow from 2.1.7, distinguishing the cases A1 $\vdash t = t'$ to A5 $\vdash t = t'$, and using induction on the structure of t.

2.1.11 INITIAL ALGEBRA

Let us say two closed terms s and t are equivalent, notation $s \equiv_{BPA} t$, if they can be proved equal using axioms from BPA. That is: $s \equiv_{BPA} t$ iff BPA $\vdash s = t$. The **initial algebra** of BPA, called $\mathbb{A}$, now consists of equivalence classes of closed BPA terms. For instance, the terms $(a + b)c$ and $ac + bc$ are in the same class (using A4), and the terms $a(b + c)$ and $ab + ac$ are not.

Note that each equivalence class contains a basic term, by proposition 2.1.6. The equivalence relation is a congruence with respect to the operators + and ·. This follows trivially from the observation that if $s \equiv_{BPA} s'$ and $t \equiv_{BPA} t'$, then BPA $\vdash s = s'$ and BPA $\vdash t = t'$, so BPA $\vdash s + t = s' + t'$ and BPA $\vdash s{\cdot}t = s'{\cdot}t'$, i.e. $(s + t) \equiv (s' + t')$ and $(s{\cdot}t) \equiv (s'{\cdot}t')$. Therefore + and · are well-defined operators on the domain of $\mathbb{A}$.

Let us write $p,q,...$ for elements (equivalence classes that is) from $\mathbb{A}$. We define the action relations on $\mathbb{A}$ as follows:

- $p \xrightarrow{a} q \Leftrightarrow$ there are terms t,s, with t in the equivalence class p, and s in the equivalence class q, such that $t \xrightarrow{a} s$, and
- $p \xrightarrow{a} \surd$, $p \overset{\sigma}{\twoheadrightarrow} q$, $p \overset{\sigma}{\twoheadrightarrow} \surd$ likewise.

With these definitions, it follows easily from 2.1.10 and axiom A3 from BPA that $p \xrightarrow{a} q \Leftrightarrow \mathbb{A} \models p = aq + p$ and $p \xrightarrow{a} \surd \Leftrightarrow \mathbb{A} \models p = a + p$.

As in 2.1.8, we can draw the **action graph** of an element p, with nodes all elements q such that $p \overset{\sigma}{\twoheadrightarrow} q$ for some σ, and a node $\surd$ if $p \overset{\sigma}{\twoheadrightarrow} \surd$ for some σ; the edges of the action graph are given by the action relations, and the root is of course given by the element p. Then, we leave out the *names* of the nodes and obtain the following proposition.

2.1.12 PROPOSITION

Let $p,q \in \mathbb{A}$. Then p and q have the same action graph iff $p = q$.

PROOF: We use induction on the size of p and q.

$\Rightarrow$: Take two basic terms t,s such that p is the equivalence class containing t and q the equivalence class with s. Using 2.1.10, we see that for every summand at' of t, there is a summand as' of s, such that the equivalence classes p' of t' and q' of s' have the same action graph. Thus, by induction, $p' = q'$, which implies BPA $\vdash t' = s'$. Hence BPA $\vdash at' = as' \leq s$. From 2.1.10 it also follows that every summand a of t is also a summand of s. Thus $t \leq s$. For the same reasons $s \leq t$, whence BPA $\vdash t = s$ (exercise 7), and $\mathbb{A} \models p = q$.

$\Leftarrow$: Trivial.

2.1.13 EXERCISES

1. A man (M) is playing a game of Russian roulette. After pulling the trigger either a bang or a click follows. We have the following atomic actions:

   t = he pulls the trigger;

   b = a bang;

   c = a click.

Describe the behaviour of M by means of a term in BPA. Compare this example with the example in 2.1.4.

2. A simple vending machine (SV) dispenses coffee and hot chocolate. After inserting a quarter the customer chooses between the two. We have the following atomic actions:

   q = a quarter is inserted

   c = the machine dispenses coffee

   h = the machine dispenses hot chocolate.

Describe the behaviour of SV by means of a term in BPA.

3. Prove that BPA $\vdash$ $a(b + b) = ab + ab$.
4. Reduce the following terms to a normal form, using the term rewrite system in the proof of 2.1.6: $a(b + c)a$, $(a + b)(a + b)$, $ab + (a + b)b$.
5. Draw a graph as in 2.1.8.4 for the following terms: $a(b + c)a$, $ab + a(b + b)$.
6. Prove that the three axioms A1-3 are equivalent to the following *two* axioms:

$$(x + y) + z = y + (z + x)$$
$$x + x = x.$$

7. i. Prove: $x \leq y \Leftrightarrow$ there is z such that BPA $\vdash$ $x + z = y$.
ii. Prove that $\leq$ is a partial ordering on processes (terms modulo BPA-equality), i.e.
 1. $x \leq x$;
 2. $x \leq y$ and $y \leq x$ imply BPA $\vdash$ $x = y$;
 3. $x \leq y$ and $y \leq z$ imply $x \leq z$.
iii. Give two closed terms t,s such that not $s \leq t$ and not $t \leq s$.
iv. Prove: $x \leq y \Rightarrow x+z \leq y+z$ and $x \cdot z \leq y \cdot z$.
v. Give two closed terms t,s such that $s \leq t$ but not $as \leq at$.
8. Give the proof of lemma 2.1.10 i, ii.
9. A more complicated vending machine than the one in exercise 2 (V) charges 25 ¢ for coffee and 20 ¢ for hot chocolate. This machine also accepts dimes and nickels beside quarters, and therefore we have atomic actions d and n. Write down a BPA term for V. (In order to do this, you must answer several questions, for instance: is it allowed to insert too much money, can coins be inserted in arbitrary order, where are the moments of choice?)

2.1.14 NOTES AND COMMENTS

The operator + for alternative composition appears in CCS, see MILNER [1980]. There, we also find laws A1-3. CCS uses prefix multiplication instead of general multiplication. We do find general multiplication in topological process theory (see DE BAKKER & ZUCKER [1982]), denoted $\circ$, and in parts of CSP, see HOARE [1980], denoted ;. The system BPA comprises the first five laws of the system PA, introduced in BERGSTRA & KLOP [1982]. The notion of a basic term is used in BERGSTRA & KLOP [1985]. Action relations, and the representation of processes by graphs, appear in MILNER [1980] and PLOTKIN [1983], but the basic ideas are much older. In the setting of process algebra, action relations are discussed in VAN GLABBEEK [1987]. Exercise 2.1.13.6 was suggested by H. Goeman. Vending machines, and recursive equations for them, appear in HOARE [1985].

2.2 DEADLOCK AND TERMINATION

In this section we will introduce an important feature into our algebras, which is the distinction between successful and unsuccessful termination. Consider a process $x \cdot y$, where x describes the behaviour of a system consisting of a number of processors that jointly perform some parallel computation. It may occur that at some point during the execution of x a state of *deadlock* is reached, i.e. all processors are waiting for each other, before the computation is finished.

Although x has reached a state where no further actions are possible, y usually is not allowed to start in such a situation: it can only start when x has terminated successfully. This leads us to distinguish between successful and unsuccessful termination.

2.2.1 DEADLOCK

First let us consider a process which has stopped executing actions and, for whatever reason, cannot proceed. Such a process (or state) is usually referred to as *deadlock* (though others prefer the name *lock* or *inaction*) and in our algebra it will be denoted by the constant symbol δ.

2.2.2 DEFINITION

The equational specification BPA_δ has operators +, ·, a set A of constants, and a special constant δ in its signature. We assume $\delta \notin A$. Apart from axioms A1-A5 of BPA, BPA_δ consists of the axioms from table 9.

$x + \delta = x$	A6
$\delta x = \delta$	A7

TABLE 9. Deadlock.

So BPA_δ = BPA + A6-A7. Equation A6 says that no deadlock will occur as long as there is an alternative that can proceed, and axiom A7 says that after a deadlock has occurred, no other actions can possibly follow. By A6, δ is the neutral element for alternative composition. The process $a \cdot \delta$ is *not* the same as process a, since $a \cdot \delta$ ends in a state of deadlock, whereas a terminates successfully.

2.2.3 BASIC TERMS

A **basic term** over BPA_δ is defined as follows (compare with 2.1.5):

i. every atomic action a is a basic term, and δ is a basic term;
ii. if t is a basic term, and a an atomic action, then $a \cdot t$ is a basic term;
iii. if t,s are basic terms, then t + s is a basic term.

As in 2.1.5, if we consider terms that only differ in the order of the summands to be identical, we find that the basic terms are exactly the terms of the form

$$t \equiv a_0t_0 + ... + a_{n-1}t_{n-1} + b_0 + ... + b_{k-1},$$

for atomic actions a_i, $b_j \in A$ and basic terms t_i (where $i<n$, $j<k$). The symbol ≡ stands for syntactical equality. We usually abbreviate these expressions using a sum notation. So we obtain

$$t \equiv \sum_{i<n} a_i \cdot t_i + \sum_{j<k} b_j.$$

Empty summations can simply be deleted from t. In the presence of δ however, we have the convention that:

$$\sum_{i<0} a_i \cdot t_i + \sum_{j<0} b_j \equiv \delta.$$

2.2.4 LEMMA

For every closed BPA_δ-term t, there is a basic term s over BPA_δ such that $BPA_\delta \vdash t=s$.

The proof of this lemma is left to the reader (cf. 2.1.6).

2.2.5 IMMEDIATE TERMINATION

In the action relations of BPA, the process a will first execute the a-step and then terminate successfully, expressed by $t \xrightarrow{a} \surd$, so we already have a representation for successful termination. In many situations however, it is useful to have a special constant denoting immediate successful termination, as a counterpart of δ. This is the process ε, the process that is only capable of terminating successfully, also referred to as the **empty process**.

2.2.6 DEFINITION

The equational specification BPA_ε has operators $+$, $\cdot$, a set A of constants, and a special constant ε in its signature. We assume $\varepsilon \notin A$. Apart from the axioms A1-A5 from BPA (see table 6 in 2.1.1), BPA_ε has the axioms from table 10.

$x\varepsilon = x$	A8
$\varepsilon x = x$	A9

TABLE 10. Empty process.

So BPA_ε := BPA + A8-A9. The equations A8 and A9 say that ε is the neutral element for sequential composition.

Note that the process $a + \varepsilon$ is *not* the same process as a, since $a + \varepsilon$ is the process which either executes a or terminates immediately. So, BPA_ε is a non-trivial extension of BPA.

In the sequel we will allow the constants ε and δ to be present in the algebra at the same time. In that case we write $BPA_{\delta\varepsilon}$:= BPA + A6-A9.

2.2.7 BASIC TERMS

A **basic term** over BPA_ε is defined as follows:

i. ε is a basic term;
ii. if t is a basic term, and a an atomic action, then $a \cdot t$ is a basic term;
iii. if t,s are basic terms, then $t + s$ is a basic term.

A **basic term** over $BPA_{\delta\varepsilon}$ is defined as follows:

i. δ and ε are basic terms;
ii. if t is a basic term, and a an atomic action, then $a \cdot t$ is a basic term;
iii. if t,s are basic terms, then $t + s$ is a basic term.

Observe that the structure of this definition is a little different from those of 2.1.5 and 2.2.3. The presence of ε allows us to eliminate the constants a from the set of basic terms, since $a = a \cdot \varepsilon$. Again, if we consider terms that differ only in the order of the summands to be identical, basic terms over BPA_ε (or $BPA_{\delta\varepsilon}$) are of the general form

$$t \equiv \sum_{i<n} a_i \cdot t_i + \sum_{j<m} \varepsilon .$$

for atomic actions $a_i \in A$ and basic terms t_i (where $i<n$). Again we use the convention of 2.2.3, and we put

$$\sum_{j<m} \varepsilon \equiv \varepsilon,$$

whenever $m>0$.

2.2.8 LEMMA

i. For every closed BPA_ε-term t, there is a basic term s over BPA_ε such that $BPA_\varepsilon \vdash t=s$.

ii. For every closed $BPA_{\delta\varepsilon}$-term t, there is a basic term s over $BPA_{\delta\varepsilon}$ such that $BPA_{\delta\varepsilon} \vdash t=s$.

It is left to the reader to prove lemma 2.2.8. As is done for BPA in 2.1.6, we can turn the algebras BPA_δ, BPA_ε and $BPA_{\delta\varepsilon}$ into rewriting systems.

2.2.9 ACTION RELATIONS

The presence of δ in our signature does not change the action relations that we established in section 2.1. The new constant can simply be added and has no transitions.

In the case of ε things are different. As ε represents successful termination, the unary predicate $\xrightarrow{a} \surd$ can be divided into two parts, $\xrightarrow{a} \varepsilon$ and $\varepsilon\downarrow$, where $\downarrow$ is a predicate indicating whether or not a process has a termination option. The new rules, involving both ε and $\downarrow$, are given in table 11 below.

$a \xrightarrow{a} \varepsilon$	
$x \xrightarrow{a} x'$	$\Rightarrow x+y \xrightarrow{a} x'$ and $y+x \xrightarrow{a} x'$
$x \xrightarrow{a} x'$	$\Rightarrow xy \xrightarrow{a} x'y$
$x\downarrow$ and $y \xrightarrow{a} y'$	$\Rightarrow x \cdot y \xrightarrow{a} y'$
$\varepsilon\downarrow$	
$x\downarrow$	$\Rightarrow (x+y)\downarrow$ and $(y+x)\downarrow$
$x\downarrow$ and $y\downarrow$	$\Rightarrow (x \cdot y)\downarrow$

TABLE 11. Action relations for BPA_ε.

Note that the action relations for $BPA_{\delta\varepsilon}$ can be found by adding δ to the signature, without adding any relations.

2.2.10 INITIAL ALGEBRA

As in 2.1.11, we can construct the initial algebra $\mathbb{A}_\delta$ of BPA_δ. Its domain consists of equivalence classes of closed terms from BPA_δ. Note that by 2.2.4 in each equivalence class, there is a basic term. We define the action relations on $\mathbb{A}_\delta$ as in 2.1.11.

In case ε is involved, we have different action relations, and we need the analogue of lemma 2.1.10.

2.2.11 LEMMA

Let t be a basic term over BPA_ε. Then:

i. $t \xrightarrow{a} s \Leftrightarrow$ t has a summand as.

ii. $t\downarrow \Leftrightarrow$ t has a summand ε.

Let t,t' be a closed BPA_ε-terms, and $BPA_\varepsilon \vdash t = t'$. Then:

iii. $t \xrightarrow{a} s \Rightarrow$ there is a closed term s' such that $BPA_\varepsilon \vdash s = s'$ and $t' \xrightarrow{a} s'$,

iv. $t\downarrow \Leftrightarrow t'\downarrow$.

PROOF: Left to the reader.

Using this lemma it is easy to define the action graphs for BPA_ε, just as in 2.1.11.

2.2.12 EXERCISES

1. Show that in BPA_ε the axiom $x + x = x$ is equivalent to $\varepsilon + \varepsilon = \varepsilon$. More precisely, show that A3 $\vdash \varepsilon + \varepsilon = \varepsilon$, and A4, A9, $\varepsilon + \varepsilon = \varepsilon \vdash$ A3.
2. Show that in $BPA_{\delta\varepsilon}$ the axiom $x + \delta = x$ is equivalent to $\varepsilon + \delta = \varepsilon$. More precisely, show that A6 $\vdash \varepsilon + \delta = \varepsilon$ and A4, A7, A9, $\varepsilon + \delta = \varepsilon \vdash$ A6.
3. Prove lemma 2.2.4.
4. Prove the analogue of lemma 2.1.10 for BPA_δ.
5. Give proper definitions for action graphs involving δ (see 2.1.11), and prove the analogue of proposition 2.1.12.
6. Prove lemma 2.2.8.
7. Prove lemma 2.2.11.
8. Give proper definitions for action graphs involving ε, and prove the analogue of proposition 2.1.12.
9. Define for closed BPA_δ-terms t the following:

   t has deadlock $\Leftrightarrow$ there is a basic term s in which δ occurs, such that BPA $\vdash$ t = s.

   Show the following:

i. t has deadlock and $a \in A \Rightarrow a \cdot t + s$ has deadlock;

ii. t has deadlock $\Rightarrow t \cdot s$ and $s \cdot t$ have deadlock;

iii. s,t have no deadlock $\Rightarrow s \cdot t$ and $s + t$ have no deadlock;

   Give a counterexample for the following:

iv. t has deadlock $\Rightarrow s + t$ has deadlock.

2.2.13 NOTES AND COMMENTS

The constant δ was introduced in BERGSTRA & KLOP [1984b], and corresponds to NIL (MILNER [1980]) or 0 (MILNER [1989]) of CCS or STOP of CSP (HOARE [1985]). The constant ε, sometimes called SKIP, first appeared in KOYMANS & VRANCKEN [1985]. The action relations in table 11 are from BAETEN & VAN GLABBEEK [1987b].

The present framework, with *two* kinds of termination, is different from the situation in CCS or CSP, where only *one* kind of termination is present (NIL and STOP respectively). More about the different approaches to termination can be found in BAETEN & VAANDRAGER [1989].

2.3 RECURSION

Let us consider a very simple vending machine VSV, even simpler than the one in 2.1.13.2, that can only give coffee. We start by writing down

$$VSV = q \cdot c,$$

but one could object that this is not completely correct: after handing out a cup of coffee, VSV has returned to its original state, and so another quarter can be inserted. Therefore, we would like to write:

$$VSV = q \cdot c \cdot VSV.$$

In this equation the object to be defined (VSV) occurs again in the right-hand side, a so-called **recursive** equation. In this section we consider recursive equations over the theory BPA. By convention, we use capital letters for variables in recursive equations.

2.3.1 SOLVING EQUATIONS

Let us consider the recursive equation

$$X = a{\cdot}X$$

where a is an atomic action). Then, for the X in the right-hand side we can substitute $a{\cdot}X$, and obtain $X = aaX$,

and, continuing in this fashion:

$$X = aaaX = aaaaX = ...$$

This gives us the idea that the **solution** for X is the infinite process that will keep on executing action a, i.e.

$$X = aaaaa....,$$

usually abbreviated by $X = a^{\omega}$.

In this way we have motivated the idea that some recursive equations determine a process (that is usually infinite). Note that processes like a^{ω} do not exist in the initial algebra $\mathbb{A}$.

2.3.2 NOTE

Not all recursive equations over BPA can determine a process. For instance, *all* processes satisfy the equation $X = X$. What is needed is a criterion that tells us which recursive equations do determine a process.

2.3.3 DEFINITION

i. A **recursive equation** over BPA is an equation of the form

$$X = s(X),$$

where $s(X)$ is a term is over BPA containing the variable X, but no other variable.

ii. A **recursive specification** E over BPA is a set of recursion equations over BPA. By this, we mean that we have a set of variables V, and an equation of the form

$$X = s_X(V)$$

for each $X \in V$, where s_X is a term over BPA containing variables from the set V.

V contains one distinguished variable called the **root variable**, usually the first variable in the textual presentation.

Usually, the set V is *finite*. In this case, there is an $n \geq 1$ and variables $X_1,....,X_n$, such that E consists of equations

$$X_1 = s_1(X_1,....,X_n)$$
$$X_2 = s_2(X_1,....,X_n)$$
.....
$$X_n = s_n(X_1,....,X_n).$$

X_1 is the root variable. For $i=1,...,n$, s_i is a term containing some of $X_1,....,X_n$ (not necessarily all of them).

iii. A **solution** of a recursive equation $X = s(X)$ is a process p (in some model of BPA) by which the equation is satisfied, i.e. we have that $p = s(p)$ holds in the model. We also talk about a solution of a recursive specification E in a certain model. A process p is a solution of E in that model, if after substituting p for the root variable of E, there exist other processes for the other variables of E such that all equations of E turn into true statements.

We will now define what it means for a recursive specification to be *guarded*. Later, we will see that we can assume that every guarded recursive specification determines a process, i.e. the specification has a unique solution. We are not saying here that *only* guarded recursive specifications can determine processes; guardedness just is a useful criterion to prove that a certain specification does determine a process.

2.3.4 DEFINITION

i. Let s be a term over BPA containing a variable X. We call an occurrence of X in s **guarded** if s has a subterm of the form $a \cdot t$, where a is an atomic action and t a term containing this occurrence of X; otherwise, we call the occurrence of X in s **unguarded.**

ii. We call a term s **completely guarded** if all occurrences of all variables in s are guarded, and we call a recursive specification E **completely guarded** if all right hand sides of all equations of E are completely guarded terms.

2.3.5 EXAMPLES

1. In term $s_1 \equiv aXX + Ya + a(b + X)$, every occurrence of X is guarded, but Y occurs unguarded. Therefore, s_1 is not completely guarded.
2. In term $s_2 \equiv aX + YX$, X occurs both guarded and unguarded. s_2 is not completely guarded.
3. In term $s_3 \equiv (a + b)X$, X is unguarded. s_3 is not completely guarded.
4. In term $s_4 \equiv aX + bX$, all occurrences of X are guarded. s_4 is completely guarded.
5. The recursive specification $E \equiv \{X = aX, Y = X\}$ is not completely guarded, because X occurs unguarded in the right-hand side of the second equation.
6. The recursive specification $E' \equiv \{X = aX, Y = aX\}$ is completely guarded.

2.3.6 DEFINITION

The examples just given motivate us to broaden the scope of definition 2.3.4 somewhat: term s_3 in 2.3.5.3 may not be completely guarded, but since BPA $\vdash s_3=s_4$, and s_4 is completely guarded (see 2.3.5.4), s_3 should be guarded too. Also, the recursive specification E of 2.3.5.5 may not be completely guarded, but by substituting aX for X we obtain E' of 2.3.5.6, which is completely guarded. This leads us to the following definitions:

i. A term s is **guarded**, if we can rewrite s to a completely guarded term by use of the axioms.

ii. A recursive specification E is **guarded**, if we can rewrite E to a completely guarded specification, by use of the axioms and by (repeatedly) replacing variables by the right-hand side of their equations. Otherwise, E is called **unguarded.**

2.3.7 NOTE

The presence of δ or ε does not make any difference in our definition, and so recursive specifications over BPA_ε, BPA_δ or $BPA_{\delta\varepsilon}$ are treated just as those over BPA. Thus by definition, the constants ε and δ cannot serve as a guard for a variable since only atomic actions can. As a consequence, the term δX is *not* completely guarded and neither is εX. Applying A7 to the first term we obtain $\delta X = \delta$, and hence δX *is* guarded in BPA_δ since using the axioms it can be written as a completely guarded term. Observe that εX is not guarded in BPA_ε.

2.3.8 EXAMPLES

1. The recursive specification $\{X=Y, Y=Z, Z=aY\}$ is guarded.
2. The recursive specification $\{X=Y, Y=aX + X\}$ is unguarded.

2.3.9 NOTE

The following criterion can be used to prove that a recursive specification is guarded.

Let E be a recursive specification over variables V. Write $X \xrightarrow{u} Y$ (for $X,Y \in V$) if Y occurs unguarded in the equation of X. Then it is easy to verify the following claim:

CLAIM: If the relation $\xrightarrow{u}$ is well-founded, then E is guarded.

We say $\xrightarrow{u}$ is **well-founded** if there is no infinite sequence $X_0, X_1, \ldots$ in V such that

$$X_0 \xrightarrow{u} X_1 \xrightarrow{u} X_2 \xrightarrow{u} \ldots\ldots$$

If V is finite, this amounts to the absence of cycles

$$X \xrightarrow{u} \ldots\ldots \xrightarrow{u} X.$$

2.3.10 NOTE

In the sequel, we will show that intuitively, every guarded recursive specification has a unique solution, and that most unguarded specifications have infinitely many solutions.

2.3.11 DEFINITION

It will be useful to have a notation for a solution of a recursive specification. If E is a recursive specification with root variable X, then $\langle X \mid E \rangle$ denotes a solution of this specification. Likewise, if Y is another variable of E, then $\langle Y \mid E \rangle$ denotes a solution of E with Y as root variable. We will even use a more general notation $\langle t \mid E \rangle$ for arbitrary (open) terms t, where the variables in t are interpreted as their solutions in E. As a consequence, the term $\langle aX \mid \{X = bX\} \rangle$ stands for the process a(bbb...) and so on.

Therefore, we need to add some obvious equations between the new terms $\langle X \mid E \rangle$ corresponding to the intuitive meaning of the operators and the recursive equations. First of all, we want to have that

$$\langle a \cdot t \mid E \rangle = a \cdot \langle t \mid E \rangle$$

and

$$\langle s + t \mid E \rangle = \langle s \mid E \rangle + \langle t \mid E \rangle$$

following the structure of terms as usual. But apart from that, we also want to express the possibility of iteratively substituting terms for variables in recursive specifications, as shown in the examples in 2.3.5. So if $E \equiv \{X = aX\}$, we have the equation

$$\langle X \mid E \rangle = a \cdot \langle X \mid E \rangle.$$

$\langle X \mid E \rangle$ can be considered as a kind of variable ranging over the set of solutions of E. If something holds for $\langle X \mid E \rangle$, this means that it holds for all solutions of E. Another notation that for this purpose is often used in the literature is $\mu X.E$. Abusing language, we will often simply write X for $\langle X \mid E \rangle$.

In BPA or BPA_δ, the action relations of the process $\langle X \mid E \rangle$ can be found by adding the rules from table 12 to table 7 (in 2.1.7). Here $\langle t_X \mid E \rangle$ is the right hand side of the equation for X in E, with every occurring variable Y replaced by $\langle Y \mid E \rangle$.

$\langle t_X \mid E \rangle \xrightarrow{a} \surd \Rightarrow \langle X \mid E \rangle \xrightarrow{a} \surd$
$\langle t_X \mid E \rangle \xrightarrow{a} y \Rightarrow \langle X \mid E \rangle \xrightarrow{a} y$

TABLE 12. Action relations and recursion in BPA_δ.

Observe that the label a in table 12 is from A and, as before, cannot be equal to δ. To find similar rules in the presence of ε is left to the exercises.

2.3.12 EXERCISES

1. Determine whether in the following terms the occurrences of X are guarded, unguarded, or both: bX, YX, XX, Xa, $aX + Xa$, $a(X + Y)a$, $aXXa$.
2. Determine whether the following specifications are guarded or unguarded:
(i) $\{X=X\}$; (ii) $\{X=Y, Y=aX\}$; (iii) $\{X = aX + Xa\}$; (iv) $\{X = (a + b)(X + c)\}$.
3. Give a recursive specification of the simple vending machine SV of 2.1.13.2.
4. Likewise for the vending machine V of 2.1.13.9.
5. Define action relations for $\langle X \mid E \rangle$ in case we have ε. That is, find rules as in table 12 in order to add recursion to table 11 in 2.2.9.

2.3.13 NOTES AND COMMENTS

Recursion is investigated in most concurrency theories. We see algebraic treatments in CCS (MILNER [1980]), CSP (HOARE [1985]), topological process theory (DE BAKKER & ZUCKER [1982]) and other places. In KRANAKIS [1987] recursive specifications with parameters (extra variables) are considered.

The notion of guardedness is found in MILNER [1980] and MILNE [1982], but is derived from older ideas such as the Greibach normal form of context-free languages due to GREIBACH [1965]. Guardedness in process algebra is found in BERGSTRA & KLOP [1984a]. The relation $\xrightarrow{u}$ was defined in BAETEN, BERGSTRA & KLOP [1987b]. The notation $\langle X \mid E \rangle$ appears in BERGSTRA & KLOP [1988]. The action rules of table 12, based on MILNER [1980], are taken from VAN GLABBEEK [1987].

2.4 PROJECTION AND BOUNDED NON-DETERMINISM

In this section we define some syntax that can be used to determine if guarded recursive specifications have unique solutions. They are also interesting in their own right. We look at the finite projections of a process and define when a process displays "bounded non-determinism". Up to 2.4.20, the definitions and results all concern the theory BPA. The introduction of δ or ε leads to some new definitions that will be presented starting in 2.4.21.

2.4.1 PROJECTION

We define the projection functions in order to obtain finite approximations of infinite processes. To that end, we define unary functions π_n, for each $n \geq 1$, with the equations in table 13. We assume we have a signature without constant ε.

$\pi_n(a) = a$	PR1
$\pi_1(ax) = a$	PR2
$\pi_{n+1}(ax) = a \cdot \pi_n(x)$	PR3
$\pi_n(x + y) = \pi_n(x) + \pi_n(y)$	PR4

TABLE 13. Projection.

In this table, the letter a stands for an arbitrary atomic action, so axiom PR1 says that $\pi_n(a) = a$ holds for every $a \in A$ (and for every $n \geq 1$). In case δ is in the signature, we also allow a to be equal to δ, i.e. we assume $a \in A \cup \{\delta\}$. Letters x,y are variables over processes. The theory obtained by enlarging the signature of BPA with the π_n operators, and adding axioms PR1-4, is called BPA + PR. Likewise, we have BPA$_\delta$ + PR. Note that the axioms follow the inductive definition of basic terms from 2.1.5. Therefore, by 2.1.6, we can calculate the projections of each closed term.

Later on (see 2.4.21), we will define a variant of the projection function, that also gives a projection for $n=0$, in order to simplify inductive proofs.

2.4.2 INTUITION

π_n is the operator that stops a process after n steps are executed, and is called the **projection operator**. For example, we have $\pi_1(abc) = a$, $\pi_2(abc) = ab$, and $\pi_n(abc) = abc$ for $n \geq 3$. Since π_n distributes over + (by axiom PR4), π_n is applied to every alternative, in case we have a sum of terms.

2.4.3 THEOREM

i. For every closed BPA+PR term t there is a basic BPA term s, such that

$$\text{BPA+PR} \vdash s=t.$$

This theorem says we can *eliminate* the π_n operators from closed terms.

ii. If t,s are two closed BPA terms, then

$$\text{BPA} \vdash s=t \iff \text{BPA+PR} \vdash s=t.$$

This theorem says BPA+PR is a **conservative extension** of BPA.

PROOF: i. We consider the following term rewriting system, that has rules corresponding to axioms A3-5 and PR1-4:

$$x + x \to x$$
$$(x + y)z \to xz + yz$$
$$(xy)z \to x(yz)$$
$$\pi_n(a) \to a$$
$$\pi_1(ax) \to a$$
$$\pi_{n+1}(ax) \to a \cdot \pi_n(x)$$
$$\pi_n(x + y) \to \pi_n(x) + \pi_n(y).$$

It is not hard to see that this term rewriting system is strongly normalizing, and that a normal form of a closed BPA+PR term must be a basic BPA term. Therefore, given a closed term t, we can find s by reducing t until a normal form is reached.

ii. Let s,t be closed BPA terms so that BPA+PR $\vdash s=t$. Now consider a proof of this equality. Each step in this proof corresponds to a one-step reduction in the term rewriting system above, or is an application of A1 or A2. Now we can show that this term rewriting system is confluent, even working modulo A1 and A2 (we do not spell out exactly what this means). As a consequence, we find that s and t have the same normal form (modulo A1, A2). Moreover, a rewriting never *introduces* a projection operator, so since s,t do not contain projection operators, the reductions of s,t to normal form must only use the first two rules. Replacing each $\to$ in these reductions by a = gives us a proof in BPA of the equality of s and t.

This theorem tells us that we can add the projection operators and their axioms to the theory BPA without changing any of our results. This is the reason we feel free to use projection operators whenever convenient, without explicitly enlarging the signature first. It is straightforward to prove the analogue of theorem 2.4.3 for the theory BPA_δ.

2.4.4 PROPOSITION

For each closed BPA+PR term t, there is an $n \geq 1$ such that for all $k \geq n$ we have

$$BPA+PR \vdash \pi_k(t) = t.$$

PROOF: By the previous theorem, it is enough to prove this proposition for all basic terms t. The proof uses induction on the structure of basic terms, as defined in 2.1.5. Since there are many such proofs in process algebra, this proof will be given in some detail.

We consider the three cases of 2.1.5:

CASE 1: t is an atomic action a. We can take $n=1$, since $\pi_k(a) = a$ for all $k \geq 1$.

CASE 2: t is of the form $a \cdot s$, with $a \in A$, and the proposition holds for s.
Let $n' \geq 1$ be such that $\pi_k(s) = s$ holds for all $k \geq n'$. Then we can take $n=n'+1$, since $k \geq n$ implies $k-1 \geq n'$, and therefore

$$\pi_k(as) = a \cdot \pi_{k-1}(s) = as.$$

CASE 3: t is of the form $s + r$, and the proposition holds for s and r.
Let $n' \geq 1$ be such that $\pi_k(s) = s$ for all $k \geq n'$, and let $n'' \geq 1$ be such that $\pi_k(r) = r$ for all $k \geq n''$. Then we can take $n=\max(n',n'')$. For $k \geq n$ then implies $k \geq n'$ and $k \geq n''$, whence

$$\pi_k(s + r) = \pi_k(s) + \pi_k(r) = s + r.$$

2.4.5 DEFINITION

A process p (in a certain model of BPA) is **finite** if there is a closed term t (not involving recursion constructs is in 2.3.11) such that p is the interpretation of a closed term. Note that the previous proposition implies that for every finite process p, there is an $n \geq 1$ such that for all $k \geq n$ we have $\pi_k(p) = p$.

In 2.3.1, we looked at the recursive equation $X = aX$, and found that the solution of this equation is the process that repeatedly executes the action a. Using the projection operators π_n, we can express this as follows:

$$X = aX \text{ implies } \pi_n(X) = a^n.$$

(where a^n is defined in the obvious way, see exercise 6). Since all the projections of a solution are different, we have by 2.4.5, that any solution must be an *infinite* process, so cannot be given by a closed BPA term.

We do have that all finite projections of a solution are given by a closed term. This is always the case, as we will see in theorem 2.4.8. First, we need a couple of definitions and a lemma.

2.4.6 DEFINITION

i. We say a process p **has a head normal form** if there are $n,m \in \mathbb{N}$, with $n+m>0$, atomic actions a_i $(i<n)$, b_j $(j<m)$ and processes p_i $(i<n)$ such that

$$p = \sum_{i<n} a_i \cdot p_i + \sum_{j<m} b_j.$$

By 2.1.6, we see that every closed term has a head normal form.

ii. A process p is **definable** if p can be obtained from the atomic actions A by means of the operators of BPA and guarded recursion (i.e. we can define p if we are allowed to use the constants $\langle X \mid E\rangle$ of 2.3.11 for each *guarded* recursive specification E).
iii. A process p is **finitely definable** if p can be obtained from the atomic actions A by means of the operators of BPA and *finite* guarded recursion (the constants $\langle X \mid E\rangle$ of 2.3.11 can only be used for guarded specifications E with finitely many equations).

Formally, the process p in definition 2.4.6 is an element from the domain of the model under consideration. Also, the operators $\cdot$ and $+$ have interpretations in that model. Note that this way, the properties of having a head normal form and of definability become model-dependent, since the validity of equations as given in (i) is model-dependent. These properties become model-independent, i.e. hold in all models of BPA, once the equation in (i) is derivable from BPA.

2.4.7 LEMMA
Each definable process has a head normal form.

PROOF: We need to prove that the set of definable processes is closed under $+$, $\cdot$ and guarded recursion. The case of $+$ is trivial.

For $\cdot$, suppose processes p and q have a head normal form. Let

$$p = \sum_{i<n} a_i \cdot p_i + \sum_{j<m} b_j,$$

where $n,m \in \mathbb{N}$, with $n+m>0$, the a_i, b_j are atomic actions, and the p_i processes.
Then $p\cdot q = (\sum_{i<n} a_i\cdot p_i + \sum_{j<m} b_j)\cdot q = \sum_{i<n} a_i\cdot p_i\cdot q + \sum_{j<m} b_j\cdot q$, so also $p\cdot q$ has a head normal form.

Finally, suppose that E is a guarded recursive specification with root variable X. By definition 2.3.6, we can assume that the right hand side of the equation for X, call it t, is completely guarded. By applying the two rewrite rules in the proof of proposition 2.1.6, we can rewrite t, such that t is a sum of terms, each of which is either an atomic action, or a product $t'\cdot t''$, where t' is not a product or a sum. That means t' must be a variable or an atomic action. But t' cannot be a variable, for it would occur unguarded. Thus t' is an atomic action, and we have written t in head normal form.

Note that the set of definable processes is also closed under projections π_n. Also note, that if p is definable, then p has a head normal form $\sum_{i<n} a_i\cdot p_i + \sum_{j<m} b_j$ with all the p_i definable.

2.4.8 THEOREM
All projections of a definable process are equal to a closed term.

PROOF: By induction on k we prove that for all definable processes p, $\pi_k(p)$ is equal to a closed term. First consider $k=1$. Let p be a definable process. By the previous lemma, p has a head normal form $\sum_{i<n} a_i\cdot p_i + \sum_{j<m} b_j$. We see immediately that $\pi_1(p) = \sum_{i<n} a_i + \sum_{j<m} b_j$, a closed term.

For the induction step, again let p be a definable process, with head normal form $\sum_{i<n} a_i\cdot p_i + \sum_{j<m} b_j$. From the above note we can assume that all the p_i are definable. Then $\pi_{k+1}(p) = \sum_{i<n} a_i\cdot\pi_k(p_i) + \sum_{j<m} b_j$. By induction hypothesis, all the $\pi_k(p_i)$ are equal to closed terms. Then it is immediate that also $\pi_{k+1}(p)$ is equal to a closed term.

2.4.9 COROLLARY
Let E be a guarded recursive specification with solutions p and q. Then for all $n \geq 1$ we have $\pi_n(p) = \pi_n(q)$. This is the so-called **projection theorem.**

2.4.10 EXAMPLE
We consider the guarded recursive specification

$$E \equiv \{X = aX + bcX\}.$$

This specification is completely guarded, so we immediately have a head normal form for X, and we can calculate $\pi_1(X)$:

$$\pi_1(X) = \pi_1(aX + bcX) = \pi_1(aX) + \pi_1(bcX) = a + b.$$

Next, we calculate $\pi_2(X)$:

$$\pi_2(X) = \pi_2(aX + bcX) = a \cdot \pi_1(X) + b \cdot \pi_1(cX) = a(a + b) + bc.$$

Continuing in this fashion, we can calculate $\pi_n(X)$ as a closed term for every n.

We see in corollary 2.4.9 that every solution of a guarded recursive specification has the same finite projections. If we assume that every recursive specification has a solution, and further that a process is determined by its finite projections, then it follows that guarded recursive specifications have unique solutions. These two assumptions are stated explicitly below in 2.4.11-12.

2.4.11 DEFINITION
The **Recursive Definition Principle** (**RDP**) is the following assumption:

every recursive specification has a solution

2.4.12 DEFINITION
The **Approximation Induction Principle** (**AIP**) is the following assumption:

a process is determined by its finite projections, i.e. $\forall n \geq 1 \;\; \pi_n(x) = \pi_n(y) \;\; \Rightarrow \;\; x = y$.

2.4.13 EXAMPLE
Unfortunately, the principles RDP and AIP, if they are combined, clash with our intuition about processes, as the following example shows.

Consider the (unguarded!) recursive equation $X = Xa + a$, and assume (using RDP), that p is a solution of this equation. Then $p = pa + a$, so $a \leq p$. This implies $aa \leq pa \leq pa + a = p$, so $aa \leq p$. Continuing like this, we obtain that $a^n \leq p$ for each $n \geq 1$ (for the notation $\leq$ see exercise 2.1.13.7).

We see that the process $p = \sum_{n \geq 1} a^n$ that only has summands a^n, and no others, is a solution of the recursive equation. Let process $q = a^\omega$ be a solution of the equation $X = aX$ (already considered in 2.3.1). It follows, using AIP, that $p = p + q$. This, however, is counterintuitive, since in p, every execution sequence will terminate successfully after finitely many steps, but q has an infinite execution sequence, that never terminates.

2.4.14 THREE ALTERNATIVES

We will consider three possible solutions to the problem sketched in 2.4.13, and will have a model for each alternative.

i. We can weaken the principle RDP to the principle RDP$^-$. RDP$^-$ states that all ***guarded*** recursive specifications have a solution. Notice that when we talk about definable processes, we implicitly assume that RDP$^-$ holds.

ii. We can weaken the principle AIP to the principle AIP$^-$ which states that all processes that display *bounded non-determinism*, are determined by their finite projections. The notion of bounded non-determinism will be explained in the sequel.

iii. We can maintain both principles RDP and AIP, and accept that $p = p + q$ and similar equations hold.

2.4.15 DEFINITION

A process p (in a certain model of BPA) has **bounded non-determinism** if for each sequence of atomic actions σ, the set of processes q with $p \overset{\sigma}{\twoheadrightarrow} q$ is finite.

This definition depends on the model, and since we have a preference for model-independent reasoning, we will give an axiomatization of this notion. As an auxiliary notion we need **bounded non-determinism up to depth n**: process p has bounded non-determinism up to depth n, $B_n(p)$, iff for each sequence σ of length less than n, $\{q : p \overset{\sigma}{\twoheadrightarrow} q\}$ is finite. The predicates B_n are axiomatized in the following table.

$B_1(x)$
$B_n(a)$
$B_n(x) \Rightarrow B_{n+1}(ax)$
$B_n(x)$ and $B_n(y) \Rightarrow B_n(x + y)$

TABLE 14. Bounded non-determinism.

Thus, x has bounded non-determinism iff $B_n(x)$ for all $n \geq 1$.

2.4.16 LEMMA

Let p be a definable process. Then p has bounded non-determinism.

PROOF: By induction on k we prove that for all definable processes p, $B_k(p)$ holds. For $k=1$, it follows immediately from table 14. For the induction step, let p be a definable process. By lemma 2.3.7, p has a head normal form $\sum_{i<n} a_i \cdot p_i + \sum_{j<m} b_j$, such that all p_i are definable. By induction hypothesis, $B_k(p_i)$ for all $i<n$. Using table 14, we obtain $B_{k+1}(a_i p_i)$ for each $i<n$, and $B_{k+1}(b_j)$ for each $j<m$, from which it follows that $B_{k+1}(p)$.

2.4.17 EXAMPLE

Lemma 2.4.16 shows that the class of processes with bounded non-determinism is fairly large. An example of a process with unbounded non-determinism is the process $p = \sum_{n\geq 1} a^n$ from 2.4.14, for $p \overset{a}{\rightarrow} a^n$ for each n.

2.4.18 DEFINITION

The **Recursive Specification Principle** (**RSP**) is the following assumption:

a guarded recursive specification has at most one solution

For reasons of clarity, we repeat the definitions of RDP^- and AIP^-:
The **Restricted Recursive Definition Principle, RDP^-** is:

every guarded recursive specification has a solution

The **Restricted Approximation Induction Principle, AIP^-** is:

$\forall n \geq 1 \;\; \pi_n(x) = \pi_n(y) \;\&\; B_n(x) \;\; \Rightarrow \;\; x = y$

2.4.19 THEOREM
AIP^- implies RSP.

PROOF: Suppose that a guarded recursive specification E has solutions p and q. By the projection theorem 2.4.9 we have $\pi_n(p) = \pi_n(q)$ for all $n \geq 1$. By 2.4.16, p and q display bounded non-determinism. Then it follows from AIP^- that $p = q$.

It follows that in every model that satisfies RDP^- and AIP^-, guarded recursive specifications have unique solutions. In the following sections, we will define such models. The term model $\mathbb{P}/\underline{\leftrightarrow}$ of section 2.5, and the graph model $\mathbb{G}^\infty/\underline{\leftrightarrow}$ of 2.7, satisfy RDP and AIP^-. The projective limit model $\mathbb{A}^\infty$ of section 2.6 satisfies RDP and AIP (and thus identifies the processes p and $p+q$ of 2.4.15), and the graph model $\mathbb{G}/\underline{\leftrightarrow}$ of 2.7 satisfies RDP^- and AIP.

2.4.20 EXAMPLES
As an example, let us consider the principles RDP, AIP and RSP in $\mathbb{A}$, the initial algebra of BPA.
i. $\mathbb{A} \not\models RDP^-$, because infinite processes do not exist in $\mathbb{A}$: no closed term over BPA satisfies the equation $X = aX$.
ii. $\mathbb{A} \models$ AIP, because all processes in $\mathbb{A}$ are finite (use 2.4.4).
iii. $\mathbb{A} \models$ RSP. This follows from 2.4.19.

2.4.21 PROJECTION AND TERMINATION
In the presence of ε things are a little different. Since ε represents immediate termination, it has no possibility of performing any action, and so according to our intuition we expect to see that it has depth 0. That is: $\pi_0(\varepsilon) = \varepsilon$. Then we can also define a projection π_n for $n=0$, by putting $\pi_0(x) = \varepsilon$. In BPA_ε we can define the projection operator π_n as in table 15 below, for $n \geq 0$ and $a \in A$. This set of axioms will be called PRE, i.e. projection with empty process.

$\pi_n(\varepsilon) = \varepsilon$	PRE1
$\pi_0(x) = \varepsilon$	PRE2
$\pi_{n+1}(ax) = a \cdot \pi_n(x)$	PRE3
$\pi_n(x + y) = \pi_n(x) + \pi_n(y)$	PRE4

TABLE 15. Projection with ε.

Note that we do not need to include the axioms PR1 and PR2 from table 13, since they have become derivable (see exercise 10). Axiom PRE3 is the same as PR3, PRE4 is the same as PR4 (but now also for $n=0$). Observe that the equations from table 15 follow the structure of basic terms as given in 2.2.7, and so the projection operator is defined on all closed terms in BPA_ε.

We will not go over all the results in this section again in order to establish them in the presence of ε. All definitions and proofs in this section apply in the same way to BPA_ε with the definition of π_n as in table 15 and the definitions adapted in a straightforward way.

2.4.22 DEADLOCK

In order to define projection in the setting of $BPA_{\delta\varepsilon}$, we can just use 2.4.21. The only difference is that in axiom PRE3 from table 15 we have $a \in A \cup \{\delta\}$ instead of $a \in A$.

2.4.23 EXERCISES

1. Prove the analogue of theorem 2.4.3 for the theory BPA_δ.
2. For $X = aX + bcX$, calculate $\pi_3(X)$ (see 2.4.10).
3. For $X = (aX + b)cX$, calculate $\pi_1(X)$, $\pi_2(X)$, $\pi_3(X)$.
4. Prove (using AIP−) that if $X = aXb$, then also $X = aX$.
5. Does the equation $X = a + X$ have a solution in $\mathbb{A}$ (or more than one)? What about the equation $X = aX + X$?
6. For a process p, and for $n \geq 1$, define p^n (using induction on n). Then, prove that $\pi_n(a^\omega) = a^n$ (a^ω as defined in 2.3.1).
7. Given the equation $X = aX + bX$, determine $\pi_n(X)$ for every $n \geq 1$. Which notation can we use for X?
8. Prove by structural induction (for an example of this technique see 2.4.4) that for all closed terms t,s in BPA the following holds $(n,m \geq 1)$:

i. $\pi_n(\pi_m(t)) = \pi_{\min(n,m)}(t)$

ii. $\pi_1(t \cdot s) = \pi_1(t)$

iii. $\pi_{n+1}(t \cdot s) = \pi_{n+1}(\pi_{n+1}(t) \cdot \pi_n(s))$.

9. Prove that the equations of exercise 8 hold for all definable processes.
10. Prove PR1 and PR2 from the axioms in table 15.
11. Reformulate definition 2.4.6 in case we also have ε. Then, using this new definition, prove lemma 2.4.7 and theorem 2.4.8.
12. From 2.4.1 we find that π_n $(n \geq 1)$ has the following action relations:

$x \xrightarrow{a} \surd$	$\Rightarrow$	$\pi_n(x) \xrightarrow{a} \surd$
$x \xrightarrow{a} x'$	$\Rightarrow$	$\pi_1(x) \xrightarrow{a} \surd$
$x \xrightarrow{a} x'$	$\Rightarrow$	$\pi_{n+1}(x) \xrightarrow{a} \pi_n(x')$

TABLE 16. Action relations for projection.

Define the action relations for π_n with δ and/or ε.

13. Observe that if we change the second equation in table 15 to $\pi_0(ax) = \varepsilon$, then we obtain a definition for π_n on BPA_ε without δ. Check that all results in section 2.4 still hold in this new setting, after having made the obvious adaptations.

14. A different way to look at projection is as follows. The n-th projection of x is the same as x except that all of its parts with depth larger than n are replaced by δ. That is: the process is blocked after being executed up to depth n. So, as an alternative we obtain the following axioms ($n \geq 0$):

$\tilde{\pi}_0(a) = \delta$
$\tilde{\pi}_{n+1}(a) = a$
$\tilde{\pi}_0(ax) = \delta$
$\tilde{\pi}_{n+1}(ax) = a \cdot \tilde{\pi}_n(x)$
$\tilde{\pi}_n(x + y) = \tilde{\pi}_n(x) + \tilde{\pi}_n(y)$

TABLE 17. Alternative projection function.

Note that with this definition, we can define a projection function for $n \geq 0$ on BPA_δ.

i. Prove theorem 2.4.8 using these projection axioms instead of the ones in table 13.
ii. Find axioms for $\tilde{\pi}_n$ involving the empty process ε, in the same fashion as is done in 2.4.21.

2.4.24 NOTES AND COMMENTS

Projection operators occur in many places in the literature, see e.g. DE BAKKER & ZUCKER [1982], BERGSTRA & KLOP [1982]. The definition of $\tilde{\pi}_n$ in exercise 2.4.23.12 is taken from VAN GLABBEEK [1987]. The notion of head normal form first appeared in BAETEN & VAN GLABBEEK [1987a]. The projection theorem is from BAETEN, BERGSTRA & KLOP [1987a]. The principles RDP, AIP and RSP were formulated in BERGSTRA & KLOP [1986a]. Example 2.4.14, and a formulation of AIP⁻ that is a little more restrictive than the present one, can be found in BAETEN, BERGSTRA & KLOP [1987b]. The present version of AIP⁻, and the notion of bounded non-determinism, are from VAN GLABBEEK [1987]. Exercise 8 is from BERGSTRA & KLOP [1982].

2.5 THE TERM MODEL

In the following sections (2.5, 2.6, 2.7), we will present a number of models of which BPA is a *complete axiomatization* (see 1.3.6). That is, in such a model every equation between closed terms is valid iff it is derivable from BPA. Equations between more complex elements (for instance infinite solutions of guarded recursive specifications) may not be derivable however, which will be an argument to consider additional principles such as AIP, AIP⁻, RDP, RDP⁻ or RSP. As we will see, these principles need not all be valid in any 'reasonable' model of BPA. We will find models in which some are valid, and others are not, illustrating that using these principles is not without further implications as to the nature of processes and their semantics.

In constructing models for BPA, we will stick closely to the intuitions of choice and sequential composition as presented in 2.1.2 and 2.1.3. The idea is that equivalent processes do not only perform the same sequences (traces) of actions but also their *branching structure* is identical, that is the moments of choice cannot be distinguished as for instance in 2.1.3 and 2.1.4. A way to define such an equivalence can be found in 2.5.2, where the notion of *bisimulation* is introduced.

The first model, presented in this section, will be one in which the principles RDP, AIP$^-$ and RSP hold. Therefore, every guarded recursive specification has a unique solution in this model. We will extend our results to the setting with δ or ε.

2.5.1 DEFINITION
The set $\mathbb{P}$ of process expressions is constructed inductively as follows:
i. each atomic action is a process expression;
ii. if E is a recursive specification, and X a variable of E, then $\langle X \mid E \rangle$ is a process expression;
iii. if p,q are process expressions, then $p+q$, $p \cdot q$ and $\pi_n(p)$ are process expressions.

So $\mathbb{P}$ is the set of all terms that we can construct from BPA and the constructs $\langle t \mid E \rangle$ for every BPA term t and recursive specification E (see 2.3.11). In order to turn $\mathbb{P}$ into a model of BPA, we must determine which expressions denote the same process. Roughly, two expressions denote the same process if the same action relations hold. Note that the projection operator π_n has action relations from exercise 2.4.23.12.

2.5.2 DEFINITION
A **bisimulation** is a binary relation R on $\mathbb{P}$, satisfying:
i. if R(p,q) and $p \xrightarrow{a} p'$, then there is a q' such that $q \xrightarrow{a} q'$ and R(p',q')
ii. if R(p,q) and $q \xrightarrow{a} q'$, then there is a p' such that $p \xrightarrow{a} p'$ and R(p',q')
iii. if R(p,q) then: $p \xrightarrow{a} \surd$ if and only if $q \xrightarrow{a} \surd$.

Process expressions p and q are **bisimilar**, notation $p \leftrightarrow q$, if there exists a bisimulation R on $\mathbb{P}$ with R(p,q). We denote the set $\{q \in \mathbb{P} : p \leftrightarrow q\}$ by $p/\leftrightarrow$.

Intuitively, bisimilarity guarantees that the branching structure of two processes is equal, provided that equal branches may be identified (obeying the law $x + x = x$). The idea is, that if one process is capable of performing an a-step to a new state, then any equivalent process should be able to do an a-step to a corresponding state.

2.5.3 EXAMPLE
We can think of the notion of bisimulation in terms of a two-person game. Suppose two players each have a process expression. Then one makes a move, performing an a-step to a certain expression. The other player must be able to match this move, also by performing an a-step. Next, one of the players makes the next move (not necessarily the same one who made the first move). The other must match this move, and so on.

If both players can play so that every sequence of moves can be matched, the starting expressions will bisimulate. If, on the other hand, a sequence of moves can be devised that cannot be matched, the expressions will not be bisimilar.

For instance, consider $\langle X \mid X = aX + aY, Y = aY + aaY \rangle$ and $\langle Z \mid Z = aZ \rangle$ as two expressions. We must find a bisimulation relation R between X and Z if one exists. The question is: if we start playing the game from either X or Z, are we always capable of matching every sequence of moves? The question can be rephrased as: do we have that R(X,Z)?

Clearly, the answer is 'yes', for assume we start by performing $X \xrightarrow{a} X$ then a possible answer is $Z \xrightarrow{a} Z$ and both players have returned in the positions X and Z respectively, and we already had R(X,Z). Alternatively, assume we start with $X \xrightarrow{a} Y$, then the answer is $Z \xrightarrow{a} Z$ and so we need R(Y,Z). If we start from the other side, we proceed as in the first case. Now we have $Y \xrightarrow{a} aY$ and $Z \xrightarrow{a} Z$ so we need to have $R(aY,Z)$, which follows from the fact that $aY \xrightarrow{a} Y$ and $Z \xrightarrow{a} Z$ as we already have $R(Y,Z)$.

Thus we find that $R(X,Z)$, $R(Y,Z)$ and $R(aY,Y)$. One easily finds that R is a bisimulation relation between $\langle X \mid X = aX + aY,\ Y = aY + aaY\rangle$ and $\langle Z \mid Z = aZ\rangle$ according to definition 2.5.2.

Warning: this method does not provide us with a way to *decide* on bisimulation equivalence between processes, because the 'game' need not be terminating. If we restrict ourselves to finite specifications however, it is.

2.5.4 PROPOSITION
$\underline{\leftrightarrow}$ is a congruence relation on $\mathbb{P}$ with respect to $+,\cdot$ and π_n.

PROOF: Left as an exercise.

2.5.5 THEOREM
$\mathbb{P}/\underline{\leftrightarrow}$ is a model of BPA + PR1-PR4.

PROOF: Follows easily using 2.1.7 and 2.3.11.

2.5.6 THEOREM
$\mathbb{P}/\underline{\leftrightarrow}$ satisfies RDP.

PROOF: A specification E has $\langle X \mid E\rangle/\underline{\leftrightarrow}$ as a solution.

The model $\mathbb{P}/\underline{\leftrightarrow}$ will be referred to as the **term model**.

Recall that an expression $p \in \mathbb{P}$ has bounded non-determinism if $\{q \in \mathbb{P} : p \xrightarrow{\sigma}\!\!\!\!\rightarrow q\}$ is finite for any sequence σ of atomic actions. Likewise a process $P \in \mathbb{P}/\underline{\leftrightarrow}$ has bounded non-determinism if $\{Q \in \mathbb{P}/\underline{\leftrightarrow} : P \xrightarrow{\sigma}\!\!\!\!\rightarrow Q\}$ is finite, where $P \xrightarrow{\sigma}\!\!\!\!\rightarrow Q$ iff $p \xrightarrow{\sigma}\!\!\!\!\rightarrow q$ for some $p \in P$, $q \in Q$. Define the predicates B_n on $\mathbb{P}/\underline{\leftrightarrow}$ in the obvious way: $B_n(P)$ iff $\{Q \in \mathbb{P}/\underline{\leftrightarrow} : P \xrightarrow{\sigma}\!\!\!\!\rightarrow Q\}$ is finite for any σ of length $<n$.

2.5.7 LEMMA
i. If $p \in \mathbb{P}$ has bounded non-determinism and $p \xrightarrow{\sigma}\!\!\!\!\rightarrow q$, then also q has bounded non-determinism;
ii. If $P \in \mathbb{P}/\underline{\leftrightarrow}$ has bounded non-determinism, then there is a $p \in P$ with bounded non-determinism.

PROOF: i. Immediate.
ii. We write a guarded recursive specification E for P as follows: we have a root variable X associated with P; for each process Q_i such that $P \xrightarrow{a_i} Q_i$ for some $a_i \in A$, we introduce a variable X_i. Then, the equation for X in E is

$$X = \sum_i a_i X_i + \sum_j b_j,$$

where the second sum is taken over all $b_j \in A$ such that $P \xrightarrow{b_j} \surd$. Continuing in this fashion, we then add equations for the processes Q_i, and so on.

In this way, we obtain a guarded recursive specification E, and the process $p \equiv \langle X \mid E\rangle$ has bounded non-determinism by 2.4.16. Finally, check that $p \in P$.

2.5.8 THEOREM

The model $\mathbb{P}/\underline{\leftrightarrow}$ satisfies AIP$^-$.

PROOF: Let $P,Q \in \mathbb{P}/\underline{\leftrightarrow}$, such that for all $n \geq 1$ we have $B_n(Q)$ and $\pi_n(P) = \pi_n(Q)$. It has to be proved that $P = Q$. Take $p \in P$ and $q \in Q$ such that q has bounded non-determinism (such a q exists by the previous lemma). We have $\pi_n(p) \underline{\leftrightarrow} \pi_n(q)$ for all n, and we must prove that $p \underline{\leftrightarrow} q$, i.e. that there is a bisimulation R on $\mathbb{P}$ with $R(p,q)$.

CLAIM: R can be defined by:

$R(u,v) \Leftrightarrow$ for all $n \geq 1$ $\pi_n(u) \underline{\leftrightarrow} \pi_n(v)$, and v has bounded non-determinism.

PROOF OF THE CLAIM: Suppose $R(u,v)$ and $u \xrightarrow{a} u'$ for some $a \in A$. Now define, for $n>1$, $S_n = \{v^* \in \mathbb{P} : v \xrightarrow{a} v^*$ and $\pi_n(u') \underline{\leftrightarrow} \pi_n(v^*)\}$. We can make the following observations:

1. $S_1 \supseteq S_2 \supseteq \ldots$, since $\pi_{n+1}(u') \underline{\leftrightarrow} \pi_{n+1}(v^*)$ implies $\pi_n(u') \underline{\leftrightarrow} \pi_n(v^*)$;
2. each S_n is non-empty, since $\pi_{n+1}(u) \underline{\leftrightarrow} \pi_{n+1}(v)$;
3. each S_n is finite, since v has bounded non-determinism (use the previous lemma).

From these observations, we can conclude that the sequence $S_1,S_2,\ldots,S_n,\ldots$ must remain constant from some n onwards, and so $\bigcap_{n \geq 1} S_n$ is non-empty. Choose v' in this intersection, then $v \xrightarrow{a} v'$ and $R(u',v')$. This verifies the first part of the bisimulation.

For the second part, suppose $R(u,v)$ and $v \xrightarrow{a} v'$ for some $a \in A$. Define, analogously to the previous case, $S_n = \{u^* \in \mathbb{P} : u \xrightarrow{a} u^*$ and $\pi_n(u^*) \underline{\leftrightarrow} \pi_n(v')\}$ (for $n \geq 1$). We can again observe that $S_1,S_2,\ldots$ form a decreasing sequence, and are non-empty (but not that they are finite). Now, for each $n \geq 1$, pick a term $u_n \in S_n$. By the first part of this proof, there are $v_n \in \mathbb{P}$ such that $v \xrightarrow{a} v_n$ and $R(u_n,v_n)$. But since v has bounded non-determinism, there must be a term v^* that occurs infinitely many times in the sequence $v_1,v_2,\ldots,v_n,\ldots$. Let k be an index such that $v^* \equiv v_k$. We claim that $R(u_k,v')$, thereby proving the second part of the bisimulation. To prove this fact, fix $n \geq 1$. Choose an index $m > n$ such that $v^* \equiv v_m$. Then $\pi_n(u_m) \underline{\leftrightarrow} \pi_n(v')$, since $u_m \in S_m \subseteq S_n$. Furthermore $R(u_m,v^*)$ and $R(u_k,v^*)$, so $\pi_n(u_k) \underline{\leftrightarrow} \pi_n(v^*) \underline{\leftrightarrow} \pi_n(u_m) \underline{\leftrightarrow} \pi_n(v')$. We have shown that $\pi_n(u_k) \underline{\leftrightarrow} \pi_n(v')$ holds for any $n \geq 1$, and thus $R(u_k,v')$.

Finally, note that if $R(u,v)$ holds then $u \xrightarrow{a} \surd \Leftrightarrow \pi_1(u) \xrightarrow{a} \surd \Leftrightarrow \pi_1(v) \xrightarrow{a} \surd \Leftrightarrow v \xrightarrow{a} \surd$.

This finishes the proof of the claim, and thereby also the proof of the theorem.

2.5.9 LEMMA

1. The (unrestricted) AIP does not hold in $\mathbb{P}/\underline{\leftrightarrow}$.
2. The model $\mathbb{P}/\underline{\leftrightarrow}$ satisfies RSP.

PROOF: 1. The proof is along the lines of example 2.4.14. Let $p \equiv \langle X \mid X = Xa + a\rangle$ and $q \equiv \langle X \mid X = aX\rangle$, then it is easy to show that $\pi_n(p) \underline{\leftrightarrow} \sum_{k \leq n} a^k \underline{\leftrightarrow} \pi_n(p + q)$ for each $n \geq 1$. On the other hand, we cannot have $p \underline{\leftrightarrow} p + q$, for $(p + q) \xrightarrow{a} q$ but not $p \xrightarrow{a} q$. Note that p does not have bounded non-determinism, since $p \xrightarrow{a} a^n$ for each $n \geq 1$.

2. By theorem 2.4.19.

The following theorem is the completeness theorem for $\mathbb{P}/\underline{\leftrightarrow}$ with respect to BPA.

2.5.10 THEOREM

Let s,t be two closed BPA terms (i.e. not containing recursion constants $\langle X \mid E\rangle$). Then:

$$\text{BPA} \vdash s=t \Leftrightarrow s \underline{\leftrightarrow} t.$$

PROOF: $\Rightarrow$: This is theorem 2.5.5.
$\Leftarrow$: By proposition 2.1.6 there are basic terms s', t' such that BPA $\vdash$ s' = s and BPA $\vdash$ t' = t. Using the first part of this proof, we find that s' $\underline{\leftrightarrow}$ s and t' $\underline{\leftrightarrow}$ t. As $\underline{\leftrightarrow}$ is an equivalence relation we find s' $\underline{\leftrightarrow}$ t' and so it is sufficient to prove $\Leftarrow$ only for basic terms. We use induction on the structure of s and t. Thus, let s,t be two basic terms and suppose s $\underline{\leftrightarrow}$ t. Consider a summand s' of s. If s' is of the form as* (for certain a$\in$A) we have s $\xrightarrow{a}$ s*. Since s $\underline{\leftrightarrow}$ t, there must be a term t* with t $\xrightarrow{a}$ t* and s* $\underline{\leftrightarrow}$ t*. By 2.1.10, at* is a summand of t. By induction hypothesis, BPA $\vdash$ s* = t*. Thus, s' $\equiv$ as* = at* $\leq$ t. The case that s' is of the form a (a$\in$A) is easier, and thus every summand of s is a BPA-summand of t, or s $\leq$ t. By symmetry it follows that t $\leq$ s, and so BPA $\vdash$ s = t.

2.5.11 DEADLOCK
It is quite easy to define the term model including the constant δ: from paragraph 2.2.9 we know that the introduction of δ does not change the action relations. Thus we can simply add δ to $\mathbb{P}$ as an additional constant in definition 2.5.1.i, obtaining $\mathbb{P}_\delta$. Using the definition of bisimulation from 2.5.2 we then find the following theorem.

2.5.12 THEOREM
i. $\underline{\leftrightarrow}$ is a congruence relation on $\mathbb{P}_\delta$;
ii. $\mathbb{P}_\delta/\underline{\leftrightarrow}$ is a model for BPA_δ.

It is left to the reader to prove that $\mathbb{P}_\delta/\underline{\leftrightarrow}$ satisfies RDP, AIP^- and RSP, and that BPA_δ is a sound and complete axiomatization of $\mathbb{P}_\delta/\underline{\leftrightarrow}$ with respect to closed terms.

2.5.13 TERMINATION
Concerning ε we find different action relations (see 2.2.9) and hence need a new definition of bisimulation on terms including this constant. As before, one can easily extend the domain $\mathbb{P}$ to $\mathbb{P}_\varepsilon$. We consider the action relations as defined in table 11 in 2.2.9.

2.5.14 DEFINITION
A **bisimulation** on $\mathbb{P}_\varepsilon$ is a binary relation R, satisfying:
i. if R(p,q) and p $\xrightarrow{a}$ p', then there is a q' such that q $\xrightarrow{a}$ q' and R(p',q')
ii. if R(p,q) and q $\xrightarrow{a}$ q', then there is a p' such that p $\xrightarrow{a}$ p' and R(p',q')
iii. if R(p,q) then p$\downarrow$ if and only if q$\downarrow$.
Again, process expressions p and q are **bisimilar**, notation p $\underline{\leftrightarrow}$ q, if there exists a bisimulation R on $\mathbb{P}$ with R(p,q).

2.5.15 THEOREM
i. $\underline{\leftrightarrow}$ is a congruence relation on $\mathbb{P}_\varepsilon$;
ii. $\mathbb{P}_\varepsilon/\underline{\leftrightarrow}$ is a model for BPA_ε.

Again, we leave it to the reader to check that $\mathbb{P}_\varepsilon/\underline{\leftrightarrow}$ satisfies RDP, AIP^- and RSP, and that BPA_ε is a sound and complete axiomatization of $\mathbb{P}_\varepsilon/\underline{\leftrightarrow}$ with respect to closed terms. A similar result can be found if both δ and ε are included in the signature. Note that, following 2.2.9, the action relations do not change by the introduction of δ, and hence the model $\mathbb{P}_{\delta\varepsilon}/\underline{\leftrightarrow}$ can be constructed along the same lines. It is easy to verify the analogue to theorem 2.5.15 in this case.

2.5.16 EXERCISES

1. Try to make the game-theoretic definition of bisimulation of 2.5.3 somewhat more precise.
2. Prove proposition 2.5.4.
3. Let $p,q,r \in \mathbb{P}$. Give bisimulations on $\mathbb{P}$ to show the following:
i. $p + q \underline{\leftrightarrow} q + p$; ii. $p + p \underline{\leftrightarrow} p$; iii. $(p + q)r \underline{\leftrightarrow} pr + qr$.
4. Show that $\mathbb{P}/\underline{\leftrightarrow}$ satisfies the equations in table 13 (in 2.4.1).
5. Fill in the details in the proof of 2.5.9.
6. Show that the model $\mathbb{P}/\underline{\leftrightarrow}$ also is sound and complete for closed terms containing the operators π_n (see 2.4.3).
7. Check that $\mathbb{P}/\underline{\leftrightarrow} \models \langle X \mid X = X + a\rangle = a$, using the definitions 2.3.11 and 2.5.2.
8. Prove theorem 2.5.12.
9. Prove theorem 2.5.15.

2.5.17 NOTES AND COMMENTS

The material of this section is taken from VAN GLABBEEK [1987]. The proof of 2.5.8 is a reconstruction of a proof in BAETEN, BERGSTRA & KLOP [1987b], which shows that a slightly different version of AIP$^-$ holds in an (isomorphic) graph model. A reference for exercise 2.5.16.1 is OGUZTUZUN [1989].

2.6 PROJECTIVE LIMIT MODEL

In this section, we present a model for the theory BPA, that satisfies the principles RDP and AIP. Therefore, guarded recursive specifications have unique solutions.

The starting point for this model is corollary 2.4.9: a solution of a guarded recursive specification has a fixed sequence of closed terms as its projections. These projections can be considered the finite approximations of the solution. We now take the view that a process is completely determined by this sequence of closed terms, and so the elements of the model to be presented now are all infinite sequences of closed terms that 'fit together'. (This is comparable to the construction of the real numbers by use of Cauchy sequences.) Again we start off without δ or ε.

2.6.1 DEFINITION

The algebraic structure $\mathbb{A}^\infty$ has the set of infinite sequences $(p_1, p_2, p_3, ...)$ of elements of the initial algebra $\mathbb{A}$ as its domain. These terms must however "fit", i.e. it must be possible that they are successive projections of the same process. That is why we have the following restriction:

$$\text{for all } n\geq 1,\ \pi_n(p_{n+1}) = p_n \qquad (*).$$

An infinite sequence that satisfies (*) is called a **projective sequence**, and we call $\mathbb{A}^\infty$, the structure with the set of projective sequences as its domain, the **projective limit model.**

On $\mathbb{A}^\infty$, we define equality, and the operators $+,\cdot,\pi_n$ as follows:

i. $(p_1,p_2,p_3,...) = (q_1,q_2,q_3,...) \Leftrightarrow$ for all $n\geq 1$ $\mathbb{A} \models p_n = q_n$,

ii. $(p_1,p_2,p_3,...) + (q_1,q_2,q_3,...) = (p_1+q_1, p_2+q_2, p_3+q_3, ...)$,

iii. $(p_1,p_2,p_3,...) \cdot (q_1,q_2,q_3,...) = (\pi_1(p_1 \cdot q_1), \pi_2(p_2 \cdot q_2), \pi_3(p_3 \cdot q_3), ...)$,
iv. $\pi_n(p_1,p_2,...,p_n,p_{n+1},...) = (p_1,p_2,...,p_{n-1},p_n,p_n,p_n,...)$.

Note that, in the definition of $\cdot$, we have to take projections, since otherwise the result need not be a projective sequence.

2.6.2 EXAMPLES

1. The interpretation in $\mathbb{A}^\infty$ of the atomic process a is $(a,a,a,...)$. Similarly, the interpretation in $\mathbb{A}^\infty$ of a process $p \in \mathbb{A}$ is the sequence $(\pi_1(p), \pi_2(p), \pi_3(p), ...)$.
2. $(a, a^2, a^3, ...) \in \mathbb{A}^\infty$ is the process a^ω of 2.3.1.
3. $(a, a + a^2, a + a^2 + a^3, ...) \in \mathbb{A}^\infty$ is the process $\Sigma_{n \geq 1}\, a^n$ of 2.4.14.

2.6.3 THEOREM

$\mathbb{A}^\infty$ is a model of BPA.

PROOF: Axioms A1-4 are easy to verify. In order to show that A5 holds, namely $(xy)z = x(yz)$, we make the following observations:

1. If $(p_1,p_2,...,p_n,...) \in \mathbb{A}^\infty$, then $\pi_n(p_n) = p_n$.
2. If $p,q \in \mathbb{A}$, then $\pi_n(p \cdot q) = \pi_n(\pi_n(p) \cdot \pi_n(q))$.

Fact 1 is a simple consequence of exercise 2.4.23.7.i:

$$\pi_n(p_n) = \pi_n(\pi_n(p_{n+1})) = \pi_n(p_{n+1}) = p_n.$$

Fact 2 is a weaker version of 2.4.23.7.ii and iii. Using these two facts it is easy to prove that A5 holds in $\mathbb{A}^\infty$.

2.6.4 THEOREM

The principles AIP and RDP hold in $\mathbb{A}^\infty$.

PROOF: The fact that AIP holds is an immediate consequence of the definition of $\mathbb{A}^\infty$. RDP holds as a consequence of the projection theorem (2.4.9), but this requires a very complicated proof.

2.6.5 DEFINITION

Let $n \geq 1$. We define the *finite* model $\mathbb{A}^n$ of BPA as follows: $\mathbb{A}^n$ has domain $\{\pi_n(p) : p \in \mathbb{A}\}$, with equality from $\mathbb{A}$, and operations $+_n$, $\cdot_n$ defined by $p +_n q = p + q$ and $p \cdot_n q = \pi_n(p \cdot q)$. Then, the model $\mathbb{A}^\infty$ is the *projective limit* of the models $\mathbb{A}^n$.

2.6.6 NOTE

We can turn the model $\mathbb{A}^\infty$ into a metric space by defining the following metric: if $p \equiv (p_1,p_2,...)$ and $q \equiv (q_1,q_2,...)$ are elements of $\mathbb{A}^\infty$, then we define their distance by $d(p,q) = 2^{-n}$, where n is the smallest number such that $\mathbb{A} \models p_n \neq q_n$, and $d(p,q) = 0$ if for all n we have $p_n = q_n$. Then, we can prove that $\mathbb{A}^\infty$ is a metric space, which is the completion of the space $\mathbb{A}$, that the operators are continuous mappings, and that $\mathbb{A}^\infty$ is compact (this last statement makes use of the finiteness of the set of atomic actions A). The existence of unique solutions for guarded recursive specifications then becomes an application of the contraction theorem of Banach. We will not consider the metrical and topological aspects of $\mathbb{A}^\infty$ any further.

2.6.7 DEFINITION

A consequence of the fact that the model $\mathbb{A}^\infty$ is the metrical completion of $\mathbb{A}$ is that the following Limit Rule holds in $\mathbb{A}^\infty$. We will, however, prove this fact without reference to metrics. The Limit Rule states that all equations that hold for all basic terms, hold for all processes. The following formulation is more exact.

Let $s(x_1,...,x_n)$, $t(x_1,...,x_n)$ be two BPA terms with variables among $x_1,...,x_n$ (this means that every variable that occurs in s or t must be from the list $x_1,...,x_n$, but that not necessarily every element of the list occurs).

Then the **Limit Rule** (**LR**) is the following statement:

if for all basic terms $p_1,...,p_n$: $s(p_1,...,p_n) = t(p_1,...,p_n)$
then: $s(x_1,...,x_n) = t(x_1,...,x_n)$

2.6.8 THEOREM

LR holds in $\mathbb{A}^\infty$.

PROOF: It is easy to derive the following equations, for all $p,q \in \mathbb{A}^\infty$:

1. $\pi_n(p + q) = \pi_n(\pi_n(p) + \pi_n(q))$,
2. $\pi_n(p \cdot q) = \pi_n(\pi_n(p) \cdot \pi_n(q))$.

Now let $s(x_1,...,x_n)$, $t(x_1,...,x_n)$ be two BPA terms with variables among $x_1,...,x_n$, and suppose the premise of the Limit Rule holds. Let $p_1,...,p_n$ be elements of $\mathbb{A}^\infty$. Let $k \geq 1$. Then

$\pi_k(s(p_1,...,p_n)) = \pi_k(s(\pi_k(p_1), ..., \pi_k(p_n)))$

(by the equations above)

$= \pi_k(t(\pi_k(p_1), ..., \pi_k(p_n)))$

(by the hypothesis in LR, since the $\pi_k(p_i) \in \mathbb{A}$ they are basic terms)

$= \pi_k(t(p_1,...,p_n))$.

Now it follows from AIP that $s(p_1,...,p_n) = t(p_1,...,p_n)$, which finishes the proof.

2.6.9 DEADLOCK AND TERMINATION

The introduction of deadlock and termination in the projective limit model is straightforward along the lines of this section. We will not go over the details again.

2.6.10 EXERCISES

1. Show that in $\mathbb{A}^\infty$ we have $a^\omega \cdot b^\omega = a^\omega$ (as defined in 2.6.2.2).
2. Show that in $\mathbb{A}^\infty$ the projection axioms of table 13 (2.4.1) hold. Also, derive the two equations in 2.6.8.
3. Show that the process $\sum a^n$, defined in 2.6.2.3, is a solution of the (unguarded!) recursive equation $X = a + Xa$.
4. Prove that $\mathbb{A}^\infty \models$ RDP$^-$.
5. Which process in $\mathbb{A}^n$ is a solution of the recursive equation $X = aX$?
6. Prove that $\mathbb{A}^n \models$ BPA, AIP, RDP$^-$, RSP for every $n \geq 1$.
7. Prove the statements in 2.6.6 (only if you know something about metric spaces).

2.6.11 NOTES AND COMMENTS

The projective limit model, called the standard model, is introduced in BERGSTRA & KLOP [1982]. An isomorphic structure, obtained by metric completion, appears in DE BAKKER &

ZUCKER [1982]. In BERGSTRA & KLOP [1982] we find a full proof of theorem 2.6.4. We refer to these papers for an extensive discussion of the metrical and topological aspects mentioned in 2.6.6. For another reference, see KRANAKIS [1987]. The Limit Rule mentioned here was formulated in BAETEN & BERGSTRA [1988], and the short proof in 2.6.8 was taken from BAETEN & VAN GLABBEEK [1987b] (of course, the theorem holds since $\mathbb{A}^\infty$ is a metrical completion).

2.7 PROCESS GRAPHS

In this section, we present two more models in which guarded recursive specifications have unique solutions. First, there is the model $\mathbb{G}^\infty/\underline{\leftrightarrow}$, that is isomorphic to the model $\mathbb{P}_{\delta\varepsilon}/\underline{\leftrightarrow}$ of section 2.5. Thus, in this model we have RDP and AIP$^-$. Then, we have the model $\mathbb{G}/\underline{\leftrightarrow}$. In this model, RDP$^-$ and AIP hold. In all of these models we immediately include δ and ε as special constants. Hence they all are models of BPA$_{\delta\varepsilon}$. By restricting their signature one can easily find models for BPA, BPA$_\delta$ or BPA$_\varepsilon$.

We also define two other models of BPA$_{\delta\varepsilon}$, namely the model of regular processes $\mathbb{R}/\underline{\leftrightarrow}$, that will be considered in more detail in the following section, and the model of finite processes $\mathbb{F}/\underline{\leftrightarrow}$, that is isomorphic to the initial algebra $\mathbb{A}$.

All these models are **graph models**, sets of process graphs modulo bisimulation, that provide a convenient visualization of the notion of a process.

2.7.1 DEFINITIONS

A **graph** consists of **nodes** and **edges**. An edge **goes from** a node **to** another node (or the same node); more than one edge can start from or arrive at a node; we have one special node called the **root**. Thus, we consider *rooted directed multi-graphs.*

A **path** in a graph is an alternating series of nodes and edges, such that each edge goes from the node before it to the node after it. We only consider graphs in which every node can be reached from the root by a finite path. A **cycle** is a path from some node back to the same node. A graph is **cyclic** if it contains a cycle, otherwise it is **acyclic**. A node is **cyclic** if it lies on a cycle. An **endnode** or **endpoint** in a graph is a node with no outgoing edges. All other nodes are called **internal**. The **trivial graph** $\mathbb{O}$ has one node and no edges. If g is a graph, and s a node in g, then $(g)_s$ is the **subgraph** of g obtained by leaving out all edges and nodes that cannot be reached by a finite path from s.

A **finitely branching** graph has only finitely many edges leaving from each node; a **countably branching** graph may also have a countable number of edges starting at a node. We do not consider graphs with uncountable branchings. A **finite** or **regular** graph has only finitely many nodes and edges. A **tree** is a graph that is acyclic, and in which every node has at most one incoming edge.

2.7.2 DEFINITIONS

A **process graph** is a graph in which each edge has a **label** from A, and in which the nodes may carry a label $\downarrow$. This label $\downarrow$ indicates whether or not the state represented by the node has a termination option (see section 2.2). If s is a node in a graph then we will write $s\downarrow$ if s carries label $\downarrow$, and say that s is a **termination node**. Similarly, if g is a graph then we write $g\downarrow$ iff the root node of g has label $\downarrow$.

$\mathbb{G}^\infty(\mathsf{B})$ is the set of (countably branching) process graphs with edge labels from the set B. Here, we only consider the class $\mathbb{G}^\infty(\mathsf{A})$, with edges labeled by atomic actions. We will write $\mathbb{G}^\infty$ instead of $\mathbb{G}^\infty(\mathsf{A})$. An edge with label a is often called an **a-step**. Analogously to the definitions in 2.1.7, we write $n \xrightarrow{a} m$ if there is an a-step from node n to node m, and $n \overset{\sigma}{\twoheadrightarrow} m$ if there is a path from node n to node m, whose edge-labels form the sequence σ.

Two graphs g,h are **isomorphic** iff there is an isomorphism between them, a bijective relation R between the nodes of g and h such that:

1. The roots of g and h are related by R
2. If R(s,t) and R(s',t') then $s \xrightarrow{a} s'$ is an edge in g iff $t \xrightarrow{a} t'$ is an edge in h ($a \in A$)
3. If R(s,t) then $s\downarrow$ iff $t\downarrow$.

In that case g and h differ only with respect to the identity of the nodes. We will always consider process graphs modulo isomorphism, and write g=h if g,h are isomorphic.

We will also consider the following subsets of $\mathbb{G}^\infty$:

1. $\mathbb{G}$ is the set of finitely branching process graphs;
2. $\mathbb{R}$ is the set of finite or regular process graphs;
3. $\mathbb{F}$ is the set of finite acyclic process graphs.

The following inclusions are immediate: $\mathbb{F} \subset \mathbb{R} \subset \mathbb{G} \subset \mathbb{G}^\infty$.
We will make these four structures into models of BPA.

2.7.3 EXAMPLES

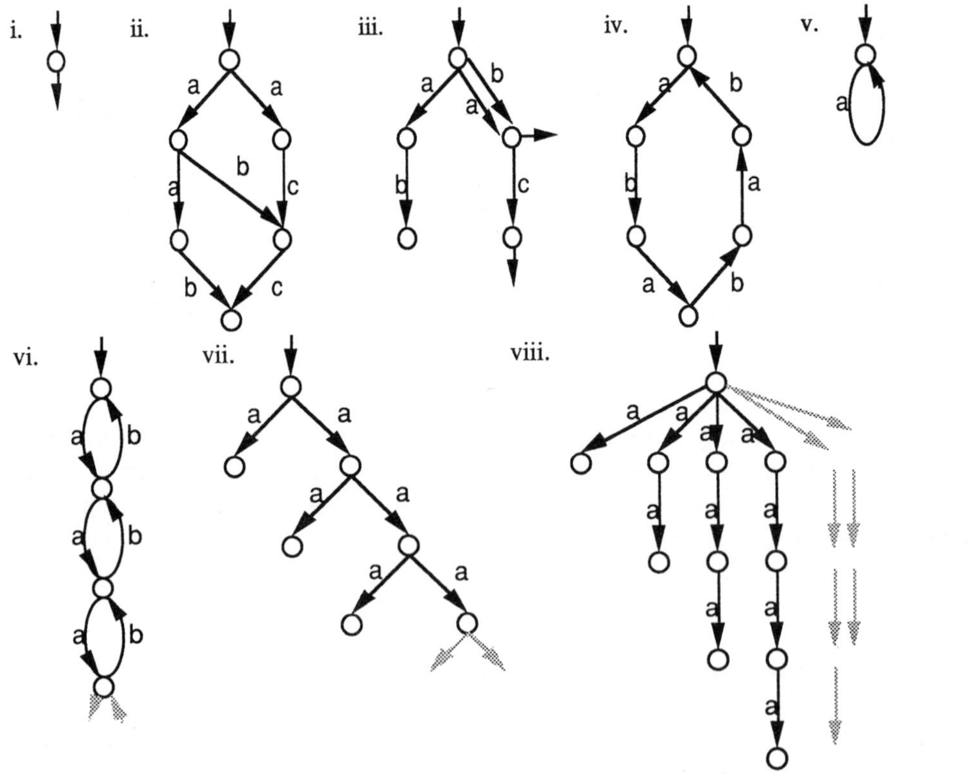

FIGURE 4.

In fig. 4, i, ii and iii are elements of $\mathbb{F}$; iv and v are elements of $\mathbb{R}$, but not of $\mathbb{F}$; vi and vii are elements of $\mathbb{G}$, but not of $\mathbb{R}$; and finally, viii is an element of $\mathbb{G}^\infty$, but not of $\mathbb{G}$. i, vii and viii are the only process graphs in fig. 4 that are trees.

2.7.4 NOTE

In pictures, we use circles for nodes, arrows for edges, and grey tones to indicate an infinite progression. We indicate the root node by an incoming unlabeled arrow, and indicate a termination node by an outgoing unlabeled arrow.

Of course, the action graph of an element of the initial algebra $\mathbb{A}_{\delta\varepsilon}$, defined in 2.1.11 and 2.2.12.8, is a finite acyclic process graph. Therefore, we can consider $\mathbb{A}_{\delta\varepsilon}$ to be a part of $\mathbb{F}$. Conversely, we can associate a closed term with each element of $\mathbb{F}$.

2.7.5 EXAMPLE

Many different process graphs can be used to denote the same process. That is why we will define a notion of bisimulation on process graphs, as we did in 2.5.2 and in 2.5.13.

As an example, the five graphs in fig. 5 all denote the process a^ω. For, from each node in these graphs, we can do infinitely many a-steps and nothing else.

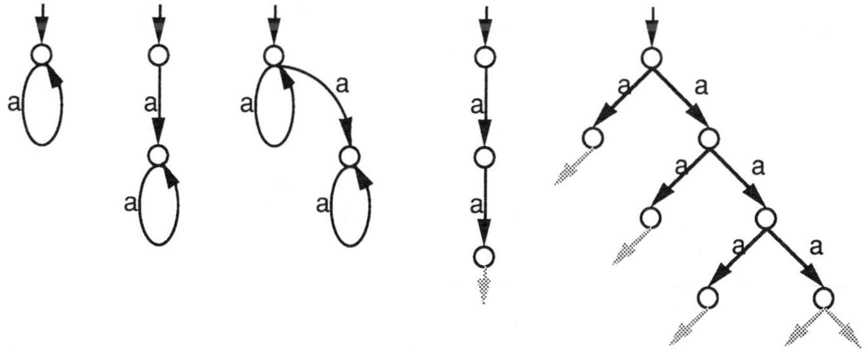

FIGURE 5. a^ω.

2.7.6 DEFINITION

Let $g,h \in \mathbb{G}^\infty$ and let R be a relation between the nodes of g and the nodes of h. R is a **bisimulation** between g and h, notation $R: g \underline{\leftrightarrow} h$, when the following four conditions hold.

i. The roots of g and h form a pair in relation R.

ii. If $s \xrightarrow{a} s'$ is an edge in g and R(s,t) (so t is a node in h), then there is an edge $t \xrightarrow{a} t'$ in h such that R(s',t') holds. See fig. 6.

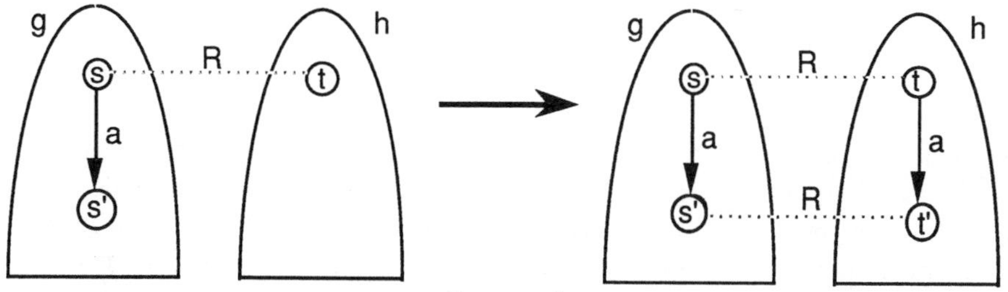

FIGURE 6.

iii. Vice versa: if $t \xrightarrow{a} t'$ is an edge in h and R(s,t), then there is an edge $s \xrightarrow{a} s'$ in g such that R(s',t'). See fig. 7.

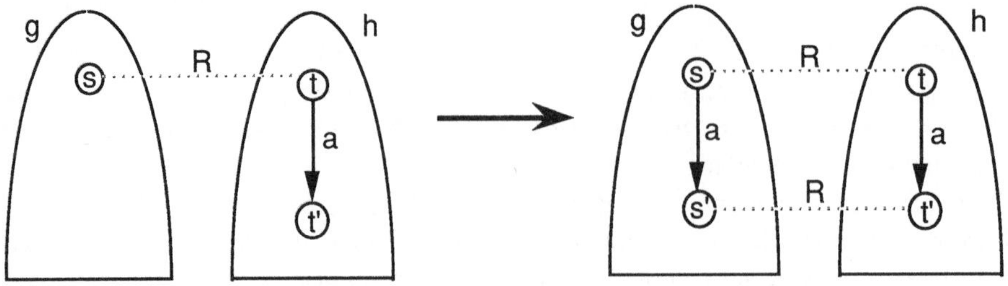

FIGURE 7.

iv. If R(s,t), then s↓ iff t↓.

We say that g and h **bisimulate**, or **are bisimilar**, notation $g \underline{\leftrightarrow} h$, if there is a bisimulation between g and h. It can be seen that this definition is analogous to the one in 2.5.13.

Note that if R and S are bisimulations, then so is $R \cup S$ (however, $R \cap S$ need not be a bisimulation). Thus, there is always a *maximal* bisimulation between two bisimulating graphs.

2.7.7 EXAMPLES

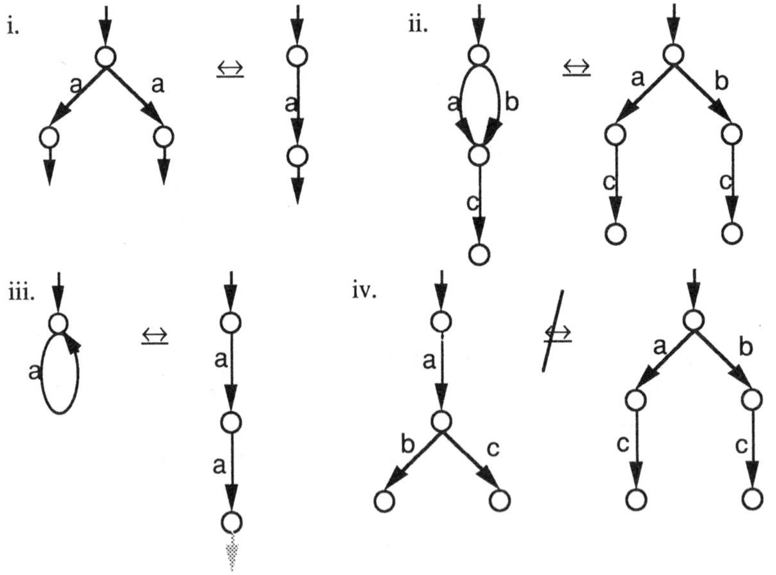

FIGURE 8.

The difference between graph isomorphism and graph bisimulation lies in two operations: we can identify two edges with the same label between the same nodes, and we can identify nodes with identical subgraphs. This difference is also expressed in axioms A3 and A4 of BPA.

Before we continue analyzing bisimulation relations, let us first look at an alternative characterization.

2.7.8 COLOURED TRACES

An alternative definition of bisimulation equivalence of 2.7.6 can be found as follows.

Let C be some arbitrary set, the set of **colours.** A **colouring** of a graph, is a mapping from its nodes to C (hence a colouring of its nodes), and a graph together with such a colouring is called a **coloured graph.** In a coloured graph there are **coloured traces** of the form $(C_0,a_1,C_1,a_2,C_2,...,a_k,C_k)$, for each path $s_0 \xrightarrow{a_1} s_1 \xrightarrow{a_2} s_2 \ldots s_{k-1} \xrightarrow{a_k} s_k$, starting from the root node s_0, such that s_i has colour C_i. The coloured traces of a node s in a graph are those of the subgraph having s as its root node, $(g)_s$.

Colours can be looked upon as characterizations of *states* or *potentials*: if two nodes have the same colour then they will be considered equivalent. Note that a coloured trace contains a lot of information: not just its execution sequence (i.e. the labels in the path), but it also carries information about the nature of its intermediate states.

The question remains how to detect the colour of a node in a graph, or – to put it differently – how to define the concept of 'potential in a node' properly. There are several ways to do this. Probably the shortest definition is the following:

2.7.9 DEFINITION

A **consistent colouring** of a graph is a colouring with the property that:

i. two nodes have the same colour only if they have the same coloured trace set;
ii. if nodes s and t have the same colour, then $s\downarrow$ iff $t\downarrow$.

So, in a consistent colouring the potentials (colours) of two nodes may only coincide if at least their coloured traces are the same.

Obviously, the *trivial* colouring (in which every node has a different colour) is consistent on any graph. Note that – even apart from the choice of the colours – a graph can have more than one consistent colouring. For instance, consider an infinite graph representing a^ω, then obviously the *homogeneous* colouring – in which every node has the same colour – is consistent, as well as the alternating or the trivial colouring.

2.7.10 DEFINITION

We say two graphs g and h are **coloured trace equivalent** if for some consistent colouring they have the same coloured trace set. Then we have the following important characterization.

2.7.11 THEOREM

$g \underline{\leftrightarrow} h$ if and only if g,h are coloured trace equivalent.

PROOF: $\Rightarrow$: suppose R is the *maximal* bisimulation relation between g and h. Let $\overline{R}$ be the reflexive, symmetric and transitive closure of R, then $\overline{R}$ is an equivalence relation on the set of nodes from g and h. Let C be the set of equivalence classes induced by $\overline{R}$ and label every node with its own equivalence class. Then this colouring is consistent with respect to both g and h.

To see this let s_0 be a node in g, and $(C_0,a_1,C_1,a_2,C_2,...,a_k,C_k)$ be a coloured trace which corresponds to a path $s_0 \xrightarrow{a_1} s_1 \xrightarrow{a_2} s_2 \ldots s_{k-1} \xrightarrow{a_k} s_k$, starting from s_0. Now suppose for some node t_0 in h we have $R(s_0,t_0)$, then we find from definition 2.7.6 that $t_0 \xrightarrow{a_1} t_1$ for some t_1 such that $R(s_1,t_1)$. Thus s_1 and t_1 have the same colour C_1. By induction we find that

t_0 has the same coloured trace $(C_0,a_1,C_1,a_2,C_2,...,a_k,C_k)$. So R preserves coloured trace sets, hence so does $\overline{R}$.

$\Leftarrow$: suppose that g and h have the same coloured trace sets, then consider the relation R which relates two nodes of g and h iff they are labeled with the same colour. It is easy to prove that R is a bisimulation between g and h.

Thus, the notion of coloured trace equivalence precisely coincides with the notion of bisimulation from definition 2.7.6.

2.7.12 NORMAL FORMS

From the idea of coloured nodes, it is easy to find a normal form representation of graphs modulo bisimulation. First note, that every **autobisimulation** – i.e. a bisimulation relating a graph with itself – can be considered as a colouring on the nodes of the graph: any autobisimulation relation is an equivalence relation, and its equivalence classes can be looked upon as a colouring. Using part $\Rightarrow$ of the proof of theorem 2.7.11, we find that this colouring is consistent.

Let $g \in \mathbb{G}^\infty$ and consider the *maximal autobisimulation* on g (note that such a relation exists), and consider its equivalence classes as colours. This colouring will be referred to as the **canonical colouring** of g. Next, identify all nodes that have the same colour in this canonical colouring, where the node resulting from such a contraction inherits all the incoming and outgoing edges from the previously existing nodes, and it has label $\downarrow$ iff the previously existing nodes did. The result of this identification will be denoted by N(g), the **normal form** of g.

2.7.13 PROPOSITION

i. $g \underline{\leftrightarrow} N(g)$

ii. $g \underline{\leftrightarrow} h \Leftrightarrow N(g) = N(h)$.

PROOF: i. Use theorem 2.7.11.

ii. Using i, it is left to prove that $N(g) \underline{\leftrightarrow} N(h) \Leftrightarrow N(g) = N(h)$.

Now if $R: N(g) \underline{\leftrightarrow} N(h)$, then R is a bijective relation between the nodes of N(g) and N(h):

a. it is surjective because every node in N(g) or N(h) can be reached from the root, and hence by definition 2.7.6 one directly finds that every node is related to some node in the other graph;

b. it is injective since every node is related with at most one other node; if a node in g is related to two nodes in h, then one can easily check that these two nodes in h are also related by the *maximal* autobisimulation on h, and so with respect to the canonical colouring they have the same colour. By 2.7.12 these nodes are identical.

Finally, if R(s,t) and R(s',t'), and $s \xrightarrow{a} s'$ is an edge in g, then, since R is a bisimulation, for some node t" in h $t \xrightarrow{a} t''$ and R(s',t"). Using the bijectivity of R we find t'=t". If R(s,t) then we find from definition 2.7.6 that $s\downarrow$ iff $t\downarrow$. Hence R is a graph isomorphism.

The converse implication is immediate.

We can apply theorem 2.7.13 in the examples in 2.7.7. In the next part of this section we will see how we may turn the graph domain $\mathbb{G}^\infty$ into a model for BPA.

2.7.14 THEOREM
Bisimulation is an equivalence relation on $\mathbb{G}^\infty$.

PROOF: Immediate from 2.7.13.

Now $\mathbb{G}^\infty/\underline{\leftrightarrow}$, the set of bisimulation classes of process graphs, is the domain of the graph model of $BPA_{\delta\varepsilon}$.

Next, we will define the operators +, · and the constants δ, ε and $a \in A$ on $\mathbb{G}^\infty$, and we will verify that $\underline{\leftrightarrow}$ is a congruence (as defined in 1.3.8). The idea for the definition of + is simple: we add two graphs by identifying their roots. However there is a complication, which is illustrated in the following example.

2.7.15 EXAMPLE
We consider the process $a^\omega + b$. This process cannot be represented by the graph on the right in fig. 9.i, because in that graph, a b-step can still be done after any number of a-steps. Rather, this process is represented by the graph on the right in fig. 9.ii. The graphs on the left in these figures are both representations of the process a^ω. The difference is, that in the representation of fig. 9.i we have a cyclic root, and in fig. 9.ii an acyclic root. That is why we will define a mapping that will make the root of a graph acyclic.

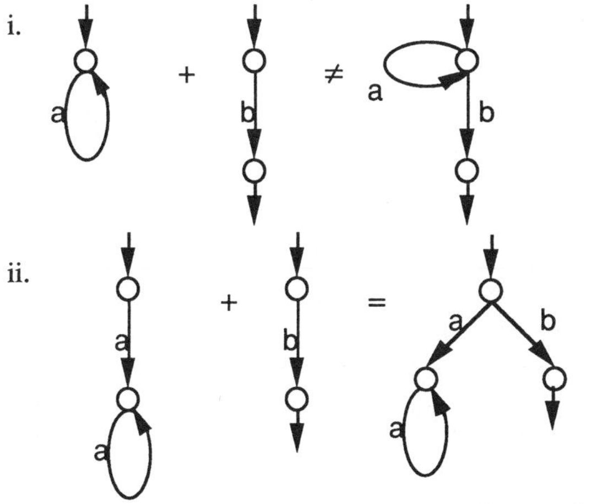

FIGURE 9.

2.7.16 DEFINITION
We define the **root unwinding map** ρ: $\mathbb{G}^\infty \to \mathbb{G}^\infty$ as follows:
Given a process graph $g \in \mathbb{G}^\infty$, we obtain $\rho(g)$ by adding a new node r' to g, which will be the root of $\rho(g)$ and which has label $\downarrow$ iff the root node r of g has (hence we put $r'\downarrow$ iff $r\downarrow$). Then we add an edge $r' \xrightarrow{a} s$ for every edge $r \xrightarrow{a} s$ in g, and finally we leave out all nodes and edges that cannot be reached from the new root node r'.

2.7.17 EXAMPLES

i.

ii.

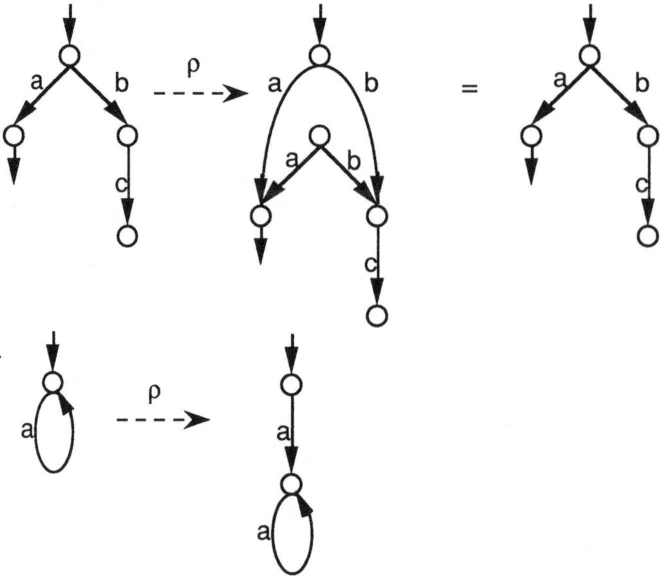

FIGURE 10.

2.7.18 THEOREM

Let $g \in \mathbb{G}^\infty$.

i. If the root of g is acyclic, then $g = \rho(g)$.

ii. The root of $\rho(g)$ is acyclic.

iii. $g \leftrightarrow \rho(g)$.

PROOF: Note that the root of a graph is acyclic if and only if it has no incoming edges.

i. We add a node in $\rho(g)$ that has the same outgoing edges as the root of g. Since the root of g is acyclic, it has no incoming edges, just like the new node of $\rho(g)$. Next, the (old) root of g is discarded, because it cannot be reached from the new root (the added node). The result is a graph, in which the added node has exactly the same incoming and outgoing edges as the discarded node.

ii. The root of $\rho(g)$ is acyclic because it has no incoming edges.

iii. By ii, we may assume that the root of g is cyclic (otherwise g and $\rho(g)$ are even isomorphic). Therefore, g is a subgraph of $\rho(g)$. Define the relation R between nodes of g and nodes of $\rho(g)$ to be the identity on g, augmented with the pair consisting of the root of g and the added node. Then, it is an exercise to verify that $R: g \leftrightarrow \rho(g)$.

2.7.19 DEFINITION

Now we define the constants and operators on $\mathbb{G}^\infty$.

i. For an atomic action $a \in A$, $[a]$, the interpretation of a in $\mathbb{G}^\infty$, is the graph consisting of two nodes with an a-edge between them. Furthermore, the endnode of $[a]$ has a label $\downarrow$ whereas its root node does not.

ii. $[\delta]$ is the trivial graph *without* label $\downarrow$, and $[\varepsilon]$ is the trivial graph *with* label $\downarrow$.

iii. For process graphs g, h, we obtain g + h by first unwinding the roots of g and h (making ρ(g), ρ(h)), and then identifying the obtained roots. Furthermore we have (g + h)↓ iff g↓ and h↓.
iv. g·h is defined by identifying every node in g having label ↓ with the root node of a distinct copy of ρ(h). Every node emerging from such identification has label ↓ iff h↓. If g has no labels ↓, then the result is just g.

2.7.20 EXAMPLES

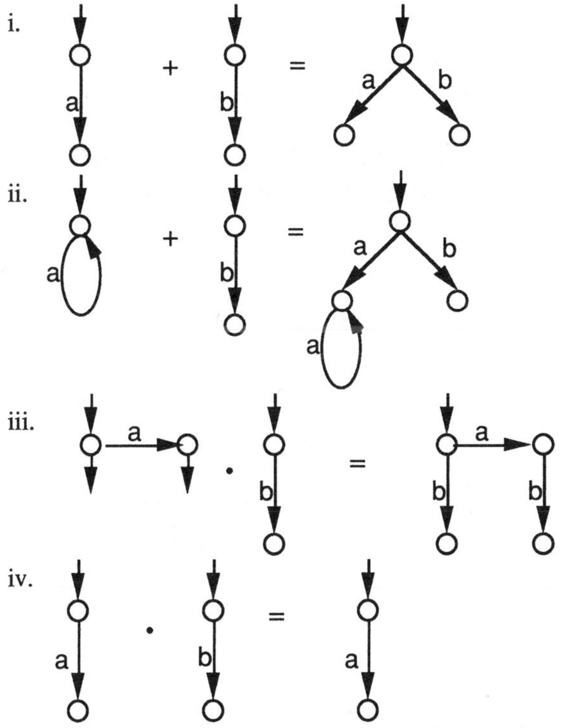

FIGURE 11.

2.7.21 DEFINITION
In order to define the operator π_n on graphs, it is necessary to be able to unwind a graph completely to a tree. This can be done by applying the mapping ρ of 2.7.16 successively to every node of a graph, but there is also a more direct way. This is what we describe now.
Let a process graph g∈$\mathbb{G}^\infty$ be given. We define the tree tree(g) as follows:
1. tree(g) has a node for every finite path of g, that starts at the root of g. Such a node has label ↓ iff the last node in this path does.
2. There is an edge labeled a between p and p' if the path p' is an extension of the path p with an edge labeled a.
3. The root of tree(g) is the node corresponding to the empty path in g.

2.7.22 LEMMA
Let g∈$\mathbb{G}^\infty$.

i. If g is a tree, then $g = tree(g)$.
ii. $tree(g)$ is a process tree.
iii. $tree(g) \leftrightarrow g$.

PROOF: Straightforward.

2.7.23 EXAMPLE
In fig. 5 (in 2.7.5), the image under tree of the first graph is the fourth graph.

2.7.24 DEFINITION
Let $g \in \mathbb{G}^\infty$, and let s be a node of g. We say s has **depth** n ($n \in \mathbb{N}$) if there is a path of length n (i.e. a path containing n edges) from the root of g to s. Note that in general, a node may have several depths. However, in a process *tree*, every node has a unique depth.

We call a bisimulation between two process graphs **layered** if it only relates nodes of same depth. We will need the following lemma, which says that we can always find a layered bisimulation between two bisimulating graphs.

2.7.25 LEMMA
Let $g,h \in \mathbb{G}^\infty$ and $R: g \leftrightarrow h$. Then there is a layered bisimulation $S \subseteq R$, $S: g \leftrightarrow h$.

PROOF: Let $g,h \in \mathbb{G}^\infty$ and $R: g \leftrightarrow h$. Define $S = \{(s,t) : R(s,t)$ and there is an $n \in \mathbb{N}$ such that s and t have depth $n\}$. It is easy to verify that S is a bisimulation. It is immediate that S is layered.

Now we have collected all the ingredients needed to define the operator π_n on process graphs, and to prove that bisimulation becomes a congruence relation on process graphs.

2.7.26 DEFINITION
Let $g \in \mathbb{G}^\infty$. We obtain $\pi_n(g)$ ($n \geq 0$) as follows.
1. Unwind g to a tree, so form $tree(g)$;
2. Remove all edges leaving from a node at depth n, replacing them by a label $\downarrow$;
3. Remove all inaccessible nodes and edges.

2.7.27 THEOREM
$\leftrightarrow$ is a congruence relation on $\mathbb{G}^\infty$ (as defined in 1.3.8).

PROOF: We know from 2.7.14 that $\leftrightarrow$ is an equivalence relation. Now let $g_1, g_2, h_1, h_2 \in \mathbb{G}^\infty$ such that $g_1 \leftrightarrow h_1$ and $g_2 \leftrightarrow h_2$. We have to prove the following:
1. $(g_1 + g_2) \leftrightarrow (h_1 + h_2)$;
2. $g_1 \cdot g_2 \leftrightarrow h_1 \cdot h_2$;
3. $\pi_n(g_1) \leftrightarrow \pi_n(h_1)$.

To prove 1, let $R: \rho(g_1) \leftrightarrow \rho(h_1)$ and $S: \rho(g_2) \leftrightarrow \rho(h_2)$ be bisimulations such that in R and S root nodes are not related to non-root nodes (such bisimulations exist by lemma 2.7.25, since root nodes are the only nodes of depth 0). The relation $R \cup S$, the union of R and S, will now be a bisimulation between $\rho(g_1) + \rho(g_2)$ and $\rho(h_1) + \rho(h_2)$, and therefore, by definition of +, also between $g_1 + g_2$ and $h_1 + h_2$.

For 2, let $R: g_1 \leftrightarrow h_1$ and $S: \rho(g_2) \leftrightarrow \rho(h_2)$ be bisimulations such that in S root nodes are not related to non-root nodes. The relation T between nodes of $g_1 \cdot g_2$ and nodes of $h_1 \cdot h_2$ consists of all pairs from R, plus all pairs from all copies of S except for the root pair. It is an exercise to show that $T: g_1 \cdot g_2 \leftrightarrow h_1 \cdot h_2$.

Finally, to prove 3, let $R: \mathrm{tree}(g_1) \leftrightarrow \mathrm{tree}(h_1)$ be a layered bisimulation (R exists by lemma 2.7.25), then R', the restriction of R to nodes of $\pi_n(g_1)$ and $\pi_n(h_1)$, is a (layered) bisimulation between $\pi_n(g_1)$ and $\pi_n(h_1)$.

Now we can define the operators $+$, $\cdot$ and π_n on $\mathbb{G}^\infty/\leftrightarrow$ as indicated in 1.3.9, obtaining the **graph model** $\mathbb{G}^\infty/\leftrightarrow$. Next, we prove that $\mathbb{G}^\infty/\leftrightarrow$ is a model of BPA$_{\delta\varepsilon}$ + PRE (see 2.4.21). We will prove this, and more, by exhibiting an isomorphism between the model $\mathbb{P}_{\delta\varepsilon}/\leftrightarrow$ of 2.5 and $\mathbb{G}^\infty/\leftrightarrow$.

2.7.28 DEFINITION

We can associate a recursive specification to each process graph. First, let g be a finitely branching process graph, i.e. $g \in \mathbb{G}$. Associate a variable to each node of g. Then, if node X has outgoing edges labeled $a_0,\ldots,a_{n-1}$ to nodes $X_0,\ldots,X_{n-1}$ ($n \geq 0$), respectively, we have the equation

$$X = \sum_{i<n} a_i X_i + \sum_{j<m} \varepsilon$$

with $m>0$ iff $X\downarrow$. As in 2.2.7 the sum over an empty index set equal to δ, so X has a summand ε iff $X\downarrow$.

In case a node has infinitely many outgoing edges, we associate a countable sequence of variables with it. Thus, if the node with variables Y_0, Y_1, ... has outgoing edges $a_0, a_1, \ldots$ to nodes with (first) variables $X_0, X_1, \ldots$ we have (unguarded!) equations

$$Y_i = a_i X_i + Y_{i+1} + \sum_{j<m} \varepsilon$$

for each $i \in \mathbb{N}$ and with $m>0$ iff $Y_i\downarrow$. It is not hard to see that each process graph is a solution of the associated recursive specification. It follows that each element of $\mathbb{G}$ is definable.

If g is a process graph, call the recursive specification associated with g in this way E_g. Then this gives a mapping term from the set of process graphs $\mathbb{G}^\infty$ to the set of terms $\mathbb{P}_{\delta\varepsilon}$: $\mathrm{term}(g) = \langle X \mid E_g \rangle$, if X is the (first) variable corresponding to the root of g.

2.7.29 LEMMA

Let $g,h \in \mathbb{G}^\infty$. Then in $\mathbb{G}^\infty$ $g \leftrightarrow h$ iff $\mathrm{term}(g) \leftrightarrow \mathrm{term}(h)$ in $\mathbb{P}_{\delta\varepsilon}$.

PROOF: $\Rightarrow$: Suppose g,h are process graphs and $R: g \leftrightarrow h$. Define a binary relation R^* on $\mathbb{P}_{\delta\varepsilon}$ as follows: $R^*(\mathrm{term}((g)_s), \mathrm{term}((h)_t))$ whenever $R(s,t)$, where s is a node in g, t a node in h. For the definition of $(g)_s$ see 2.7.1. We leave it to the reader to check that R^* is a bisimulation on $\mathbb{P}_{\delta\varepsilon}$ (see 2.5.13).

$\Leftarrow$: Suppose g,h are process graphs and R^* is a bisimulation on $\mathbb{P}_{\delta\varepsilon}$ with $R^*(\mathrm{term}(g), \mathrm{term}(h))$. Define a relation R between nodes of g and nodes of h as follows: $R(s,t)$ iff $R^*(\langle X_s \mid E_g \rangle, \langle X_t \mid E_h \rangle)$, where X_s is a variable corresponding to node s in the specification E_g, and likewise for X_t. Note that because of the form of the specifications E_g and E_h, whenever $\langle X \mid E_g \rangle \xrightarrow{a} p$ for some process p, then there is a node s in g such that p is of the form $\langle X_s \mid E_g \rangle$. Now we leave it to the reader to check that R is a bisimulation between g and h.

2.7.30 DEFINITION

We can associate a process graph to each element of $\mathbb{P}_{\delta\varepsilon}$. We do this as follows: suppose $p \in \mathbb{P}_{\delta\varepsilon}$. For each process q such that for some sequence σ $p \overset{\sigma}{\twoheadrightarrow} q$, and for p itself, we create a node in graph(p), the graph to be constructed. The node corresponding to p will be the root node, and there is an edge labeled a between two nodes when the relation $\overset{a}{\rightarrow}$ holds between the corresponding processes. Finally, a node in graph(p) corresponding to a process q has label $\downarrow$ iff $q\downarrow$.

2.7.31 LEMMA

Let $p,q \in \mathbb{P}_{\delta\varepsilon}$. Then $p \leftrightarrow q \Leftrightarrow \text{graph}(p) \leftrightarrow \text{graph}(q)$.

PROOF: Obvious, by the definition of the mapping graph.

2.7.32 LEMMA

i. For $g \in \mathbb{G}^\infty$, $\text{graph}(\text{term}(g)) \leftrightarrow g$

ii. For $p \in \mathbb{P}_{\delta\varepsilon}$, $\text{term}(\text{graph}(p)) \leftrightarrow p$.

PROOF: i. By 2.7.31, graph(term(g)) has a node node(q) for every process q such that for some sequence σ $\text{term}(g) \overset{\sigma}{\twoheadrightarrow} q$, and it has an edge $\text{node}(q) \overset{a}{\rightarrow} \text{node}(r)$ whenever $q \overset{a}{\rightarrow} r$. Now use definition 2.7.28 to see that every sequence $\text{term}(g) \overset{\sigma}{\twoheadrightarrow} q$ corresponds to a finite path starting from the root in g – hence so does every node in graph(term(g)) – and that every edge $\text{node}(q) \overset{a}{\rightarrow} \text{node}(r)$ corresponds to an extension of the path corresponding to node(q). Hence, from 2.7.21 we find that $\text{graph}(\text{term}(g)) = \text{tree}(g)$. Now apply lemma 2.7.22.iii.

ii. By 2.7.28, $\text{term}(\text{graph}(p)) = \langle X \mid E_{\text{graph}(p)} \rangle$ where X is the (first) variable corresponding to the root of graph(p). Let Y be a variable from $E_{\text{graph}(p)}$. Using lemma 2.1.10 and the construction of $E_{\text{graph}(p)}$, we find that whenever $\langle Y \mid E_{\text{graph}(p)} \rangle \overset{a}{\rightarrow} Y_i$, graph(p) has an edge $Y \overset{a}{\rightarrow} Y_i$ where the variables stand for the nodes in graph(p) with which they are associated (see 2.7.28). Then, using definition 2.7.30, every such edge corresponds to a transition $p(Y) \overset{a}{\rightarrow} p(Y_j)$, where $p(X) = p$ and all p(Y) are descendants of p. Vice versa, for descendants q, r of p every transition $q \overset{a}{\rightarrow} r$ corresponds to an edge in graph(p) and hence to a transition from $\langle X \mid E_{\text{graph}(p)} \rangle$. Now define the bisimulation relation R: $\text{term}(\text{graph}(p)) \leftrightarrow p$ by relating every process p(Y) with $\langle Y \mid E_{\text{graph}(p)} \rangle$, for variables Y from $E_{\text{graph}(p)}$.

2.7.33 THEOREM

$\mathbb{P}_{\delta\varepsilon}/\leftrightarrow$ and $\mathbb{G}^\infty/\leftrightarrow$ are isomorphic.

PROOF: From lemma 2.7.32 we find that term is a bijection on bisimulation equivalence classes and that term is the inverse of graph. It is left as an exercise to prove that term respects +, · and π_n in order to conclude that it is an isomorphism.

2.7.34 COROLLARY

$\mathbb{G}^\infty/\leftrightarrow$, with +, ·, π_n, and constants as defined in 2.7.15 and 2.7.22 is a complete model for $BPA_{\delta\varepsilon}$ + PRE (see 2.4.21, 2.5.10) and RDP, AIP⁻ and RSP.

The proof of this corollary follows immediately from theorem 2.5.4, 2.5.14, exercise 2.5.15.6 and theorem 2.7.33.

2.7.35 OTHER GRAPH MODELS

One can also prove that $\mathbb{G}/\underline{\leftrightarrow}$, $\mathbb{R}/\underline{\leftrightarrow}$ and $\mathbb{F}/\underline{\leftrightarrow}$ are models of BPA$_{\delta\varepsilon}$ + PRE by showing that they are submodels of $\mathbb{G}^\infty/\underline{\leftrightarrow}$ (i.e. their domains are closed under +, · and π_n). Then, RSP follows immediately, whereas one still has to prove AIP$^-$ and RDP. Using 2.1.11 and 2.7.28 we find that $\mathbb{F}/\underline{\leftrightarrow}$ and the initial algebra $\mathbb{A}_{\delta\varepsilon}$ are identical (i.e. isomorphic).

As a corollary to 2.7.34 we see that $\mathbb{G}^\infty/\underline{\leftrightarrow}$ satisfies the principles RDP, AIP$^-$ and RSP. In the following we prove that the algebra $\mathbb{G}/\underline{\leftrightarrow}$ satisfies the principles RDP$^-$, AIP and RSP (see 2.4.12, 2.4.13 and 2.4.18). So also in $\mathbb{G}/\underline{\leftrightarrow}$ every guarded recursive specification has a unique solution.

2.7.36 THEOREM

$\mathbb{G}/\underline{\leftrightarrow} \models$ AIP.

PROOF (Difficult!): Let g and h be graphs such that $\pi_n(g) \underline{\leftrightarrow} \pi_n(h)$ for all $n \geq 0$. We have to prove that $g \underline{\leftrightarrow} h$. For every n consider all bisimulations between $\pi_n(g)$ and $\pi_n(h)$. All such such bisimulation relations can be partially ordered as follows: there is an edge from R: $\pi_n(g) \underline{\leftrightarrow} \pi_n(h)$ to R': $\pi_{n+1}(g) \underline{\leftrightarrow} \pi_{n+1}(h)$ if and only if $R \subseteq R'$. In this way we find a finitely branching, but infinite tree, and thus by König's lemma it contains an infinite path. The union of all bisimulations along such an infinite path yields a bisimulation between g and h.

Note that it is essential in this proof to consider finitely branching process graphs only: AIP does *not* hold when allowing infinitely branching graphs, as is shown by the following example.

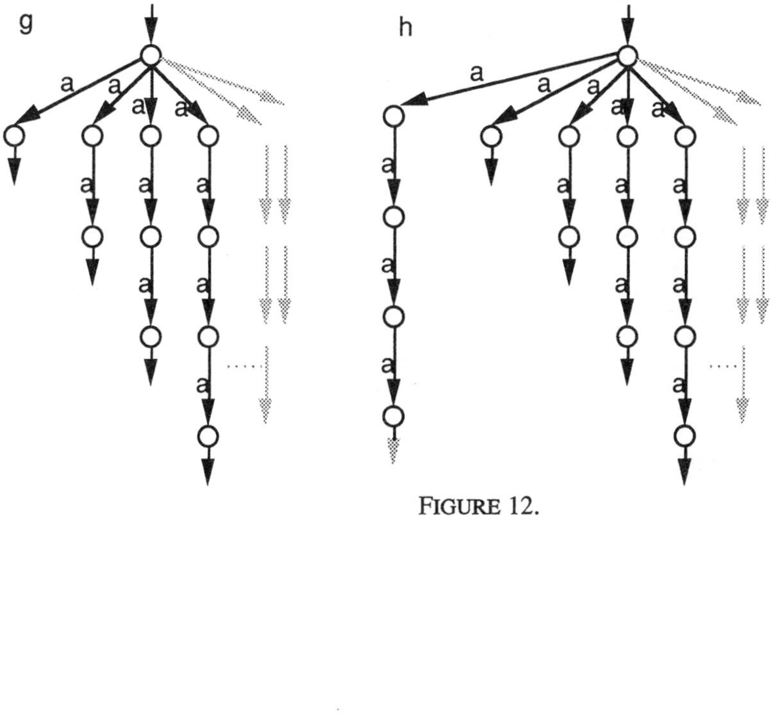

FIGURE 12.

2.7.37 EXAMPLE

Let $g = \sum_{n\geq 0} a^n$ and $h = a^\omega + g$ be the two graphs in fig. 12 (this is example 2.4.14).

Clearly $g,h \in \mathbb{G}^\infty$, but $g,h \notin \mathbb{G}$. Observe that g and h are not bisimilar, since g only has finite branches whereas h has an infinite branch. However, $\pi_n(g) \underline{\leftrightarrow} \pi_n(h)$ for all $n\geq 0$, and so we find that $\mathbb{G}^\infty/\underline{\leftrightarrow} \not\models$ AIP. We do have $\mathbb{R}/\underline{\leftrightarrow} \models$ AIP and $\mathbb{F}/\underline{\leftrightarrow} \models$ AIP, since $\mathbb{R}, \mathbb{B} \subset \mathbb{G}$.

2.7.38 THEOREM

$\mathbb{G}/\underline{\leftrightarrow} \models$ RSP.

The proof of theorem 2.7.38 follows immediately from 2.4.19 and the previous theorem.

2.7.39 THEOREM

$\mathbb{G}/\underline{\leftrightarrow} \models$ RDP$^-$.

PROOF: In 2.7.30, we constructed a process graph for each element of $\mathbb{P}$. We do the same thing here. Let E be a guarded recursive specification with root variable X. By 2.4.7, X has a head normal form, say

$$X = \sum_{i<n} a_i p_i + \sum_{j<m} \varepsilon,$$

for definable processes p_i. Now the node corresponding to X in the graph has an edge labeled a_i to the node corresponding to p_i, and a label $\downarrow$ if $m>0$. We continue in the same way with the head normal forms of the p_i. We see immediately that the resulting graph is in $\mathbb{G}$.

Then we need to prove that the resulting graph g actually is a solution of the specification E. The equation for X in E is $X = t(X_1,...,X_k)$, for certain variables $X_1,...,X_k$. For $X_1,...,X_k$ we have graphs $g_1,...,g_k$, respectively, in the same way. It is left to show that $g \underline{\leftrightarrow} t(g_1,...,g_k)$.

Assume we have a fixed number $n\geq 0$. By 2.4.8 we may assume every variable in t to be n times guarded. Hence $\pi_n(t)$ is independent from $g_1,...,g_k$, and by construction equal to $\pi_n(g)$. Hence $\pi_n(g) \underline{\leftrightarrow} \pi_n(t(g_1,...,g_k))$ for every $n\geq 0$, and by AIP $g \underline{\leftrightarrow} t(g_1,...,g_k)$.

2.7.40 COMPARISON WITH OTHER MODELS

Note that RDP$^-$ does *not* hold in $\mathbb{R}/\underline{\leftrightarrow}$ or $\mathbb{F}/\underline{\leftrightarrow}$ (exercise 21).

Now we know that every guarded recursive specification determines a unique element of $\mathbb{G}/\underline{\leftrightarrow}$. On the other hand, for every element in $\mathbb{G}/\underline{\leftrightarrow}$ we can find a guarded recursive specification having this particular element as a solution (see 2.7.28).

The model $\mathbb{A}^\infty$ cannot be considered a submodel of $\mathbb{G}/\underline{\leftrightarrow}$, since in $\mathbb{A}^\infty$ there are infinitely branching elements like $\sum a^n$, defined in 2.4.14. However, $\mathbb{G}/\underline{\leftrightarrow}$ can be seen as a submodel of $\mathbb{A}^\infty$. Furthermore, $\mathbb{A}^\infty$ cannot be seen as a submodel of $\mathbb{G}^\infty/\underline{\leftrightarrow}$, since in $\mathbb{A}^\infty$ processes are identified that are distinguished in $\mathbb{G}^\infty/\underline{\leftrightarrow}$ (like the two processes in fig. 12, in 2.7.37).

2.7.41 GRAPH MODELS WITHOUT TERMINATION

It is possible to define graph models for BPA without δ or ε. In order to do this, restrict the graph domains as follows:

i. In order to obtain a model in the signature with only δ, consider only those graphs in which *none* of the internal nodes has label $\downarrow$.

ii. To define a model in the signature with only ε, consider only those graphs in which *all* endnodes have label ↓.
iii. A model without δ or ε can be found by taking the intersection of (i) and (ii).

It is left to the reader to check that all the results in this section can be easily extended to either of these three cases.

2.7.42 EXERCISES

1. Prove that the graphs in fig. 5 (2.7.5) are all bisimilar.
2. Are graphs (iii) and (v) in 2.7.3 bisimilar? And (iv) and (vi)?
3. Find bisimulation relations for cases 2.7.8.i, ii, iii. Show why in 2.7.8.iv there exists no bisimulation.
4. Check that the relations R' and T defined in 2.7.9, are bisimulations.
5. Unwind the root of the graphs (iii), (iv), (v) in 2.7.3.
6. Check that the relation R, defined in 2.7.18.iii is a bisimulation.
7. Construct the sum and product of every pair of graphs in 2.7.3.
8. Prove lemma 2.7.22.
9. Prove that between any two bisimulating graphs there exists a layered bisimulation.
10. Check that the relations defined in 2.7.27 are bisimulations.
11. Prove $\mathbb{G}/\underline{\leftrightarrow} \models$ A3 and $\mathbb{G}/\underline{\leftrightarrow} \models$ A4.
12. Which graph is a solution of the specification $\{X = (a + b)X\}$ (see 2.4.21.6)?
13. Which graph is a solution of the specification $\{X = aX + bcX\}$?
14. Find two non-bisimulating graphs in $\mathbb{G}$ that are both a solution of the (unguarded!) specification $\{X = Xa + Xb\}$.
15. Give a plausible argument why the (unguarded!) specification $\{X = Xa + a\}$ has no solution in $\mathbb{G}$.
16. Prove that the relations defined in 2.7.29 are bisimulations.
17. Prove lemma 2.7.31.
18. Prove theorem 2.7.33.
19. Prove that AIP holds in $\mathbb{R}/\underline{\leftrightarrow}$ and $\mathbb{F}/\underline{\leftrightarrow}$.
20. Show that the specification $\{X = aX\}$ has no solution in $\mathbb{F}/\underline{\leftrightarrow}$ (but in $\mathbb{R}/\underline{\leftrightarrow}$ it does).
21. Show that the specification $\{X_n = bX_{n+1} + a^n : n=1,2,...\}$ does not have a solution in $\mathbb{R}/\underline{\leftrightarrow}$ (but in $\mathbb{G}/\underline{\leftrightarrow}$ it does).
22. Show that $\mathbb{G}/\underline{\leftrightarrow} \models x + x = x$, with the definition of + as in 2.7.19.
23. Prove that $\mathbb{G}/\underline{\leftrightarrow} \models$ A6-A9.
24. Show that on every graph g there exists a unique colouring of its nodes (apart from the choice of the colours), such that two nodes have the same colour iff they have the same coloured trace set. Prove that this colouring is equal to the canonical colouring of g.

2.7.43 NOTES AND COMMENTS

The graph models presented in this section are based on Milner's model of *synchronization trees* (MILNER [1980]). Process graphs were introduced in BERGSTRA & KLOP [1985]. A definition with node labels can be found in BAETEN, BERGSTRA & KLOP [1987b]. The notion of bisimulation is from PARK [1981], but coincides in the present setting with the notion of observational congruence of MILNER [1980]. The presentation with coloured traces is from VAN GLABBEEK & WEIJLAND [1989]. The root-unwinding map of 2.7.16 can be found in

BERGSTRA & KLOP [1986b]. Theorem 2.7.33 is from VAN GLABBEEK [1987], theorem 2.7.36 from BERGSTRA & KLOP [1986b].

2.8 REGULAR PROCESSES

In this section we will take a closer look at the model $\mathbb{R}/\underline{\leftrightarrow}$, the model of regular graphs. We restrict $\mathbb{R}/\underline{\leftrightarrow}$ to the model without δ or ε (see 2.7.41). We define the notion of regular process, and present a few different characterizations. What we call a regular process, is often referred to as a **finite automaton** in the literature.

2.8.1 DEFINITION

Let p be a process in some model $\mathbb{M}$ of BPA. Define the relations $\xrightarrow{a}$ on this model (as in 2.1.11) as follows:

$p \xrightarrow{a} q \Leftrightarrow \mathbb{M} \models p = p + aq$

$p \xrightarrow{a} \surd \Leftrightarrow \mathbb{M} \models p = p + a.$

As usual, we define the relations $\xrightarrow{\sigma}\!\!\!\rightarrow$ (see table 8, in 2.1.7). A process q such that $p \xrightarrow{\sigma}\!\!\!\rightarrow q$ is called a **subprocess** or a **state** of process p. We call p a **regular process** if p has only finitely many subprocesses, or only finitely many states.

Note that this notion of regularity depends on the model involved, so that a certain process can be regular in one model, but not regular in another.

2.8.2 DEFINITION

Let E be a recursive specification with variables from the set V. E is called **linear** if every equation in E has the following form:

$$X = \sum_{i<n} a_i X_i + \sum_{j<k} b_j,$$

for certain atomic actions a_i, b_j and variables X, $X_i \in V$ (n+k>0).

Note that every linear specification is guarded.

2.8.3 CANONICAL GRAPH

Now if a process p is given as the solution of a linear specification, then it is easy to find a graph for p: the graph has a node corresponding to each variable, and the edges are determined by the equations (cf. 2.7.30). We call this graph G(p).

But also the other way around, for every graph g in $\mathbb{G}$ there exists a linear recursive specification, having this graph as a solution (see 2.7.28).

2.8.4 EXAMPLES

Let the process X be given as a solution of the linear specification

$E \equiv \{X = aX + bY,\ Y = aZ + b,\ Z = a\}.$

Then G(X) is given in fig. 13.i.

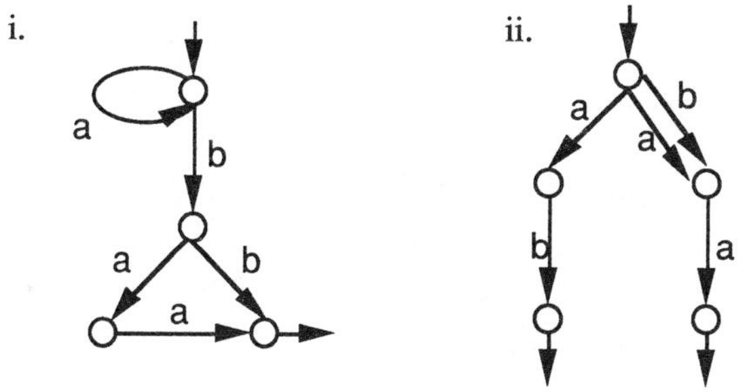

FIGURE 13.

Let g be the graph given in fig. 13.ii. With g we associate the linear specification

$E' \equiv \{X = aY + aZ + bZ, Y = b, Z = a\}$.

The proof of the following lemma can be extracted from the preceding observations.

2.8.5 LEMMA

Let p be a process in a model $\mathbb{M}$. Then the following statements are equivalent:

1. p can be represented by a graph in $\mathbb{R}$;
2. p is the solution of a finite linear specification.

It is obvious that a regular process has the properties mentioned in lemma 2.8.5, as a finite graph can be constructed as in 2.7.30. The converse implication need not be true however, as certain identifications in a model may cause extra action relations to hold. The models presented in 2.5 through 2.7 are well-behaved in this respect, however.

2.8.6 THEOREM

Let p be a process in the term model (2.5), the projective limit model (2.6) or one of the graph models (2.7). If p is given as the solution of a finite linear specification, then p is a regular process.

PROOF: Left to the reader.

2.8.7 EXERCISES

1. Let the process X be given by the recursive specification

   $E_1 \equiv \{X = (a+b)X + a + bY, Y = aY\}$.

Determine G(X).

2. Let the process X_0 be given by $E_2 \equiv \{X_n = aX_{n+1} + b : n \geq 0\}$ in one of the models of 2.5 - 2.7. Is this a regular process?
3. Similarly for Y_0 given by $E_3 \equiv \{Y_0 = aY_1\} \cup \{Y_n = aY_{n+1} + bY_{n-1} : n \geq 1\}$.
4. Prove theorem 2.8.6.
5. Consider a vending machine F for refreshing drinks (no coffee for a change). This machine is able to accept only quarters and dimes. It asks for a dime first, and next for two quarters. When a wrong coin is inserted, the action re (reject) is performed. Sometimes, the machine does not accept a good coin, and then the action n (not accepted) is performed. Other possible actions are: q (insert a quarter), d (insert a dime), a (accept the coin) and r (return refreshment).

i. Draw a finite graph, representing the behaviour of F.
ii. Find a linear specification for F.

2.8.8. NOTES AND COMMENTS
Material for this section was taken from BERGSTRA & KLOP [1984a]. Also see MILNER [1984].

2.9 STACK

As a first practical example of the use of recursive specifications we will consider the example of the **stack**. A stack consists of a sequence of data elements; at only one side of this sequence elements can be added or deleted. This side is called the **top** of the stack.

First we look at the case in which we only have two data elements, 0 and 1 say.

2.9.1 DEFINITION
We have the following atomic actions:

push(0) = add a 0 to the stack;
pop(0) = delete 0 from, the stack.

Similarly, we have push(1) and pop(1).

2.9.2 INFINITE SPECIFICATION
To begin with, we give an infinite specification of the stack. The content of the stack is a sequence of 0's and 1's, in which the first element is considered the top of the stack. We use the following notations:

- the symbols σ, ρ stand for sequences of 0's and 1's;
- if σ, ρ are such sequences and d is 0 or 1, then $\sigma\rho$, σd and $d\rho$ are **concatenations**, i.e. the sequence σ followed by the sequence ρ, the sequence consisting of σ followed by the element d, and the sequence with first element d followed by the sequence σ, respectively.
- λ is the empty sequence.

The following specification has variables S_σ, representing the stack containing σ.

$$S_\lambda = \mathsf{push}(0)\cdot S_0 + \mathsf{push}(1)\cdot S_1$$
$$S_{d\sigma} = \mathsf{push}(0)\cdot S_{0d\sigma} + \mathsf{push}(1)\cdot S_{1d\sigma} + \mathsf{pop}(d)\cdot S_\sigma$$
(for d=0 or d=1, and every sequence σ)

TABLE 18. Stack over {0,1} (1st).

2.9.3 GRAPH
We can determine a graph of this linear specification as indicated in 2.8. In fig. 14 we have the graph for S_λ. Here we use the abbreviation 0 for push(0) and $\underline{0}$ for pop(0) (similarly 1, $\underline{1}$).

One can easily see that the stack is an example of a process which (in the graph model) is not regular, since every node in the graph has a unique shortest path to the root; therefore this graph cannot bisimulate with any finite graph.

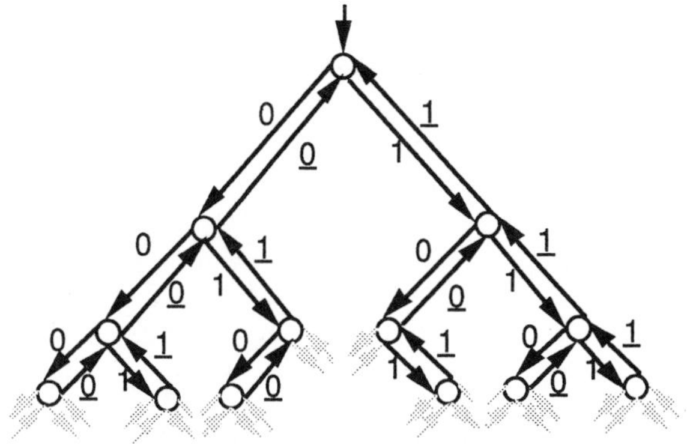

FIGURE 14. Stack.

2.9.4 FINITE SPECIFICATION

Now we present a *finite* recursive specification of the stack. As we saw before, this cannot be a linear specification. This specification has variables S, T, T_0 and T_1 and the following equations.

$S = T \cdot S$
$T = push(0) \cdot T_0 + push(1) \cdot T_1$
$T_0 = pop(0) + T \cdot T_0$
$T_1 = pop(1) + T \cdot T_1$

TABLE 19. Stack over {0,1} (2nd).

We can easily see that this specification is guarded. We will also use the symbol S for the solution of this specification.

2.9.5 THEOREM

$S = S_\lambda$.

PROOF: Let σ be some arbitrary sequence of 0's and 1's, $\sigma \equiv d_0 d_1 \ldots d_k$ say. We will prove that in general the following holds:

$$S_\sigma = T_{d_0} \cdot T_{d_1} \cdot \ldots \cdot T_{d_k} \cdot S.$$

We do this by showing that the processes $R_\sigma \equiv T_{d_0} \cdot T_{d_1} \cdot \ldots \cdot T_{d_k} \cdot S$ satisfy the specification of table 17 (in 2.9.2).

i. $R_\lambda = S = T \cdot S = (push(0) \cdot T_0 + push(1) \cdot T_1) \cdot S =$
$= push(0) \cdot T_0 \cdot S + push(1) \cdot T_1 \cdot S = push(0) \cdot R_0 + push(1) \cdot R_1.$

ii. $R_{d\sigma} = T_d \cdot R_\sigma = (pop(d) + T \cdot T_d) \cdot R_\sigma =$
$= pop(d) \cdot R_\sigma + (push(0) \cdot T_0 + push(1) \cdot T_1) \cdot T_d \cdot R_\sigma =$
$= pop(d) \cdot R_\sigma + push(0) \cdot T_0 \cdot R_{d\sigma} + push(1) \cdot T_1 \cdot R_{d\sigma} =$
$= pop(d) \cdot R_\sigma + push(0) \cdot R_{0d\sigma} + push(1) \cdot R_{1d\sigma}.$

So the processes R_σ are a solution of the specification in table 18, and by RSP (guarded specifications have at most one solution) it follows that $R_\sigma = S_\sigma$.

2.9.6 TERMINATING STACK

We see that the process T_0 from table 17 represents the stack with single element 0, and T_1 with single element 1. The process T is called the **terminating stack**, which stops as soon as it is empty. The graph of T is shown in fig. 15.

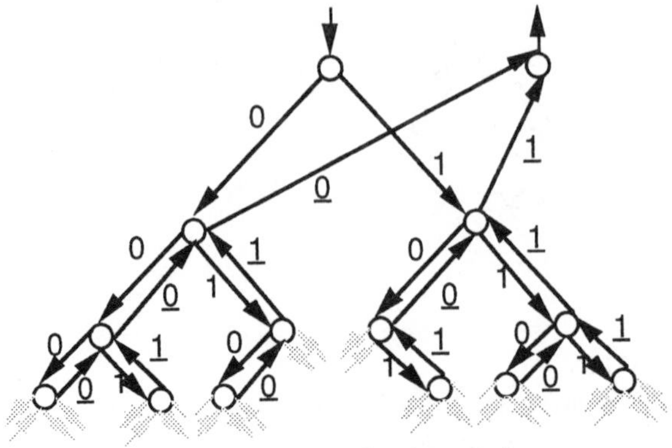

FIGURE 15. Terminating stack.

2.9.7 STACK OVER D

A stack over an arbitrary set of data elements can be described by means of the sum-notation. If the set of data is some finite set D, then we have the specification from table 20.

$$S = T \cdot S$$
$$T = \sum_{d \in D} push(d) \cdot T_d$$
$$T_d = pop(d) + T \cdot T_d \qquad \text{(for every } d \in D)$$

TABLE 20. Stack over D.

2.9.8 DEFINITION

We use sum-notations like in 2.9.7 as abbreviations. If $D = \{d_1, d_2, ..., d_n\}$, then the second line in table 19 means the following:

$$T = push(d_1) \cdot T_{d_1} + push(d_2) \cdot T_{d_2} + ... + push(d_n) \cdot T_{d_n}.$$

2.9.9 COUNTER

We obtain a **counter** by considering the equations from 2.9.7, with D only having one element. After renaming, we obtain table 21.

$$C = T \cdot C$$
$$T = plus \cdot T'$$
$$T' = min + T \cdot T'$$

TABLE 21. Counter.

2.9.10 EXERCISES

1. Rewrite the equations from table 18 into a completely guarded recursive specification (see 2.3.4).

2. Calculate $\pi_1(S_\lambda)$, $\pi_2(S_\lambda)$, $\pi_3(S_\lambda)$ for S_λ in table 18. Also calculate $\pi_1(S)$, $\pi_2(S)$, $\pi_3(S)$ for S in table 19, and show that these terms are pairwise equal.
3. Which process in table 19 corresponds to S_{011} in table 18?
4. Draw a process graph for the counter C.
5. Eliminate the variable T in the specification of the counter.
6. If D = {a,b,c}, then write down the specification of table 20 without sum-notation and draw a process graph of its solution.
7. In BPA_ε the specification of a stack over a finite set of data elements D can be given in only three equations, no matter how large D is. Show that the specification in table 22 is such a specification.

$$S = T \cdot S$$
$$T = \sum_{d \in D} push(d) \cdot R \cdot pop(d)$$
$$R = \varepsilon + T \cdot R$$

TABLE 22. Stack over D (3rd).

2.9.11 NOTES AND COMMENTS

The specification of the stack in table 20 can be found in BERGSTRA & KLOP [1986b]. The one in table 22 is from KOYMANS & VRANCKEN [1985].

Chapter 3
Concurrent processes

3.1 INTERLEAVING

In order to be able to describe processes that occur in parallel, concurrently, we introduce the **merge** operator $\|$.

The process $x \| y$ is the process that executes processes x and y in parallel. If we assume that the observation of an atomic action has no duration, and that two actions cannot happen simultaneously, then it appears that in $x \| y$ the atomic actions of x are *merged* or *interleaved* with those of y: every time we either see the next action of x, or the next action of y. Thus, in $a \| b$ ($a,b \in A$) we either see a first, followed by b, or we see b first, followed by a. We obtain the following identity:

$$a \| b = ab + ba.$$

This approach to the merge operator is called **arbitrary interleaving** or **shuffle** in the literature. Notice that we do not assert that the first action has terminated when the second one starts. This can depend on the implementation of a process (on a sequential or a parallel machine). We can however, if we want to, explicitly state that two actions can overlap in time: if g and h are two events having some duration, we can introduce atomic actions $begin(g)$, $end(g)$, $begin(h)$ and $end(h)$, and then we can describe process $g \| h$ by

$$(begin(g) \cdot end(g)) \| (begin(h) \cdot end(h)).$$

This process has $begin(g) \cdot begin(h) \cdot end(g) \cdot end(h)$ as one of its possible execution sequences.

Note that in this theory, we cannot mention time explicitly, contrary to theories like temporal logic.

In 3.1.2 we will expand the system BPA from chapter 2 with this merge operator. In order to specify the merge in finitely many equations, we need an auxiliary operator. This auxiliary operator is $⫦$, the **left-merge**. $x ⫦ y$ has the same meaning as $x \| y$, but with the restriction that the first step must come from x.

3.1.1 EXAMPLES

The following equalities can be derived with the intuition of 3.1.

1. $a \| b = ab + ba$.
2. $(ab) \| c = a(bc + cb) + cab$.

3. $(a + b) \| c = ac + bc + c(a + b)$.

3.1.2 SYNTAX

The signature of the equational specification PA contains the following binary operators:

$+$	alternative composition, sum
$\cdot$	sequential composition, product
$\|$	**parallel composition, merge**
$\mathbin{\|\!\!\lfloor}$	**left-merge**

and, furthermore, a set of constants A (a,b,c,....∈ A). (Here, we do not use the constants δ or ε of 2.9; we do consider them in 3.3.) PA stands for Process Algebra.

PA has the equations in table 24.

$x + y = y + x$	A1
$(x + y) + z = x + (y + z)$	A2
$x + x = x$	A3
$(x + y)z = xz + yz$	A4
$(xy)z = x(yz)$	A5
$x \| y = x \mathbin{\|\!\!\lfloor} y + y \mathbin{\|\!\!\lfloor} x$	M1
$a \mathbin{\|\!\!\lfloor} x = ax$	M2
$ax \mathbin{\|\!\!\lfloor} y = a(x \| y)$	M3
$(x + y) \mathbin{\|\!\!\lfloor} z = x \mathbin{\|\!\!\lfloor} z + y \mathbin{\|\!\!\lfloor} z$	M4

TABLE 23. PA.

In this table, a is an arbitrary element of A. Axioms M2 and M3 are in fact axiom *schemes:* there is such an axiom for each element of A.

3.1.3 COMMENTS

The merge in this system does not contain a possibility of communication (that will be considered in the next chapter) and is often called the **free merge**.

Axioms A1-5 are the axioms of BPA (see 2.1). Axiom M1 defines the merge in terms of the left-merge: when we merge processes x and y, then either the first step will come from x, or the first step will come from y. The axioms M2-4 define the left-merge, depending on the form of the process on the left. Here, we use the structure of basic terms of 2.1.5.

We often leave out brackets, as for instance in M1 or M3, assuming that · will always bind stronger than $\|$ and $\mathbin{\|\!\!\lfloor}$, which in turn bind stronger than +. Thus, the left-hand side of M3 stands for $(a \cdot x) \mathbin{\|\!\!\lfloor} y$.

3.1.4 EXAMPLES

We use the laws of PA in the following examples:

1. $a \| b = a \mathbin{\|\!\!\lfloor} b + b \mathbin{\|\!\!\lfloor} a =$ (M1)
   $= ab + ba$ (M2).
2. $ab \| c = ab \mathbin{\|\!\!\lfloor} c + c \mathbin{\|\!\!\lfloor} ab$ (M1)
   $= a(b \| c) + cab$ (M3, M2)
   $= a(bc + cb) + cab$ (by example 1).
3. $(a + b) \| c = (a + b) \mathbin{\|\!\!\lfloor} c + c \mathbin{\|\!\!\lfloor} (a + b)$ (M1)

$$= a \mathbin{|\!\!\lfloor} c + b \mathbin{|\!\!\lfloor} c + c \mathbin{|\!\!\lfloor} (a + b) \qquad \text{(M4)}$$
$$= ac + bc + c(a + b) \qquad \text{(M2).}$$

3.1.5 ACTION RELATIONS

Having new operators, we can try to find an intuitive operational meaning of the terms involving merge and left-merge. We obtain the following simple rules, which form an extension of the ones for BPA (see 2.1.7).

$$
\begin{array}{lll}
a \xrightarrow{a} \surd & & \\
x \xrightarrow{a} x' & \Rightarrow & x+y \xrightarrow{a} x' \text{ and } y+x \xrightarrow{a} x' \\
x \xrightarrow{a} \surd & \Rightarrow & x+y \xrightarrow{a} \surd \text{ and } y+x \xrightarrow{a} \surd \\
x \xrightarrow{a} x' & \Rightarrow & xy \xrightarrow{a} x'y \\
x \xrightarrow{a} \surd & \Rightarrow & xy \xrightarrow{a} y \\
 & & \\
x \xrightarrow{a} x' & \Rightarrow & x \| y \xrightarrow{a} x' \| y \text{ and } y \| x \xrightarrow{a} y \| x' \\
x \xrightarrow{a} \surd & \Rightarrow & x \| y \xrightarrow{a} y \text{ and } y \| x \xrightarrow{a} y \\
x \xrightarrow{a} x' & \Rightarrow & x \mathbin{|\!\!\lfloor} y \xrightarrow{a} x' \| y \\
x \xrightarrow{a} \surd & \Rightarrow & x \mathbin{|\!\!\lfloor} y \xrightarrow{a} y
\end{array}
$$

TABLE 24. Action relations for PA.

The first five rules are action relations from BPA. The last four rules define new relations on terms involving the additional operators $\|$ and $\mathbin{|\!\!\lfloor}$.

3.1.6 EXERCISES

1. Use the axioms of PA to eliminate $\|$, $\mathbin{|\!\!\lfloor}$ from the following terms.

i. $aa \| bb$; ii. $(a + b) \| (a + b)$; iii. $aaa \| aaa$; iv. $abc \| (d + e)$.

2. Prove that PA $\vdash x \| y = y \| x$.
3. Is the equality $(x \| y) \| z = x \| (y \| z)$ derivable from PA?
4. We consider a vending machine K' where coffee costs 40 ¢. A quarter, a dime and a nickel need to be inserted (in arbitrary order), and then coffee is dispensed. Describe K' by means of a recursive equation, using the merge operator.
5. Try to describe the operator $\|$ in equations *without* the use of an auxiliary operator like $\mathbin{|\!\!\lfloor}$.
6. Draw the action graph of the following PA terms, using the rules from table 24.

i. $(a + b) \| c$; ii. $ab \| c(d + e)$; iii. $(a + b) \| (c + d)e$; iv. $ab \| ab$; v. $(ab + c)d \mathbin{|\!\!\lfloor} e$.

7. Use definition 2.5.2 and the rules in table 24 to prove that: i. $x \| y \underline{\leftrightarrow} x \mathbin{|\!\!\lfloor} y + y \mathbin{|\!\!\lfloor} x$;

ii. $a \mathbin{|\!\!\lfloor} x \underline{\leftrightarrow} ax$; iii. $ax \mathbin{|\!\!\lfloor} y \underline{\leftrightarrow} a(x \| y)$; iv. $(x + y) \mathbin{|\!\!\lfloor} z \underline{\leftrightarrow} x \mathbin{|\!\!\lfloor} z + y \mathbin{|\!\!\lfloor} z$.

8. Give an example which shows that $(x + y) \| z \underline{\leftrightarrow} x \| z + y \| z$ does *not* hold.
9. Show that $x \| z \underline{\leftrightarrow} y \| z$ implies that $x \underline{\leftrightarrow} y$.

3.1.7 NOTES AND COMMENTS

The axiom system PA was introduced in BERGSTRA & KLOP [1982]. The interleaving approach to parallel composition prevails in many theories of concurrency, e.g. in CCS and CSP. MOLLER [1989] showed that the merge operator cannot be axiomatized in finitely many equations without using an auxiliary operator (this was conjectured before in BERGSTRA & KLOP [1982]). The left-merge has similarities to an operator of BEKIC [1984]. The action rules of 3.1.5 appear in VAN GLABBEEK [1987]. Exercise 3.1.6.9 was inspired by MOLLER [1989].

3.2 SOME THEOREMS ON PA

In this section we present some of the basic results on PA, such as a theorem for eliminating the merge operator from closed terms, and the so-called expansion theorem.

3.2.1 THEOREM

i. For every closed PA term t there is a basic BPA term s, such that $PA \vdash t=s$.
This is called the **elimination theorem** (since the operators $\|$ and $\lfloor\!\lfloor$ are eliminated from t).
ii. If t,s are two closed terms without $\|$ and $\lfloor\!\lfloor$, then

$$PA \vdash t=s \ \Rightarrow\ BPA \vdash t=s.$$

This theorem says that PA is a **conservative extension** of BPA.

PROOF: i. We consider the following term rewriting system, that has rules corresponding to axioms A3-5 and M1-4:

$$x + x \to x$$
$$(x + y)z \to xz + yz$$
$$(xy)z \to x(yz)$$
$$x \| y \to x \lfloor\!\lfloor y + y \lfloor\!\lfloor x$$
$$a \lfloor\!\lfloor x \to ax$$
$$ax \lfloor\!\lfloor y \to a(x \| y)$$
$$(x + y) \lfloor\!\lfloor z \to x \lfloor\!\lfloor z + y \lfloor\!\lfloor z.$$

We can prove that this term rewriting system is strongly normalizing, and that a normal form of a closed term must be a basic term. For if a closed term s has an occurrence of $\|$, then the third rule can still be applied. Furthermore, if s has an occurrence of $\lfloor\!\lfloor$, then consider the smallest subterm with an occurrence of $\lfloor\!\lfloor$. Such a subterm has the form $t_1 \lfloor\!\lfloor t_2$, with t_1, t_2 terms without $\lfloor\!\lfloor$, i.e. BPA terms. Then rewrite t_1 into a normal form and we obtain one of the cases mentioned in 2.1.5. In each case, one of the last three rewrite rules is applicable.

We see that if s contains either $\|$ or $\lfloor\!\lfloor$, then there is a rule applicable, and so s cannot be in normal form. Hence the normal forms of t do not contain occurrences of $\|, \lfloor\!\lfloor$, and must be BPA terms. Using 2.1.6 we obtain a basic term.

As in 2.4.3, we can show that the term rewriting system is confluent modulo A1 and A2, so that terms that are equal in the theory PA have normal forms that are identical up to A1, A2, i.e. up to the order of the summands.

ii. Let t,s be closed terms such that $PA \vdash t=s$. Reduce t and s to basic terms by means of the term rewriting system above. By i, these basic terms must be equal up to A1, A2. Since t and s do not contain $\|$ or $\lfloor\!\lfloor$, each reduction is an instance of the first two rules. This is because no rewrite rule *introduces* $\|$ or $\lfloor\!\lfloor$ in its right-hand side if it was not already there in its left-hand side. So in the reductions of t and s there are no occurrences of $\|$ or $\lfloor\!\lfloor$ and the reduction of t into a normal form, followed by the reverse of the reduction of s into a normal form, is a proof of s=t in BPA.

3.2.2 THEOREM

The following equalities hold for all closed terms:

1. $(x \lfloor\!\lfloor y) \lfloor\!\lfloor z = x \lfloor\!\lfloor (y \| z)$
2. $(x \| y) \| z = x \| (y \| z)$

PROOF: We may assume that x, y and z are basic terms (see 3.2.1). We use induction on the sum of the number of symbols in x, y, and z. If k=3 then it is left to the reader to check 1. and 2. Suppose this number is k (>3) and we know 1. and 2. for all numbers less than k. By 2.1.5 we can write x as a basic term

$$\sum_{i<n} a_i x_i + \sum_{j<m} b_j \quad (n+m>0).$$

Then:

1. $(x \lfloor\!\lfloor y) \lfloor\!\lfloor z = (\sum_{i<n} a_i x_i \lfloor\!\lfloor y + \sum_{j<m} b_j \lfloor\!\lfloor y) \lfloor\!\lfloor z = (\sum_{i<n} a_i (x_i \| y) + \sum_{j<m} b_j y) \lfloor\!\lfloor z =$

$= \sum_{i<n} a_i (x_i \| y) \lfloor\!\lfloor z + \sum_{j<m} b_j y \lfloor\!\lfloor z = \sum_{i<n} a_i ((x_i \| y) \| z) + \sum_{j<m} b_j (y \| z) =$

$= \sum_{i<n} a_i (x_i \| (y \| z)) + \sum_{j<m} b_j (y \| z) = \sum_{i<n} a_i x_i \lfloor\!\lfloor (y \| z) + \sum_{j<m} b_j \lfloor\!\lfloor (y \| z) =$

$= (\sum_{i<n} a_i x_i + \sum_{j<m} b_j) \lfloor\!\lfloor (y \| z) = x \lfloor\!\lfloor (y \| z).$

Now we know that 1. holds for all triples x, y and z having a total of k symbols. We use this in the second part of the proof.

2. $(x \| y) \| z = (x \| y) \lfloor\!\lfloor z + z \lfloor\!\lfloor (x \| y) = (x \lfloor\!\lfloor y + y \lfloor\!\lfloor x) \lfloor\!\lfloor z + z \lfloor\!\lfloor (x \| y) =$

$= (x \lfloor\!\lfloor y) \lfloor\!\lfloor z + (y \lfloor\!\lfloor x) \lfloor\!\lfloor z + z \lfloor\!\lfloor (y \| x) = x \lfloor\!\lfloor (y \| z) + y \lfloor\!\lfloor (x \| z) + (z \lfloor\!\lfloor y) \lfloor\!\lfloor x =$

$= x \lfloor\!\lfloor (y \| z) + y \lfloor\!\lfloor (z \| x) + (z \lfloor\!\lfloor y) \lfloor\!\lfloor x = x \lfloor\!\lfloor (y \| z) + (y \lfloor\!\lfloor z) \lfloor\!\lfloor x + (z \lfloor\!\lfloor y) \lfloor\!\lfloor x =$

$= x \lfloor\!\lfloor (y \| z) + (y \lfloor\!\lfloor z + z \lfloor\!\lfloor y) \lfloor\!\lfloor x = x \lfloor\!\lfloor (y \| z) + (y \| z) \lfloor\!\lfloor x = x \| (y \| z).$

3.2.3 REMARK

The equalities in 3.2.2 are often referred to as **axioms for standard concurrency**. Although these axioms do not appear in our system PA, and are not derivable from it (we can only prove them for *closed* terms), we will often assume them to be valid. Thus we usually do not write parentheses in expressions as $x \| y \| z$.

3.2.4 THEOREM

In PA with standard concurrency we have

$$x_1 \| \ldots\ldots \| x_n = \sum_{1 \le i \le n} x_i \lfloor\!\lfloor (x_1 \| \ldots\ldots \| x_{i-1} \| x_{i+1} \| \ldots\ldots \| x_n) \qquad (n \ge 2)$$

This is the so-called **expansion theorem**, that can be considered as a generalization of M1 to a merge of n processes. We will also use the following notation:

$$\|_{1 \le i \le n} x_i = \sum_{1 \le i \le n} x_i \lfloor\!\lfloor (\|_{1 \le j \le n, j \ne i} x_j) \qquad (n \ge 2)$$

PROOF: By induction on n. The case n=2 is precisely axiom M1. The induction step is as follows:

$x_1 \| \ldots\ldots \| x_{n+1} = (x_1 \| \ldots\ldots \| x_n) \| x_{n+1} =$

$$
\begin{aligned}
&= (x_1 \| \ldots \| x_n) \mathbin{\|\!\!\lfloor} x_{n+1} + x_{n+1} \mathbin{\|\!\!\lfloor} (x_1 \| \ldots \| x_n) = \\
&= \Big(\sum_{1 \le i \le n} x_i \mathbin{\|\!\!\lfloor} \big(\mathop{\Big\|}_{1 \le j \le n. j \ne i} x_j \big)\Big) \mathbin{\|\!\!\lfloor} x_{n+1} + x_{n+1} \mathbin{\|\!\!\lfloor} \big(\mathop{\Big\|}_{1 \le j \le n} x_j \big) = \\
&= \sum_{1 \le i \le n} x_i \mathbin{\|\!\!\lfloor} \Big(\big(\mathop{\Big\|}_{1 \le j \le n. j \ne i} x_j \big) \| x_{n+1} \Big) + x_{n+1} \mathbin{\|\!\!\lfloor} \big(\mathop{\Big\|}_{1 \le j \le n} x_j \big) = \\
&= \sum_{1 \le i \le n} x_i \mathbin{\|\!\!\lfloor} \big(\mathop{\Big\|}_{1 \le j \le n+1. j \ne i} x_j \big) + x_{n+1} \mathbin{\|\!\!\lfloor} \big(\mathop{\Big\|}_{1 \le j \le n} x_j \big) = \\
&= \sum_{1 \le i \le n+1} x_i \mathbin{\|\!\!\lfloor} \big(\mathop{\Big\|}_{1 \le j \le n+1. j \ne i} x_j \big)
\end{aligned}
$$

3.2.5 GUARDED TERMS

Although working in an extended signature – involving new operators $\|$ and $\mathbin{\|\!\!\lfloor}$ – we stick to our previous definition on **guarded** and **completely guarded** terms over PA, as well as over any other extension of the theory BPA (see definition 2.3.4). As a consequence, PA has many more guarded terms than BPA has. In the sequel we will see however, that the number of guarded recursive specifications – and hence the number of **definable** processes – over PA does not really exceed that of BPA.

Some examples:

i. All occurrences of X in $a(X \| X) + aX \| Y + a \| Y$ are guarded, whereas those of Y are unguarded.

ii. The recursive equation $X = a \mathbin{\|\!\!\lfloor} X$ is guarded because of axiom M2.

3.2.6 THEOREM

Each definable process over PA has a head normal form.

PROOF: Following the proof of theorem 2.4.7 we only need to prove that the set of definable processes is closed under $\|$ and $\mathbin{\|\!\!\lfloor}$. Now suppose that p has a head normal form $p = \sum_{i<n} a_i p_i + \sum_{j<m} b_j$, then:

$$p \mathbin{\|\!\!\lfloor} q = \Big(\sum_{i<n} a_i p_i + \sum_{j<m} b_j \Big) \mathbin{\|\!\!\lfloor} q = \sum_{i<n} a_i (p_i \mathbin{\|\!\!\lfloor} q) + \sum_{j<m} b_j q,$$

which is in head normal form.

Furthermore, $p \| q = p \mathbin{\|\!\!\lfloor} q + q \mathbin{\|\!\!\lfloor} p$ and since the set of definable processes is closed under +, we find that it is also closed with respect to $\|$.

3.2.7 THEOREM

A process is definable in PA if and only if it is definable in BPA.

PROOF: $\Rightarrow$: According to 3.2.6 we may assume every definable process p in PA to be in head normal form: $p = \sum_{i<n} a_i p_i + \sum_{j<m} b_j$. From this head normal form one immediately obtains a *linear* equation $p = \sum_{i<n} a_i X_i + \sum_{j<m} b_j$, adding new equations of the form $X_i = p_i$ $(i<n)$. Thus all p_i are definable. Repeating this procedure we obtain an (infinite) guarded recursive specification over BPA. Hence p is definable in BPA.

$\Leftarrow$: Immediate.

Thus we have proved that PA is not more expressive with respect to infinitely definable processes. With respect to *finitely* definable processes it is, as we will see later on in this chapter.

3.2.8 EXERCISES

1. Rewrite the following terms into normal form.

i. $(a \| b) \| c$; ii. $a \| (b \| c)$; iii. $(a ⌊\!⌊ b) ⌊\!⌊ c$; iv. $a ⌊\!⌊ (b \| c)$.

2. Prove the expansion theorem in detail for the case $n=3$.
3. Rewriting terms into normal form may involve a lot of effort. For instance, see example 3.2.9 where a combinatorial explosion of the number of summands is visualized. Verify that the length of a normal form may grow exponentially with respect to the length of the input term.
4. Describe the initial algebra of PA.
5. For every process x and any natural number $n \geq 1$, define the **n-merge** of x, $x^{\underline{\underline{n}}}$, recursively in n:

$$x^{\underline{\underline{1}}} = x$$
$$x^{\underline{\underline{n+1}}} = x^{\underline{\underline{n}}} \| x \qquad \text{(for } n \geq 1\text{)}.$$

Prove that for an atomic action a we have that $a^{\underline{\underline{n}}} = a^n$ (for $n \geq 1$). Find a closed term t such that $t^{\underline{\underline{n}}} \neq t^n$.

3.2.9 EXAMPLE

The normal form of $(a^3 \| b^3 \| c^3)$ is as follows:

a(a(a(b(b(bccc + c(bcc + c(bc + cb))) + c(b(bcc + c(bc + cb)) + c(b(bc + cb) + cbb))) + c(b(b(bcc + c(bc + cb)) + c(b(bc + cb) + cbb)) + c(b(b(bc + cb) + cbb) + cbbb))) + b(a(b(bccc + c(bcc + c(bc + cb))) + c(b(bcc + c(bc + cb)) + c(b(bc + cb) + cbb))) + b(a(bccc + c(bcc + c(bc + cb))) + b(accc + c(acc + c(ac + ca))) + c(a(bcc + c(bc + cb)) + b(acc + c(ac + ca)) + c(a(bc + cb) + b(ac + ca) + c(ab + ba)))) + c(a(b(bcc + c(bc + cb)) + c(b(bc + cb) + cbb)) + b(a(bcc + c(bc + cb)) + b(acc + c(ac + ca)) + c(a(bc + cb) + b(ac + ca) + c(ab + ba))) + c(a(b(bc + cb) + cbb) + b(a(bc + cb) + b(ac + ca) + c(ab + ba)) + c(abb + b(ab + ba))))) + c(a(b(b(bcc + c(bc + cb)) + c(b(bc + cb) + cbb)) + c(b(b(bc + cb) + cbb) + cbbb)) +b(a(b(bcc + c(bc + cb)) + c(b(bc + cb) + cbb)) + b(a(bcc + c(bc + cb)) + b(acc + c(ac + ca)) + c(a(bc + cb) + b(ac + ca) + c(ab + ba))) + c(a(b(bc + cb) + cbb) + b(a(bc + cb) + b(ac + ca) + c(ab + ba)) + c(abb + b(ab + ba)))) + c(a(b(b(bc + cb) + cbb) + cbbb) + b(a(b(bc + cb) + cbb) + b(a(bc + cb) + b(ac + ca) + c(ab + ba)) + c(abb + b(ab + ba))) + c(abbb + b(abb + b(ab + ba)))))) + b(a(a(b(bccc + c(bcc + c(bc + cb))) + c(b(bcc + c(bc + cb)) + c(b(bc + cb) + cbb))) + b(a(bccc + c(bcc + c(bc + cb))) + b(accc + c(acc + c(ac + ca))) + c(a(bcc + c(bc + cb)) + b(acc + c(ac + ca)) + c(a(bc + cb) + b(ac + ca) + c(ab + ba)))) + c(a(b(bcc + c(bc + cb)) + c(b(bc + cb) + cbb)) + b(a(bcc + c(bc + cb)) + b(acc + c(ac + ca)) + c(a(bc + cb) + b(ac + ca) + c(ab + ba))) + c(a(b(bc + cb) + cbb) + b(a(bc + cb) + b(ac + ca) + c(ab + ba)) + c(abb + b(ab + ba))))) + b(a(a(bccc + c(bcc + c(bc + cb))) + b(accc + c(acc + c(ac + ca))) + c(a(bcc + c(bc + cb)) + b(acc + c(ac + ca)) + c(a(bc + cb) + b(ac + ca) + c(ab + ba)))) + b(a(accc + c(acc + c(ac + ca))) + c(a(acc + c(ac + ca)) + c(a(ac + ca) + caa))) + c(a(a(bcc + c(bc + cb)) + b(acc + c(ac + ca)) + c(a(bc + cb) + b(ac + ca) + c(ab + ba))) + b(a(acc + c(ac + ca)) + c(a(ac + ca) + caa)) + c(a(a(bc + cb) + b(ac + ca) + c(ab + ba)) + b(a(ac + ca) + caa) + c(a(ab + ba) + baa)))) + c(a(a(b(bcc + c(bc + cb)) + c(b(bc + cb) + cbb)) + b(a(bcc + c(bc + cb)) + b(acc + c(ac + ca)) + c(a(bc + cb) + b(ac + ca) + c(ab + ba))) + c(a(b(bc + cb) + cbb) + b(a(bc + cb) + b(ac + ca) + c(ab + ba)) + c(abb + b(ab + ba)))) + b(a(a(bcc + c(bc + cb)) + b(acc + c(ac + ca)) + c(a(bc + cb) + b(ac + ca) + c(ab + ba))) + b(a(acc + c(ac + ca)) + c(a(ac + ca) + caa)) + c(a(a(bc + cb) + b(ac + ca) + c(ab + ba)) + b(a(ac + ca) + caa) + c(a(ab + ba) + baa))) + c(a(a(b(bc + cb) + cbb) + b(a(bc + cb) + b(ac + ca) + c(ab + ba)) + c(abb + b(ab + ba))) + b(a(a(bc + cb) + b(ac + ca) + c(ab + ba)) + b(a(ac + ca) + caa) + c(a(ab + ba) + baa)) + c(a(abb + b(ab + ba)) + b(a(ab + ba) + baa))))) + c(a(a(b(b(bcc + c(bc + cb)) + c(b(bc + cb) + cbb)) + c(b(b(bc + cb) + cbb) + cbbb)) + b(a(b(bcc + c(bc + cb)) + c(b(bc + cb) + cbb)) + b(a(bcc + c(bc + cb)) + b(acc + c(ac + ca)) + c(a(bc + cb) + b(ac + ca) + c(ab + ba))) + c(a(b(bc + cb) + cbb) + b(a(bc + cb) + b(ac + ca) + c(ab + ba)) + c(abb + b(ab + ba)))) + c(a(b(b(bc + cb) + cbb) + cbbb) + b(a(b(bc + cb) + cbb) + b(a(bc + cb) + b(ac + ca) + c(ab + ba)) + c(abb + b(ab + ba))) + c(abbb + b(abb + b(ab + ba))))) + b(a(a(b(bcc + c(bc + cb)) + c(b(bc + cb) + cbb)) + b(a(bcc + c(bc + cb)) + b(acc + c(ac + ca)) + c(a(bc + cb) + b(ac + ca) + c(ab + ba))) + c(a(b(bc + cb) + cbb) + b(a(bc + cb) + b(ac + ca) + c(ab + ba)) + c(abb + b(ab + ba)))) + b(a(a(bcc + c(bc + cb)) + b(acc + c(ac + ca)) + c(a(bc + cb) + b(ac + ca) + c(ab + ba))) + b(a(acc + c(ac + ca)) + c(a(ac + ca) + caa)) + c(a(a(bc + cb) + b(ac

+ ca) + c(ab + ba)) + b(a(ac + ca) + caa) + c(a(ab + ba) + baa))) + c(a(a(b(bc + cb) + cbb) + b(a(bc + cb) + b(ac + ca) + c(ab + ba)) + c(abb + b(ab + ba))) + b(a(a(bc + cb) + b(ac + ca) + c(ab + ba)) + b(a(ac + ca) + caa) + c(a(ab + ba) + baa)) + c(a(abb + b(ab + ba)) + b(a(ab + ba) + baa)))) + c(a(a(b(b(bc + cb) + cbb) + cbbb) + b(a(b(bc + cb) + cbb) + b(a(bc + cb) + b(ac + ca) + c(ab + ba)) + c(abb + b(ab + ba))) + c(abbb + b(abb + b(ab + ba)))) + b(a(a(b(bc + cb) + cbb) + b(a(bc + cb) + b(ac + ca) + c(ab + ba)) + c(abb + b(ab + ba))) + b(a(a(bc + cb) + b(ac + ca) + c(ab + ba)) + b(a(ac + ca) + caa) + c(a(ab + ba) + baa)) + c(a(abb + b(ab + ba)) + b(a(ab + ba) + baa))) + c(a(abbb + b(abb + b(ab + ba))) + b(a(abb + b(ab + ba)) + b(a(ab + ba) + baa)))))) + b(a(a(a(b(bccc + c(bcc + c(bc + cb))) + c(b(bcc + c(bc + cb)) + c(b(bc + cb) + cbb))) + b(a(bccc + c(bcc + c(bc + cb))) + b(accc + c(acc + c(ac + ca))) + c(a(bcc + c(bc + cb)) + b(acc + c(ac + ca)) + c(a(bc + cb) + b(ac + ca) + c(ab + ba)))) + c(a(b(bcc + c(bc + cb)) + c(b(bc + cb) + cbb)) + b(a(bcc + c(bc + cb)) + b(acc + c(ac + ca)) + c(a(bc + cb) + b(ac + ca) + c(ab + ba))) + c(a(b(bc + cb) + cbb) + b(a(bc + cb) + b(ac + ca) + c(ab + ba)) + c(abb + b(ab + ba))))) + b(a(a(bccc + c(bcc + c(bc + cb))) + b(accc + c(acc + c(ac + ca))) + c(a(bcc + c(bc + cb)) + b(acc + c(ac + ca)) + c(a(bc + cb) + b(ac + ca) + c(ab + ba)))) + b(a(accc + c(acc + c(ac + ca))) + c(a(acc + c(ac + ca)) + c(a(ac + ca) + caa))) + c(a(a(bcc + c(bc + cb)) + b(acc + c(ac + ca)) + c(a(bc + cb) + b(ac + ca) + c(ab + ba))) + b(a(acc + c(ac + ca)) + c(a(ac + ca) + caa)) + c(a(a(bc + cb) + b(ac + ca) + c(ab + ba)) + b(a(ac + ca) + caa) + c(a(ab + ba) + baa)))) + c(a(a(b(bcc + c(bc + cb)) + c(b(bc + cb) + cbb)) + b(a(bcc + c(bc + cb)) + b(acc + c(ac + ca)) + c(a(bc + cb) + b(ac + ca) + c(ab + ba))) + c(a(b(bc + cb) + cbb) + b(a(bc + cb) + b(ac + ca) + c(ab + ba)) + c(abb + b(ab + ba)))) + b(a(a(bcc + c(bc + cb)) + b(acc + c(ac + ca)) + c(a(bc + cb) + b(ac + ca) + c(ab + ba))) + b(a(acc + c(ac + ca)) + c(a(ac + ca) + caa)) + c(a(a(bc + cb) + b(ac + ca) + c(ab + ba)) + b(a(ac + ca) + caa) + c(a(ab + ba) + baa))) + c(a(a(b(bc + cb) + cbb) + b(a(bc + cb) + b(ac + ca) + c(ab + ba)) + c(abb + b(ab + ba))) + b(a(a(bc + cb) + b(ac + ca) + c(ab + ba)) + b(a(ac + ca) + caa) + c(a(ab + ba) + baa)) + c(a(abb + b(ab + ba)) + b(a(ab + ba) + baa))))) + b(a(a(a(bccc + c(bcc + c(bc + cb))) + b(accc + c(acc + c(ac + ca))) + c(a(bcc + c(bc + cb)) + b(acc + c(ac + ca)) + c(a(bc + cb) + b(ac + ca) + c(ab + ba)))) + b(a(accc + c(acc + c(ac + ca))) + c(a(acc + c(ac + ca)) + c(a(ac + ca) + caa))) + c(a(a(bcc + c(bc + cb)) + b(acc + c(ac + ca)) + c(a(bc + cb) + b(ac + ca) + c(ab + ba))) + b(a(acc + c(ac + ca)) + c(a(ac + ca) + caa)) + c(a(a(bc + cb) + b(ac + ca) + c(ab + ba)) + b(a(ac + ca) + caa) + c(a(ab + ba) + baa)))) + b(a(a(accc + c(acc + c(ac + ca))) + c(a(acc + c(ac + ca)) + c(a(ac + ca) + caa))) + c(a(a(acc + c(ac + ca)) + c(a(ac + ca) + caa)) + c(a(a(ac + ca) + caa) + caaa))) + c(a(a(a(bcc + c(bc + cb)) + b(acc + c(ac + ca)) + c(a(bc + cb) + b(ac + ca) + c(ab + ba))) + b(a(acc + c(ac + ca)) + c(a(ac + ca) + caa)) + c(a(a(bc + cb) + b(ac + ca) + c(ab + ba)) + b(a(ac + ca) + caa) + c(a(ab + ba) + baa))) + b(a(a(acc + c(ac + ca)) + c(a(ac + ca) + caa)) + c(a(a(ac + ca) + caa) + caaa)) + c(a(a(a(bc + cb) + b(ac + ca) + c(ab + ba)) + b(a(ac + ca) + caa) + c(a(ab + ba) + baa)) + b(a(a(ac + ca) + caa) + caaa) + c(a(a(ab + ba) + baa) + baaa)))) + c(a(a(a(b(bcc + c(bc + cb)) + c(b(bc + cb) + cbb)) + b(a(bcc + c(bc + cb)) + b(acc + c(ac + ca)) + c(a(bc + cb) + b(ac + ca) + c(ab + ba))) + c(a(b(bc + cb) + cbb) + b(a(bc + cb) + b(ac + ca) + c(ab + ba)) + c(abb + b(ab + ba)))) + b(a(a(bcc + c(bc + cb)) + b(acc + c(ac + ca)) + c(a(bc + cb) + b(ac + ca) + c(ab + ba))) + b(a(acc + c(ac + ca)) + c(a(ac + ca) + caa)) + c(a(a(bc + cb) + b(ac + ca) + c(ab + ba)) + b(a(ac + ca) + caa) + c(a(ab + ba) + baa))) + c(a(a(b(bc + cb) + cbb) + b(a(bc + cb) + b(ac + ca) + c(ab + ba)) + c(abb + b(ab + ba))) + b(a(a(bc + cb) + b(ac + ca) + c(ab + ba)) + b(a(ac + ca) + caa) + c(a(ab + ba) + baa)) + c(a(abb + b(ab + ba)) + b(a(ab + ba) + baa)))) + b(a(a(a(bcc + c(bc + cb)) + b(acc + c(ac + ca)) + c(a(bc + cb) + b(ac + ca) + c(ab + ba))) + b(a(acc + c(ac + ca)) + c(a(ac + ca) + caa)) + c(a(a(bc + cb) + b(ac + ca) + c(ab + ba)) + b(a(ac + ca) + caa) + c(a(ab + ba) + baa))) + b(a(a(acc + c(ac + ca)) + c(a(ac + ca) + caa)) + c(a(a(ac + ca) + caa) + caaa)) + c(a(a(a(bc + cb) + b(ac + ca) + c(ab + ba)) + b(a(ac + ca) + caa) + c(a(ab + ba) + baa)) + b(a(a(ac + ca) + caa) + caaa) + c(a(a(ab + ba) + baa) + baaa))) + c(a(a(a(b(bc + cb) + cbb) + b(a(bc + cb) + b(ac + ca) + c(ab + ba)) + c(abb + b(ab + ba))) + b(a(a(bc + cb) + b(ac + ca) + c(ab + ba)) + b(a(ac + ca) + caa) + c(a(ab + ba) + baa)) + c(a(abb + b(ab + ba)) + b(a(ab + ba) + baa))) + b(a(a(a(bc + cb) + b(ac + ca) + c(ab + ba)) + b(a(ac + ca) + caa) + c(a(ab + ba) + baa)) + b(a(a(ac + ca) + caa) + caaa) + c(a(a(ab + ba) + baa) + baaa)) + c(a(a(abb + b(ab + ba)) + b(a(ab + ba) + baa)) + b(a(a(ab + ba) + baa) + baaa))))) + c(a(a(a(b(b(bcc + c(bc + cb)) + c(b(bc + cb) + cbb)) + c(b(b(bc + cb) + cbb) + cbbb)) + b(a(b(bcc + c(bc + cb)) + c(b(bc + cb) + cbb)) + b(a(bcc + c(bc + cb)) + b(acc + c(ac + ca)) + c(a(bc + cb) + b(ac + ca) + c(ab + ba))) + c(a(b(bc + cb) + cbb) + b(a(bc + cb) + b(ac + ca) + c(ab + ba)) + c(abb + b(ab + ba)))) + c(a(b(b(bc + cb) + cbb) + cbbb) + b(a(b(bc + cb) + cbb) + b(a(bc + cb) + b(ac + ca) + c(ab + ba)) + c(abb + b(ab + ba))) + c(abbb + b(abb + b(ab + ba))))) + b(a(a(b(bcc + c(bc + cb)) + c(b(bc + cb) + cbb)) + b(a(bcc + c(bc + cb)) + b(acc + c(ac + ca)) + c(a(bc + cb) + b(ac + ca) + c(ab + ba))) + c(a(b(bc + cb) + cbb) + b(a(bc + cb) + b(ac + ca) + c(ab + ba)) + c(abb + b(ab + ba)))) + b(a(a(bcc + c(bc + cb)) + b(acc + c(ac + ca)) + c(a(bc + cb) + b(ac + ca) + c(ab + ba))) + b(a(acc + c(ac + ca)) + c(a(ac + ca) + caa)) + c(a(a(bc + cb) + b(ac + ca) + c(ab + ba)) + b(a(ac + ca) + caa) + c(a(ab + ba) + baa))) + c(a(a(b(bc + cb) + cbb) + b(a(bc + cb) + b(ac + ca) + c(ab + ba)) + c(abb + b(ab + ba))) + b(a(a(bc + cb) + b(ac + ca) + c(ab + ba)) + b(a(ac + ca) + caa) + c(a(ab + ba) + baa)) + c(a(abb + b(ab + ba)) + b(a(ab + ba) + baa)))) + c(a(a(b(b(bc + cb) + cbb) + cbbb) + b(a(b(bc + cb) + cbb) + b(a(bc + cb) + b(ac + ca) + c(ab + ba)) + c(abb + b(ab + ba))) + c(abbb + b(abb + b(ab + ba)))) + b(a(a(b(bc + cb) + cbb) + b(a(bc + cb) + b(ac + ca) + c(ab + ba)) + c(abb + b(ab + ba))) + b(a(a(bc + cb) + b(ac + ca) + c(ab + ba)) + b(a(ac + ca) + caa) + c(a(ab + ba) + baa)) + c(a(abb + b(ab + ba)) + b(a(ab + ba) + baa))) + c(a(abbb +

b(abb + b(ab + ba))) + b(a(abb + b(ab + ba)) + b(a(ab + ba) + baa))))) + b(a(a(a(b(bcc + c(bc + cb)) + c(b(bc + cb) + cbb)) + b(a(bcc + c(bc + cb)) + b(acc + c(ac + ca)) + c(a(bc + cb) + b(ac + ca) + c(ab + ba))) + c(a(b(bc + cb) + cbb) + b(a(bc + cb) + b(ac + ca) + c(ab + ba)) + c(abb + b(ab+ ba)))) + b(a(a(bcc + c(bc + cb)) + b(acc + c(ac + ca)) + c(a(bc + cb) + b(ac + ca) + c(ab + ba))) + b(a(acc + c(ac + ca)) + c(a(ac + ca) + caa)) + c(a(a(bc + cb) + b(ac + ca) + c(ab + ba)) + b(a(ac + ca) + caa) + c(a(ab + ba) + baa))) + c(a(a(b(bc + cb) + cbb) + b(a(bc + cb) + b(ac + ca) + c(ab + ba)) + c(abb + b(ab + ba))) + b(a(a(bc + cb) + b(ac + ca) + c(ab + ba)) + b(a(ac + ca) + caa) + c(a(ab + ba) + baa)) + c(a(abb + b(ab + ba)) + b(a(ab + ba) + baa)))) + b(a(a(a(bcc + c(bc + cb)) + b(acc + c(ac + ca)) + c(a(bc + cb) + b(ac + ca) + c(ab + ba))) + b(a(acc + c(ac + ca)) + c(a(ac + ca) + caa)) + c(a(a(bc + cb) + b(ac + ca) + c(ab + ba)) + b(a(ac + ca) + caa) + c(a(ab + ba) + baa))) + b(a(a(acc + c(ac + ca)) + c(a(ac + ca) + caa)) + c(a(a(ac + ca) + caa) + caaa)) + c(a(a(a(bc + cb) + b(ac + ca) + c(ab + ba)) + b(a(ac + ca) + caa) + c(a(ab + ba) + baa)) + b(a(a(ac + ca) + caa) + caaa) + c(a(a(ab + ba) + baa) + baaa))) + c(a(a(a(b(bc + cb) + cbb) + b(a(bc + cb) + b(ac + ca) + c(ab + ba)) + c(abb + b(ab + ba))) + b(a(a(bc + cb) + b(ac + ca) + c(ab + ba)) + b(a(ac + ca) + caa) + c(a(ab + ba) + baa)) + c(a(abb + b(ab + ba)) + b(a(ab + ba) + baa))) + b(a(a(a(bc + cb) + b(ac + ca) + c(ab + ba)) + b(a(ac + ca) + caa) + c(a(ab + ba) + baa)) + b(a(a(ac + ca) + caa) + caaa) + c(a(a(ab + ba) + baa) + baaa)) + c(a(a(abb + b(ab + ba)) + b(a(ab + ba) + baa)) + b(a(a(ab + ba) + baa) + baaa)))) + c(a(a(a(b(b(bc + cb) + cbb) + cbbb) + b(a(b(bc + cb) + cbb) + b(a(bc + cb) + b(ac + ca) + c(ab + ba)) + c(abb + b(ab + ba))) + c(abbb + b(abb + b(ab + ba)))) + b(a(a(b(bc + cb) + cbb) + b(a(bc + cb) + b(ac + ca) + c(ab + ba)) + c(abb + b(ab + ba))) + b(a(a(bc + cb) + b(ac + ca) + c(ab + ba)) + b(a(ac + ca) + caa) + c(a(ab + ba) + baa)) + c(a(abb + b(ab + ba)) + b(a(ab + ba) + baa))) + c(a(abbb + b(abb + b(ab + ba))) + b(a(abb + b(ab + ba)) + b(a(ab + ba) + baa)))) + b(a(a(a(b(bc + cb) + cbb) + b(a(bc + cb) + b(ac + ca) + c(ab + ba)) + c(abb + b(ab + ba))) + b(a(a(bc + cb) + b(ac + ca) + c(ab + ba)) + b(a(ac + ca) + caa) + c(a(ab + ba) + baa)) + c(a(abb + b(ab + ba)) + b(a(ab + ba) + baa))) + b(a(a(a(bc + cb) + b(ac + ca) + c(ab + ba)) + b(a(ac + ca) + caa) + c(a(ab + ba) + baa)) + b(a(a(ac + ca) + caa) + caaa) + c(a(a(ab + ba) + baa) + baaa)) + c(a(a(abb + b(ab + ba)) + b(a(ab + ba) + baa)) + b(a(a(ab + ba) + baa) + baaa))) + c(a(a(abbb + b(abb + b(ab + ba))) + b(a(abb + b(ab + ba)) + b(a(ab + ba) + baa))) + b(a(a(abb + b(ab + ba)) + b(a(ab + ba) + baa)) + b(a(a(ab + ba) + baa) + baaa))))).

3.2.10 NOTES AND COMMENTS

Most of the material in this section already appears in BERGSTRA & KLOP [1982]. Also see BERGSTRA & KLOP [1984b], [1986b]. Example 3.2.9 was generated by a Pascal-program written by L. Bouma and J. Bruijning. The formulation of the expansion theorem is from BERGSTRA & TUCKER [1984].

3.3 MERGE AND TERMINATION

In this section we will extend the signature of PA in order to include the special constants δ, ε.

3.3.1 DEADLOCK

The constant δ can be included in PA by simply adding its basic axioms to it. That is, we set PA_δ := PA + A6-A7 and stipulate that in the axiom schemes M2 and M3 of PA, the constant a ranges over $A \cup \{\delta\}$, instead of just over A.

3.3.2 THEOREM

i. $PA_\delta \vdash \delta \mathbin{|\!\!\lfloor} x = \delta$.

ii. For all closed terms x we have $PA_\delta \vdash x \| \delta = x \mathbin{|\!\!\lfloor} \delta = x\delta$.

PROOF: i. By M2 and A7.

ii. The first equation is immediate: $x \| \delta = x \mathbin{|\!\!\lfloor} \delta + \delta \mathbin{|\!\!\lfloor} x = x \mathbin{|\!\!\lfloor} \delta + \delta = x \mathbin{|\!\!\lfloor} \delta$. For the second equation we use induction on the structure of x.

CASE 1: x is an atomic action or δ. Then apply M2.

CASE 2: $x \equiv ay$, for some atomic action a and closed term y, and we may assume the theorem holds for y. Then $x \mathbin{|\!\!\lfloor} \delta = ay \mathbin{|\!\!\lfloor} \delta = a(y \| \delta) = a(y \mathbin{|\!\!\lfloor} \delta) = ay\delta = x\delta$.

CASE 3: $x \equiv y + z$, for some closed terms y and z, and we assume the theorem holds for y and z. Then $x \mathbin{⌊\!⌊} \delta = (y + z) \mathbin{⌊\!⌊} \delta = y \mathbin{⌊\!⌊} \delta + z \mathbin{⌊\!⌊} \delta = y\delta + z\delta = (y + z)\delta = x\delta$.

3.3.3 EMPTY PROCESS

We can also add ε to the theory PA, although this involves a few changes in the axioms. It turns out that there are several ways to introduce ε to our algebra, in particular concerning the axioms on the interaction between $⌊\!⌊$ and ε.

Intuitively, it seems plausible that we want to have that $\varepsilon \| x = x$, in particular $\varepsilon \| \varepsilon = \varepsilon$. From the axiom $x \| y = x \mathbin{⌊\!⌊} y + y \mathbin{⌊\!⌊} x$ of PA we find that the last equation can be achieved by postulating $\varepsilon \mathbin{⌊\!⌊} \varepsilon = \varepsilon$. Including this axiom will lead to a few troublesome complications, since the interpretation of $x \mathbin{⌊\!⌊} y$ is that of $x \| y$, except that $x \mathbin{⌊\!⌊} y$ has its first step from x. Obviously, if x is equal to ε then x is unable to perform any action and hence it becomes doubtful whether $x \mathbin{⌊\!⌊} y$ is able to proceed or not. If not, then $\varepsilon \mathbin{⌊\!⌊} x = \delta$ would be much more plausible.

In this section we will assume that $\varepsilon \mathbin{⌊\!⌊} x = \delta$, thus choosing the second of the two possible interpretations of $⌊\!⌊$ involving ε. With respect to the main axiom for interleaving $x \| y = x \mathbin{⌊\!⌊} y + y \mathbin{⌊\!⌊} x$ this is a drawback: together with $\varepsilon \mathbin{⌊\!⌊} x = \delta$ we can derive $\varepsilon \| \varepsilon = \varepsilon \mathbin{⌊\!⌊} \varepsilon + \varepsilon \mathbin{⌊\!⌊} \varepsilon = \delta + \delta = \delta$ which is not what we want. We deal with this problem by considering the termination behaviour of a process separately.

3.3.4 THE TERMINATION OPERATOR

In order to solve the problem mentioned in the previous paragraph, we introduce a unary operator $\surd$, the **termination operator**. Roughly speaking, $\surd$ indicates whether or not a process has a termination option. If so, then the result will be ε, and otherwise δ. For instance, $\surd(x + \varepsilon) = \varepsilon$ whereas $\surd(a + b) = \delta$. The axioms for $\surd$ are given in the next paragraph.

3.3.5 PA_ε.

Since we have $\varepsilon \mathbin{⌊\!⌊} x = \delta$ as an axiom, δ becomes definable in the presence of ε and hence we cannot consider PA with ε without having δ. Then, the equational specification PA_ε has binary operators $+$, $\cdot$, $\|$, $⌊\!⌊$, a unary operator $\surd$, a set of constants A, and special constants ε and δ. PA_ε has the axioms from table 25 below, where $a \in A \cup \{\delta\}$, and x, y and z are arbitrary processes.

The first nine axioms in table 25 are the axioms of $BPA_{\delta\varepsilon}$ (see section 2.2). Axioms TM3 and TM4 are the same as M3, M4 of table 23 in 3.1.2. Observe that for closed terms x we can prove that $\surd(x)$ is either δ or ε, and therefore $\surd(x) \cdot \surd(y) = \surd(y) \cdot \surd(x)$.

$x + y = y + x$	A1
$(x + y) + z = x + (y + z)$	A2
$x + x = x$	A3
$(x + y)z = xz + yz$	A4
$(xy)z = x(yz)$	A5
$\delta + x = x$	A6
$\delta x = \delta$	A7
$x\varepsilon = x$	A8
$\varepsilon x = x$	A9
$x \| y = x ⫦ y + y ⫦ x + \surd(x)\cdot\surd(y)$	TM1
$\varepsilon ⫦ x = \delta$	TM2
$ax ⫦ y = a(x \| y)$	TM3
$(x + y) ⫦ z = x ⫦ z + y ⫦ z$	TM4
$\surd(\varepsilon) = \varepsilon$	TE1
$\surd(a) = \delta$	TE2
$\surd(x + y) = \surd(x) + \surd(y)$	TE3
$\surd(xy) = \surd(x)\cdot\surd(y)$	TE4

TABLE 25. PA_ε.

3.3.6 THEOREM

For every closed PA_ε-term s there exists a basic term t over $BPA_{\delta\varepsilon}$ such that $PA_\varepsilon \vdash s = t$.

This is the elimination theorem for PA_ε. Its proof proceeds as the one in 3.2.1.

3.3.7 LEMMA

For all closed PA_ε-terms x, y, z we have that:

i. $x ⫦ \varepsilon = x$

ii. $x \| \varepsilon = x$

iii. $\surd(x) = \varepsilon$ if and only if $x + \varepsilon = x$.

PROOF: The proofs are by induction on the structure of the PA_ε-terms. By 2.2.8 it is sufficient to consider the following three cases only for a closed term x:

1. $x = \varepsilon$;
2. $x = ay$, for $a \in A \cup \{\delta\}$ and a closed term y;
3. $x = y + z$, for closed terms y,z.

We leave the proofs for the exercises. It is recommended to prove (i) and (ii) at the same time by means of simultaneous induction.

3.3.8 THEOREM

For closed PA terms x and y (hence without ε or δ) we have: $PA_\varepsilon \vdash x = y$ iff $PA \vdash x = y$.

Note that PA_ε is not a conservative extension of the theory PA, since the axiom $x \| y = x ⌊\!⌊ y + y ⌊\!⌊ x$ is not preserved. However, with respect to closed terms without ε or δ we have that PA_ε does not yield any equations different from those that can be derived from PA.

3.3.9 THEOREM

The following equations of standard concurrency are valid for all closed PA_ε-terms:

1. $x \| y = y \| x$
2. $(x ⌊\!⌊ y) ⌊\!⌊ z = x ⌊\!⌊ (y \| z)$
3. $(x \| y) \| z = x \| (y \| z)$.

PROOF: Analogously to the proof of 3.2.2. Check the case $x=\varepsilon$ and use the representation $x = \sum_{i<n} a_i x_i + \surd(x)$.

3.3.10 THEOREM

In PA_ε with standard concurrency we have the following expansion theorem:

$$x_1 \| \ldots\ldots \| x_n = \sum_{1 \le i \le n} x_i ⌊\!⌊ \left(\mathop{\|}_{1 \le j \le n, j \ne i} x_j \right) + \prod_{1 \le i \le n} \surd(x_i) \qquad (n \ge 2).$$

PROOF: Just like 3.2.4.

3.3.11 THEOREM

A process is definable in PA_ε if and only if it is definable in $BPA_{\delta\varepsilon}$.

The proof of this theorem proceeds along the lines of the proof of theorem 3.2.7. We do not present it here, leaving it to the reader.

3.3.12 EXERCISES

1. Prove by means of induction on their structure that for all closed PA_ε-terms x, y the following equations are derivable:

i. $a ⌊\!⌊ x = ax$; ii. $x ⌊\!⌊ y\delta = (x ⌊\!⌊ y)\delta = x\delta ⌊\!⌊ y$; iii. $x \| y\delta = (x \| y)\delta$.

2. Prove the following equations for all head normal forms in PA_ε:

i. $x \| y = y \| x$; ii. $\surd(x) ⌊\!⌊ y = \delta$; iii. $\surd(x ⌊\!⌊ y) = \delta$; iv. $\surd(\surd(x)) = \surd(x)$.

3. It is not a good idea to include the axiom $\varepsilon ⌊\!⌊ x = x$ in PA.

Show that $PA + \varepsilon ⌊\!⌊ x = x \nvdash ((a + \varepsilon) \| b) \| c = (a + \varepsilon) \| (b \| c)$ $(a,b,c \in A)$, so the merge operator would not be associative.

4. Prove 3.3.6.
5. Prove 3.3.8
6. Prove 3.3.9.
7. One can also extend the action relations from table 11 (see 2.2.9) with terms involving the additional operators of PA_ε. The extra rules (defined on top of the ones in table 11) are shown in table 24 below.

Note that these rules do not match with the ones in table 24 for PA, because of the different treatment of termination.

$x \xrightarrow{a} x'$	$\Rightarrow$	$x \parallel y \xrightarrow{a} x' \parallel y$ and $y \parallel x \xrightarrow{a} y \parallel x'$
$x \xrightarrow{a} x'$	$\Rightarrow$	$x \lfloor\!\lfloor y \xrightarrow{a} x' \parallel y$
$x\downarrow$ and $y\downarrow$	$\Rightarrow$	$(x \parallel y)\downarrow$
$x\downarrow$	$\Rightarrow$	$\surd(x)\downarrow$

TABLE 26. Action relations for PA_ε.

Draw the action graphs of the following terms:

i. $(a + \varepsilon) \parallel (b + \varepsilon)$; ii. $\varepsilon \parallel ab$; iii. $a(b + \varepsilon) \lfloor\!\lfloor c$; iv. $a(b + \varepsilon) \parallel c$; v. $\varepsilon \lfloor\!\lfloor a$.

8. Use the previous exercise and definition 2.5.14 to prove that:

i. $x \parallel y \; \underline{\leftrightarrow} \; x \lfloor\!\lfloor y + y \lfloor\!\lfloor x + \surd(x) \cdot \surd(y)$; ii. $\varepsilon \lfloor\!\lfloor x \; \underline{\leftrightarrow} \; \delta$; iii. $\surd(xy) \; \underline{\leftrightarrow} \; \surd(x) \cdot \surd(y)$.

9. Define the 0-merge of a process x, $x^{\underline{0}}$, in a way consistent with 3.2.8.5.

10. Extend the definition of the property to *have deadlock* to all closed PA_ε-terms t as follows:

t has deadlock $\Leftrightarrow$ there is a basic $BPA_{\delta\varepsilon}$-term s in which δ occurs such that $PA_\varepsilon \vdash t = s$.

Then extend the definition to all definable processes p as follows (using 2.4.8):

p has deadlock $\Leftrightarrow$ there is an $n \geq 0$ such that $\pi_n(p)$ has deadlock.

Prove the following:

i. If $a \in A$, then the process a does not have deadlock.

ii. If p is definable and has no deadlock, and if $a \in A$, then the process $a \cdot p$ has no deadlock.

iii. If definable p and q have no deadlock, then neither has the process $p+q$.

11. Let p,q be definable processes. Prove the following:

i. if $p \parallel q$ has deadlock, then either p or q has deadlock;

ii. if p and q are finite, and p or q has deadlock, then so has $p \parallel q$;

iii. give an example of definable p and q, so that p has deadlock, but $p \parallel q$ does not.

12. Let p,q be definable processes.

Prove: i. if $p \cdot q$ has deadlock, then either p or q has deadlock;

ii. if p is finite, and either p or q has deadlock, then so has $p \cdot q$.

iii. give an example of definable p and q, so that q has deadlock, but $p \cdot q$ does not.

3.3.13 NOTES AND COMMENTS

The first treatment of PA with ε was given in KOYMANS & VRANCKEN [1985]. There we see the non-associative merge operator mentioned in 3.3.3 and 3.3.12.3. The first axiomatization of an associative merge with ε is in VRANCKEN [1986]. The present axiomatization, and most of the material of this section, is based on BAETEN & VAN GLABBEEK [1987b].

3.4 MODELS

In this section we will define several models which are completely axiomatized by PA_ε. This way we gain some more intuition on the nature of the constructs that were suggested in the former paragraphs, and we obtain an instrument for proving statements about PA_ε (derivability in PA_ε is equivalent to validity in the models).

We will only define models for PA_ε. A model for PA or PA_δ can be found from each of these models by restricting its domain and by showing that the smaller domain is closed under the operations. Nevertheless it is important to have a completeness result for the latter theories as well as for the former one.

3.4.1 INITIAL ALGEBRA

It follows from the elimination theorem 3.3.6 that the initial algebra of PA_ε does not contain any more elements than the one of $BPA_{\delta\varepsilon}$. The only difference is the size of the equivalence classes, which in the case of PA_ε contain more elements than in the case of $BPA_{\delta\varepsilon}$. We will neglect this difference, and refer to the initial algebra of PA_ε by $\mathbb{A}_{\delta\varepsilon}$. The definition of the operators $\|$ and $\llfloor$ on $\mathbb{A}_{\delta\varepsilon}$ is given by the axioms of PA_ε.

3.4.2 THE TERM MODEL

As before, the term model is constructed from the terms of PA_ε and the action relations (see exercise 3.3.12.6), by dividing out bisimulation equivalence as defined in definition 2.5.14. Hopefully, the reader has already proved in exercise 3.3.12.8 that the axioms of PA_ε are valid in this model. Furthermore, using theorem 3.3.11 we find that this domain does not contain any more elements than the term model of $BPA_{\delta\varepsilon}$. Hence, modulo bisimulation we obtain the same model, as is stated in the following theorem.

3.4.3 THEOREM

$\mathbb{P}_{\delta\varepsilon}/\underline{\leftrightarrow} \models PA_\varepsilon$.

3.4.4 PROJECTIVE LIMIT MODEL

As in 2.6, the projective limit model $\mathbb{A}^\infty$ can be constructed from the initial algebra $\mathbb{A}$. Then $\|$ and $\llfloor$ are defined in the obvious way. Namely, if $(p_1,p_2,p_3,...)$ and $(q_1,q_2,q_3,...)$ are projective sequences, then we define:

i. $(p_1,p_2,p_3,...) \| (q_1,q_2,q_3,...) = (\pi_1(p_1 \| q_1), \pi_2(p_2 \| q_2), \pi_3(p_3 \| q_3),...)$;

ii. $(p_1,p_2,p_3,...) \llfloor (q_1,q_2,q_3,...) = (\pi_1(p_1 \llfloor q_1), \pi_2(p_2 \llfloor q_2), \pi_3(p_3 \llfloor q_3), ...)$.

The proof that $\mathbb{A}^\infty$ is a model of PA_ε, is left for the exercises.

3.4.5 THE GRAPH MODEL

In order to turn the graph model $\mathbb{G}^\infty/\underline{\leftrightarrow}$ of $BPA_{\delta\varepsilon}$ (see 2.7) into a model for PA_ε, we have to define the operators $\|$, $\llfloor$ and $\surd$ on process graphs.

So let g,h be two graphs ($g,h \in \mathbb{G}^\infty$). Then the graph $g\|h$ is the **cartesian product** of the graphs g and h. To be more precise:

i. the nodes of $g\|h$ are all pairs of nodes from g and nodes from h;

ii. a node (s,t) in $g\|h$ has label $\downarrow$ iff both s and t have;

iii. there is an edge $(s,t) \xrightarrow{a} (s',t)$ in $g\|h$ precisely if there is an edge $s \xrightarrow{a} s'$ in g;
there is an edge $(s,t) \xrightarrow{a} (s,t')$ in $g\|h$ precisely if there is an edge $t \xrightarrow{a} t'$ in g;
these edges together form all edges of $g\|h$;

iv. the root node of $g\|h$ is the pair of roots from g and h.

The graph $g\llfloor h$ can be obtained as follows:

i. construct the cartesian product of g and h (i.e. construct $g\|h$);

ii. unwind the root of $g\|h$, hence obtaining $\rho(g\|h)$;

iii. if (s,t) is the root of $\rho(g \| h)$, then remove all edges $(s,t) \xrightarrow{a} (s,t')$ (that is, edges that originate from h);
iv. remove all parts of the graph that have become inaccessible from the root node, and remove a possibly existing label $\surd$ at the root node;

The graph $\surd(g)$ is the 'root node of g', that is the one-node graph without edges having label $\surd$ iff the root node of g has label $\surd$.

3.4.6 EXAMPLE

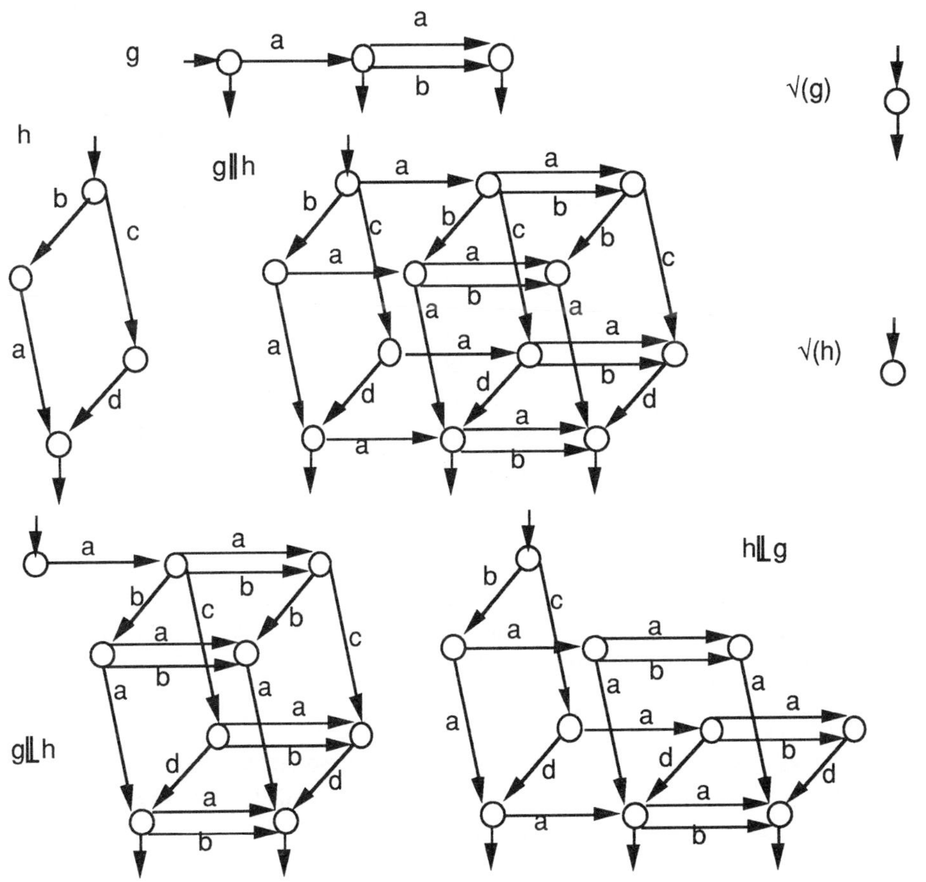

FIGURE 16.

3.4.7 THEOREM
Bisimulation is a congruence relation with respect to the operators $\|$, $\underline{\|}$ and $\surd$.
That is, if g, h, k and l are process graphs such that $g \underline{\leftrightarrow} k$ and $h \underline{\leftrightarrow} l$, then

$$g \| h \underline{\leftrightarrow} k \| l,\ g \underline{\|} h \underline{\leftrightarrow} k \underline{\|} l \text{ and } \surd(g) \underline{\leftrightarrow} \surd(h).$$

PROOF: To prove the first statement, let $R: g \underline{\leftrightarrow} h$ and $S: k \underline{\leftrightarrow} l$ be two bisimulations. The relation $T = R \times S$, the cartesian product of R and S (defined by $T(\langle s,t \rangle, \langle u,v \rangle)$ iff $R(s,u)$ and $S(t,v)$), will now be a bisimulation between $g \| h$ and $k \| l$.

For the second statement, a bisimulation $T: g \| h \leftrightarrow k \| l$ induces a bisimulation $T^*: \rho(g \| h) \leftrightarrow \rho(k \| l)$ in which a root node is not related to a non-root node (cf. 2.7.27). The restriction of T^* to the graphs $g ⌊⌊ h$ and $k ⌊⌊ l$ will then be a bisimulation between $g ⌊⌊ h$ and $k ⌊⌊ l$.

Finally, for the third part, note that $\surd(g)$ and $\surd(h)$ are one-node graphs. The relation relating the two nodes is a bisimulation.

Because of theorem 3.4.7, the structure $(\mathbb{G}^\infty/\leftrightarrow, +, \cdot, \|, ⌊⌊, \surd)$ is an ***algebra*** (in the sense of 1.3.9).

3.4.8 THEOREM
$\mathbb{G}^\infty/\leftrightarrow \models PA_\varepsilon$.

PROOF: By theorem 2.7.33 and 3.4.3 it is left to prove that term respects the extension operators $\|$ and $⌊⌊$ of PA_ε. If so, then term is an isomorphism between $\mathbb{G}^\infty/\leftrightarrow$ and $\mathbb{P}_{\delta\varepsilon}/\leftrightarrow$, even with respect to the signature of PA_ε.
Again, we leave the proof as an exercise.

3.4.9 COROLLARY
$\mathbb{G}^\infty/\leftrightarrow \models$ AIP$^-$, RSP, RDP.

Note that, as a corollary of theorem 3.4.8, we also obtain another proof of the fact that PA_ε is a conservative extension of $BPA_{\delta\varepsilon}$ (cf. 3.2.1): if an equation between two $BPA_{\delta\varepsilon}$-terms is derivable from PA_ε, it holds in the model $\mathbb{G}^\infty/\leftrightarrow$; but then it also holds in the restriction of $\mathbb{G}^\infty/\leftrightarrow$ to the signature of $BPA_{\delta\varepsilon}$; finally, since this model is complete for $BPA_{\delta\varepsilon}$, it must be derivable from $BPA_{\delta\varepsilon}$.

3.4.10 OTHER GRAPH MODELS
In the same way as before (2.7.35) one can prove that $\mathbb{G}/\leftrightarrow$, $\mathbb{R}/\leftrightarrow$ and $\mathbb{F}/\leftrightarrow$ are models of PA. Again we have that $\mathbb{F}/\leftrightarrow$ is isomorphic to the initial algebra $\mathbb{A}_{\delta\varepsilon}$, and again AIP holds in $\mathbb{R}/\leftrightarrow$, $\mathbb{F}/\leftrightarrow$ and $\mathbb{G}/\leftrightarrow$. RSP holds in all models and RDP$^-$ holds in $\mathbb{G}/\leftrightarrow$, but not in $\mathbb{R}/\leftrightarrow$ or $\mathbb{F}/\leftrightarrow$.

3.4.11 CONCLUSION
Every guarded recursive specification over PA_ε has a unique solution in the models $\mathbb{P}_{\delta\varepsilon}/\leftrightarrow$, $\mathbb{A}^\infty$, $\mathbb{G}/\leftrightarrow$ and $\mathbb{G}^\infty/\leftrightarrow$. Therefore, we may assume that every guarded recursive specification uniquely determines a process in these models.

3.4.12 COMPLETENESS
We can easily conclude that all models of PA discussed in this section are also ***complete*** with respect to the theory PA: by the elimination theorem 3.2.1, all closed terms are provably equal to a basic BPA term. Thus, the proof for PA reduces to the proof for BPA. For BPA, the results were already established in chapter 2 (see 2.5.10 and 2.6.9).

Using theorem 3.3.6, we obtain similar results for PA_ε using the completeness theorems for $BPA_{\delta\varepsilon}$.

3.4.13 EXERCISES

1. Show that for all closed PA_ε-terms p,q we have:
i. $\pi_1(p \mathbin{⌊\!⌊} q) = \pi_1(p)$;
ii. $\pi_{n+1}(p \mathbin{⌊\!⌊} q) = \pi_{n+1}(\pi_{n+1}(p) \mathbin{⌊\!⌊} \pi_n(q))$;
iii. $\pi_n(p \| q) = \pi_n(\pi_n(x) \| \pi_n(y))$.
2. Prove that $\mathbb{A}^\infty \models PA_\varepsilon$, using 2.6.3.
3. Prove theorem 3.4.7.
4. Prove theorem 3.4.8.
5. Let g be the graph corresponding to $a + \varepsilon$, and h the graph corresponding to $b + \varepsilon$. Construct the graphs $g \| h$, $g \mathbin{⌊\!⌊} h$, $h \mathbin{⌊\!⌊} g$ and $\sqrt{}(g)\cdot\sqrt{}(h)$, and check that the results are in agreement with the algebraic results.
6. Consider the processes $aa\delta$ and b+c. Find graphs g and h, that represent these processes and construct graphs $g \| h$, $g \mathbin{⌊\!⌊} h$, $h \mathbin{⌊\!⌊} g$, $\sqrt{}(g)$ and $\sqrt{}(h)$ using 3.4.5.

Do the same thing for the processes a^ω and bc, as well as for a^ω and b^ω. Note that $a^\omega \| b^\omega$ and $(a + b)^\omega$ are equal.
7. Given the specification $\{X=Y \| Z, Y=aY, Z=bZ\}$, find $\pi_1(X)$, $\pi_2(X)$ and in general $\pi_n(X)$ as a closed term. What is the process graph of X? Do the same for the specification $\{X = aX \| bcX\}$ and the specification $\{X = a(X \| X)\}$.

3.4.14 NOTES AND COMMENTS

As general references for this section, we mention BERGSTRA & KLOP [1984b] and [1986b].

3.5 BAG

As an example of a guarded recursive specification in PA we consider the example of a **bag** of unbounded capacity. A bag is a process, able to input data elements that reappear in some arbitrary order. Let us first take a look at the equations in case we have only two data elements, say 0 and 1.

3.5.1 INFINITE SPECIFICATION

We have the following atomic actions:

in(0) = put a 0 in the bag;
out(0) = remove a 0 from the bag.

Likewise, we have in(1), out(1).

We first present an infinite linear recursive specification. The order in which data elements are put into the bag is not important: only the number of occurrences in the bag counts. The specification in table 27 has variables $B_{n,m}$ $(n,m \geq 0)$, where $B_{n,m}$ is the bag with n occurrences of 0 and m occurrences of 1.

$B_{0,0} = in(0) \cdot B_{1,0} + in(1) \cdot B_{0,1}$
$B_{0,m+1} = in(0) \cdot B_{1,m+1} + in(1) \cdot B_{0,m+2} + out(1) \cdot B_{0,m}$
$B_{n+1,0} = in(0) \cdot B_{n+2,0} + in(1) \cdot B_{n+1,1} + out(0) \cdot B_{n,0}$
$B_{n+1,m+1} = in(0) \cdot B_{n+2,m+1} + in(1) \cdot B_{n+1,m+2} +$
$\quad + out(0) \cdot B_{n,m+1} + out(1) \cdot B_{n+1,m}$
(for every $n,m \geq 0$)

TABLE 27. Bag over {0,1} (1st).

In figure 17 we draw the graph of $B_{0,0}$ (we write 0 instead of in(0) and $\underline{0}$ instead of out(0). Similarly 1, $\underline{1}$).

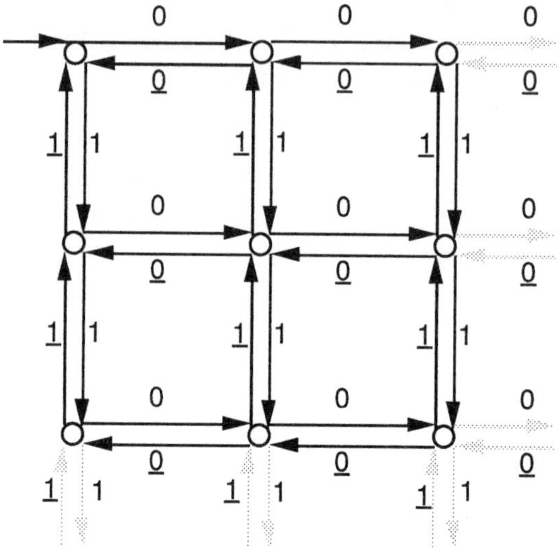

FIGURE 17.

3.5.2 FINITE SPECIFICATION

Next we will present a *finite* recursive specification of a bag. This specification has only one equation with variable B.

$B = in(0) \cdot (B \parallel out(0)) + in(1) \cdot (B \parallel out(1))$

TABLE 28. Bag over {0,1} (2nd).

Immediately we see that this is a guarded equation. We will also use the letter B for the solution of this equation.

3.5.3 THEOREM

$B = B_{0,0}$.

PROOF: Define the processes $D_{n,m}$ $(n,m \geq 0)$ as follows:

i. $D_{0,0} = B$

ii. $D_{0,m+1} = B \parallel out(1)^{m+1}$

iii. $D_{n+1,0} = B \parallel out(0)^{n+1}$

iv. $D_{n+1,m+1} = B \parallel out(1)^{m+1} \parallel out(0)^{n+1}$.

We will prove that $D_{n,m} = B_{n,m}$ for all n,m. We do this by showing that $D_{n,m}$ satisfies the equations of the specification in table 27 in 3.5.1.

i. $D_{0,0} = B = in(0)\cdot(B \| out(0)) + in(1)\cdot(B \| out(1)) = in(0)\cdot D_{1,0} + in(1)\cdot D_{0,1}$.

ii. $D_{0,m+1} = B \| out(1)^{m+1} = B ⌊⌊ out(1)^{m+1} + out(1)^{m+1} ⌊⌊ B =$
$= (in(0)\cdot D_{1,0} + in(1)\cdot D_{0,1}) ⌊⌊ out(1)^{m+1} + out(1)^{m+1} ⌊⌊ B =$
$= in(0)\cdot(D_{1,0} \| out(1)^{m+1}) + in(1)\cdot(D_{0,1} \| out(1)^{m+1}) +$
$+ out(1)\cdot(out(1)^m \| B) =$
$= in(0)\cdot D_{1,m+1} + in(1)\cdot D_{0,m+2} + out(1)\cdot D_{0,m}$

(in the middle term we use 3.2.8.5; the term $out(1)^m$ equals ε when $m=0$).

iii. As ii.

iv. $D_{n+1,m+1} = B \| out(1)^{m+1} \| (out(0))^{n+1} =$
$= B ⌊⌊ (out(1)^{m+1} \| out(0)^{n+1}) + out(1)^{m+1} ⌊⌊ (B \| out(0)^{n+1}) +$
$+ out(0)^{n+1} ⌊⌊ (B \| out(1)^{m+1})$ (use theorem 3.2.6) $=$
$= (in(0)\cdot D_{1,0} + in(1)\cdot D_{0,1}) ⌊⌊ (out(1)^{m+1} \| out(0)^{n+1}) +$
$+ out(1)^{m+1} ⌊⌊ (B \| out(0)^{n+1}) + out(0)^{n+1} ⌊⌊ (B \| out(1)^{m+1}) =$
$= in(0)\cdot(D_{1,0} \| out(1)^{m+1} \| out(0)^{n+1}) + in(1)\cdot(D_{0,1} \| out(1)^{m+1} \| out(0)^{n+1}) +$
$+ out(1)\cdot(out(1)^m \| B \| out(0)^{n+1}) + out(0)\cdot(out(0)^n \| B \| out(1)^{m+1}) =$
$= in(0)\cdot D_{n+2,m+1} + in(1)\cdot D_{n+1,m+2} + out(0)\cdot D_{n,m+1} + out(1)\cdot D_{n+1,m}$.

The processes $D_{n,m}$ form a solution of the specification in table 27, and hence by RSP it follows that $D_{n,m} = B_{n,m}$, in particular $B = B_{0,0}$.

3.5.4 BAG OVER D

A bag over an arbitrary number of data elements is written by means of a sum notation. If the set of data is some finite set D, then the equation for the bag over D reads as follows.

$$B = \sum_{d \in D} in(d)\cdot(B \| out(d))$$

TABLE 29. Bag over D.

3.5.5 REMARK (without proof)

A bag over more than one data element cannot be given by means of a finite recursive specification over BPA. Therefore, over PA more processes are finitely definable than over BPA.

3.5.6 COUNTER

The bag over one data element will give us the counter from 2.9.9. Writing the two atomic actions as plus and min respectively, we obtain the specification in table 30.

$$D = plus\cdot(D \| min)$$

TABLE 30. Counter (2nd).

3.5.7 THEOREM

Let C be given by the recursive specification

$$C = T\cdot C$$
$$T = plus\cdot T'$$
$$T' = min + T\cdot T'$$

from table 21 in 2.9.9 and let D be given by the equation in table 30. Then C=D.

PROOF: We can give this proof by showing that C and D satisfy the same (infinite) linear specification. To illustrate another proof technique, this time we will prove it by applying AIP$^-$. Since both specifications are guarded, the processes are definable, and thus have bounded non-determinism (2.4.16); this means AIP$^-$ can be applied.

We will prove that $C = D$, and at the same time that $(T')^n\cdot C = D\|min^n$, for every $n\geq 1$. By AIP$^-$ it is sufficient to prove that all finite projections are equal. We prove this by induction.

The basis of the induction:

$\pi_1(C) = \pi_1(T\cdot C) = \pi_1(plus\cdot T'\cdot C) = plus$, and

$\pi_1(D) = \pi_1(plus\cdot(D\|min)) = plus$.

Further, if $n\geq 1$:

$$\pi_1((T')^n\cdot C) = \pi_1((min + plus\cdot T'\cdot T')\cdot(T')^{n-1}\cdot C) =$$
$$= \pi_1(min\cdot(T')^{n-1}\cdot C + plus\cdot(T')^{n+1}\cdot C) = min + plus$$

(where the term $(T')^{n-1}$ equals ε when $n=1$), and

$$\pi_1(D\|min^n) = \pi_1(D \mathbin{\|\!\_} min^n + min^n \mathbin{\|\!\_} D) =$$
$$= \pi_1(plus\cdot(D\|min^{n+1}) + min\cdot(D\|min^{n-1})) = min + plus$$

(and the term min^{n-1} equals ε when $n=1$).

The induction step: assume that the claim holds for k, then we obtain for k+1:

$$\pi_{k+1}(C) = \pi_{k+1}(plus\cdot T'\cdot C) = plus\cdot\pi_k(T'\cdot C) = plus\cdot\pi_k(D\|min) =$$
$$= \pi_{k+1}(plus\cdot(D\|min) = \pi_{k+1}(D).$$

Further, if $n\geq 1$,

$$\pi_{k+1}((T')^n\cdot C) = \pi_{k+1}(min\cdot(T')^{n-1}\cdot C + plus\cdot(T')^{n+1}\cdot C) =$$
$$= min\cdot\pi_k((T')^{n-1}\cdot C) + plus\cdot\pi_k((T')^{n+1}\cdot C) =$$
$$= min\cdot\pi_k(D\|min^{n-1}) + plus\cdot\pi_k(D\|min^{n+1}) =$$
$$= \pi_{k+1}(min\cdot(D\|min^{n-1}) + plus\cdot(D\|min^{n+1})) =$$
$$= \pi_{k+1}(min^n \mathbin{\|\!\_} D + D \mathbin{\|\!\_} min^n) = \pi_{k+1}(D\|min^n).$$

3.5.8 EXERCISES

1. Calculate $\pi_1(B)$, $\pi_2(B)$, $\pi_3(B)$ for B in 3.5.2.
2. If D={a,b,c}, then write down the equations for B from 3.5.4 without sum notation, and draw the graph of its solution.
3. Describe a biscuit-tin with two kinds of biscuits (with unbounded capacity) by means of a guarded recursive specification over PA.
4. Let p be a closed term in PA. The ω-merge of p, $p\|p\|p\|p\|$....., cannot be given by the equation $x=p\|x$, which is unguarded and has infinitely many solutions. Which guarded recursive specification *does* have the ω-merge of p as its unique solution?
5. Show that the graph that you found in 2.9.10.4 is equal to the graph of 3.5.6.
6. Find a bisimulation between the graph g in fig. 17 and the graph of

$$in(0)\cdot(g\|out(0)) + in(1)\cdot(g\|out(1)).$$

3.5.9 NOTES AND COMMENTS
The specification of the bag in 3.5.4 is from BERGSTRA & KLOP [1984a]. There, also the proof of remark 3.5.5 can be found. Exercise 3.5.8.4 is based on BERGSTRA & KLOP [1982].

3.6 RENAMING

It will be useful to have the possibility of ***renaming*** atomic actions. An example of such a renaming is the function that renames certain atoms into δ, leaving others as they are. In this section we will present a general treatment of this notion.

3.6.1 DEFINITION
Let f be a function from the set A of atomic actions to the set of processes. Then there is a unary operator ρ_f, the **renaming** operator, replacing every occurrence of a constant $a \in A$ by $f(a)$. We will only consider renamings to constants, so $f: A \to A \cup C$, where C is the set of special constants (containing δ, ε and perhaps others, depending on which constants are in the signature considered).

The operator ρ_f can be defined by means of the equations from table 31.

$\rho_f(\gamma) = \gamma$	RN0
$\rho_f(a) = f(a)$	RN1
$\rho_f(x + y) = \rho_f(x) + \rho_f(y)$	RN2
$\rho_f(xy) = \rho_f(x) \cdot \rho_f(y)$	RN3
$\rho_{id}(x) = x$	RR1
$\rho_f \circ \rho_g(x) = \rho_{f \circ g}(x)$	RR2

TABLE 31. Renaming.

In this table, we have $a \in A$, $\gamma \in C$, id is the identity function ($id(a)=a$ for all a) and $\circ$ is composition of functions or operators, so $f \circ g(x) = f(g(x))$, but we put $f \circ g(a) = g(a)$ if $g(a) \in C$.

3.6.2 SIMPLE RENAMINGS
In practical applications we often use a specialization of this scheme: let $t \in A \cup C$ and $H \subseteq A$. Define the function t_H on A by means of the equations

$t_H(a) = a$ if $a \notin H$

$t_H(a) = t$ if $a \in H$.

(Note that $t_\varnothing = id$ for every t.) The resulting renaming operator ρ_{t_H} is called a **simple renaming operator**, and usually denoted by t_H.

3.6.3 THEOREM
The following equations are derivable from the system PA with renaming (for $t \in A \cup C$).

i. $t_{H \cup K}(x) = t_H \circ t_K(x)$

ii. if $H \cap K = \varnothing$, $s \notin H$ and $t \notin K$, then $t_H \circ s_K(x) = s_K \circ t_H(x)$

iii. $t_{\{s\}} \circ s_H(x) = t_{H \cup \{s\}}(x)$

iv. if $s \in H$ and $s \neq u$, then $t_{\{s\}} \circ u_H(x) = u_H(x)$

PROOF: see exercises.

3.6.4 ENCAPSULATION

One particular simple renaming operator will be of special importance, which is δ_H, the **encapsulation operator**. In fact it can be seen as an indispensable feature in process algebra. In the following chapters we will find some of its applications.

The axioms of this operator can be derived from table 31 and 3.6.2.

$\delta_H(a) = a$	if $a \notin H$	D1
$\delta_H(a) = \delta$	if $a \in H$	D2
$\delta_H(x + y) = \delta_H(x) + \delta_H(y)$		D3
$\delta_H(xy) = \delta_H(x) \cdot \delta_H(y)$		D4

TABLE 32. Encapsulation.

Sometimes we will consider BPA or PA with only this operator and without general renamings. In order to avoid confusion between occurrences of the constant δ and the encapsulation operator δ_H, we often write ∂_H instead of δ_H. This way the distinction between the constant and the operator becomes more manifest.

3.6.5 EXAMPLE

As an example, consider the behaviour of a machine performing the process $a(b + c)$ but which for some reason is unable to execute the atomic action c. Then after having performed a it will continue with b, as it does not have any other choice available.

On the other hand, consider a similar machine performing $ab + ac$ then this machine will perform an a-step and next it will either perform b, or it will be in the position that it can only continue with c, which is blocked. Hence it will end in deadlock.

Using the encapsulation operator, this feature can be modeled by renaming c into δ, that is, by putting $H \equiv \{c\}$. We obtain

$$\partial_H(a(b + c)) = \partial_H(a) \cdot \partial_H(b + c) = a(\partial_H(b) + \partial_H(c)) = a(b + \delta) = ab,$$

and

$$\partial_H(ab + ac) = \partial_H(ab) + \partial_H(ac) = \partial_H(a)\partial_H(b) + \partial_H(a)\partial_H(c) = ab + a\delta.$$

We remark that the process $ab + a\delta$ has a deadlock, whereas the process $a(b + \delta)$ does not. We refer to exercise 2.2.12.9 for a formal definition of this notion.

3.6.6 RECURSION

For renamings ρ_f with $f: A \to A \cup \{\delta\}$, we can keep the same definition of guardedness as before, and all previously established results still hold. We have to be careful however, when we have $f(a) = \varepsilon$, for in this case a guard may be renamed away. To give an example, the equation

$$X = \varepsilon_{\{a\}}(aX)$$

cannot be guarded, as any process in which a does not occur is a solution. Therefore, we will not allow any renaming operator in a recursive specification, that will rename an atomic action into ε.

3.6.7 MODELS

The definition of ρ_f in the initial model and the projective limit model can be found in a straightforward way by means of the axioms of table 31. The definition of ρ_f in the term model without ε requires the introduction of new action relations involving ρ_f, as shown in the following table.

$x \xrightarrow{a} x'$ and $f(a) \in A$	$\Rightarrow$	$\rho_f(x) \xrightarrow{f(a)} \rho_f(x')$
$x \xrightarrow{a} \surd$ and $f(a) \in A$	$\Rightarrow$	$\rho_f(x) \xrightarrow{f(a)} \surd$

TABLE 33. Action relations for renaming.

It is left for the exercises to prove that the term model satisfies the axioms for renaming. The case of the term model with ε is harder, since renaming actions into ε is difficult to define. A possible formulation of action relations is given in the following table.

$x \xrightarrow{a} x'$ and $f(a) \in A$	$\Rightarrow$	$\rho_f(x) \xrightarrow{f(a)} \rho_f(x')$
$x \xrightarrow{a} \surd$, $f(a)=\varepsilon$, $\rho_f(x) \xrightarrow{b} y$	$\Rightarrow$	$\rho_f(x) \xrightarrow{b} y$
$x \xrightarrow{a} \surd$, $f(a)=\varepsilon$, $\rho_f(x)\downarrow$	$\Rightarrow$	$\rho_f(x)\downarrow$
$x\downarrow$	$\Rightarrow$	$\rho_f(x)\downarrow$

TABLE 34. Action relations for renaming with termination.

Finally, on the graph model the definition of ρ_f reads as follows:

$\rho_f(g)$ is obtained from g as follows:

- for all labels a with $f(a) \in A$, replace them by $f(a)$;
- for all edges with labels a with $f(a)=\delta$, remove the edges;
- for all edges with labels a with $f(a)=\varepsilon$, remove the edges and put a $\downarrow$-label at the starting node.

Again one can prove that the axioms for renaming are satisfied in the graph model.

3.6.8 EXERCISES

1. Why is it impossible to have for some $a \in A$ that $\rho_f(\delta) = a$ or $\rho_f(\varepsilon) = a$?
2. Prove theorem 3.6.3.
3. The general renaming operator is more powerful than just simple renaming. In other words, there exists a function $f: A \to A \cup C$ such that ρ_f cannot be defined by means of a composition of simple renaming operators. Give an example of such a function f. Prove that ρ_f can be written as a composition of simple renaming operators iff $f = id$ or $A \not\subseteq f(A)$.
4. Prove that for closed PA terms, the axioms RR1-2 follow from the others.
5. Prove that the axioms of renaming are valid in the term model. Prove the same thing for the graph model.
6. Define the renaming operators on the projective limit model and prove that the axioms in table 31 hold.
7. Show that the operators $\surd$ of 3.3.5 and ∂_A (*all* atoms encapsulated) have the same axioms. Thus, we can consider them to be the same.
8. Calculate the process $\partial_{\{a\}}(a\delta + b)$. Note that the process $a\delta + b$ has deadlock, but $\partial_{\{a\}}(a\delta + b)$ does not. Hence, encapsulation can cause the loss of deadlock possibilities.

Conversely, it is easy to find a process x and a set of atoms H such that x is without deadlock, whereas $\partial_H(x)$ is not.

9. Describe the behaviour of the vending machine K from 2.1.13.9, if due to some mechanical defect it is impossible to insert any dimes. Does this machine K have any deadlock?

10. Prove by induction on the structure of all closed PA_ε-terms x,y that the following statements are valid:

i. $\partial_H(x \mathbin{\|\!\_} y) = \partial_H(x) \mathbin{\|\!\_} \partial_H(y)$; ii. $\partial_H(x \| y) = \partial_H(x) \| \partial_H(y)$.

3.6.9 NOTES AND COMMENTS

This section was based on BAETEN & BERGSTRA [1988], with improvements by VAANDRAGER [1986]. Renaming operators occur in most concurrency theories, see e.g. MILNER [1980] and HOARE [1985]. Encapsulation, and the notation ∂_H, is from BERGSTRA & KLOP [1984b].

Chapter 4
Communication

4.1 COMMUNICATION FUNCTION

A central issue in concurrency theory is that of modelling communication. The method that we present here yields **synchronous communication**. That is, the occurrence of communication between two processes is the result of the simultaneous performance of corresponding actions. For instance, one process may perform a send action, whereas the other performs a receive action, and if these actions take place simultaneously the result is a communicate action. Later on, we will also consider examples of asynchronous communication in process algebra.

In synchronous communication, every communication action has two parts. This can be denoted as follows: suppose an atomic action comm(5) represents the communication between send(5) and receive(5), then we write

$$\gamma(\mathsf{send}(5), \mathsf{receive}(5)) = \mathsf{comm}(5).$$

If two actions do *not* communicate, then their communication is not defined. For example:

$$\gamma(\mathsf{send}(5), \mathsf{receive}(6)) \text{ is not defined.}$$

This will be formalized in the next paragraph.

4.1.1 DEFINITION

Let A be the set of atomic actions. A **communication function** on A is a partial binary function γ on A satisfying the following conditions:

1. for every $a,b \in A$: $\gamma(a,b) = \gamma(b,a)$, that is, communication is **commutative**;
2. for every $a,b,c \in A$: $\gamma(\gamma(a,b),c) = \gamma(a,\gamma(b,c))$: communication is **associative**.

When we write such an equation for a partial function, we also imply that one side of the equation is defined exactly when the other side is. Also, γ is not defined when one of its arguments is not defined or is not in A.

It follows from the properties of γ that we can leave out brackets in expressions as $\gamma(a,\gamma(\gamma(b,c),d))$, and simply write $\gamma(a,b,c,d)$.

If for $a,b \in A$ $\gamma(a,b)$ is not defined, then we say that a and b **do not communicate**. An action $a \in A$ such that $a = \gamma(b,c)$ for certain b,c will be called a **communication action** or **communication step**. A communication $\gamma(a,b)$ is called a **binary** communication; a communication $\gamma(a,b,c)$ is called a **ternary** communication, in which case the communication action has three components, three actions take part of it. In most of the applications we only have binary communication and higher order communication does not occur. That case is called **handshaking**, which can be expressed by the following statement:

$$\text{for all } a,b,c \in A \quad \gamma(a,b,c) \text{ is not defined.}$$

4.1.2 Conventions

Since most examples of communication involve the transmission of data at ports, it is useful to have some standardized notation. In general we have a set of **locations**, that are interconnected by **ports**, or **channels**. An example is given in fig. 18.

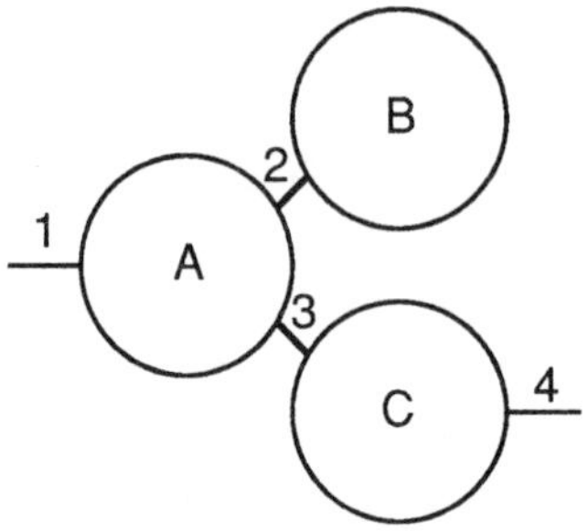

FIGURE 18.

Here, we have locations A, B, C and ports 1, 2, 3, 4. Locations are always given by processes (by means of a closed term or a guarded recursive specification). We assume binary communication only. Ports that connect two locations are called **internal**, ports attached to one location only are **external**. Here, 2, 3 are internal, and 1,4 external.

In general we then have the following atomic actions

- $s_j(d)$ = send d at port j;
- $r_j(d)$ = receive d at port j;
- $c_j(d)$ = transmit d by communication at port j.

On these atomic actions we define the following communication function:

$$\gamma(s_j(d),r_j(d)) = c_j(d),$$

and γ is not defined otherwise. For instance, the process A in fig. 18 could perform an action $s_2(d)$, and B an action $r_2(d)$, and assuming both actions are performed simultaneously, the result is $c_2(d)$.

4.1.3 Exercises

1. Find a recursive specification for the stack with input port 1 and output port 2, using the formalism of 4.1.2.
2. Do the same for the bag.
3. Find a statement describing the situation where only binary and ternary communication are possible, and none of higher order.
4. Can we describe the situation where only ternary communication is possible, and not binary?

4.1.4 Notes and comments

HENNESSY [1981] has a communication function with 1 as a neutral element. Communication in CCS is a special kind of handshaking with $\gamma(a,\bar{a}) = \tau$ for all a, and in CSP we have the format $\gamma(a,a) = a$ for all a. WINSKEL [1982] discusses various communication formats. The conventions of 4.1.2 were introduced in BERGSTRA & KLOP [1986a].

4.2 ACP

If we now consider the merge of two processes, $x \| y$, then there are not just two possibilities to proceed (as in PA, see 3.1.2) but three: either we start with a first step from x (given by $x \mathbin{⌊\!⌊} y$), or a first step from y ($y \mathbin{⌊\!⌊} x$), or we start with a communication step, with 'halves' from x and y (this possibility is denoted by $x|y$).

$x|y$ thus represents the merge of two processes x and y with the restriction that the first step is a communication step between x and y. This way we obtain a binary operator $|$ on processes, the so-called **communication merge**. This communication merge is an extension of the communication *function* on atomic actions. In case the communication function is not defined, we set the communication merge equal to δ. Thus, for the definition of the communication merge we need the constant δ in our signature. We get that ACP will be an extension of the theory BPA_δ. For now we omit the empty process however, as it is not needed in the basic definitions.

Now we present the axiom system ACP (the Algebra of Communicating Processes) incorporating this communication merge.

4.2.1 SYNTAX

The equational specification ACP has in its signature:

- a set of constants A, and on A a given partial communication function γ which is commutative and associative;

• a constant	δ	deadlock ($\delta \notin A$)
• binary operators	$+$	alternative composition
	$\cdot$	sequential composition
	$\|$	merge
	$⌊\!⌊$	left-merge
	$\|$	communication merge
• unary operators	∂_H	encapsulation, where $H \subseteq A$.

REMARK: the communication merge will be considered as an *extension* of the communication function that we have on A. So we have two different mappings: a fixed partial function γ: $A \times A \rightarrow A$ on the set of atomic actions, and an operator $|$ on processes such that $a|b = \gamma(a,b)$ whenever γ is defined.

The equations of ACP are given in table 35. The symbols a,b,c range over $A \cup \{\delta\}$, and we assume $H \subseteq A$.

4.2.2 COMMENTS

Axioms A1-7 are the axioms of BPA_δ, which have been discussed in chapter 2. The axiom CF1 expresses that $|$ is an extension of γ. Since δ is not in A, γ is not defined if one of its arguments is δ, and so axiom CF2 implies that $a|\delta = \delta|a = \delta$ for all $a \in A$.

$x + y = y + x$		A1
$(x + y) + z = x + (y + z)$		A2
$x + x = x$		A3
$(x + y)z = xz + yz$		A4
$(xy)z = x(yz)$		A5
$x + \delta = x$		A6
$\delta x = \delta$		A7
$a \mid b = \gamma(a,b)$	if γ defined	CF1
$a \mid b = \delta$	otherwise	CF2
$x \parallel y = x ⌊\!⌊ y + y ⌊\!⌊ x + x \mid y$		CM1
$a ⌊\!⌊ x = ax$		CM2
$ax ⌊\!⌊ y = a(x \parallel y)$		CM3
$(x + y) ⌊\!⌊ z = x ⌊\!⌊ z + y ⌊\!⌊ z$		CM4
$ax \mid b = (a \mid b) \cdot x$		CM5
$a \mid bx = (a \mid b) \cdot x$		CM6
$ax \mid by = (a \mid b) \cdot (x \parallel y)$		CM7
$(x + y) \mid z = x \mid z + y \mid z$		CM8
$x \mid (y + z) = x \mid y + x \mid z$		CM9
$\partial_H(a) = a$	if $a \notin H$	D1
$\partial_H(a) = \delta$	if $a \in H$	D2
$\partial_H(x + y) = \partial_H(x) + \partial_H(y)$		D3
$\partial_H(xy) = \partial_H(x) \cdot \partial_H(y)$		D4

TABLE 35. ACP.

Axiom CM1 presents the three possibilities of the merge as mentioned above, thus extending the axiom M1 of PA_δ (see 3.1.2 and 3.3.1) with a third summand. Axioms CM2-4 are the same as M2-4 of PA_δ. Axioms CM5-9 define the extension of the communication function to arbitrary processes, using the inductive definition of basic terms. D1-4 are the encapsulation axioms of table 32 in 3.6.4.

4.2.3 EXAMPLES

Some examples of how to use ACP are the following:
Let $A = \{a,b\}$ with $\gamma(a,a) = b$, γ not defined otherwise, and $H = \{a\}$. Then

1. $\partial_H(a \parallel a) = \partial_H(a ⌊\!⌊ a + a ⌊\!⌊ a + \gamma(a,a)) = \partial_H(aa + b) = b$.
2. $\partial_H(ba \parallel ab) = \partial_H(ba ⌊\!⌊ ab + ab ⌊\!⌊ ba + ba \mid ab) =$
   $= \partial_H(b(a \parallel ab) + a(b \parallel ba) + (b \mid a)(a \parallel b)) =$
   $= b \cdot \partial_H(a ⌊\!⌊ ab + ab ⌊\!⌊ a + a \mid ab) + \delta + \delta =$
   $= b \cdot \partial_H(aab + a(b \parallel a) + \gamma(a,a)b) = b(\delta + \delta + bb) = bbb$.

4.2.4 ACTION RELATIONS

Let us adjust the rules defining action relations on terms (see 3.1.5). The following rules are an extension of the ones for BPA in 2.1.7. Here $a,b,c \in A$.

The first seven rules are action relations from PA. The last three define new relations for terms involving communication actions.

$$
\begin{array}{ll}
a \xrightarrow{a} \surd & \\
x \xrightarrow{a} x' & \Rightarrow x+y \xrightarrow{a} x' \text{ and } y+x \xrightarrow{a} x' \\
x \xrightarrow{a} \surd & \Rightarrow x+y \xrightarrow{a} \surd \text{ and } y+x \xrightarrow{a} \surd \\
x \xrightarrow{a} x' & \Rightarrow xy \xrightarrow{a} x'y \\
x \xrightarrow{a} \surd & \Rightarrow xy \xrightarrow{a} y \\
 & \\
x \xrightarrow{a} x' & \Rightarrow x \| y \xrightarrow{a} x' \| y,\ y \| x \xrightarrow{a} y \| x' \\
 & \qquad \text{and } x \mathbin{|\!\!\lfloor} y \xrightarrow{a} x' \| y \\
x \xrightarrow{a} \surd & \Rightarrow x \| y \xrightarrow{a} y,\ y \| x \xrightarrow{a} y \text{ and } x \mathbin{|\!\!\lfloor} y \xrightarrow{a} y \\
x \xrightarrow{a} x',\ y \xrightarrow{b} y' \text{ and } \gamma(a,b) = c & \Rightarrow \\
 & x \| y \xrightarrow{c} x' \| y' \text{ and } x | y \xrightarrow{c} x' \| y' \\
x \xrightarrow{a} x',\ y \xrightarrow{b} \surd \text{ and } \gamma(a,b) = c & \Rightarrow \\
 & x \| y \xrightarrow{c} x',\ x | y \xrightarrow{c} x',\ y \| x \xrightarrow{c} x' \\
 & \qquad \text{and } y | x \xrightarrow{c} x' \\
x \xrightarrow{a} \surd,\ y \xrightarrow{b} \surd \text{ and } \gamma(a,b) = c & \Rightarrow \\
 & x \| y \xrightarrow{c} \surd \text{ and } x | y \xrightarrow{c} \surd
\end{array}
$$

TABLE 36. Action relations for ACP.

4.2.5 EXERCISES

1. Let $\gamma(a,b)=c$ be the only defined communication, and $H = \{a,b\}$. Then calculate:
i. $aa \| bb$; ii. $\partial_H(aa \| bb)$; iii. $\partial_H(ba \| bb)$; iv. $a\delta \| ba$; v. $\partial_H(ca \| cbb)$.
2. Describe a relay race in ACP, by first finding a closed term representing the behaviour of each runner, and then compose these closed terms by means of an encapsulated merge. Calculate the resulting process as a term in BPA.
3. Give an example illustrating that $\partial_H(x \| y) \neq \partial_H(x) \| \partial_H(y)$.
4. Let $\gamma(a,b)=c$ be the only defined communication and let $H = \{a,b\}$. Show that $\partial_H((ca + cb) \| b)$ has deadlock, and that $\partial_H(c(a + b) \| b)$ has not. This again illustrates the difference between $ca + cb$ and $c(a + b)$.
5. Prove that for all closed terms x,y in BPA$_\delta$:
i. $x | y = y | x$; ii. $x \| y = y \| x$.
6. Find a formula for $x \| y$ without $\mathbin{|\!\!\lfloor}$ and $|$, if

$$x = \sum_{1 \le i \le n} a_i x_i + \sum_{1 \le j \le m} b_j \text{ and } y = \sum_{1 \le k \le p} c_k y_k + \sum_{1 \le \ell \le q} d_\ell .$$

7. Let $\gamma(a,b) = \gamma(c,d) = e$ and $H = \{a,b,c,d\}$, γ undefined otherwise. Then draw the action graph of the following ACP-terms:
i. $a \| c(b + d)$; ii. $(a + da) \mathbin{|\!\!\lfloor} cb$; iii. $\partial_H(ac \| (c + bd)$; iv. $(a + ca | db)$.
8. Prove that the following terms bisimulate, using definition 2.5.2 and table 36:
i. $x \| y = x \mathbin{|\!\!\lfloor} y + y \mathbin{|\!\!\lfloor} x + x | y$; ii. $ax \mathbin{|\!\!\lfloor} y = a(x \| y)$; iii. $(ax \| by) = (a | b) \cdot (x \| y)$;

iv. $(x + y)|z \leftrightarrow xz + yz$.

4.2.6 NOTES AND COMMENTS

The system ACP was introduced in BERGSTRA & KLOP [1984b]. HENNESSY [1988a] uses an operator γ, where $x\gamma y$ corresponds to $x \Vert\!\_ \, y + x|y$. The action relations are taken from VAN GLABBEEK [1987].

4.3 SOME THEOREMS ON ACP

In this section we will go over the main theorems again that we already proved for PA in chapter 3. We start off with the elimination theorem and continue with new axioms for standard concurrency and the expansion theorem.

4.3.1 THEOREM

i. **Elimination**: for every closed ACP-term t there is a basic term s (hence without operators $\Vert$, $\Vert\!\_$, $|$ or ∂_H) such that ACP $\vdash$ t=s.

ii. ACP is a **conservative extension** of BPA_δ, in other words: for all closed BPA_δ-terms t,s we have that ACP $\vdash$ t=s iff $BPA_\delta \vdash$ t=s.

PROOF: We consider ACP as a term rewriting system, with rules as follows:

$x + x \to x$	$a|b \to \gamma(a,b)$ if γ defined
$(x + y)z \to xz + yz$	$a|b \to \delta$ otherwise
$(xy)z \to x(yz)$	$x \Vert y \to x \Vert\!\_\, y + y \Vert\!\_\, x + x|y$
$x + \delta \to x$	$a \Vert\!\_\, x \to ax$
$\delta x \to \delta$	$ax \Vert\!\_\, y \to a(x \Vert y)$
$x|\delta \to \delta$	$(x + y) \Vert\!\_\, z \to x \Vert\!\_\, z + y \Vert\!\_\, z$
$\delta|x \to \delta$	$ax|b \to (a|b)x$
$\partial_H(a) \to a$ if $a \notin H$	$a|bx \to (a|b)x$
$\partial_H(a) \to \delta$ if $a \in H$	$ax|by \to (a|b)(x \Vert y)$
$\partial_H(x + y) \to \partial_H(x) + \partial_H(y)$	$(x + y)|z \to x|z + y|z$
$\partial_H(xy) \to \partial_H(x) \cdot \partial_H(y)$	$x|(y + z) \to x|y + x|z$.

This TRS is strongly normalizing and confluent modulo A1, A2, and the normal form of a closed term is a BPA_δ basic term. We need to add the extra rewrite rules $x|\delta \to \delta$ and $\delta|x \to \delta$ in order to obtain confluence for open terms. The equations $x|\delta = \delta$ and $\delta|x = \delta$ are easily derivable for all closed terms. The rest of the proof is analogous to the proof of 3.2.1.

4.3.2 LEMMA

For all $a,b,c \in A \cup \{\delta\}$ we have

i. $a|b = b|a$;

ii. $a|(b|c) = (a|b)|c$;

iii. $a|\delta = \delta$.

PROOF: Straightforward, using the properties of the communication function.

4.3.3 THEOREM

For all closed ACP-terms the following axioms of **standard concurrency** hold:

1. $x|y = y|x$
2. $x \| y = y \| x$
3. $(x|y)|z = x|(y|z)$
4. $(x |\!\!\lfloor y) |\!\!\lfloor z = x |\!\!\lfloor (y \| z)$
5. $x|(y |\!\!\lfloor z) = (x|y) |\!\!\lfloor z$
6. $x \| (y \| z) = (x \| y) \| z$

PROOF: Because of theorem 4.3.1 we may assume x,y,z to be closed BPA_δ-terms. Therefore the proof of the equalities 1 and 2 is already given in 4.2.5.5. For the equalities 3-6, we use induction on the total number of symbols in x,y and z. We write x,y,z in sum notation, as follows:

$$x = \sum_i a_i x_i + \sum_j a'_j, \quad y = \sum_k b_k y_k + \sum_\ell b'_\ell, \quad z = \sum_m c_m z_m + \sum_n c'_n.$$

We prove 3-6 by simultaneous induction.

3. Write $x = x' + x''$, with $x' = \sum_i a_i x_i$ and $x'' = \sum_j a'_j$.

Similarly $y = y' + y''$ and $z = z' + z''$. Then:

$$x|(y|z) = x'|(y'|z') + x'|(y''|z') + x'|(y'|z'') + x'|(y''|z'') + \\ + x''|(y'|z') + x''|(y''|z') + x''|(y'|z'') + x''|(y''|z'').$$

Then we have

$$x'|(y'|z') = \sum_{i,k,m} (a_i|(b_k|c_m))(x_i \| (y_k \| z_m)) = \sum_{i,k,m} ((a_i|b_k)|c_m)((x_i \| y_k) \| z_m) = (x'|y')|z',$$

using lemma 4.3.2.ii and the induction hypothesis for 6. The other summands of $x|(y|z)$ can be rewritten in a similar way, and so $x|(y|z) = (x|y)|z$.

4. As in 3.2.2.1.

5. Again let $x = x' + x''$ and $y = y' + y''$ be as in the proof of 3. Then

$$x|(y |\!\!\lfloor z) = x'|(y' |\!\!\lfloor z) + x'|(y'' |\!\!\lfloor z) + x''|(y' |\!\!\lfloor z) + x''|(y'' |\!\!\lfloor z).$$

Further

$$x'|(y' |\!\!\lfloor z) = (\sum_i a_i x_i)|((\sum_k b_k y_k) |\!\!\lfloor z) = (\sum_i a_i x_i)|(\sum_k b_k \cdot (y_k \| z)) =$$

$$= \sum_{i,k} (a_i|b_k) \cdot (x_i \| (y_k \| z)) = \sum_{i,k} (a_i|b_k) \cdot ((x_i \| y_k) \| z) \quad \text{(using 6)}$$

$$= \Big(\sum_{i,k} (a_i|b_k)(x_i \| y_k)\Big) |\!\!\lfloor z = (x'|y') |\!\!\lfloor z.$$

The other three summands can be treated in the same way, and so $x|(y |\!\!\lfloor z) = (x|y) |\!\!\lfloor z$.

6. $x \| (y \| z) = x |\!\!\lfloor (y \| z) + (y \| z) |\!\!\lfloor x + x|(y \| z) =$

$$= x |\!\!\lfloor (y \| z) + (y |\!\!\lfloor z) |\!\!\lfloor x + (z |\!\!\lfloor y) |\!\!\lfloor x + (y|z) |\!\!\lfloor x + x|(y |\!\!\lfloor z) + x|(z |\!\!\lfloor y) + x|(y|z) =$$

$$= (x |\!\!\lfloor y) |\!\!\lfloor z + y |\!\!\lfloor (z \| x) + z |\!\!\lfloor (y \| x) + (z|y) |\!\!\lfloor x + (x|y) |\!\!\lfloor z + (x|z) |\!\!\lfloor y + (x|y)|z =$$

$$= (x |\!\!\lfloor y) |\!\!\lfloor z + y |\!\!\lfloor (x \| z) + z |\!\!\lfloor (y \| x) + z|(y |\!\!\lfloor x) + (x|y) |\!\!\lfloor z + (z|x) |\!\!\lfloor y + z|(x|y) =$$

$$= (x |\!\!\lfloor y) |\!\!\lfloor z + (y |\!\!\lfloor x) |\!\!\lfloor z + z |\!\!\lfloor (x \| y) + z|(y |\!\!\lfloor x) + (x|y) |\!\!\lfloor z + z|(x |\!\!\lfloor y) + z|(x|y) =$$

$$= (x \| y) |\!\!\lfloor z + z |\!\!\lfloor (x \| y) + z|(x \| y) = (x \| y) \| z.$$

4.3.4 HANDSHAKING

In the system ACP, we can reformulate the principle of handshaking of 4.1.1 with the axiom $a|b|c = \delta$. From this axiom, it follows that for all closed terms $x|y|z = \delta$. This last equation will be called the **Handshaking Axiom.**

4.3.5 THEOREM

In ACP with standard concurrency and handshaking the following **expansion** theorem holds:

$$x_1 \parallel \ldots \parallel x_n = \sum_{1\le i\le n} x_i \mathbin{\underline{\|}} \Big(\mathop{\|}_{1\le j\le n\ j\ne i} x_j \Big) + \sum_{1\le i<j\le n} (x_i|x_j) \mathbin{\underline{\|}} \Big(\mathop{\|}_{1\le k\le n\ k\ne i,j} x_k \Big) \qquad (n\ge 3).$$

For sake of clarity we write out this term in full for the case $n=3$:

$$x\parallel y\parallel z = x \mathbin{\underline{\|}} (y\parallel z) + y \mathbin{\underline{\|}} (x\parallel z) + z \mathbin{\underline{\|}} (x\parallel y) + (x|y) \mathbin{\underline{\|}} z + (x|z) \mathbin{\underline{\|}} y + (y|z) \mathbin{\underline{\|}} x.$$

PROOF: By induction on n. We leave it to the reader to prove the theorem for $n=3$. The induction step follows:

$$x_1 \parallel \ldots \parallel x_{n+1} = (x_1 \parallel \ldots \parallel x_n) \parallel x_{n+1} =$$
$$= (x_1 \parallel \ldots \parallel x_n) \mathbin{\underline{\|}} x_{n+1} + x_{n+1} \mathbin{\underline{\|}} (x_1 \parallel \ldots \parallel x_n) + (x_1 \parallel \ldots \parallel x_n) | x_{n+1}.$$

We will write out these terms separately; the first:

$$(x_1 \parallel \ldots \parallel x_n) \mathbin{\underline{\|}} x_{n+1} =$$
$$= \Big(\sum_{1\le i\le n} x_i \mathbin{\underline{\|}} \Big(\mathop{\|}_{1\le j\le n\ j\ne i} x_j \Big) + \sum_{1\le i<j\le n} (x_i|x_j) \mathbin{\underline{\|}} \Big(\mathop{\|}_{1\le k\le n\ k\ne i,j} x_k \Big)\Big) \mathbin{\underline{\|}} x_{n+1} =$$
$$= \sum_{1\le i\le n} \Big(x_i \mathbin{\underline{\|}} \Big(\mathop{\|}_{1\le j\le n\ j\ne i} x_j \Big)\Big) \mathbin{\underline{\|}} x_{n+1} + \sum_{1\le i<j\le n} \Big((x_i|x_j) \mathbin{\underline{\|}} \Big(\mathop{\|}_{1\le k\le n\ k\ne i,j} x_k \Big)\Big) \mathbin{\underline{\|}} x_{n+1} =$$
$$= \sum_{1\le i\le n} x_i \mathbin{\underline{\|}} \Big(\Big(\mathop{\|}_{1\le j\le n\ j\ne i} x_j \Big) \mathbin{\underline{\|}} x_{n+1}\Big) + \sum_{1\le i<j\le n} (x_i|x_j) \mathbin{\underline{\|}} \Big(\Big(\mathop{\|}_{1\le k\le n\ k\ne i,j} x_k \Big) \mathbin{\underline{\|}} x_{n+1}\Big) =$$

(because of 4.3.3.4)

$$= \sum_{1\le i\le n} x_i \mathbin{\underline{\|}} \Big(\mathop{\|}_{1\le j\le n+1\ j\ne i} x_j \Big) + \sum_{1\le i<j\le n} (x_i|x_j) \mathbin{\underline{\|}} \Big(\mathop{\|}_{1\le k\le n+1\ k\ne i,j} x_k \Big).$$

The second term is $x_{n+1} \mathbin{\underline{\|}} \Big(\mathop{\|}_{1\le j\le n+1\ j\ne n+1} x_j \Big)$, and the third:

$$(x_1 \parallel \ldots \parallel x_n) | x_{n+1} =$$
$$= \Big(\sum_{1\le i\le n} x_i \mathbin{\underline{\|}} \Big(\mathop{\|}_{1\le j\le n\ j\ne i} x_j \Big) + \sum_{1\le i<j\le n} (x_i|x_j) \mathbin{\underline{\|}} \Big(\mathop{\|}_{1\le k\le n\ k\ne i,j} x_k \Big)\Big) \mid x_{n+1} =$$
$$= \sum_{1\le i\le n} \Big(x_i \mathbin{\underline{\|}} \Big(\mathop{\|}_{1\le j\le n\ j\ne i} x_j \Big)\Big) | x_{n+1} + \sum_{1\le i<j\le n} \Big((x_i|x_j) \mathbin{\underline{\|}} \Big(\mathop{\|}_{1\le k\le n\ k\ne i,j} x_k \Big)\Big) | x_{n+1} =$$
$$= \sum_{1\le i\le n} (x_i|x_{n+1}) \mathbin{\underline{\|}} \Big(\mathop{\|}_{1\le j\le n\ j\ne i} x_j \Big) + \sum_{1\le i<j\le n} (x_i|x_j|x_{n+1}) \mathbin{\underline{\|}} \Big(\mathop{\|}_{1\le k\le n\ k\ne i,j} x_k \Big) =$$

(because of 4.3.3.1, 3 and 5)

$$= \sum_{1\le i\le n} (x_i|x_{n+1}) \mathbin{\underline{\|}} \Big(\mathop{\|}_{1\le j\le n+1\ j\ne i} x_j \Big) \qquad \text{(by handshaking, 4.3.4).}$$

By the summation of the three terms we obtain the formula we were looking for.

Again, we stick to our previous definition on **guarded** and **completely guarded** terms over ACP. We will see that the number of guarded recursive specifications – and hence the number of **definable** processes – over ACP does not really exceed that over BPA.

4.3.6 THEOREM
Each definable process over ACP has a head normal form.

PROOF: As the proof of 3.2.6.

4.3.7 THEOREM
A process is definable in ACP if and only if it is definable in BPA.

PROOF: As the proof of 3.2.7.

Thus we have proved that ACP is not more expressive with respect to infinitely definable processes. With respect to *finitely* definable processes it is more expressive, however, as we will see later on in this chapter.

4.3.8 EXERCISES
1. Assume that $a,b,c \in A$ with $\gamma(a,b) = \gamma(b,a) = d$, $\gamma(a,c) = \gamma(c,a) = e$, and γ is undefined otherwise. Reduce the following terms to a normal form with the term rewriting system in 4.3.1:
i. $a \| b$; ii. $b \| a$; iii. $(a \mathbin{\lfloor\!\lfloor} b) \mathbin{\lfloor\!\lfloor} c$; iv. $a \mathbin{\lfloor\!\lfloor} (b \| c)$; v. $a | (b \mathbin{\lfloor\!\lfloor} c)$; vi. $(a | b) \mathbin{\lfloor\!\lfloor} c$; vii. $a \| (b \| c)$; viii. $(a \| b) \| c$.
2. Prove the claim in 4.3.4.
3. Write out the full proof of the expansion theorem in the case $n=3$, without sum notation.
4. Prove that the following equalities hold for all closed terms in ACP:
i. $x \| \delta = x \mathbin{\lfloor\!\lfloor} \delta = x\delta$; ii. $x | \delta = \delta$; iii. $x \| y\delta = (x \| y)\delta$; iv. $x \mathbin{\lfloor\!\lfloor} y\delta = (x \mathbin{\lfloor\!\lfloor} y)\delta = x\delta \mathbin{\lfloor\!\lfloor} y$;
v. $x | y\delta = (x | y)\delta$.
5. Describe the initial algebra of ACP.
6. Define the n-merge of x, $x^{\underline{n}}$, as in 3.2.8.5. Let $a \in A$. Under which conditions do we also have in ACP that $a^{\underline{n}} = a^n$?
7. Give the proofs of 4.3.6 and 4.3.7.

4.3.9 NOTES AND COMMENTS
ACP, and theorem 4.3.1 appeared first in BERGSTRA & KLOP [1984b]. The axioms of standard concurrency, the handshaking axiom and the given formulation of the expansion theorem are taken from BERGSTRA & TUCKER [1984]. A full analysis of the term rewriting system in 4.3.1 appears in AKKERMAN [1987], who uses an algorithm of PETERSON & STICKEL [1981].

4.4 TERMINATION

Let us extend the theory ACP with the additional constant ε, or to put it differently, let us extend PA_ε (see 3.3.5) with a communication operator on processes.

4.4.1 DEFINITION

ACP_ε has in its signature binary operators $+, \cdot, \|, \mathbin{|\!\!\lfloor}, |$, unary operators ∂_H, a set A of constants and special constants ε and δ. On A, a partial, commutative and associative communication function γ is given.

ACP_ε has the axioms in table 37. Here we have $a,b,c \in A \cup \{\delta\}$, $H \subseteq A$ and x,y,z are arbitrary processes.

$x + y = y + x$	A1	$x + \delta = x$	A6
$(x + y) + z = x + (y + z)$	A2	$\delta x = \delta$	A7
$x + x = x$	A3	$\varepsilon x = x$	A8
$(x + y)z = xz + yz$	A4	$x\varepsilon = x$	A9
$(xy)z = x(yz)$	A5		
$x \| y = x \mathbin{|\!\!\lfloor} y + y \mathbin{|\!\!\lfloor} x + x \mid y + \surd(x)\cdot\surd(y)$			CTM1
$\varepsilon \mathbin{|\!\!\lfloor} x = \delta$	TM2	$\varepsilon \mid x = \delta$	TM5
$ax \mathbin{|\!\!\lfloor} y = a(x \| y)$	TM3	$x \mid \varepsilon = \delta$	TM6
$(x + y) \mathbin{|\!\!\lfloor} z = x \mathbin{|\!\!\lfloor} z + y \mathbin{|\!\!\lfloor} z$	TM4	$ax \mid by = (a \mid b)(x \| y)$	CM7
$a \mid b = \gamma(a,b)$ if defined	CF1	$(x + y) \mid z = x \mid z + y \mid z$	CM8
$a \mid b = \delta$ otherwise	CF2	$x \mid (y + z) = x \mid y + x \mid z$	CM9
$\partial_H(\varepsilon) = \varepsilon$	D0		
$\partial_H(a) = a$ if $a \notin H$	D1	$\surd(\varepsilon) = \varepsilon$	TE1
$\partial_H(a) = \delta$ if $a \in H$	D2	$\surd(a) = \delta$	TE2
$\partial_H(x + y) = \partial_H(x) + \partial_H(y)$	D3	$\surd(x + y) = \surd(x) + \surd(y)$	TE3
$\partial_H(xy) = \partial_H(x)\cdot\partial_H(y)$	D4	$\surd(xy) = \surd(x)\cdot\surd(y)$	TE4

TABLE 37. ACP_ε.

4.4.2 COMMENT

Comparing to table 25 in 3.3.5, and table 35 in 4.2.1, only the axioms for $\mathbin{|\!\!\lfloor}$ and $|$ need some further explanation, in particular the equations concerning ε.

Now recall that ε represents a process which terminates immediately. In $\varepsilon \mathbin{|\!\!\lfloor} x$, the left-hand process should commence by executing an atomic action. This it cannot do, since ε can only terminate (successfully). Therefore, we put $\varepsilon \mathbin{|\!\!\lfloor} x = \delta$. The axiom $\varepsilon \mid x = \delta$ states that it is not possible to communicate with a process which has only the capability of terminating.

The axiom D0 is added to conform to 3.6. Observe that this time a does not have the constant ε in its range and therefore it has to be included explicitly. Finally, we can easily prove that the operator $\surd$ is the same as ∂_A (see exercise 3.6.8.7).

The next four results can be proved analogously to the ones in section 4.3 and in chapter 3. The proofs are not given here, but left to the reader.

4.4.3 LEMMA

For all closed terms in ACP_ε the statements in lemma 3.3.7 hold:

i. $x \mathbin{|\!\!\lfloor} \varepsilon = x$

ii. $x \parallel \varepsilon = x$

iii. $\surd(x) = \varepsilon$ if and only if $x + \varepsilon = x$.

4.4.4 THEOREM

i. For every closed ACP_ε-term t there is a basic term s over $BPA_{\delta\varepsilon}$ such that $ACP_\varepsilon \vdash t=s$.

ii. ACP_ε is a conservative extension of $BPA_{\delta\varepsilon}$.

4.4.5 THEOREM

The axioms of standard concurrency (4.3.3) hold for all closed terms in ACP_ε.

4.4.6 THEOREM

The expansion theorem generalizes to ACP_ε as follows:

$$x_1 \parallel \ldots \parallel x_n = \sum_{1 \le i \le n} x_i \mathbin{|\!\!\lfloor} \Big(\mathop{\Big\|}_{1 \le j \le n\ j \ne i} x_j \Big) + \sum_{1 \le i < j \le n} (x_i | x_j) \mathbin{|\!\!\lfloor} \Big(\mathop{\Big\|}_{1 \le k \le n\ k \ne i,j} x_k \Big) + \prod_{1 \le i \le n} \surd(x_i) \qquad (n \ge 2)$$

(compare with theorem 3.3.10 and theorem 4.3.5).

4.4.7 EXERCISES

1. Show that $ACP_\varepsilon \vdash x | \delta = \delta$.
2. Show that the following equations are derivable from ACP_ε plus extra axiom $\varepsilon \parallel x = x$: i. $x = x \mathbin{|\!\!\lfloor} \varepsilon + \surd(x)$; ii. $x \parallel \varepsilon = x$; iii. $a \mathbin{|\!\!\lfloor} x = ax$; iv. $a | bx = ax | b = (a|b)x$; v. $ax | by = (a|b)(x \parallel y)$.
3. Show that for all processes with head normal form the following equations hold: i. $\surd(x) = \varepsilon$ iff $x = x + \varepsilon$, and $\surd(x) = \delta$ otherwise; ii. $x \parallel y = y \parallel x$; iii. $\surd(x) \mathbin{|\!\!\lfloor} y = \surd(x) | y = \delta$; iv. $\surd(x \mathbin{|\!\!\lfloor} y) = \surd(x | y) = \delta$; v. $\surd(\surd(x)) = \surd(x)$.
4. Show by induction on their structure that for all closed terms x,y in ACP_ε the following statements hold: i. $x \mathbin{|\!\!\lfloor} y\delta = (x \mathbin{|\!\!\lfloor} y)\delta = x\delta \mathbin{|\!\!\lfloor} y$; ii. $x | y\delta = (x|y)\delta$; iii. $x \parallel y\delta = (x \parallel y)\delta$.
5. Prove 4.4.3.
6. Prove 4.4.4.
7. Prove that for all closed terms x,y: $ACP_\varepsilon + ax|y = (a|y) \mathbin{|\!\!\lfloor} x \models$ CM5-7.
8. Below, we find new rules (on top of the rules from 2.2.9 for $BPA_{\delta\varepsilon}$) – not compatible with the ones in 4.2.4 – defining action relations for ACP_ε-terms.

$x \xrightarrow{a} x'$	$\Rightarrow x \parallel y \xrightarrow{a} x' \parallel y,\ y \parallel x \xrightarrow{a} y \parallel x'$ and $x \mathbin{|\!\!\lfloor} y \xrightarrow{a} x' \parallel y$
$x\downarrow$ and $y\downarrow$	$\Rightarrow (x \parallel y)\downarrow$
$x\downarrow$	$\Rightarrow \surd(x)\downarrow$
$x \xrightarrow{a} x',\ y \xrightarrow{b} y'$ and $\gamma(a,b) = c$	$\Rightarrow x \parallel y \xrightarrow{c} x' \parallel y'$

TABLE 38. Action relations for ACP_ε.

Observe that these rules are a straightforward extension of the ones in 3.3.12.7 for PA_ε. Now check that the axioms of ACP_ε hold, when replacing '=' by '$\underline{\leftrightarrow}$' (i.e. ACP holds in the *term model*, see next section).

4.4.8 NOTES AND COMMENTS

Most of this section is taken from BAETEN & VAN GLABBEEK [1987b]. The first formulation of ACP with empty step was in VRANCKEN [1986].

4.5 MODELS

4.5.1 INITIAL ALGEBRA

In 4.3, we found that every closed term in ACP is equal to a term in BPA_δ, and therefore the initial algebra of ACP does not contain more elements than the one for BPA_δ. The only difference is that in the case of ACP the equivalence classes of closed terms contain more elements. Therefore, we will denote the initial algebra of ACP by $\mathbb{A}_\delta$ as before. The definition of the operators in $\mathbb{A}_\delta$ is given by the axioms in ACP.

4.5.2 TERM MODEL

Again, the term model is constructed from the terms of ACP_ε and the action relations in 4.4.7.8, by dividing out bisimulation equivalence as defined in definition 2.5.14. In exercise 4.4.7.8 we already proved the soundness of the axioms of ACP_ε. It then follows from the analogue of theorem 3.3.11 (see also 4.3.7) that the domain of ACP_ε-terms modulo bisimulation is equal to the one for $BPA_{\delta\varepsilon}$-terms. Thus the term model for ACP_ε can be written as $\mathbb{P}_{\delta\varepsilon}/\underline{\leftrightarrow}$.

4.5.3 THEOREM

The axioms of standard concurrency (of 4.3.3) hold in $\mathbb{P}_{\delta\varepsilon}/\underline{\leftrightarrow}$.

PROOF: Let us first look at the first two equations. Define the relation R on process expressions as follows: R will relate each expression to itself, and further will relate each expression $x^* \| y^*$ to $y^* \| x^*$, where x^* is a subprocess of x, y^* a subprocess of y (as defined in 2.8.1). Moreover, R relates $x|y$ to $y|x$. Showing that R is a bisimulation proves that equations 1 and 2 of 4.3.3 hold.

For equations 3 through 6, we consider the relation S that relates each process expression to itself, relates each expression $x^* \| (y^* \| z^*)$ to $(x^* \| y^*) \| z^*$ (with x^* a subprocess of x, y^* a subprocess of y, z^* a subprocess of z), and further relates each left-hand side of 3-6 with its right-hand side. Showing that S is a bisimulation proves that equations 3 through 6 hold.

4.5.4 PROJECTIVE LIMIT MODEL

As before, we build a projective limit model $\mathbb{A}_\delta^\infty$ for ACP from the initial algebra $\mathbb{A}_\delta$. The operators are defined as follows. Let $(p_1,p_2,p_3,...)$ and $(q_1,q_2,q_3,...)$ be projective sequences, then we define:

i. $(p_1,p_2,p_3,...) \| (q_1,q_2,q_3,...) = (\pi_1(p_1 \| q_1), \pi_2(p_2 \| q_2), \pi_3(p_3 \| q_3), ...)$;

ii. $(p_1,p_2,p_3,...) \mathbin{⌊\!\!⌊} (q_1,q_2,q_3,...) = (\pi_1(p_1 \mathbin{⌊\!\!⌊} q_1), \pi_2(p_2 \mathbin{⌊\!\!⌊} q_2), \pi_3(p_3 \mathbin{⌊\!\!⌊} q_3), ...)$;

iii. $(p_1,p_2,p_3,...) \mid (q_1,q_2,q_3,...) = (\pi_1(p_1|q_1), \pi_2(p_2|q_2), \pi_3(p_3|q_3), ...)$;
iv. $\partial_H((p_1,p_2,p_3,...)) = (\partial_H(p_1),\partial_H(p_2),\partial_H(p_3),...)$.

The proof that $\mathbb{A}_\delta^\infty$ is a model of ACP, is left as an exercise. The proof that $\mathbb{A}_\delta^\infty \models$ AIP, RSP, RDP proceeds as before.

4.5.5 THE GRAPH MODEL

In order to turn the graph model of $BPA_{\delta\varepsilon}$ (see section 2.7) into a model of ACP_ε, we have to define the operators $\|, \lfloor\!\lfloor, |$ and ∂_H.

4.5.6 DEFINITION

1. $g \| h$ is the graph, which is the cartesian product of graphs g, h with diagonal edges added for every communication action. To be precise: let g, h be two process graphs, then $g\|h$ is the graph with nodes consisting of pairs of nodes from g and h, such that for $a,b \in A$:
i. The root of $g\|h$ is the pair of root nodes of g and h.
ii. A node (r,s) in $g\|h$ has label $\downarrow$ iff both r and s do.
iii. For every edge $r \xrightarrow{a} r'$ in g, and $s \xrightarrow{b} s'$ in h, there are edges $(r,s) \xrightarrow{a} (r',s)$ and $(r,s) \xrightarrow{b} (r,s')$ in $(g\|h)$.
If moreover $\gamma(a,b) = c$, then $g\|h$ also has an edge $(r,s) \xrightarrow{c} (r',s')$.
2. $g \lfloor\!\lfloor h$ is as defined in 3.4.5, but with the following adjustment:
If (r,s) is the root node of $\rho(g\|h)$, then all edges $(r,s) \xrightarrow{b} (r,s')$, where $s \xrightarrow{b} s'$ is an edge in h, and all communication edges $(r,s) \xrightarrow{c} (r',s')$ are left out. A possible root label $\downarrow$ is removed.
3. $g|h$ is again $\rho(g\|h)$ but with a similar adjustment:
If (r,s) is the root node, then all edges $(r,s) \xrightarrow{a} (r',s)$ and $(r,s) \xrightarrow{b} (r,s')$ are left out. A possible root label $\surd$ is removed.
4. $\surd(g)$ is as defined in 3.4.5.
5. $\partial_H(g)$ is as defined in 3.6.7: all edges with labels from H are removed.

Finally, in the graphs resulting from definitions 2, 3, 5 all nodes and edges that are inaccessible from the root node are left out.

4.5.7 EXAMPLES

We suppose $\gamma(a,b) = c$, and γ is not defined otherwise.

Let g = 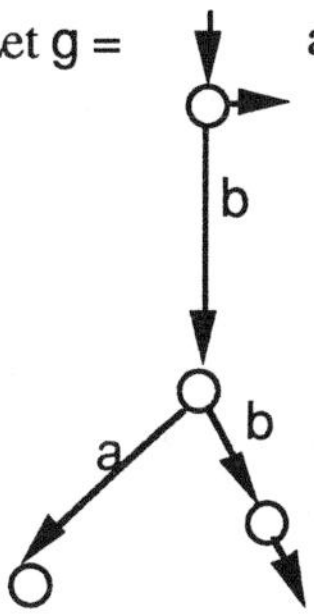

and h = 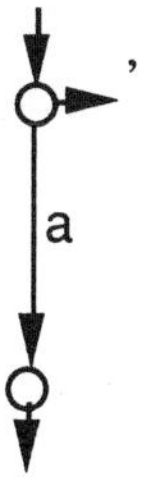

, then $g\|h$ = 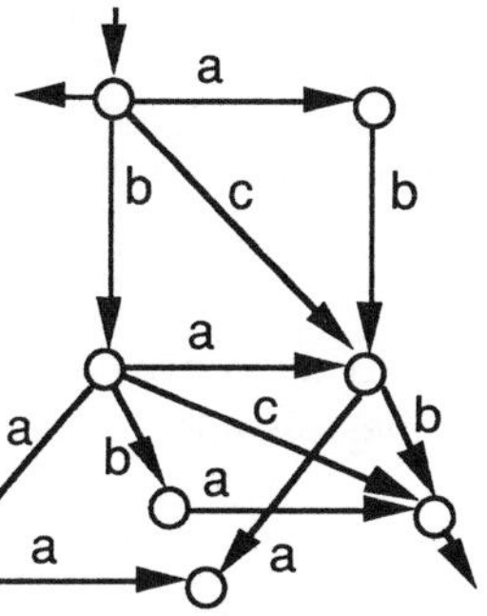

FIGURE 19 (first part).

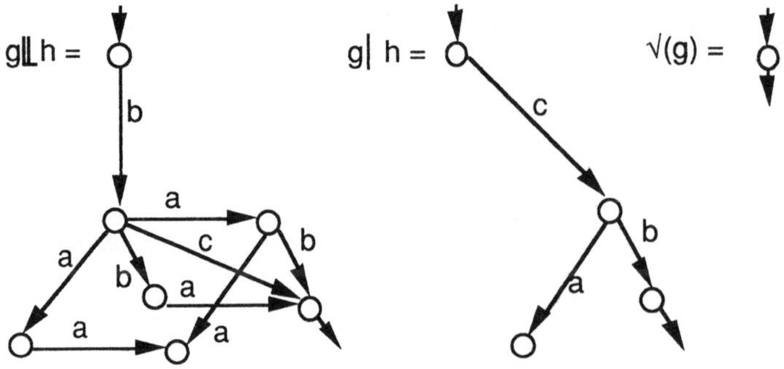

FIGURE 19 (second part).

4.5.8 THEOREM

Bisimulation is a congruence relation with respect to the operators $\|, \lfloor\!\lfloor, |, \partial_H$.
That is, if g,h,k,l are process graphs such that $g \underline{\leftrightarrow} k$ and $h \underline{\leftrightarrow} l$, then:

$$g \| h \underline{\leftrightarrow} k \| l,\ g \lfloor\!\lfloor h \underline{\leftrightarrow} k \lfloor\!\lfloor l,\ g|h \underline{\leftrightarrow} k|l \text{ and } \partial_H(g) \underline{\leftrightarrow} \partial_H(k).$$

PROOF: As in 3.4.7. Details are left for the exercises.

Because of theorem 4.5.8 we can define the parallel operators and the encapsulation operators on the model $\mathbb{G}^\infty/\leftrightarrow$ as indicated in 1.3.9.

4.5.9 THEOREM

$\mathbb{G}^\infty/\underline{\leftrightarrow}$ is a model of ACP_ε.

PROOF: As in 3.4.8.

4.5.10 THEOREM

i. $\mathbb{G}^\infty/\underline{\leftrightarrow}$ is a model of RDP, RSP, AIP^-.
ii. $\mathbb{G}/\underline{\leftrightarrow}$ is a model of RDP^-, RSP, AIP.
iii. $\mathbb{R}/\underline{\leftrightarrow}$ and $\mathbb{F}/\underline{\leftrightarrow}$ are models of RSP, AIP.

PROOF: as before (see 2.7.35, 3.4.10).

4.5.11 NOTE

We find that $\mathbb{G}/\underline{\leftrightarrow}$, $\mathbb{R}/\underline{\leftrightarrow}$ and $\mathbb{F}/\underline{\leftrightarrow}$ are models of ACP with standard concurrency. Again we see that $\mathbb{F}/\underline{\leftrightarrow}$ is isomorphic to the initial algebra $\mathbb{A}$.

4.5.12 COROLLARY

Every guarded recursive specification over ACP has a unique solution in the graph models $\mathbb{G}/\underline{\leftrightarrow}$ and $\mathbb{G}^\infty/\underline{\leftrightarrow}$. Thus we may assume that each such specification uniquely determines a process.

4.5.13 COMPLETENESS

As before (see 3.4.12), we can establish that the models discussed in this section are *complete* for the theory ACP resp. ACP_ε.

4.5.14 EXERCISES

1. Let $A = \{a,b,c\}$ with only defined communication $\gamma(a,b) = c$. Consider the processes $a(a + b)$ and bc. Find graphs g and h, representing these processes, and construct graphs $g \| h$, $g \lfloor\!\lfloor h$, $h \lfloor\!\lfloor g$ and $g | h$. Also do this for a^ω and b^ω (defined in 2.3.1), and find a linear recursive equation for $a^\omega \| b^\omega$.
2. Show that for all closed terms p,q in ACP:
i. $\pi_1(p \lfloor\!\lfloor q) = \pi_1(p)$;
ii. $\pi_{n+1}(p \lfloor\!\lfloor q) = \pi_{n+1}(\pi_{n+1}(p) \lfloor\!\lfloor \pi_n(q))$;
iii. $\pi_n(p | q) = \pi_n(\pi_n(p) | \pi_n(q))$;
iv. $\pi_n(p \| q) = \pi_n(\pi_n(p) \| \pi_n(q))$.
3. Prove that $\mathbb{A}^\infty \models$ ACP.
4. Prove that the relations R,S defined in the proof of theorem 4.5.3 are bisimulations.
5. Give the proof of theorem 4.5.8.
6. Show that the models $\mathbb{P}_{\delta\varepsilon}/\underline{\leftrightarrow}$ and $\mathbb{G}^\infty/\underline{\leftrightarrow}$ are isomorphic (compare 3.4.13.4).

4.5.15 NOTES AND COMMENTS

References for this section are BERGSTRA & KLOP [1984b], [1986b]. There, these model constructions were discussed in a setting without empty step.

4.6 EXAMPLES

In this section we present some examples of recursive specifications in ACP, and calculations with them. We present a process that is finitely definable in ACP, but not in PA.

4.6.1 ONE-BIT BUFFER

A linear specification of a **one-bit buffer**, with input port 1 and output port 2, is not hard to give:

$$B = r_1(0) \cdot s_2(0) \cdot B + r_1(1) \cdot s_2(1) \cdot B.$$

In case not just bits, but more generally, elements of some finite data set D are buffered, we get the following equation:

$$B^{12} = \sum_{d \in D} r_1(d) \cdot s_2(d) \cdot B^{12}.$$

Here, we write the names of the ports of the process in superscript.

To describe a buffer with capacity 2, we need a specification with two equations:

$$B_2^{12} = \sum_{d \in D} r_1(d) \cdot B_d$$

$$B_d = s_2(d) \cdot B_2^{12} + \sum_{e \in D} r_1(e) \cdot s_2(d) \cdot B_e.$$

4.6.2 COUPLING BUFFERS

Assume we have a communication network as given in fig. 20, and a finite data set D.

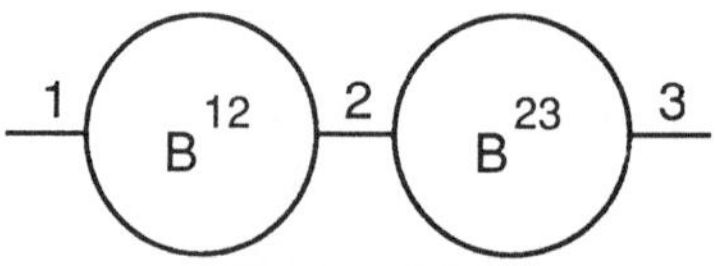

FIGURE 20.

The processes B^{12} and B^{23} are one element buffers as defined above:

$$B^{12} = \sum_{d\in D} r_1(d)\cdot s_2(d)\cdot B^{12}$$

$$B^{23} = \sum_{d\in D} r_2(d)\cdot s_3(d)\cdot B^{23}.$$

Communication between the buffers follows the format of 4.1.2. When we compose the buffers by means of a parallel operator, we encapsulate 'halves' of communication at internal ports. Thus, we put $H = \{r_2(d), s_2(d) : d\in D\}$, and look at the process $\partial_H(B^{12} \parallel B^{23})$. We will derive a set of guarded recursive equations for this process.

Define $X = \partial_H(B^{12} \parallel B^{23})$, and for $d\in D$ $X_d = \partial_H(B^{12} \parallel s_3(d)B^{23})$. Then

$$\begin{aligned}
X &= \partial_H(B^{12} \parallel B^{23}) = \partial_H(B^{12} \lfloor\!\lfloor B^{23}) + \partial_H(B^{23} \lfloor\!\lfloor B^{12}) + \partial_H(B^{12} \mid B^{23}) = \\
&= \partial_H\Big(\sum_{d\in D} r_1(d)\cdot(s_2(d)B^{12} \parallel B^{23})\Big) + \delta + \delta = \\
&= \sum_{d\in D} r_1(d)\cdot\partial_H\big(s_2(d)B^{12} \lfloor\!\lfloor B^{23} + B^{23} \lfloor\!\lfloor s_2(d)B^{12} + s_2(d)B^{12} \mid B^{23}\big) = \\
&= \sum_{d\in D} r_1(d)\cdot\big(\delta + \delta + c_2(d)\cdot\partial_H(B^{12} \parallel s_3(d)B^{23})\big) = \\
&= \sum_{d\in D} r_1(d)\cdot c_2(d)\cdot X_d
\end{aligned}$$

and

$$\begin{aligned}
X_d &= \partial_H(B^{12} \parallel s_3(d)B^{23}) = \\
&= \partial_H(B^{12} \lfloor\!\lfloor s_3(d)B^{23}) + \partial_H(s_3(d)B^{23} \lfloor\!\lfloor B^{12}) + \partial_H(B^{12} \mid s_3(d)B^{23}) = \\
&= \sum_{e\in D} r_1(e)\cdot\partial_H(s_2(e)B^{12} \parallel s_3(d)B^{23}) + s_3(d)\cdot\partial_H(B^{12} \parallel B^{23}) + \delta = \\
&= \sum_{e\in D} r_1(e)\cdot\big(\delta + s_3(d)\cdot\partial_H(s_2(e)B^{12} \parallel B^{23}) + \delta\big) + s_3(d)\cdot X = \\
&= \sum_{e\in D} r_1(e)\cdot s_3(d)\cdot\big(\delta + \delta + c_2(e)\cdot\partial_H(B^{12} \parallel s3(e)B^{23})\big) + s3(d)\cdot X = \\
&= \sum_{e\in D} r_1(e)\cdot s_3(d)\cdot c_2(e)\cdot X_e + s_3(d)\cdot X.
\end{aligned}$$

Hence a system of two connected one-bit buffers is given by the recursive specification

$$X = \sum_{d\in D} r_1(d)\cdot c_2(d)\cdot X_d$$

$$X_d = s_3(d)\cdot X + \sum_{e\in D} r_1(e)\cdot s_3(d)\cdot c_2(e)\cdot X_e.$$

Comparing this specification to the one for the two-element buffer in 4.6.1, we see that they are the same if we leave out the atoms $c_2(d)$ (for $d\in D$). These atoms are communication actions at internal ports. If we look at a process from the outside, we only want to see halves of communications at external ports, and want to 'hide' communications at internal ports. We will return to this issue later on.

4.6.3 REMARK

Very often, a process will be of the following form:

$\partial_H(P_1 \| P_2 \| ..... \| P_n)$,

where $H = \{a \in A \mid$ for some $b \in A$ in one of the P_i we have $a|b \neq \delta\}$. In case communication follows the format of 4.1.2, this specializes to:

$H = \{s_i(d), r_i(d) \mid d \in D$, i an internal port$\}$.

This is why ∂_H is called the *encapsulation* operator: actions from $P_1 \| .... \| P_n$ that are to communicate with one another, are encapsulated, screened from interaction with the outside world.

Next, we will present an example of a process P which is finitely definable in ACP but is not in PA, thus showing that ACP has greater expressive power than PA. We do not prove the claim, however.

4.6.4 DEFINITION

Consider the process P defined by the infinite specification in table 39.

$P = P_1$	
$P_n = b \cdot a^n \cdot b \cdot a^{n+1} \cdot P_{n+1}$	(for $n \geq 1$)

TABLE 39.

Informally speaking, we have: $P = ba(ba^2)^2(ba^3)^2(ba^4)^2....$

4.6.5 FINITE SPECIFICATION

Now we present a finite specification for P in ACP. Let $c,d \in A$ such that $\gamma(c,c) = a$ and $\gamma(d,d) = b$ are the only defined communications. Further, let $H = \{c,d\}$. Then consider the recursive specification in table 40.

$Q = \partial_H(dcY \| Z)$	$Y = dXY$
$X = cXc + d$	$Z = dXcZ$

TABLE 40.

4.6.6 THEOREM

$P = Q$.

PROOF: Define $Q_n = \partial_H(dc^nY \| Z)$, for $n \geq 1$. We will prove that $P_n = Q_n$ for every $n \geq 1$. Because of RSP it is sufficient to prove that the processes Q_n satisfy the specification in table 39.

$$Q_n = \partial_H(dc^nY \| Z) = \partial_H(dc^nY \| dXcZ) = \partial_H(dc^nY | dXcZ) = b \cdot \partial_H(c^nY \| XcZ) =$$
$$= b \cdot \partial_H(c^nY \| (cXc + d)cZ) = b \cdot \partial_H(c^nY | cXc^2Z) =$$
$$= b \cdot a \cdot \partial_H(c^{n-1}Y \| Xc^2Z) = ... = ba^n \cdot \partial_H(Y \| Xc^{n+1}Z) =$$
$$= ba^n \cdot \partial_H(dXY \| (cXc + d)c^{n+1}Z) = ba^n \cdot \partial_H(dXY | dc^{n+1}Z) =$$

$= ba^nb \cdot \partial_H(XY \| c^{n+1}Z) = ba^nb \cdot \partial_H((cXc + d)Y \| c^{n+1}Z) =$
$= ba^nb \cdot \partial_H(cXcY | c^{n+1}Z) = ba^nba \cdot \partial_H(XcY \| c^nZ) = ... =$
$= ba^nba^{n+1} \cdot \partial_H(Xc^{n+1}Y \| Z) = ba^nba^{n+1} \cdot \partial_H((cXc + d)c^{n+1}Y \| dXcZ) =$
$= ba^nba^{n+1} \cdot \partial_H(dc^{n+1}Y \| dXcZ) = ba^nba^{n+1} \cdot \partial_H(dc^{n+1}Y \| Z) =$
$= ba^nba^{n+1} \cdot Q_{n+1}.$

4.6.7 EXERCISES

1. Give a specification of an n-element buffer, for $n \in \mathbb{N}$.
2. Show that $\varepsilon_I(\partial_H(B^{12} \| B^{23})) = B_2^{13}$, if $I = \{c_2(d) \mid d \in D\}$, and other items are as defined in 4.6.1-2. Thus, renaming internal steps into ε gives the correct external behaviour, in this case.

On the other hand, observe that process $i \cdot \delta + a$ has deadlock but process $\varepsilon_{\{i\}}(i \cdot \delta + a)$ does not. Thus, ε-renaming can alter deadlock behaviour.

3. Consider again the communication network from fig. 20, but now with the processes S and R given by the equations:

$$S = \sum_{d \in D} r_1(d) \cdot s_2(d) \cdot r_2(ack) \cdot S,$$

$$R = \sum_{d \in D} r_2(d) \cdot s_3(d) \cdot s_2(ack) \cdot R.$$

Here ack is a special element denoting an *acknowledgement*. It is advisable to take $ack \notin D$. Let $H = \{r_2(x), s_2(x) \mid x \in D \text{ or } x \equiv ack\}$ and find a recursive equation for $\partial_H(S \| R)$.

4. Add all missing steps in the proof of theorem 4.6.6.

4.6.8 NOTES AND COMMENTS

Buffers occur in every treatment of concurrency theory, see for instance REM [1987]. The example in 4.6.4 - 4.6.6 is from BERGSTRA & KLOP [1984a]. There, also the proof can be found that this process is not definable in PA.

4.7 ALTERNATING BIT PROTOCOL (SPECIFICATION)

In this section we will present an extensive example of a process algebra specification, namely a communication protocol. This protocol is often referred to as the **Alternating Bit Protocol** in the literature. A communication protocol concerns the transmission of data through an unreliable channel, such that – despite the unreliability – no information will get lost. We have a configuration as in fig. 21.

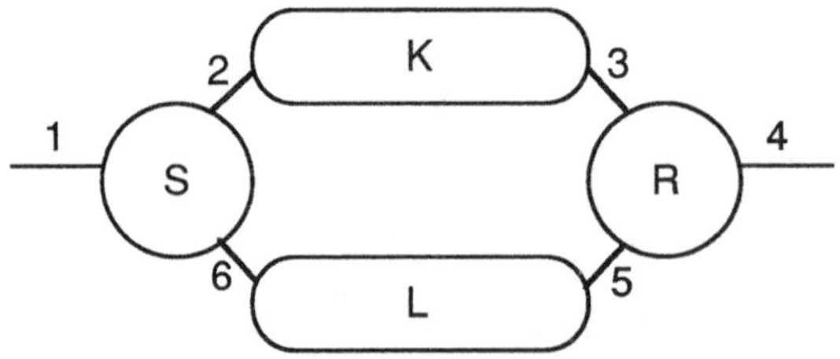

FIGURE 21.

4.7.1 COMPONENTS

In fig. 21, S is the sender, sending data elements d to the receiver R via the unreliable channel K. After having received a certain data element, R will send an acknowledgement to S via channel L which is unreliable as well (in practice we usually find that K and L are physically the same medium). The problem now is to define processes S and R such that no information will get lost, that is: the behaviour of the entire process, apart from the communications at the internal ports 2,3,5,6, satisfies the equation

$$B^{14} = \sum_{d \in D} r_1(d) \cdot s_4(d) \cdot B^{14},$$

i.e. the process behaves externally as a one-element buffer.

4.7.2 SOLUTION

We solve this problem as follows: S will read a datum d at port 1 and passes on a sequence d0, d0, d0,.... of copies of this datum, appended with a bit 0, to K until an acknowledgement 0 is received at port 6. Then, the next datum is read, and sent on together with a bit 1; the acknowledgement then is the reception of 1. The following data element has 0 in turn, and so 0, 1 form the alternating bit.

K is the data transmission channel, passing on frames of the form d0, d1. K may corrupt data, however, passing on $\perp$ (an error message; thus we assume that the incorrect transmission of d can be recognized, for instance using a *checksum*).

R is the receiver, receiving frames d0, d1 from K, sending on d to port 4 (if this was not done earlier), and the acknowledgement 0 resp. 1 is sent to L.

L is the acknowledgement transmission channel, and passes bits 0 or 1, received from R, on to S. L is also unreliable, and may send on $\perp$ instead of 0 or 1. Now we present the processes S, K, R, L by means of recursive specifications.

4.7.3 DEFINITION

Let D be a finite data set and define the set of frames by $F = \{d0, d1 : d \in D\}$. Let i be some atomic action. The channels K and L are given by the equations in table 41.

$$K = \sum_{x \in F} r_2(x)(i \cdot s_3(x) + i \cdot s_3(\perp)) \cdot K$$

$$L = \sum_{n=0,1} r_5(n)(i \cdot s_6(n) + i \cdot s_6(\perp)) \cdot L$$

TABLE 41. Channels.

The atom i serves to make the choice non-deterministic: the decision whether or not the frame will be corrupted is internal to the channel, and cannot be influenced by the environment (we will say more about this point in exercise 4.7.7.2). We still have a correctly functioning protocol, nonetheless, if the occurrences of i are removed.

The sender S and the receiver R are given by the recursive specifications in tables 42 and 43.

$$S = S0 \cdot S1 \cdot S$$
$$Sn = \sum_{d \in D} r_1(d) \cdot Sn_d$$
$$Sn_d = s_2(dn) \cdot Tn_d$$
$$Tn_d = (r_6(1\text{-}n) + r_6(\perp)) \cdot Sn_d + r_6(n)$$

TABLE 42. Sender ($n=0,1,\ d \in D$).

$$R = R1 \cdot R0 \cdot R$$
$$Rn = \Big(\sum_{d \in D} r_3(dn) + r_3(\perp)\Big) \cdot s_5(n) \cdot Rn \ +$$
$$+ \sum_{d \in D} r_3(d(1\text{-}n)) \cdot s_4(d) \cdot s_5(1\text{-}n)$$

TABLE 43. Receiver ($n=0,1$).

4.7.4 COMPOSITE SYSTEM

The composition of these four processes now is represented by

$$\partial_H(S \,\|\, K \,\|\, L \,\|\, R),$$

where $H = \{r_k(x), s_k(x) \colon x \in F \cup \{0,1,\perp\},\ k=2,3,5,6\}$. Next we will derive a recursive equation for this process. In order to do so, we introduce the following abbreviations (for every $d \in D$):

$$X = \partial_H(S \,\|\, K \,\|\, L \,\|\, R)$$
$$X1_d = \partial_H(S0_d \cdot S1 \cdot S \,\|\, K \,\|\, L \,\|\, R)$$
$$X2_d = \partial_H(T0_d \cdot S1 \cdot S \,\|\, K \,\|\, L \,\|\, s_5(0) \cdot R0 \cdot R)$$
$$Y = \partial_H(S1 \cdot S \,\|\, K \,\|\, L \,\|\, R0 \cdot R)$$
$$Y1_d = \partial_H(S1_d \cdot S \,\|\, K \,\|\, L \,\|\, R0 \cdot R)$$
$$Y2_d = \partial_H(T1_d \cdot S \,\|\, K \,\|\, L \,\|\, s_5(1) \cdot R).$$

Then we can derive the recursive specification from table 44 by means of the expansion theorem from 4.3.5. The calculations are carried out in 4.7.5.

$$\partial_H(S \,\|\, K \,\|\, L \,\|\, R) = X = \sum_{d \in D} r_1(d) \cdot X1_d$$
$$X1_d = c_2(d0)\Big(i \cdot c_3(\perp) \cdot c_5(1)(i \cdot c_6(\perp) + i \cdot c_6(1)) \cdot X1_d \ +$$
$$+ \ i \cdot c_3(d0) \cdot s_4(d) \cdot X2_d\Big)$$
$$X2_d = c_5(0)\Big(i \cdot c_6(\perp) \cdot c_2(d0)(i \cdot c_3(\perp) + i \cdot c_3(d0))X2_d + i \cdot c_6(0) \cdot Y\Big)$$

$$Y = \sum_{d \in D} r_1(d) \cdot Y1_d$$
$$Y1_d = c_2(d1)\Big(i \cdot c_3(\perp) \cdot c_5(0)(i \cdot c_6(\perp) + i \cdot c_6(0))Y1_d \ +$$
$$+ \ i \cdot c_3(d1) \cdot s_4(d) \cdot Y2_d\Big)$$
$$Y2_d = c_5(1)\Big(i \cdot c_6(\perp) \cdot c_2(d1)(i \cdot c_3(\perp) + i \cdot c_3(d1))Y2_d + i \cdot c_6(1) \cdot X\Big)$$

TABLE 44. Specification for $\partial_H(S \,\|\, K \,\|\, L \,\|\, R)$.

We have drawn the process graph (or **state transition diagram**) of the process X in fig. 22. We do not show the sum over possible data elements in the nodes corresponding to X and

Y, but just take one, arbitrary element. We indicate the nodes corresponding to the variables of the specification in table 44, by putting the name of the variable inside the node.

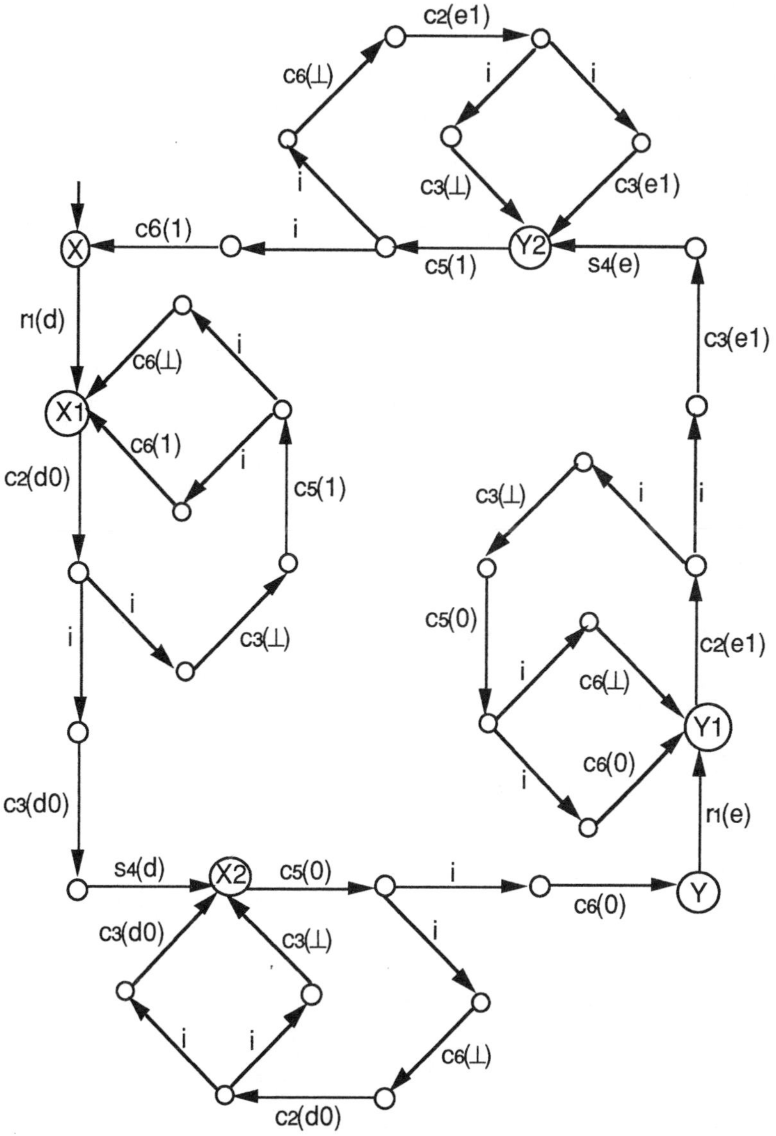

FIGURE 22.

4.7.5 CALCULATIONS

We introduce the following abbreviations:

$K'_x = (i{\cdot}s_3(x) + i{\cdot}s_3(\bot)){\cdot}K \qquad (x \in E)$

$L'_n = (i{\cdot}s_6(n) + i{\cdot}s_6(\bot)){\cdot}L \qquad (n=0,1).$

The expansion theorem (4.3.5) gives ten terms for the merge of four processes. At every step in the following calculations, nine of these terms will equal δ (either because the communication function is not defined on certain pairs, or because of encapsulation). We will indicate which of the terms will be not δ, by underlining the process (in case of a left-merge) or the two processes (in case of a communication action) involved.

$$X = \partial_H(\underline{S} \| K \| L \| R) = \sum_{d\in D} r_1(d)\cdot\partial_H(S0_d\cdot S1\cdot S \| K \| L \| R) = \sum_{d\in D} r_1(d)\cdot X1_d.$$

Next, the second equation. Let $d\in D$. Then we obtain

$$\begin{aligned}
X1_d &= \partial_H(\underline{S0_d\cdot S1\cdot S} \| \underline{K} \| L \| R) = \\
&= c_2(d0)\cdot\partial_H(T0_d\cdot S1\cdot S \| \underline{K'_{d0}} \| L \| R) = \\
&= c_2(d0)\Big(i\cdot\partial_H(T0_d\cdot S1\cdot S \| \underline{s_3(d0)\cdot K} \| L \| \underline{R}) + i\cdot\partial_H(T0_d\cdot S1\cdot S \| \underline{s_3(\bot)\cdot K} \| L \| \underline{R})\Big) = \\
&= c_2(d0)\Big(i\cdot c_3(d0)\cdot\partial_H(T0_d\cdot S1\cdot S \| K \| L \| \underline{s_4(d)\cdot s_5(0)\cdot R0\cdot R}) + \\
&\qquad + i\cdot c_3(\bot)\cdot\partial_H(T0_d\cdot S1\cdot S \| K \| \underline{L} \| \underline{s_5(1)\cdot R1\cdot R0\cdot R})\Big) = \\
&= c_2(d0)\Big(i\cdot c_3(d0)\cdot s_4(d)\cdot\partial_H(T0_d\cdot S1\cdot S \| K \| L \| s_5(0)\cdot R0\cdot R) + \\
&\qquad + i\cdot c_3(\bot)\cdot c_5(1)\cdot\partial_H(T0_d\cdot S1\cdot S \| K \| \underline{L'_1} \| R)\Big) = \\
&= c_2(d0)\Big(i\cdot c_3(d0)\cdot s_4(d)\cdot X2_d + i\cdot c_3(\bot)\cdot c_5(1)\cdot\Big\{i\cdot\partial_H(\underline{T0_d\cdot S1\cdot S} \| K \| \underline{s_6(1)\cdot L} \| R) + \\
&\qquad + i\cdot\partial_H(\underline{T0_d\cdot S1\cdot S} \| K \| \underline{s_6(\bot)\cdot L} \| R)\Big\}\Big) = \\
&= c_2(d0)\Big(i\cdot c_3(d0)\cdot s_4(d)\cdot X2_d + i\cdot c_3(\bot)\cdot c_5(1)\cdot\Big\{i\cdot c_6(1)\cdot\partial_H(S0_d\cdot S1\cdot S \| K \| L \| R) + \\
&\qquad + i\cdot c_6(\bot)\cdot\partial_H(S0_d\cdot S1\cdot S \| K \| L \| R)\Big\}\Big) = \\
&= c_2(d0)\Big(i\cdot c_3(d0)\cdot s_4(d)\cdot X2_d + i\cdot c_3(\bot)\cdot c_5(1)\cdot\Big\{i\cdot c_6(1)\cdot X1_d + i\cdot c_6(\bot)\cdot X1_d\Big\}\Big) = \\
&= c_2(d0)\Big(i\cdot c_3(d0)\cdot s_4(d)\cdot X2_d + i\cdot c_3(\bot)\cdot c_5(1)\cdot\Big\{i\cdot c_6(1) + i\cdot c_6(\bot)\Big\}\cdot X1_d\Big).
\end{aligned}$$

Thus we have derived the second equation. We continue immediately with the third. Let $d\in D$. Then

$$\begin{aligned}
X2_d &= \partial_H(T0_d\cdot S1\cdot S \| K \| \underline{L} \| \underline{s_5(0)\cdot R0\cdot R}) = \\
&= c_5(0)\cdot\partial_H(T0_d\cdot S1\cdot S \| K \| \underline{L'_0} \| R0\cdot R) = \\
&= c_5(0)\cdot\Big(i\cdot\partial_H(\underline{T0_d\cdot S1\cdot S} \| K \| \underline{s_6(0)\cdot L} \| R0\cdot R) + i\cdot\partial_H(\underline{T0_d\cdot S1\cdot S} \| K \| \underline{s_6(\bot)\cdot L} \| R0\cdot R)\Big) = \\
&= c_5(0)\cdot\Big(i\cdot c_6(0)\cdot\partial_H(S1\cdot S \| K \| L \| R0\cdot R) + i\cdot c_6(\bot)\cdot\partial_H(\underline{S0_d\cdot S1\cdot S} \| \underline{K} \| L \| R0\cdot R)\Big) = \\
&= c_5(0)\cdot\Big(i\cdot c_6(0)\cdot Y + i\cdot c_6(\bot)\cdot c_2(d0)\cdot\partial_H(T0_d\cdot S1\cdot S \| \underline{K'_{d0}} \| L \| R0\cdot R)\Big) = \\
&= c_5(0)\cdot\Big(i\cdot c_6(0)\cdot Y + i\cdot c_6(\bot)\cdot c_2(d0)\cdot\Big\{i\cdot\partial_H(T0_d\cdot S1\cdot S \| \underline{s_3(d0)\cdot K} \| L \| \underline{R0\cdot R}) + \\
&\qquad + i\cdot\partial_H(T0_d\cdot S1\cdot S \| \underline{s_3(\bot)\cdot K} \| L \| \underline{R0\cdot R})\Big\}\Big) = \\
&= c_5(0)\cdot\Big(i\cdot c_6(0)\cdot Y + i\cdot c_6(\bot)\cdot c_2(d0)\cdot\Big\{i\cdot c_3(d0)\cdot\partial_H(T0_d\cdot S1\cdot S \| K \| L \| s_5(0)\cdot R0\cdot R) + \\
&\qquad + i\cdot c_3(\bot)\cdot\partial_H(T0_d\cdot S1\cdot S \| K \| L \| s_5(0)\cdot R0\cdot R)\Big\}\Big) = \\
&= c_5(0)\cdot\Big(i\cdot c_6(0)\cdot Y + i\cdot c_6(\bot)\cdot c_2(d0)\cdot\Big\{i\cdot c_3(d0)\cdot X2_d + i\cdot c_3(\bot)\cdot X2_d\Big\}\Big) = \\
&= c_5(0)\cdot\Big(i\cdot c_6(0)\cdot Y + i\cdot c_6(\bot)\cdot c_2(d0)\cdot\Big\{i\cdot c_3(d0) + i\cdot c_3(\bot)\Big\}\cdot X2_d\Big).
\end{aligned}$$

Thus, we have derived the first three equations from table 44. The remaining three equations can be derived in the same way.

4.7.6 ABSTRACTION

Next we would like to show that somehow X satisfies the specification of B^{14} in 4.7.1, that is X, after *abstraction* of internal actions, behaves as a one-element buffer.

The set of internal steps is $I = \{c_k(x) : x \in F \cup \{0,1,\perp\}, k = 2,3,5,6\} \cup \{i\}$, i.e. all communications at internal ports and other internal actions; only the actions $r_1(d)$ and $s_4(d)$, occurring at external ports, that are to communicate with the environment, are external. Thus we want to have an *abstraction operator* τ_I, making internal steps invisible, such that

$$\tau_I(X) = B^{14}.$$

We will define such an abstraction operator in chapter 5. For now, we will try to make it plausible by means of a picture that after abstraction, X shows the intended behaviour.

In fig. 23 the boxed areas of the graph represent clusters, containing sets of internal states that are externally equivalent.

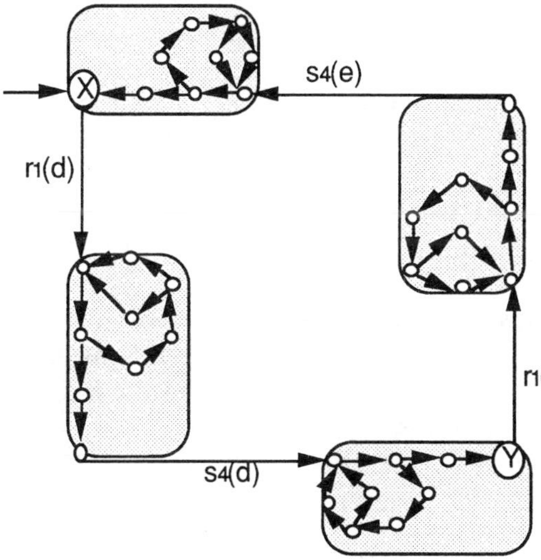

FIGURE 23.

4.7.7 EXERCISES

1. In this exercise we consider a simple communication protocol. We wish to transmit data (from some data set D) from a sender S to a receiver R through some unreliable channel K (see fig. 24).

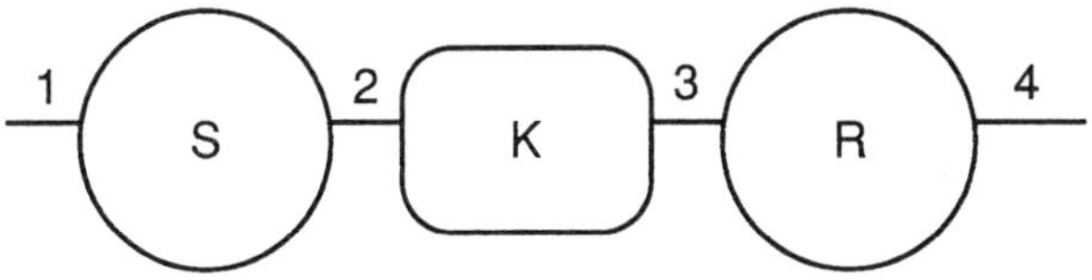

FIGURE 24.

The channel may correctly send on, or completely destroy data. The sender will send a data element until an acknowledgement ack is received. We present specifications for S, K and R:

Sender: $$S = \sum_{d \in D} r_1(d) \cdot S_d$$

$$S_d = s_2(d)\cdot S_d + r_2(ack)\cdot S \quad \text{(for every } d\in D)$$

Receiver: $$R = \sum_{d\in D} r_3(d)\cdot s_4(d)\cdot R + s_3(ack)\cdot R$$

Channel: $$K = \sum_{d\in D} r_2(d)\cdot(i\cdot K + i\cdot s_3(d)\cdot L)$$

$$L = r_3(ack)\cdot(i\cdot L + i\cdot s_2(ack)\cdot K)$$

(i is an internal atomic action).

Let $H = \{s_2(x), r_2(x), s_3(x), r_3(x): x\in D\cup\{ack\}\}$.

i. Derive a recursive specification for the process $\partial_H(S \| K \| R)$, and draw its process graph.

ii. Does this communication protocol behave correctly?

2. Consider, in the alternating bit protocol, channels *without* the internal i-steps, so:

$$K^* = \varepsilon_{\{i\}}(K), \quad L^* = \varepsilon_{\{i\}}(L).$$

Now show that the receiver can *force* channel K to behave correctly, by refusing to accept errors, i.e. consider

$$R^* = \partial_{\{r_3(\perp)\}}(R) \quad \text{(similarly } S^* = \partial_{\{r_6(\perp)\}}(S)),$$

and show that in $\partial_H(S^* \| K^* \| L^* \| R^*)$, errors $c_3(\perp)$, $c_6(\perp)$ never occur, and the protocol behaves correctly.

On the other hand, show that *with* the i's, occurrence of an error results in deadlock, i.e. process $\partial_H(S^* \| K \| L \| R^*)$ has a deadlock.

4.7.8 NOTES AND COMMENTS

The alternating bit protocol was first described in BARTLETT, SCANTLEBURY & WILKINSON [1969]. Its description in process algebra is from BERGSTRA & KLOP [1986a]. The present treatment benefits from BERGSTRA & KLOP [1986c].

A concurrent version of the ABP is discussed in KOYMANS & MULDER [1990] and VAN GLABBEEK & VAANDRAGER [1989]. Treatments in other theories can be found in LARSEN & MILNER [1987], MILNER [1989] and HALPERN & ZUCK [1987].

4.8 QUEUE

As an example of the use of renaming operators we consider the (First In, First Out, or FIFO) **queue**, transmitting incoming data while preserving their order. First, we describe a queue (with input port 1 and output port 2) over a finite data set D by means of an infinite linear specification. Here we use the same notations for finite sequences as in 2.9.2, so:

- letters σ and ρ represent words (sequences of symbols) over D, that is: $\sigma,\rho\in D^*$;
- if $\sigma,\rho\in D^*$ and $d\in D$, then $\sigma\rho$, σd and $d\sigma$ are concatenations, i.e. respectively: the sequence σ followed by ρ, the sequence σ followed by the element d, and the sequence consisting of the element d followed by σ;
- λ is the empty sequence in D^*.

4.8.1 INFINITE SPECIFICATION

In table 45 we present an infinite linear specification of a queue with input port 1 and output port 2 over D. Variables Q_σ (for $\sigma\in D^*$) will denote the queue with contents σ.

$Q = Q_\lambda = \sum_{d \in D} r_1(d) \cdot Q_d$
$Q_{\sigma d} = s_2(d) \cdot Q_\sigma + \sum_{e \in D} r_1(e) \cdot Q_{e\sigma d}$ (for every $\sigma \in D^*$ and $d \in D$)

TABLE 45. Queue over D (1st).

This specification strongly resembles the one for a stack in table 18 in 2.9.2. Therefore, the following theorem comes as a surprise:

4.8.2 THEOREM

The process Q from 4.8.1 is not finitely definable over ACP (using the conventions from 4.1.2).

The proof of this theorem is not presented here.

4.8.3 FINITE SPECIFICATION

However, we *can* find a finite recursive specification for Q in the system ACP with renamings (see 3.6). To do this, we need the following definitions: assume we have atomic actions $l(d)$ and $u(d)$ for every $d \in D$, and the only defined communication is $\gamma(l(d), l(d)) = u(d)$.

Now let $s2_u$ be the renaming operator renaming all $u(d)$ into $s_2(d)$ (leaving all other atoms fixed) and l_{s2} the renaming operator renaming all $s_2(d)$ into $l(d)$. Finally, let $H = \{l(d): d \in D\}$. Then consider the recursive specification in table 46.

$R = \sum_{d \in D} r_1(d) \cdot s2_u \circ \partial_H(l_{s2}(R) \parallel s_2(d)Z)$
$Z = \sum_{d \in D} l(d) \cdot Z$

TABLE 46. Queue over D (2nd).

In the following theorem we will prove that this specification has the same solution as the one in table 45. In order to gain some more intuition about table 46, consider the following: a queue R can also be imagined as smaller queue followed by a one-element buffer (see 4.6.1), which are interconnected by some internal communication channel called *link*. This link is watched over by a guard Z, only allowing new data to enter the buffer if it is empty. See fig. 25.i and ii.

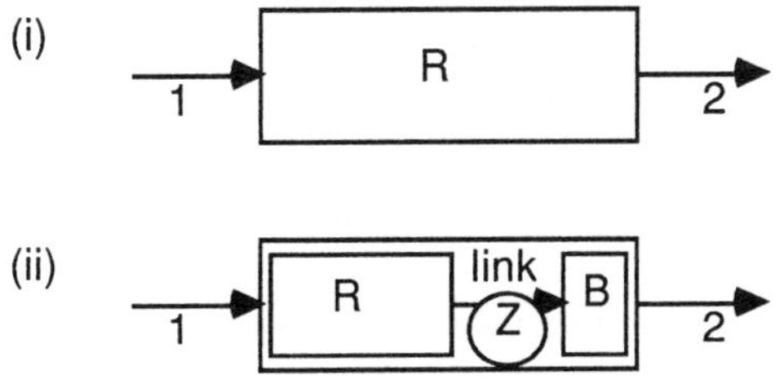

FIGURE 25.

4.8.4 THEOREM

$Q = R$ (as defined in 4.8.1 and 4.8.3 respectively)

PROOF: If $\sigma \in D^*$, the process R_σ is defined inductively as follows:

$R_\lambda = R$

$R_{\sigma d} = s2_u{}^\circ\partial_H(l_{s2}(R_\sigma) \parallel s2(d)Z)$ (if $\sigma \in D^*$ and $d \in D$).

First we prove:

(1) $R_\sigma = s2_u{}^\circ\partial_H(l_{s2}(R_\sigma) \parallel Z)$ (for $\sigma \in D^*$).

We do this by showing that both sides satisfy the same guarded recursive specification. On the one hand we have

$$R_\lambda = \sum_{d \in D} r_1(d) \cdot s2_u{}^\circ\partial_H(l_{s2}(R_\lambda) \parallel s2(d)Z) = \sum_{d \in D} r_1(d) \cdot R_d, \quad \text{and}$$

$$R_{\sigma d} = s2_u{}^\circ\partial_H(l_{s2}(R_\sigma) \parallel s2(d)Z) =$$

$$= s2_u{}^\circ\partial_H\left(l_{s2}(\sum_{e \in D} r_1(e)) \cdot [l_{s2}(R_{e\sigma}) \parallel s2(d)Z] + l_{s2}(s2(f)) \cdot [l_{s2}(R_\rho) \parallel s2(d)Z]\right) +$$

$$+ s2(d) \cdot s2_u{}^\circ\partial_H(l_{s2}(R_\sigma) \parallel Z) =$$

(the first term in this summation is obtained by induction; the second occurs if for certain σ and f: $\sigma \equiv \rho f$, and it is missing if $\sigma \equiv \lambda$)

$$= \sum_{e \in D} r_1(e) \cdot s2_u\left(\partial_H(l_{s2}(R_{e\sigma}) \parallel s2(d)Z) + \delta\right) + s2(d) \cdot s2_u{}^\circ\partial_H(l_{s2}(R_\sigma) \parallel Z) =$$

$$= \sum_{e \in D} r_1(e) \cdot R_{e\sigma d} + s2(d) \cdot s2_u{}^\circ\partial_H(l_{s2}(R_\sigma) \parallel Z),$$

and on the other hand

$$s2_u{}^\circ\partial_H(l_{s2}(R_\lambda) \parallel Z) =$$

$$= s2_u{}^\circ\partial_H\left(\sum_{d \in D} r_1(d) \cdot [l_{s2}(s2_u{}^\circ\partial_H(l_{s2}(R) \parallel s2(d)Z)) \parallel Z] + l(d) \cdot [l_{s2}(R_\lambda) \parallel Z]\right) =$$

$$= \sum_{d \in D} r_1(d) \cdot s2_u{}^\circ\partial_H(l_{s2}(R_d) \parallel Z), \quad \text{and}$$

$$s2_u{}^\circ\partial_H(l_{s2}(R_{\sigma d}) \parallel Z) =$$

$$= s2_u{}^\circ\partial_H\left(l_{s2}(s2_u{}^\circ\partial_H(l_{s2}(R_\sigma)) \parallel s2(d)Z) \parallel Z\right) =$$

$$= s2_u{}^\circ\partial_H\left(\{l_{s2}(\sum_{e \in D} r_1(e) \cdot [s2_u{}^\circ\partial_H(l_{s2}(R_{e\sigma}) \parallel s2(d)Z)]) +$$

$$+ l_{s2}(s2(d) \cdot [s2_u{}^\circ\partial_H(l_{s2}(R_\sigma) \parallel Z)])\} \parallel Z\right) =$$

$$= s2_u{}^\circ\partial_H\left(\sum_{e \in D} r_1(e)(l_{s2}(R_{e\sigma d}) \parallel Z)\right) + s2_u{}^\circ\partial_H\left(u(d)(s2_u{}^\circ\partial_H[l_{s2}(R_\sigma) \parallel Z] \parallel Z)\right) =$$

$$= \sum_{e \in D} r_1(e) \cdot s2_u{}^\circ\partial_H(l_{s2}(R_{e\sigma d}) \parallel Z) + s2(d) \cdot s2_u{}^\circ\partial_H(s2_u{}^\circ\partial_H(l_{s2}(R_\sigma) \parallel Z) \parallel Z).$$

This proves statement (1). Thus we may reduce the equations for R_λ and $R_{\sigma d}$ to:

$$R_\lambda = \sum_{d \in D} r_1(d) \cdot R_d$$

$$R_{\sigma d} = \sum_{e \in D} r_1(e) \cdot R_{e\sigma d} + s2(d) \cdot R_\sigma.$$

But these are precisely the equations for the queue. Hence $R = R_\lambda = Q_\lambda = Q$.

4.8.5 EXERCISES

1. Draw the process graph of the queue for the case $D = \{0,1\}$.
2. The queue *can* be defined in ACP (with handshaking) if we abstain from the conventions from 4.1.2. In order to do so, it is necessary to have that actions $s_2(d)$ are able to communicate in a different way. Let $l(d) \in A$ be atomic actions such that $\gamma(s_2(d),l(d)) = s_2{}^*(d)$ and $\gamma(s_2{}^*(d),l(d)) = s_2(d)$, define $H = \{s_2(d), l(d): d \in D\}$, and $H^* = \{s_2{}^*(d), l(d) \mid d \in D\}$. Show that we can define the queue by the recursive specification from table 47.

$$Q' = \sum_{d \in D} r_1(d) \cdot \partial_{H^*}(Z \| \partial_H(Q' \| s_2{}^*(d) \cdot Z))$$

$$Z = \sum_{d \in D} l(d) \cdot Z$$

TABLE 47. Queue over D (3rd).

4.8.6 NOTES AND COMMENTS

The specification of the queue in 4.8.3 is from BAETEN & BERGSTRA [1988] which also features a proof of 4.8.2, starting from results in BERGSTRA & TIURYN [1987]. Much more about queues can be found in VAN GLABBEEK & VAANDRAGER [1989]. For treatments in other concurrency theories, see DENVIR, HARWOOD, JACKSON & RAY [1985], BROY [1987], HOARE [1985] and PRATT [1982].

Chapter 5
Abstraction

5.1 ABSTRACTION AND SILENT STEP

As we argued in the previous chapter, we want to be able to *abstract* from certain actions, to *hide* them. It is important to note that it does not always work out well to simply remove steps (as what happens when we apply the operator ε_I; see for example exercise 4.6.7.2). This is because we want a process to behave precisely as it did before abstraction, apart from the actions abstracted from. For instance, a process having deadlock before abstraction, must still do so afterwards. As an example, consider the process $a+b\delta$ which has deadlock (see exercise 2.2.12.9), but after leaving out b by renaming it into ε, we obtain $a+\delta = a$, which is without deadlock because of axiom A6 from BPA_δ.

This is why we introduce the **silent step** τ, which can be removed in some cases, but in other cases it cannot. Abstraction now means renaming into τ. So, abstracting from b in the process $a+b\delta$, we obtain $a+\tau\delta$, and in this case we cannot remove τ. We conclude that $\tau a \neq a$ (since $\tau a+b \neq a+b$). However, abstracting from b in the process abc, we obtain $a\tau c$, and since this τ does not occur in a choice context, it *can* be removed: $a\tau c = ac$.

5.1.1 COLOURED TRACES

Let us allow a new symbol τ to appear as a label. As mentioned earlier, this label τ refers to a silent step: by executing τ-steps the process proceeds but observers cannot record any visible actions.

Let us again consider the coloured traces from 2.7.8, but this time with the extended set of edge-labels $A\cup\{\tau\}$. Such traces denote the execution sequences of a process together with a characterization (by means of a colour) of the potentials in every state that is passed through. Considering silent steps τ in such sequences we find two different cases:

i. either τ is between two states with the same colour: then these two states can be identified (by contracting the τ-step) as it is an invisible transition that does not change the state of the process;

ii. or τ is between two states with a different colour: the τ-step changes the current state of the process. Therefore, such τ-steps cannot be deleted.

We will return to the coloured traces in section 5.4. For now, we use these observations to illustrate the following intuition.

5.1.2 INTUITION
Rephrasing the observations about coloured traces, we find the following intuition: if during the execution of a process we can do a τ-step *without* discarding any of the options that we had before, then this τ-step is redundant. Fig. 26 illustrates this fact. Observe that the process in the right-hand diagram cannot be distinguished from the left-hand one: the right-hand process has the possibility of performing either a step from y, or one from x (after an invisible move). Assuming that the observer cannot 'see' the silent τ-step, this is equivalent to a process choosing between y and x as in the left-hand diagram. Algebraically, we find that a state in which a process can do ...$(x + y)$... cannot be distinguished from one in which it may continue with ...$(\tau(x + y) + y)$... .

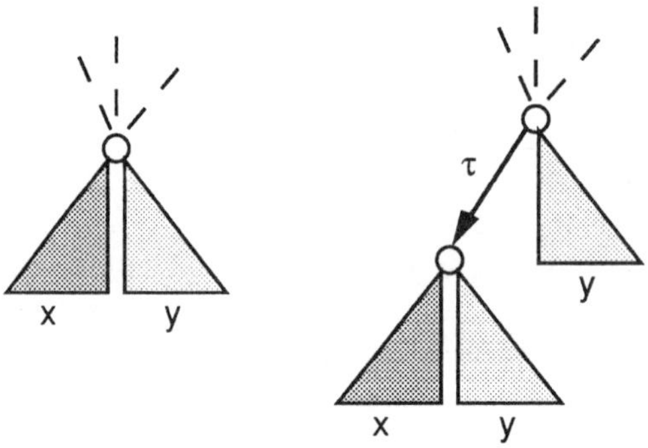

FIGURE 26.

Assume that we are watching a machine performing atomic actions, but we are only able to see an atomic step a *begin*, not end. Then we could interpret τ to be some action of which also the beginning cannot be observed. As a consequence, it is impossible to distinguish the process $a\tau$ from the process a: we see a begin, then the machine is busy for some time, and finally we see the process terminate (assuming successful termination is observable).

It follows from this intuition that we do *not* have that $\tau a = a$, as the process a will immediately start by performing a whereas τa will wait some time before showing its first observable action. This observation is important, especially since we want our definition of a silent step to be compatible with the intuitions that we had before concerning the other operators from BPA. For assume we *would* have that $\tau a = a$, then also $\tau a + b = a + b$. However, the left-hand process has a state in which it is able to perform a without having the possibility of choosing b, whereas the right-hand process has always b as an alternative option for a.

5.1.3 DEFINITION
Using the intuition from 5.1.1, we can formulate two τ-laws, describing the precise behaviour of τ. The laws are presented in table 48, for the case where the empty process ε is not in the signature.

$x\tau = x$	B1
$x(\tau(y + z) + y) = x(y + z)$	B2

TABLE 48. τ-laws.

The law B2 corresponds exactly to the situation in fig. 26. B1 is the variant of B2 where both x and y are absent. The variants where only y or only z is absent, can easily be derived.

We *cannot* consider τ to be an atomic action, so $\tau \notin A$, since PR2 and PR3 in 2.4.1 do not hold for τ instead of a (see 5.1.4). Adding τ with its laws to the system BPA_δ we obtain the system BPA_δ^τ. The behaviour of τ together with parallel composition is described in section 5.2.

5.1.4 PROJECTION

We formulate the projection laws corresponding to BPA_δ^τ to clarify some of the properties of τ once again. Here we find that we cannot assume τ to be an atomic action, since then we would have

$$a = a\tau = \pi_2(a\tau b) = \pi_2(ab) = ab,$$

which is an undesirable equation. The solution to this problem is to give τ no depth, and so we add the following laws to table 13 in 2.4.1 ($n \geq 1$), or table 15 in 2.4.21 ($n \geq 0$):

$\pi_n(\tau) = \tau$	PRT1
$\pi_n(\tau x) = \tau \cdot \pi_n(x)$	PRT2

TABLE 49. Projection and τ.

5.1.5 ABSTRACTION

For any set I of atomic actions (the set of *internal* actions), the **abstraction operator** τ_I is the renaming operator that renames all actions from I into τ. This operator satisfies the laws from table 50. We always have that $\delta \notin I$ (since $\delta \notin A$ and $I \subseteq A$), so δ can never be renamed into τ; we have $\tau_I(\delta) = \delta$. In the following table we assume that $a \in A \cup \{\delta, \tau\}$.

$\tau_I(a) = a$	if $a \notin I$	TI1
$\tau_I(a) = \tau$	if $a \in I$	TI2
$\tau_I(x + y) = \tau_I(x) + \tau_I(y)$		TI3
$\tau_I(xy) = \tau_I(x) \cdot \tau_I(y)$		TI4

TABLE 50. Abstraction.

5.1.6 BASIC TERMS

Inductively, we define a set of **basic terms** over BPA_δ^τ (compare with 2.2.3 or 2.2.7) as follows:

i. τ and δ are basic terms;
ii. if t is a basic term, and $a \in A \cup \{\tau\}$, then $a \cdot t$ is a basic term;
iii. if t,s are basic terms, then $t + s$ is a basic term.

We see that the basic terms over BPA_δ^τ are exactly the terms of the form

$$t = \tau \quad \text{or} \qquad t = \sum_{i<n} a_i t_i$$

for $a_i \in A \cup \{\tau\}$ and basic terms t_i ($i<n$). Recall that $t = \delta$ if $n=0$ (see 2.2.3).

As in 2.4.6 we will say that a process p is in **head normal form** if it is of the form $p = \tau$ or $p = \sum_{i<n} a_i p_i$ ($a_i \in A \cup \{\tau\}$) for arbitrary processes p_i.

5.1.7 PROPOSITION

For every closed BPA^{τ}_{δ}-term t, there is a basic term s over BPA^{τ}_{δ} such that $BPA^{\tau}_{\delta} \vdash t=s$.

PROOF: as in 2.1.6. Use the following rewrite rules to find the desired normal form:

$(x + y)z \rightarrow xy + xz$

$(xy)z \rightarrow x(yz)$

$x + \delta \rightarrow x$

$\delta x \rightarrow \delta$,

and only if the result is a single constant a, replace it by $a\tau$.

5.1.8 ACTION RELATIONS

The action relations for BPA^{τ}_{δ} are the ones from table 7 (see 2.1.7), this time allowing a to range over $A \cup \{\tau\}$.

5.1.9 EXERCISES

1. Show that $BPA^{\tau}_{\delta} \vdash x(\tau y + y) = xy$.
2. Prove that for the following terms t_i we have $\pi_1(t_i)=t_i$:

   $t_1 = a$, $t_2 = \tau$, $t_{2n+1} = t_{2n-1} + t_{2n}$ (for $n\geq 1$), $t_{2n} = \tau \cdot t_{2n-3}$ (for $n\geq 2$).

Note that we find infinitely many BPA^{τ}_{δ}-terms t satisfying $\pi_1(t)=t$, that cannot be proved equal in BPA^{τ}_{δ}. A proof of this fact will be outlined in 5.4.29.

3. Give a counterexample to show $\pi_n \circ \tau_I(x) \neq \tau_I \circ \pi_n(x)$.
4. Prove proposition 5.1.7. Hint: use 2.2.4.

5.1.10 NOTES AND COMMENTS

The approach to the silent step followed in this section was conceived in the early part of 1989 and documented in VAN GLABBEEK & WEIJLAND [1989], WEIJLAND [1989b] and VAN GLABBEEK [1990]. The silent step τ has a long history in process algebra, starting from the work of MILNER [1980] in which abstraction is introduced in CCS. There, also Milner's three τ-laws are formulated. These laws also formed the basis for the treatment of abstraction of BERGSTRA & KLOP [1985], and occur in most of the literature on process algebra. The τ-laws in 5.1.3 constitute a weakening of Milner's τ-laws, with subtly different properties. We will say more about the difference in section 5.8.

The abstraction operator in 5.1.5 and the projection axioms in 5.1.4 are from BERGSTRA & KLOP [1985]. More about exercise 5.1.9.2 can be found in BERGSTRA & KLOP [1989].

5.2 ACP^{τ}

Next, we will extend the axiom system of BPA^{τ}_{δ} with the operators and axioms of ACP. As it turns out, this does not involve many complications. As before, we assume we have some fixed partial communication function γ: $A \times A \to A$ which is commutative and associative. We do not allow the silent step to communicate with any other action and therefore we will find that $\tau | a = \delta$, for all $a \in A \cup \{\delta, \tau\}$ (axiom CF2).

The name that we will use for the resulting axiom system will be ACP^{τ}.

5.2.1 SIGNATURE

The system ACP^{τ} is parametrized by a set A of atomic actions and a communication function γ. It has the following signature:

constants	a	$a \in A$
	δ	deadlock ($\delta \notin A$)
	τ	silent step ($\tau \notin A$).
binary operators	$+$	alternative composition, sum
	$\cdot$	sequential composition, product
	$\Vert$	parallel composition, merge
	$\Vert\!\_$	left-merge
	$\vert$	communication-merge
unary operators	∂_H	encapsulation ($H \subseteq A$)
	τ_I	abstraction ($I \subseteq A$)

5.2.2 AXIOMS

ACP^{τ} has the axioms from table 51. We have $a,b,c \in A \cup \{\delta, \tau\}$, $H, I \subseteq A$ and x,y,z are arbitrary processes.

$x + y = y + x$	A1	$x\tau = x$	B1
$x + (y + z) = (x + y) + z$	A2	$x(\tau(y + z) + y) = x(y + z)$	B2
$x + x = x$	A3		
$(x + y)z = xz + yz$	A4		
$(xy)z = x(yz)$	A5		
$x + \delta = x$	A6	$a \vert b = \gamma(a,b)$ if $\gamma(a,b)\downarrow$	CF1
$\delta x = \delta$	A7	$a \vert b = \delta$ otherwise	CF2
$x \Vert y = x \Vert\!\_\, y + y \Vert\!\_\, x + x \vert y$	CM1	$ax \vert b = (a \vert b)x$	CM5
$a \Vert\!\_\, x = ax$	CM2	$a \vert bx = (a \vert b)x$	CM6
$ax \Vert\!\_\, y = a(x \Vert y)$	CM3	$ax \vert by = (a \vert b)(x \Vert y)$	CM7
$(x + y) \Vert\!\_\, z = x \Vert\!\_\, z + y \Vert\!\_\, z$	CM4	$(x + y) \vert z = x \vert z + y \vert z$	CM8
		$x \vert (y + z) = x \vert y + x \vert z$	CM9
$\partial_H(a) = a$ if $a \notin H$	D1	$\tau_I(a) = a$ if $a \notin I$	TI1
$\partial_H(a) = \delta$ if $a \in H$	D2	$\tau_I(a) = \tau$ if $a \in I$	TI2
$\partial_H(x + y) = \partial_H(x) + \partial_H(y)$	D3	$\tau_I(x + y) = \tau_I(x) + \tau_I(y)$	TI3
$\partial_H(xy) = \partial_H(x) \cdot \partial_H(y)$	D4	$\tau_I(xy) = \tau_I(x) \cdot \tau_I(y)$	TI4

TABLE 51. ACP^{τ}.

Almost all axioms in this table are from the system ACP from 4.2.1, except for the axioms B1-B2 from 5.1.2 and those for the abstraction operator from 5.1.5. We will go over the main theorems again, such as those about elimination, conservative extension, standard concurrency and expansion of terms. As it will turn out, all these theorems are straightforward corollaries from the previous ones, as ACP^{τ} does not differ from ACP other than with respect to the axioms B1 and B2.

Note that in table 51 we have $a,b,c \in A \cup \{\delta,\tau\}$, so the special constants δ and τ behave as if they were ordinary atomic actions. Note that from CF2, it follows that $a|\tau = \tau|a = a|\delta = \delta|a = \delta$ for all $a \in A \cup \{\delta,\tau\}$.

5.2.3 THEOREM

i. **Elimination:** for every closed term t from ACP^{τ}, there exists a BPA^{τ}_{δ}-term s such that $ACP^{\tau} \vdash t=s$.

ii. ACP^{τ} is a **conservative extension** of BPA^{τ}_{δ}, i.e. for all closed terms t and s from BPA^{τ}_{δ} we have $ACP^{\tau} \vdash t=s$ iff $BPA^{\tau}_{\delta} \vdash t=s$.

iii. ACP^{τ} is also a conservative extension of ACP.

PROOF: i. Consider the term rewriting system consisting of the rules in 4.3.1 (with $a \in A \cup \{\tau\}$) together with the additional rules:

$\tau_I(a) \rightarrow a \quad$ if $a \notin I$

$\tau_I(a) \rightarrow \tau \quad$ if $a \in I$

$\tau_I(x + y) \rightarrow \tau_I(x) + \tau_I(y)$

$\tau_I(xy) \rightarrow \tau_I(x) \cdot \tau_I(y)$.

Then the proof of (i) proceeds along the same lines as in theorem 4.3.1. Note that this rewriting system does not rewrite terms into basic terms over BPA^{τ}_{δ} (a is in normal form, but not a basic term over BPA^{τ}_{δ}).

ii. As in 3.2.1 and 4.3.1. Use the fact that the term rewriting system given above is confluent and terminating, and does not introduce any of the parallel or renaming operators in the rules. Then conclude that ACP^{τ} is a conservative extension of BPA^{τ}_{δ}.

iii. Consider the term rewriting system

$x + x \rightarrow x$

$(x + y)z \rightarrow xz + yz$

$(xy)z \rightarrow x(yz)$

$x + \delta \rightarrow x$

$\delta x \rightarrow \delta$

$x\tau \rightarrow x$

$x(\tau y) \rightarrow xy$

$x(\tau y + y) \rightarrow xy$

$x(\tau(y + z) + y) \rightarrow x(y + z)$.

Notice that the last four rules correspond to the τ-laws of 5.1.3. The middle two rules give the case that y resp. z is absent in rule B2, and correspond to equations easily derivable from BPA^{τ}_{δ} (see 5.1.9.1). Now we claim (without proof) that this term rewriting system is strongly terminating and confluent modulo A1,A2. It follows that if two closed terms s,t are provably equal in BPA_δ^τ (i.e. $BPA_\delta^\tau \vdash s{=}t$), then their normal forms must be equal up to the order of the summands (i.e. A1,A2 $\vdash$ s=t).

Then we can conclude that BPA_δ^τ is a conservative extension of BPA_δ.

We can extend this result in order to prove that ACP$^\tau$ is a conservative extension of ACP, but encounter some complications. Trying to complete (make terminating and confluent) the term rewriting system consisting of the rules in 4.3.1 plus the rules above, we find the following rules:

$x \mathbin{⌊\!⌊} \tau \to x$
$x \mathbin{⌊\!⌊} \tau y \to x \mathbin{⌊\!⌊} y$
$x \mathbin{⌊\!⌊} (\tau y + y) \to x \mathbin{⌊\!⌊} y$
$x \mathbin{⌊\!⌊} (\tau(y + z) + y) \to x \mathbin{⌊\!⌊} (y + z)$
$\tau | x \to \delta$
$x | \tau \to \delta$
$\tau x | y \to \delta$
$x | \tau y \to \delta.$

Now all of these rules correspond to equations that are derivable from ACP$^\tau$ for closed terms (see exercises). Then, we also find that we need the commutativity of the communication merge ($x|y = y|x$), and so we have to work modulo A1,A2 and this equation. The extra equation is also derivable for closed terms, see the following theorem. With these extra provisions, we do obtain a terminating and confluent term rewriting system, and can derive a conservativity result.

In 5.4.21, we will give a semantical proof of the same fact.

5.2.4 THEOREM

For all closed ACP$^\tau$-terms x,y,z we have the axioms of **standard concurrency** of theorem 4.3.3. That is:

1. $x|y = y|x$
2. $x \| y = y \| x$
3. $x|(y|z) = (x|y)|z$
4. $(x \mathbin{⌊\!⌊} y) \mathbin{⌊\!⌊} z = x \mathbin{⌊\!⌊} (y \| z)$
5. $(x|y) \mathbin{⌊\!⌊} z = x|(y \mathbin{⌊\!⌊} z)$
6. $x \| (y \| z) = (x \| y) \| z.$

PROOF: Precisely as the proof of theorem 4.3.3. Observe that the basic terms over BPA_δ^τ are even simpler than the ones over BPA_δ. Therefore, the proof is in fact shorter.

5.2.5 THEOREM

In ACP$^\tau$ with standard concurrency and handshaking we have the following **expansion** theorem:

$$x_1 \| \ldots\ldots \| x_n = \sum_{1\le i\le n} x_i \mathbin{⌊\!⌊} (\mathop{\|}_{1\le j\le n\ j\ne i} x_j) + \sum_{1\le i<j\le n} (x_i|x_j) \mathbin{⌊\!⌊} (\mathop{\|}_{1\le k\le n\ k\ne i,j} x_k) \qquad (n\ge 3).$$

The proof of theorem 5.2.5 is very similar to the proof of theorem 4.3.5.

5.2.6 EXERCISES

1. Prove that i. $ACP^\tau \vdash a(\tau \| x) = ax$, and ii. $ACP^\tau \vdash a(\tau x \| y) = a(x \| y)$ (for $a \in A \cup \{\delta,\tau\}$). Then use (i) to show that axiom CM6 is derivable from the other axioms of ACP^τ.
2. Prove that for $a,b \in A \cup \{\delta,\tau\}$ the following equations can be derived from ACP^τ (not just for closed terms!):
i. $\tau x \| \tau y = \tau y \| \tau x$; ii. $ax | by = by | ax$; iii. $ax \| by = by \| ax$;
iv. $(\sum_i a_i x_i) \| (\sum_j b_j y_j) = (\sum_j b_j y_j) \| (\sum_i a_i x_i)$.
We see that we can prove $x \| y = y \| x$ for all x and y in head normal form.
3. Prove the following equations for all processes x,y,z in head normal form.
i. $x | \tau = \tau | x = \delta$; ii. $x \lfloor\!\lfloor \tau = x$; iii. $x \| \tau = \tau \| x = \tau x + x$;
iv. $x \lfloor\!\lfloor \tau y = x \lfloor\!\lfloor y$; v. $x | \tau y = \tau x | y = \delta$; vi. $x \| \tau y = \tau(x \| y) + x \lfloor\!\lfloor y$;
vii. $x \lfloor\!\lfloor (\tau y + y) = x \lfloor\!\lfloor y$; viii. $x \lfloor\!\lfloor (\tau(y + z) + y) = x \lfloor\!\lfloor (y + z)$.
4. Prove theorem 5.2.4.
5. Complete the proof of 5.2.3.iii.
6. Assume that $I \subseteq A$ and that no element of I can communicate. Now prove that for all closed ACP^τ-terms x,y we have

$$\tau_I(x \| y) = \tau_I(\tau_I(x) \| \tau_I(y))$$

Assume in addition that none of the elements in I is a communication action (i.e: for all $a,b \in A$ we have $a | b \notin I$). Then prove that for all closed terms in ACP^τ:

$$\tau_I(x \| y) = \tau_I(x) \| \tau_I(y).$$

7. Prove that for all ACP^τ-terms x the following holds (in the terminology of exercise 2.2.12.9): x has deadlock $\Leftrightarrow$ $\tau_I(x)$ has deadlock.

5.2.7 NOTES AND COMMENTS

The original formulation of ACP with silent step is the axiom system ACP_τ of BERGSTRA & KLOP [1985] (see also section 5.8). It is based on Milner's τ-laws, and this necessitates the addition of extra axioms in order to describe the interaction of τ and merge. These extra axioms do not occur in the system ACP_η of BAETEN & VAN GLABBEEK [1987a], where the τ-laws are weakened. The τ-laws are weakened even further in the present setting, but otherwise the system ACP^τ presented here is the same as their system ACP_η.

5.3 TERMINATION

In this section we combine the systems ACP_ε of 4.4 and ACP^τ of 5.2 to obtain ACP^τ_ε.

5.3.1 ACP^τ_ε

The signature of ACP^τ_ε is obtained from the one of ACP^τ by adding a special constant ε and a unary operator $\surd$. The axioms are presented in table 52.

In this table we have $a \in A \cup \{\delta,\tau\}$, $H,I \subseteq A$, and x,y,z are arbitrary processes.

$x + y = y + x$	A1	$\delta + x = x$	A6
$(x + y) + z = x + (y + z)$	A2	$\delta x = \delta$	A7
$x + x = x$	A3	$\varepsilon x = x$	A8
$(x + y)z = xz + yz$	A4	$x\varepsilon = x$	A9
$(xy)z = x(yz)$	A5		
$a(\tau(x + y) + x) = a(x + y)$	BE		
$x \parallel y = x \lfloor\!\lfloor y + y \lfloor\!\lfloor x + x \mid y + \surd(x) \cdot \surd(y)$			CTM1
$\varepsilon \lfloor\!\lfloor x = \delta$	TM2	$\varepsilon \mid x = \delta$	TM5
$ax \lfloor\!\lfloor y = a(x \parallel y)$	TM3	$x \mid \varepsilon = \delta$	TM6
$(x + y) \lfloor\!\lfloor z = x \lfloor\!\lfloor z + y \lfloor\!\lfloor z$	TM4		
$ax \mid by = (a \mid b)(x \parallel y)$	CM7	$a \mid b = \gamma(a,b)$ if $\gamma(a,b)\downarrow$	CF1
$(x + y) \mid z = x \mid z + y \mid z$	CM8	$a \mid b = \delta$ otherwise	CF2
$x \mid (y + z) = x \mid y + x \mid z$	CM9		
$\partial_H(\varepsilon) = \varepsilon$	D0	$\tau_I(\varepsilon) = \varepsilon$	TI0
$\partial_H(a) = a$ if $a \notin H$	D1	$\tau_I(a) = a$ if $a \notin H$	TI1
$\partial_H(a) = \delta$ if $a \in H$	D2	$\tau_I(a) = \tau$ if $a \in H$	TI2
$\partial_H(x + y) = \partial_H(x) + \partial_H(y)$	D3	$\tau_I(x + y) = \tau_I(x) + \tau_I(y)$	TI3
$\partial_H(xy) = \partial_H(x) \cdot \partial_H(y)$	D4	$\tau_I(xy) = \tau_I(x) \cdot \tau_I(y)$	TI4
$\surd(\varepsilon) = \varepsilon$	TE1	$\surd(x + y) = \surd(x) + \surd(y)$	TE3
$\surd(a) = \delta$	TE2	$\surd(xy) = \surd(x) \cdot \surd(y)$	TE4

TABLE 52. ACP$^{\tau}_{\varepsilon}$.

5.3.2 COMMENT

ACP$^{\tau}_{\varepsilon}$ has the axioms from table 37 from 4.4.1, together with the axiom BE and the axioms for the abstraction operator τ_I. Note that we do not have axiom B1 – $x\tau = x$ – since together with A8 this would yield $\tau = \varepsilon\tau = \varepsilon$, which is not what we want. Instead we have $a(\tau(x + y) + x) = a(x + y)$, which is axiom B2 with only prefix multiplication (thus not allowing a to be equal to ε). It is left for the exercises to prove that BE, A1-A9 $\vdash a\tau = a$.

We will also write BPA$^{\tau}_{\delta\varepsilon}$ for BPA$_{\delta\varepsilon}$ + BE. BPA$^{\tau}_{\delta\varepsilon}$ has the action relations from table 11 (see 2.2.9), allowing a to range over $A \cup \{\tau\}$.

5.3.3 BASIC TERMS

The set of **basic terms** over BPA$^{\tau}_{\delta\varepsilon}$ (compare with 2.2.3 or 2.2.7) is defined as follows:

i. δ and ε are basic terms;

ii. if t is a basic term, and $a \in A \cup \{\tau\}$, then $a \cdot t$ is a basic term;

iii. if t,s are basic terms, then t + s is a basic term.
The basic terms over $BPA^{\tau}_{\delta\varepsilon}$ are of the form

$$t = \varepsilon \quad \text{or} \quad t = \sum_{i<n} a_i t_i$$

for $a_i \in A \cup \{\tau\}$ and basic terms t_i ($i<n$).

5.3.4 LEMMA
If $\varepsilon \leq x$ (x a closed ACP^{τ}_{ε}-term), then write $x = x' + \varepsilon$ where x' is such that *not* $\varepsilon \leq x'$ (if $x = \varepsilon$, then $x' = \delta$). If *not* $\varepsilon \leq x$, then write $x' = x$. Then for all closed ACP^{τ}_{ε}-terms x,y we have:
1. $x \mathbin{\|\!\!\_} \tau y = x' \mathbin{\|\!\!\_} y$
2. $x \| \tau y = \tau(x \| y) + x' \mathbin{\|\!\!\_} y$

PROOF: Use 5.3.3 to prove that x' exists. The proof of 1. and 2. is left for the exercises.

5.3.5 THEOREM
i. **Elimination:** for every closed term t from ACP^{τ}_{ε}, there exists a $BPA^{\tau}_{\delta\varepsilon}$-term s such that $ACP^{\tau}_{\varepsilon} \vdash t=s$.
ii. ACP^{τ}_{ε} is a **conservative extension** of $BPA^{\tau}_{\delta\varepsilon}$ and of ACP^{τ}.
iii. For all closed ACP^{τ}_{ε}-terms x,y,z we have the axioms of **standard concurrency** from theorem 4.3.3 (or 5.2.4).

PROOF: left for the exercises.

5.3.6 THEOREM
In ACP^{τ}_{ε} with standard concurrency and handshaking we have the following **expansion** theorem:

$$x_1 \| \ldots \| x_n = \sum_{1 \leq i \leq n} x_i \mathbin{\|\!\!\_} (\mathop{\|}_{1 \leq j \leq n,\ j \neq i} x_j) + \sum_{1 \leq i < j \leq n} (x_i | x_j) \mathbin{\|\!\!\_} (\mathop{\|}_{1 \leq k \leq n,\ k \neq i,j} x_k) + \prod_{1 \leq i \leq n} \surd(x_i)$$

(for $n \geq 3$, compare with 4.4.6).

Here, $\prod_{1 \leq i \leq n} x_i$ stands for the product $x_1 \cdot x_2 \cdot \ldots \cdot x_n$ of the processes x_i.

5.3.7 EXERCISES
1. We cannot define an operator ε_I in ACP^{τ}_{ε} in order to deal with abstraction. If we do, show that we can prove from the renaming axioms (see 3.6) and ACP^{τ}_{ε} that $\tau = \varepsilon$.
2. Prove lemma 5.3.4.
3. Prove theorem 5.3.5.
4. Prove theorem 5.3.6.
5. Prove that for all closed terms in ACP^{τ}_{ε}:
i. $x \mathbin{\|\!\!\_} \varepsilon = x \| \varepsilon = x$, and
ii. $\surd(x) = \varepsilon \Leftrightarrow x = x + \varepsilon$.
6. Check that, assuming handshaking, we can derive the expansion theorem from the axioms of standard concurrency.

7. Prove that BE, A6, A9 $\vdash$ $a\tau = a$. Prove that the axioms A3 and A6 in ACP^{τ}_{ε} can be replaced by the axioms $\varepsilon + \varepsilon = \varepsilon$ and $\delta + \varepsilon = \varepsilon$ respectively.

5.3.8 NOTES AND COMMENTS

The axiom system ACP^{τ}_{ε} is new here. It is very similar to the system ACPc in BAETEN & VAN GLABBEEK [1989] (only the τ-laws and the axioms for the communication merge are different).

5.4 MODELS

In this section we will construct models for the theories BPA^{τ}_{δ} and ACP^{τ}, that involve τ, in order to prove the consistency of the axioms we introduced for τ. Furthermore, we will again prove that $BPA^{\tau}_{\delta\varepsilon}$ is a conservative extension of $BPA_{\delta\varepsilon}$ (for closed terms), by proving that $BPA_{\delta\varepsilon}$ is complete with respect to a submodel of a model for $BPA^{\tau}_{\delta\varepsilon}$. Without much trouble, we can extend this result to prove that ACP^{τ} is a conservative extension of ACP (for closed terms).

As before, we will present models for the full theory ACP^{τ}_{ε}, and only make a few remarks on how to obtain models for the smaller theories.

Although this section is about models in general, it will strongly focus on the graph model. In this model we will present several views on the silent step. First, we will see that τ leads to a variant of the notion of bisimulation, which will be referred to as *branching bisimulation*. Next we will present a *graph reduction relation* which reduces process graphs by contracting silent steps. The resulting normal forms are unique modulo graph isomorphism. Using a graph rewriting system we present a full proof of the completeness theorem for $BPA^{\tau}_{\delta\varepsilon}$ with respect to the graph model.

As opposed to former sections, we will consider the graph model immediately after the initial algebra, and we can transfer the results of the graph model to the other models.

5.4.1 INITIAL ALGEBRA

The initial algebra of $BPA^{\tau}_{\delta\varepsilon}$, denoted by $\mathbb{A}^{\tau}_{\delta\varepsilon}$, is constructed from the axioms in the usual way. Since $BPA^{\tau}_{\delta\varepsilon}$ is a conservative extension of $BPA_{\delta\varepsilon}$ we have $\mathbb{A}_{\delta\varepsilon} \subset \mathbb{A}^{\tau}_{\delta\varepsilon}$, saying that $\mathbb{A}_{\delta\varepsilon}$ is contained in $\mathbb{A}^{\tau}_{\delta\varepsilon}$ as a proper submodel.

Because of theorem 5.3.5 the initial algebra of ACP^{τ}_{ε} has the same elements as the one of $BPA^{\tau}_{\delta\varepsilon}$, with the only difference that the equivalence classes consist of more elements. The operators on $\mathbb{A}^{\tau}_{\delta\varepsilon}$ are defined by the axioms of ACP^{τ}_{ε}.

5.4.2 GRAPH MODEL

The graph model of ACP_{ε} can be extended to a model of ACP^{τ}_{ε}. There are some complicating factors, however. For instance, we have to change the definition of bisimulation, to model the special properties of edges with label τ.

In the following paragraphs we will mainly deal with the proper introduction of the graph model with abstraction, i.e. with τ.

5.4.3 DEFINITION

A sequence $s \xrightarrow{\tau} \ldots \xrightarrow{\tau} t$ of zero or more τ-steps from s to t will be called a **generalized τ-step**. We will write $s \Rightarrow t$, if there is such a generalized step.

5.4.4 DEFINITION

Assume we allow graphs from $\mathbb{G}^\infty$ to have edges labeled with τ. Let $g,h \in \mathbb{G}^\infty$ and R be a relation between nodes of g and nodes of h. R is a **branching bisimulation** between g and h, $R: g \underline{\leftrightarrow}_b h$, if:

i. the roots of g and h are related by R;

ii. if $s \xrightarrow{a} s'$ is an edge in g ($a \in A \cup \{\tau\}$) and R(s,t), then either:

a. $a=\tau$ and R(s',t), or:

b. there exists a path $t \Rightarrow t_1 \xrightarrow{a} t'$, such that $R(s,t_1)$ and R(s',t');

iii. if $s\downarrow$ and R(s,t), then there exists a path $t \Rightarrow t'$ in h to a node t' with $t'\downarrow$ and R(s,t');

iv, v: as in ii, iii, with the roles of g and h interchanged.

Moreover, assume we have the following **root condition**:

vi. if $root(g) \xrightarrow{a} s'$ ($a \in A \cup \{\tau\}$), then there is t' with $root(h) \xrightarrow{a} t'$ and R(s',t')

vii. as vi, with g and h interchanged

viii. $root(g)\downarrow$ iff $root(h)\downarrow$

then R is called a **rooted branching bisimulation** or **rb-bisimulation.**

We will write $g \underline{\leftrightarrow}_b h$ if R exists such that $R: g \underline{\leftrightarrow}_b h$, and similarly $g \underline{\leftrightarrow}_{rb} h$ if there is an R such that $R: g \underline{\leftrightarrow}_{rb} h$. The notion of bisimulation $\underline{\leftrightarrow}$ from definition 2.7.6 will often be referred to as **strong bisimulation**.

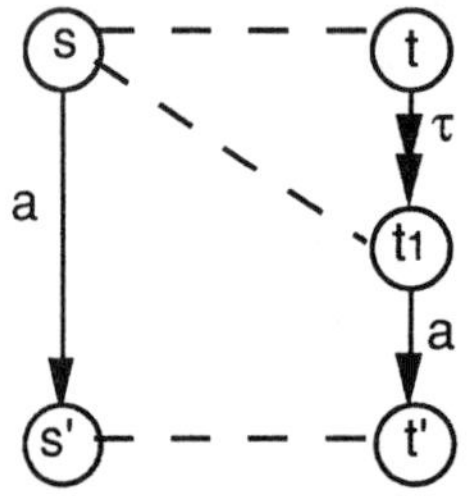

FIGURE 27. Branching bisimulation.

The basic idea behind the definition of branching bisimulation is that we may delete τ-steps from computation sequences in the way as is pictured in fig. 27. Here, it is shown that a path $t \Rightarrow t_1 \xrightarrow{a} t'$ can be related to an single a-step $s \xrightarrow{a} s'$, provided that the generalized τ-step does not yield any change of state. This is expressed by requiring the relations R(s,t) and $R(s,t_1)$. Equivalently, we could have required *all* intermediate states in $t \Rightarrow t_1$ to be related to s, as we will see later (lemma 5.4.6).

Again, (rooted) branching bisimulations are closed under arbitrary union, and so there exists a unique *maximal* branching bisimulation between two branching bisimilar graphs.

5.4.5 EXAMPLES

In the next five examples rb-bisimulations are denoted by dashed lines.

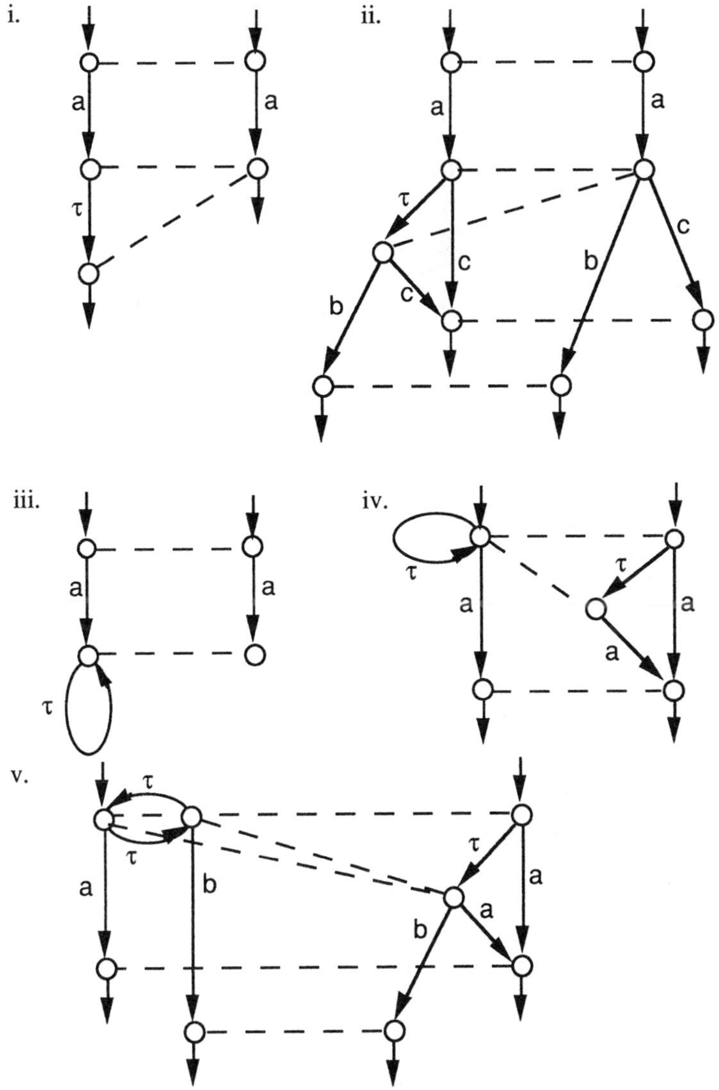

FIGURE 28, i - v.

In examples vi, vii a branching bisimulation is presented, which is *not* a rb-bisimulation; between the graphs in viii, not even a branching bisimulation exists.

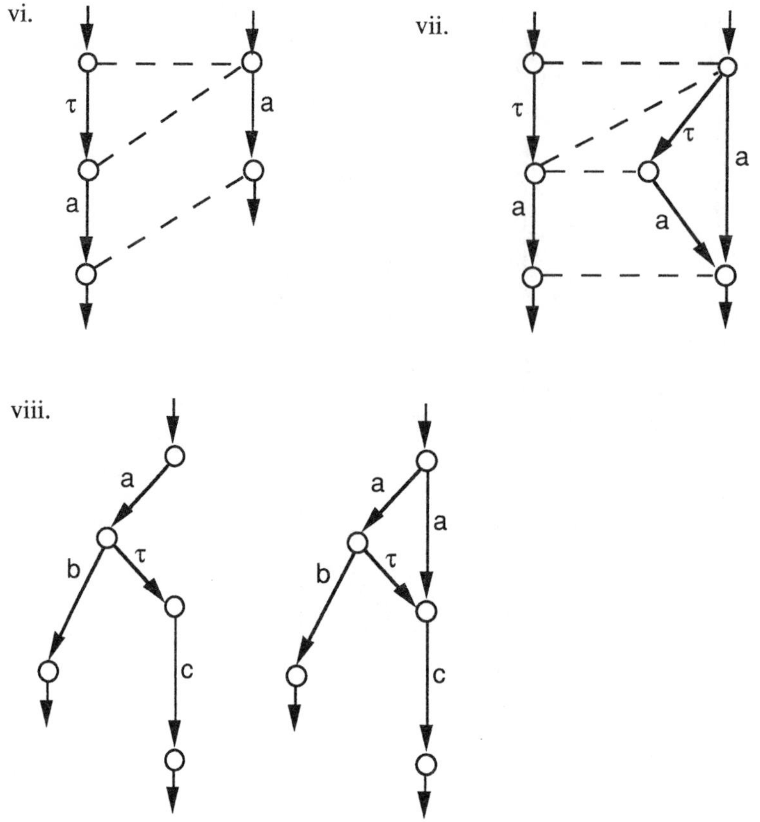

FIGURE 28, vi - viii.

5.4.6 LEMMA

Let R be the maximal branching bisimulation between g and h.
If $r \xrightarrow{\tau} r_1 \xrightarrow{\tau} r_2 \xrightarrow{\tau} \dots \xrightarrow{\tau} r_m \xrightarrow{\tau} r'$ $(m \geq 0)$ is a path in g such that $R(r,s)$ and $R(r',s)$, then for all $1 \leq i \leq m$ we have: $R(r_i,s)$.
This is the so-called **stuttering lemma**.

PROOF: First we prove lemma 5.4.6 for a slightly different kind of bisimulation, defined as follows.

A **semi-branching bisimulation** between two graphs g and h is a symmetric relation R between the nodes of g and h such that:

i. The roots are related by R
ii. If $R(s,t)$ and $s \xrightarrow{a} s'$ then either
   a. $a=\tau$ and there exists a path $t \Rightarrow t'$ such that $R(s,t')$ and $R(s',t')$, or:
   b. there exists a path $t \Rightarrow t_1 \xrightarrow{a} t'$ such that $R(s,t_1)$, $R(s',t_2)$ and $R(s',t')$.
iii. if $s\downarrow$ and $R(s,t)$, then there exists a path $t \Rightarrow t'$ in h to a node t' with $t'\downarrow$ and $R(s,t')$;
iv,v: as ii,iii with g and h interchanged.

The difference with branching bisimulation is in case (a), and is illustrated in the following picture.

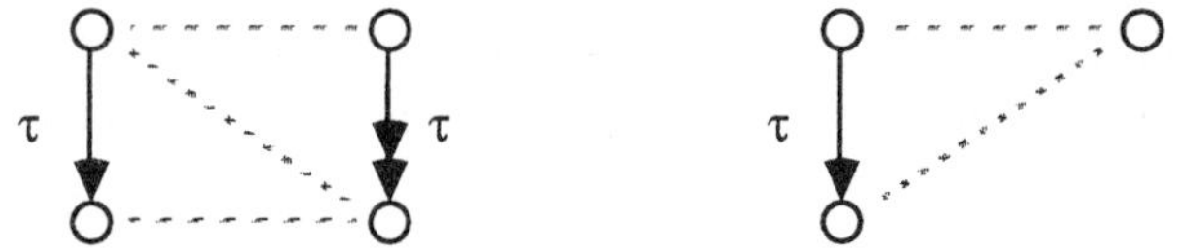

FIGURE 29. Semi-branching (left) and branching bisimulation.

Now let (*) denote the property mentioned in the lemma. Observe that any branching bisimulation is a semi-branching bisimulation and moreover, any semi-branching bisimulation satisfying (*) is a branching bisimulation. Then it is sufficient to prove the following claim.

CLAIM: The maximal semi-branching bisimulation between g and h satisfies (*).

PROOF OF THE CLAIM: Let R be the maximal semi-branching bisimulation between g and h, let s be a node and let $r \xrightarrow{\tau} r_1 \xrightarrow{\tau} \cdots \xrightarrow{\tau} r_m \xrightarrow{\tau} r'$ $(m \geq 0)$ be a path such that $R(r,s)$ and $R(r',s)$. Then we prove that $R' = R \cup \{(r_i,s) : 1 \leq i \leq m\}$ is a semi-branching bisimulation. We check the conditions:

i. Clearly, the root nodes of g and h are related by R' (since they are by R).

ii,iv. Suppose $R'(v,w)$. If also $R(v,w)$ then the conditions (ii) and (iv) are satisfied, since $R \subseteq R'$ and R is a semi-branching bisimulation.

So assume *not* $R(v,w)$, then $v=r_i$ and $w=s$.

Now if $r_i \xrightarrow{a} r''$ then $r \xrightarrow{\tau} r_1 \xrightarrow{\tau} \cdots \xrightarrow{\tau} r_i \xrightarrow{a} r''$ and since $R(r,s)$ we find that there exists a sequence $s \Rightarrow s_1 \Rightarrow \cdots \Rightarrow s_i$ such that $R(r_1,s_1),\ldots,R(r_i,s_i)$. It follows from $R(r_i,s_i)$ that either:

a. $a=\tau$ and there exists a path $s_i \Rightarrow s''$ such that $R(r_i,s'')$ and $R(r'',s'')$, and hence $R'(r_i,s'')$ and $R'(r'',s'')$ as required, or:

b. there exists a path $s_i \Rightarrow t_1 \xrightarrow{a} s''$ such that $R(r_i,t_1)$ and $R(r'',s'')$, and hence $s \Rightarrow s_i \Rightarrow t_1 \xrightarrow{a} s''$ with $R'(r_i,t_1)$ and $R'(r'',s'')$.

If $s \xrightarrow{a} s''$ then it follows from $R(r',s)$ that either:

a. $a=\tau$ and there is a path $r' \Rightarrow r''$ such that $R(r'',s)$ and $R(r'',s'')$. Hence there is a path $r_i \Rightarrow r' \Rightarrow r''$ such that $R'(r'',s)$ and $R'(r'',s'')$ as required, or:

b. there is a path $r' \Rightarrow t_1 \xrightarrow{a} r''$ such that $R(t_1,s)$ and $R(r'',s'')$ and hence $r_i \Rightarrow r' \Rightarrow t_1 \xrightarrow{a} r''$ with $R'(t_1,s)$ and $R'(r'',s'')$.

Parts iii,v proceed along the same lines. This proves that R' is a semi-branching bisimulation. Since R is maximal we find $R=R'$.

Thus, we have proved the claim. Finally, conclude that the maximal semi-branching bisimulation – as it satisfies (*) – is identical to the maximal branching bisimulation, and so we have proved the lemma. It is left to the reader to prove that the stuttering lemma holds as well for the maximal *rooted* branching bisimulation.

5.4.7 PROPOSITION

The relations $\underline{\leftrightarrow}_b$ and $\underline{\leftrightarrow}_{rb}$ are equivalences on $\mathbb{G}^\infty$.

The proof of this theorem is easy and left for the exercises. The equivalence relation, induced by $\leftrightarrow_b$ resp. $\leftrightarrow_{rb}$, will be called **(rooted) branching bisimulation equivalence**. We will return to this equivalence later.

The root condition in 5.4.4 can be simplified when restricting to *root unwound* process graphs, elements of the set $\{\rho(g) : g \in \mathbb{G}^\infty\}$ (see 2.7.16). Consider the following lemma.

5.4.8 LEMMA

Two root unwound process graphs are rooted branching bisimilar iff there exists a branching bisimulation between them relating root nodes with root nodes only.

The proof of this lemma is left for the exercises.

5.4.9 COLOURED TRACES

Let us present an alternative way of defining branching bisimulation, in order to have some more intuition about its nature. We do this by means of the coloured traces that we saw before in 2.7.8 and in 5.1.1. For convenience, we restrict ourselves to root unwound process graphs. The definitions and theorems can be adjusted to the case of arbitrary process graphs, although this involves a few minor complications.

Consider a coloured root unwound graph g. Intuitively, the colours of the nodes are considered to indicate the nature of the state that they represent. Then a τ-edge can be regarded as *inert* if it is between two nodes that have the same colour. Since such τ-step itself is invisible ('silent') and there are no changes in the current state (i.e. in its colour) of the process, there is no way of observing such inert actions. Thus they may as well be contracted.

Let us formalize this intuition in the following paragraphs. We extend the definition of a coloured trace to the setting with τ.

5.4.10 DEFINITIONS

An **abstract coloured trace** can be found from a coloured trace by replacing all subtraces of the form $(C,\tau,C,...,C,\tau,C)$ by C. Furthermore, let s be a node in a coloured graph, then we write $s\Downarrow$ if there exists a path $s=s_0 \xrightarrow{\tau} s_1 \xrightarrow{\tau} ... \xrightarrow{\tau} s_m$ such that $C(s_i) = C(s)$ $(1 \leq i \leq m)$ and $s_m\downarrow$.

A colouring of a graph is **abstract trace consistent** if:

i. two nodes have the same colour only if they have the same abstract coloured trace set;

ii. if nodes s and t have the same colour, then $s\Downarrow$ iff $t\Downarrow$.

Moreover, such a colouring is **rooted** if the root node has a colour not occurring anywhere else in the graph.

Two coloured graphs g and h are **(rooted) abstract trace equivalent** if for some (rooted) abstract trace consistent colouring, the root nodes have the same abstract coloured traces. Compare this definition with 2.7.10, where we defined similar notions for concrete coloured traces.

5.4.11 THEOREM

Let g and h be root unwound process graphs, then:

i. $g \leftrightarrow_b h$ if and only if g and h are abstract trace equivalent.

ii. $g \underline{\leftrightarrow}_{rb} h$ if and only if g and h are rooted abstract trace equivalent.

PROOF: We will only prove (ii).
$\Rightarrow$. Suppose R is a rooted branching bisimulation between g and h, not relating root nodes to internal nodes (see lemma 5.4.8). Let $\overline{R}$ be its symmetric, transitive closure and $\mathbf{C}$ the set of equivalence classes induced by $\overline{R}$. Consider the $\overline{R}$-colouring in which every node is labeled with its own equivalence class then this colouring is a rooted abstract trace consistent colouring.

To see this, let us write $C(r)$ for the colour of the node r and assume that $R(r_0,s_0)$ and r_0 has an abstract coloured trace $(C_0,a_1,C_1,a_2,C_2,...,a_k,C_k)$. Then there exists a path of the form $r_0 \xrightarrow{\tau} u_1 \xrightarrow{\tau} ... \xrightarrow{\tau} u_m \xrightarrow{a_1} r_1$ $(m \geq 0)$ such that for all i: $C(u_i) = C(r_0)$. For every edge $u_i \xrightarrow{\tau} u_{i+1}$ $(0 \leq i < m,\ u_0 = r_0)$ there exists a path $v_i \Rightarrow v_{i+1}$ $(v_0 = s_0)$ such that $R(u_i,v_i)$, and all intermediate nodes are related to either u_i or u_{i+1} (by lemma 5.4.6), hence all have the same colour, including v_i and v_{i+1}. So we find a path $s_0 \Rightarrow v_m$ with only one colour in the nodes such that $R(u_m,v_m)$.

Next, since $u_m \xrightarrow{a_1} r_1$ and $R(u_m,v_m)$ we find that either $a_1 = \tau$ and $R(r_1,v_m)$ – in which case $C_1 = C_0$ in contradiction with $(C_0,a_1,C_1,a_2,C_2,...,a_k,C_k)$ being a coloured trace – or there is a path $v_m \Rightarrow t_1 \xrightarrow{a_1} s_1$ such that $R(u_m,t_1)$ and $R(r_1,s_1)$. Again by lemma 5.4.6 we find that t_1 and all the intermediate nodes in $\Rightarrow$ have the same colour as v_m and so we find an abstract coloured trace (C_0,a_1,C_1). By repeating this argument k times, we find that s_0 has an abstract coloured trace $(C_0,a_1,C_1,a_2,C_2,..., a_k,C_k)$ and so R preserves abstract coloured trace sets.

It is left to prove that $r_0\Downarrow$ iff $s_0\Downarrow$. This proof can be found along the same lines. Thus $\overline{R}$ induces an abstract consistent colouring. Since R does not relate root nodes to non-root nodes, this colouring is rooted, and since the roots are related we find g and h are rooted abstract coloured trace equivalent.

$\Leftarrow$. Consider a rooted abstract consistent colouring such that the coloured trace sets of g and h are equal with respect to that colouring. Let R be the relation between nodes of g and h relating two nodes iff they have the same colour, then it is easy to see that R is a rooted branching bisimulation. Note again, that the root condition is satisfied.

Using the results in the previous paragraphs, we can define a graph reduction system by asserting rules for eliminating inert τ-steps. We do this as follows.

5.4.12 DEFINITION
The **abstract canonical colouring** of a root unwound graph is the rooted abstract trace consistent colouring corresponding to the maximal rooted branching autobisimulation relating the root node only with itself (compare with 2.7.12). Equivalently: it is the unique rooted colouring such that two nodes have the same colour iff they have the same abstract coloured trace set. Note that in the abstract canonical colouring the root node has a unique colour.

Let g be a process graph and consider its abstract canonical colouring with colour set $\mathbf{C}$. Then $N_a(g)$ – the **abstract normal form** of g – is the graph which can be found from g by identifying all nodes with the same colour, and next deleting all τ-loops (τ-edges that start and end in the same node). Furthermore, a node in $N_a(g)$ has label $\downarrow$ iff $s\Downarrow$ for all nodes s in g with that colour.

5.4.13 THEOREM

For all root unwound process graphs g, we have $g \leftrightarrow_{rb} N_a(g)$.

PROOF: By definition, $N_a(g)$ is found from the abstract canonical colouring on g by identifying all nodes with the same colour. From 5.4.12 we find that this colouring can be found from the maximal rooted branching autobisimulation on g. Every node in $N_a(g)$ has a colour, namely the colour of the corresponding nodes in g. Now assume two nodes from g and $N_a(g)$ are related by R iff they have the same colour. Then R is a rooted branching bisimulation relation, since it is constructed from one on g.

The following theorem tells us why these normal forms are important.

5.4.14 THEOREM

For all root unwound process graphs g and h:
$g \leftrightarrow_{rb} h$ if and only if $N_a(g) = N_a(h)$.

PROOF: By proposition 5.4.7 and theorem 5.4.13 it follows that $g \leftrightarrow_{rb} h$ iff $N_a(g) \leftrightarrow_{rb} N_a(h)$. It follows immediately from definition 5.4.12 that σ is an abstract coloured trace in $N_a(g)$ iff it is a (concrete) coloured trace and so $N_a(g)$ and $N_a(h)$ are abstract coloured trace equivalent iff they are (concrete) coloured trace equivalent. Then by proposition 2.7.13 and theorem 5.4.11 we find that $N_a(g) \leftrightarrow_{rb} N_a(h)$ iff $N_a(g) \leftrightarrow N_a(h)$, so it is left to prove that $N_a(g) \leftrightarrow N_a(h)$ iff $N_a(g) = N_a(h)$.

Now if $R: N_a(g) \leftrightarrow N_a(h)$, then R is a bijective relation between the nodes of $N_a(g)$ and $N_a(h)$:

i. it is surjective because every node in $N_a(g)$ or $N_a(h)$ can be reached from the root by a finite path, hence by the definition of bisimulation (2.7.6) one directly finds that every node is related to some node in the other graph;

ii. it is injective since every node is related with at most one other node; if two different nodes in one graph are both related to a node in the other graph, these relations also hold in the *maximal* branching autobisimulation on that graph, and so with respect to the abstract canonical colouring they have the same colour. But then by definition 5.4.11 the nodes are identical, which is a contradiction.

Finally, since R is a strong bisimulation, using the bijectivity of R we find that if R(r,s) and R(r',s') then $r \xrightarrow{a} r'$ iff $s \xrightarrow{a} s'$ and $r\downarrow$ iff $s\downarrow$. Hence R is a graph isomorphism.

On the graph domain $\mathbb{G}^\infty$, we already defined all operators of ACP_ε^τ apart from the abstraction operator τ_I.

5.4.15 DEFINITION

The abstraction operator τ_I is defined on $\mathbb{G}^\infty$ as follows: for any graph g, the graph $\tau_I(g)$ can be found by replacing all labels from I by τ.

5.4.16 REMARK

Branching bisimulation is not a congruence relation with respect to the operators of ACP_ε^τ. This is so, because we have $\tau \cdot a \leftrightarrow_b a$ (example 5.4.5.vi), but not $\tau a + b \leftrightarrow_b a + b$, not $\tau a \llbracket b \leftrightarrow_b$

$a \lfloor\!\lfloor b$ and in general not $\tau a|b \leftrightarrow_b a|b$. This was the reason for introducing the root condition, since, as will be shown in the next theorem, $\leftrightarrow_{rb}$ *is* a congruence with respect to the operators of ACP^{τ}_{ε}.

5.4.17 DEFINITION

Let g be a process graph, and s a node in g. We say that s **has depth n** ($n \geq 0$), if s can be reached from the root node, following a path in which precisely n atomic actions (hence $\neq\tau$) occur as a label.

In a process *tree* every node has a unique depth, and all nodes in $\pi_n(g)$ are of depth $\leq n$. In graphs that are not trees, one node may have several depths, however.

A **layered rooted branching bisimulation** between graphs g and h is a relation R: $g \leftrightarrow_{rb} h$, such that:

$R(s,t) \Rightarrow$ there exists n such that s and t both have depth n.

As before (see 2.7.25) there is always a layered rooted branching bisimulation between two rooted branching bisimilar graphs.

5.4.18 THEOREM

Rooted branching bisimulation equivalence is a congruence relation on $\mathbb{G}^{\infty}$.

PROOF: We know from 5.4.7 that $\leftrightarrow_{rb}$ is an equivalence relation. The operators $+$, $\cdot$ are defined in 2.7.19, π_n in 2.7.26, $\sqrt{}$ in 3.4.5, the operators $\|$, $\lfloor\!\lfloor$, $|$ and ∂_H in 4.5.6 and τ_I in 5.4.15. We will only prove theorem 5.4.18 for the operators $+$, $\cdot$ and π_n. For the other operators, it is left to the reader. Now assume g_1,g_2,h_1,h_2 are graphs such that $g_1 \leftrightarrow_{rb} h_1$ and $g_2 \leftrightarrow_{rb} h_2$.

1. $g_1 + g_2 \leftrightarrow_{rb} h_1 + h_2$.

Find relations R: $\rho(g_1) \leftrightarrow_{rb} \rho(h_1)$ and S: $\rho(g_2) \leftrightarrow_{rb} \rho(h_2)$, such that in R and S root nodes are only related to root nodes (for the definition of ρ see 2.7.16). Such relations exist because of theorem 2.7.18.iii and lemma 5.4.8. Then the relation $T = R \cup S$ is a rb-bisimulation between $\rho(g_1) + \rho(g_2)$ and $\rho(h_1) + \rho(h_2)$, hence between $g_1 + g_2$ and $h_1 + h_2$.

2. $g_1 \cdot g_2 \leftrightarrow_{rb} h_1 \cdot h_2$.

If R: $g_1 \leftrightarrow_{rb} h_1$ and S: $\rho(g_2) \leftrightarrow_{rb} \rho(h_2)$ where S relates root nodes only with root nodes, then the relation T that consists of all pairs from R, plus all pairs from all copies of S except for the root pair, is an rb-bisimulation between $g_1 \cdot \rho(g_2)$ and $h_1 \cdot \rho(h_2)$, hence between $g_1 \cdot g_2$ and $h_1 \cdot h_2$. The details are left to the reader.

3. $\pi_n(g_1) \leftrightarrow_{rb} \pi_n(h_1)$.

Recall that every node in $tree(g)$ has exactly one depth, and that in $\pi_n(g)$ every node has depth $\leq n$. Since $g_1 \leftrightarrow_{rb} h_1$, there is R: $tree(g_1) \leftrightarrow_{rb} tree(h_1)$ (using lemma 2.7.22) and we may assume R to be layered (by 5.4.17). Then the restriction R_n of R to nodes in $tree(g_1)$ and $tree(h_1)$ with depth $\leq n$ is a rb-bisimulation between $\pi_n(tree(g_1))$ and $\pi_n(tree(h_1))$. Again using 2.7.22 we then find $\pi_n(g_1) \leftrightarrow_{rb} \pi_n(h_1)$.

5.4.19 THEOREM

$\mathbb{G}^{\infty}/\leftrightarrow_{rb}$ is a model of ACP^{τ}_{ε}.

PROOF: $\mathbb{G}^\infty/\underline{\leftrightarrow}_{rb} \models ACP_\varepsilon$ follows from the fact that $\mathbb{G}^\infty/\underline{\leftrightarrow} \models ACP_\varepsilon$ (see 4.5.9). For the law BE we refer to 5.4.6.i-ii, where some 'prototypes' of this law were treated. It is not hard to see, that in TI1-TI4, both sides yield isomorphic graphs.

5.4.20 OTHER GRAPH MODELS

In the same way, one can prove $\mathbb{G}/\underline{\leftrightarrow}_{rb}$, $\mathbb{R}/\underline{\leftrightarrow}_{rb}$ and $\mathbb{B}/\underline{\leftrightarrow}_{rb}$ to be models of ACP^τ_ε. In the models mentioned here, we also have the axioms of standard concurrency of 5.3.4, so these laws hold for all process graphs, not just for closed terms.

AIP does not hold in the model $\mathbb{G}^\infty/\underline{\leftrightarrow}_{rb}$, but it does, however, hold in the models $\mathbb{G}/\underline{\leftrightarrow}_{rb}$, $\mathbb{R}/\underline{\leftrightarrow}_{rb}$ and $\mathbb{B}/\underline{\leftrightarrow}_{rb}$. RSP holds in all these models (using a proper definition of guardedness), whereas RDP does not hold in $\mathbb{G}/\underline{\leftrightarrow}_{rb}$, $\mathbb{R}/\underline{\leftrightarrow}_{rb}$ and $\mathbb{B}/\underline{\leftrightarrow}_{rb}$, but it does in $\mathbb{G}^\infty/\underline{\leftrightarrow}_{rb}$. We will return to this further on, in the next section.

5.4.21 COROLLARY

i. $BPA^\tau_{\delta\varepsilon}$ is a conservative extension of $BPA_{\delta\varepsilon}$.
ii. ACP^τ_ε is a conservative extension of ACP_ε.
iii. ACP^τ is a conservative extension of ACP.

PROOF: The domain $\mathbb{G}^\infty$ contains a subdomain consisting of all process graphs without edge-labels τ. Obviously, this subdomain coincides with the domain of the graph model that we studied in the previous chapter. Furthermore, when restricting to graphs without τ, the definition of rb-bisimulation coincides with that of strong bisimulation and therefore we find that the 'old' graph model $\mathbb{G}^\infty/\underline{\leftrightarrow}$ from chapter 4 is a submodel of the new model $\mathbb{G}^\infty_\tau/\underline{\leftrightarrow}_{rb}$, writing $\mathbb{G}^\infty_\tau$ for the extended graph domain with graphs containing τ.
i. By 2.7.34 we know that $BPA_{\delta\varepsilon}$ is a complete axiomatization of $\mathbb{G}^\infty/\underline{\leftrightarrow}$. Since $\mathbb{G}^\infty/\underline{\leftrightarrow} \subseteq \mathbb{G}^\infty_\tau/\underline{\leftrightarrow}_{rb}$ and $\mathbb{G}^\infty_\tau/\underline{\leftrightarrow}_{rb} \models BPA^\tau_{\delta\varepsilon}$ we find that $BPA^\tau_{\delta\varepsilon}$ does not force any new equations on the subdomain $\mathbb{G}^\infty/\underline{\leftrightarrow}$: it leaves $\mathbb{G}^\infty/\underline{\leftrightarrow}$ 'unchanged'. Hence $BPA^\tau_{\delta\varepsilon}$ does not force new equations between terms from $BPA_{\delta\varepsilon}$.
ii. In 5.4.19 we found that $\mathbb{G}^\infty_\tau/\underline{\leftrightarrow}_{rb} \models ACP^\tau_\varepsilon$ and so ACP^τ_ε does not force any new equations on the subdomain $\mathbb{G}^\infty/\underline{\leftrightarrow}$. Hence it does not force new equations between terms from ACP_ε, since ACP_ε is complete with respect to $\mathbb{G}^\infty/\underline{\leftrightarrow}$ (see 4.5.13).
iii. As in (ii) we find that $\mathbb{G}^\infty_\tau/\underline{\leftrightarrow}_{rb} \models ACP^\tau$ (since $ACP^\tau \subseteq ACP^\tau_\varepsilon$), and as we stated in 4.5.13 we have that ACP is complete with respect to $\mathbb{G}^\infty/\underline{\leftrightarrow}$.

5.4.22 COMPLETENESS PROOF

In the following paragraphs we will present a full proof of the completeness theorem of $BPA^\tau_{\delta\varepsilon}$ for the graph model $\mathbb{G}^\infty/\underline{\leftrightarrow}_{rb}$. The basic idea in this proof is to establish a ***graph rewriting system*** on finite process graphs, which is confluent and terminating. Next we prove that (i) two normal forms (with respect to the graph rewriting system) are rooted branching bisimilar iff they are isomorphic, and furthermore that every rewriting step in the system (ii) corresponds to a proof step in the theory, and (iii) preserves bisimulation. Then we conclude that

- two finite graphs are bisimilar iff they have the same normal form;
- if two graphs have the same normal form then they can be proved equal.

5.4.23 DEFINITION

i. A pair (r,s) of nodes in a graph g is called a pair of **double nodes** if $r \neq s$ and:

1. $r\downarrow \Leftrightarrow s\downarrow$
2. for all nodes t and labels $a \in A \cup \{\tau\}$: $r \xrightarrow{a} t \Leftrightarrow s \xrightarrow{a} t$.

ii. An edge $r \xrightarrow{\tau} s$ in a graph g is called **manifestly inert** if:

1. $r \neq root(g)$
2. $r\downarrow \Rightarrow s\downarrow$
3. for all nodes t and labels $a \in A \cup \{\tau\}$ such that either $a \neq \tau$ or $t \neq s$: $r \xrightarrow{a} t \Rightarrow s \xrightarrow{a} t$.

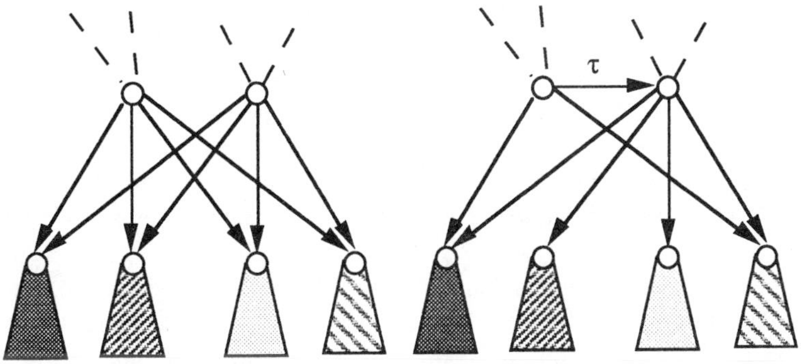

FIGURE 30. A pair of double nodes (left) and a manifestly inert τ-step.

As we can see from fig. 30, it is essential in both definitions that the equivalence between nodes can be found by investigating the outgoing edges (and labels ↓) only up to one level. For this reason, in definition 5.4.23 the τ-step is called *manifestly* inert since it can be recognized as such. Sharing and contraction turns out to be strong enough to reduce a graph to its normal form, which is a nice property since it means on finite graphs that all equivalent nodes after reduction become *manifestly* equivalent.

5.4.24 THEOREM

A finite acyclic graph g without double nodes or manifestly inert edges is in normal form.

PROOF: Let g be a finite acyclic graph which is not in normal form. Then with respect to its abstract canonical colouring (5.4.13) it has at least one pair of (different) nodes with the same colour. Now define the **norm** d(s) of a node s as the number of edges in the longest path starting from s (in finite acyclic graphs all paths are finite), and the **combined norm** of two nodes as the sum of their norms. Choose the pair (r,s) of equally coloured nodes in g with minimal combined norm. Consequently we have:

(*) $d(r')+d(s') < d(r)+d(s) \Rightarrow$ r' and s' have the same colour iff r'=s'.

Without loss of generality assume $d(s) \leq d(r)$. Then we prove the following four statements:

1. if $r \xrightarrow{a} t$ ($a \in A \cup \{\tau\}$) is an edge in g and $a \neq \tau$ or $t \neq s$, then $s \xrightarrow{a} t$ is an edge in g;
2. if $s \xrightarrow{a} t$ ($a \in A \cup \{\tau\}$) is an edge in g, then either $r \xrightarrow{\tau} s$ or $r \xrightarrow{a} t$ is an edge in g;
3. $r\downarrow \Rightarrow s\downarrow$;
4. if $r \xrightarrow{\tau} s$ is *not* an edge in g then $r\downarrow \Leftrightarrow s\downarrow$.

From these statements we find that if $r \xrightarrow{\tau} s$ is an edge in g then it is manifestly inert, and if $r \xrightarrow{\tau} s$ is not an edge in g, then (r,s) is a pair of double nodes, which proves our theorem.

1. Let $r \xrightarrow{a} t$ be an edge in g and $a \neq \tau$ or $t \neq s$. Since r and s have the same colours (hence the same abstract coloured traces) we find that either $a=\tau$ and t has the same colour as r and s, or s has the same abstract coloured trace $(C(r),a,C(t))$. Now if t has the same colour as r and s then it follows from $d(t) < d(r)$ and (*) that $s=t$, which is in contradiction with our assumption $(a,t) \neq (\tau,s)$. So s has an abstract coloured trace $(C(r),a,C(t))$ and by the same argument we find that s has no τ-edges to nodes with the same colour $C(r)=C(s)$. Hence there is a node u such that $s \xrightarrow{a} u$ and $C(t)=C(u)$, and since $d(t)+d(u) < d(r)+d(s)$ we conclude from (*) that $t=u$. Hence $s \xrightarrow{a} t$ is an edge in g.

2. Let $s \xrightarrow{a} t$ be an edge in g. If $C(s)=C(t)$ then it follows from (*), $C(s)=C(r)$ and $d(t)<d(s)$ (hence $d(r)+d(t) < d(r)+d(s)$) that $r=t$, in contradiction with $d(s)<d(r)$. So $(C(s),a,C(t))$ is an abstract coloured trace of s, and since r and s have the same colour $(C(s),a,C(t))$ is an abstract coloured trace of r. Now suppose r has an outgoing τ-edge to a node with the same colour $C(r)$, i.e. $r \xrightarrow{\tau} u$. Then it follows from $d(u)+d(s) < d(r)+d(s)$ and (*) that $u=s$. Suppose r has no such edge, then it has an edge $r \xrightarrow{a} u$ with $C(u)=C(t)$, and since $d(u)+d(t) < d(r)+d(s)$ we find that $u=t$. Thus we proved that either $r \xrightarrow{\tau} s$ or $r \xrightarrow{a} t$, which gives (2).

3. Since r and s have the same colour, we find that $r{\Downarrow}$ iff $s{\Downarrow}$ (see 5.4.10). Since (r,s) has minimal combined norm and $d(s) \leq d(r)$ we find that $s{\Downarrow}$ iff $s{\downarrow}$, for if there would be an inert step $s \xrightarrow{\tau} s'$ such that $C(s) = C(s')$, then the pair (r,s') has lower combined norm. So we find: $r{\downarrow} \Rightarrow r{\Downarrow} \Leftrightarrow s{\Downarrow} \Leftrightarrow s{\downarrow}$, hence $r{\downarrow} \Rightarrow s{\downarrow}$.

4. Now suppose $s{\downarrow}$, then we have $r{\Downarrow}$ (since $s{\Downarrow}$ and r and s have the same colour). If there is an inert step $r \xrightarrow{\tau} r'$ such that $C(r) = C(r')$ then $d(r') + d(s) < d(r) + d(s)$ and so $r'=s$. So if $r \xrightarrow{\tau} s$ is *not* an edge in g, then r has no outgoing inert steps and it follows from $r{\Downarrow}$ that $r{\downarrow}$. Hence $r{\downarrow} \Leftrightarrow s{\downarrow}$, using (3).

Theorem 5.4.24 tells us that all we need do to turn a graph g into its normal form is to share its pairs of double nodes and contract its manifestly inert edges. In the case of finite acyclic graphs (elements of $\mathbb{F}$) this can be done in finitely many steps as follows:

5.4.25 DEFINITION

For any graph g the rewriting relation $\rightarrow_{\mathbf{F}}$ is defined by the following two one-step reductions:

1. *sharing* a pair of double nodes (r,s): replace all edges $t \xrightarrow{a} r$ by $t \xrightarrow{a} s$ and remove r together with all its outgoing edges from g;
2. *contracting* a manifestly inert step $r \xrightarrow{\tau} s$: replace all edges $t \xrightarrow{a} r$ by $t \xrightarrow{a} s$ and remove r together with all its outgoing edges from g.

5.4.26 PROPOSITION

The rewriting relation $\rightarrow_{\mathbf{F}}$ has the following properties:

i. $\mathbb{F}$ is closed under applications of $\rightarrow_{\mathbf{F}}$

ii. if $g \rightarrow_{\mathbf{F}} h$ then $g \underline{\leftrightarrow}_{rb} h$

iii. $\rightarrow_{\mathbf{F}}$ is confluent and terminating.

PROOF: i. $\rightarrow_{\mathbf{F}}$ cannot increase the number of nodes and edges in g.

ii. Suppose (r,s) is a pair of double nodes in g or $r \xrightarrow{\tau} s$ is a manifestly inert edge in g which is contracted, and $g \to_F h$ identifies the nodes r and s. Let I be the identity relation on the nodes of g then $I \cup \{(r,s)\}$ is a rooted branching bisimulation between g and h. This is easy to prove from definition 5.4.23.

iii. $\to_F$ is terminating since it decreases the number of nodes, and every finite process graph has finitely many nodes. Next, suppose g has two normal forms n and n', then by definition of $\to_F$ n and n' are without pairs of double nodes and without manifestly inert edges. Thus by theorem 5.4.24 and (ii) it follows that $n \underline{\leftrightarrow}_{rb} n'$ and hence by theorem 5.4.14 we have $n=n'$.

Recall from definition 2.7.28 that we already defined a mapping term from $\mathbb{F}$ to the set of terms of $BPA^\tau_{\delta\varepsilon}$. Every $g \in \mathbb{F}$ has only finitely many paths. For this reason $term(g)$ is a closed $BPA^\tau_{\delta\varepsilon}$-term which is uniquely determined modulo equality induced by the axioms A1 and A2.

5.4.27 THEOREM
If $g \to_F h$ then $A1\text{-}A3 + BE \vdash term(g) = term(h)$.

PROOF: • Suppose (r,s) is a pair of double nodes in g such that r and s are shared in $g \to_F h$. According to definition 5.4.23 we find that r is an endnode (i.e. without outgoing edges) iff s is. Furthermore, $r\downarrow \Leftrightarrow s\downarrow$. Now suppose r and s are endnodes, then it follows from the construction in definition 2.7.28 that sharing them does not affect $term(g)$. So: if r and s are endnodes then $A1\text{-}A2 \vdash term(g) = term(h)$.

Now suppose r nor s is an endnode, then r has an edge $r \xrightarrow{a} t$ iff s has an edge $s \xrightarrow{a} t$ and so: $A1\text{-}A3 \vdash term(g_r) = term(g_s)$. Now replace $term(g_r)$ in $term(g)$ by $term(g_s)$, then it is easy to see that the result is $term(h)$ and so: $A1\text{-}A3 \vdash term(g) = term(h)$.

• Suppose $r \xrightarrow{\tau} s$ is a manifestly inert edge in g and $g \to_F h$ consists of the contraction of r and s. Then $r \neq root(g)$ and so for some $a \in A \cup \{\tau\}$ there is a 'higher' edge $t \xrightarrow{a} r$. By definition 2.7.28 we have that $term(g_t)$ has a summand $a\cdot term(g_r)$. Furthermore, $term(g_r)$ has a summand $\tau\cdot term(g_s)$ and we obtain:

1. $A1\text{-}A3 \vdash term(g_t) = a\cdot term(g_r) + term(g_t)$
2. $A1\text{-}A3 \vdash a\cdot term(g_r) = a\cdot(\tau\cdot term(g_s) + term(g_r))$.

Since for all nodes u: $r \xrightarrow{a} u \Rightarrow s \xrightarrow{a} u$ (apart from $(a,u)=(\tau,s)$), we find from definition 2.7.28 that all summands of $term(g_r)$ are summands of $term(g_s)$ as well, except for the summand $\tau\cdot term(g_s)$. Write ϕ_r for the basic term which is $term(g_r)$ *without* $\tau\cdot term(g_s)$ as a summand ($\phi_r=\delta$ if it is empty). Then we obtain:

3. $A1\text{-}A3 \vdash term(g_r) = \tau\cdot term(g_s) + \phi_r$
4. $A1\text{-}A3 \vdash term(g_s) = \phi_r + term(g_s)$.

So we derive:
$A1\text{-}A3 + BE \vdash \tau\cdot term(g_s) = \tau\cdot(\phi_r + term(g_s)) = $ (now applying BE from right to left)
$= \tau\cdot(\tau\cdot(\phi_r + term(g_s)) + \phi_r) = \tau\cdot(\tau\cdot term(g_s) + \phi_r)$ (by (4)) $=$
$= \tau\cdot term(g_r)$ (by (3)).

Then, after substitution and using $BE \vdash a\tau=a$ (see 5.3.2) we find that
$A1\text{-}A3 + BE \vdash term(g_t) = a\cdot\tau\cdot term(g_r) + term(g_t) = $ (by (1) and BE)
$= a\cdot\tau\cdot term(g_s) + term(g_t) = a\cdot term(g_s) + term(g_t)$.

Now replace term(g_r) in term(g) by term(g_s) then from (1) and definitions 2.7.28 and 5.4.25 we see that the result is term(h) and so: A1-A3 + BE $\vdash$ term(g) = term(h).

As in lemma 2.7.32 one can prove that term is a bijection from $\mathbb{F}$ to the set of finite $BPA^{\tau}_{\delta\varepsilon}$-terms modulo A1-A3. Hence every term in $BPA^{\tau}_{\delta\varepsilon}$ modulo A1-A3 is uniquely represented by a finite graph modulo graph isomorphisms. Then finally, we are in the position to prove the completeness of $BPA^{\tau}_{\delta\varepsilon}$ with respect to $\mathbb{F}/\underline{\leftrightarrow}_{rb}$:

5.4.28 THEOREM

$BPA^{\tau}_{\delta\varepsilon}$ is sound and complete with respect to $\mathbb{G}^{\infty}/\underline{\leftrightarrow}_{rb}$.

PROOF: (soundness) by 5.4.19.
(completeness) If $\mathbb{G}^{\infty}/\underline{\leftrightarrow}_{rb} \models s=t$ for two $BPA^{\tau}_{\delta\varepsilon}$-terms s,t, then it follows from 2.7.19 and 2.7.31 that graph(s) $\underline{\leftrightarrow}_{rb}$ graph(t). So N_a(graph(s)) = N_a(graph(t)) by theorem 5.4.14. So graph(s) and graph(t) have the same normal form with respect to $\rightarrow_F$ (see theorems 5.4.24 and 5.4.26.iii).

By theorem 5.4.27 we find that A1-A3 + BE $\vdash$ term(graph(s)) = term(graph(t)). Since $\mathbb{P}_{\delta\varepsilon}/\underline{\leftrightarrow} \models$ term(graph(s)) = s (2.7.32) and $BPA_{\delta\varepsilon}$ is complete with respect to $\mathbb{P}_{\delta\varepsilon}$ (2.5.10, 2.5.15) we find that $BPA_{\delta\varepsilon} \vdash$ term(graph(s)) = s.

Concluding we find that A1-A3 + BE + $BPA_{\delta\varepsilon} \vdash$ s=t, hence $BPA^{\tau}_{\delta\varepsilon} \vdash$ s=t.

Observe that the axioms A4-A9 are only needed in the last lines of the proof, where we needed a complete theory for $\mathbb{P}_{\delta\varepsilon}/\underline{\leftrightarrow}$. Obviously, term(graph(s)) = s is also valid in the models $\mathbb{P}_{\delta}/\underline{\leftrightarrow}$, $\mathbb{P}_{\varepsilon}/\underline{\leftrightarrow}$ and $\mathbb{P}/\underline{\leftrightarrow}$ (since these are submodels of $\mathbb{P}_{\delta\varepsilon}/\underline{\leftrightarrow}$), and BPA_{δ}, BPA_{ε} and BPA are the corresponding complete theories. This way we prove that BPA^{τ}_{δ}, BPA^{τ}_{ε} and BPA^{τ} are complete for $\mathbb{G}^{\infty}/\underline{\leftrightarrow}_{rb}$ as well (though with smaller signatures).

5.4.29 COROLLARY

i. $BPA^{\tau}_{\delta\varepsilon}$ is a conservative extension of BPA^{τ}, BPA^{τ}_{δ} and BPA^{τ}_{ε}.
ii. ACP^{τ}_{ε} is a conservative extension of ACP^{τ}.

PROOF: following the lines of 5.4.21, using the previous theorem.

5.4.30 NON-EXISTENCE OF A PROJECTIVE LIMIT MODEL

We cannot construct a Projective Limit Model for ACP^{τ}_{ε}, like we did for $BPA_{\delta\varepsilon}$, PA_{ε} and ACP_{ε}. The reason for this is that we cannot define the operator τ_I properly, because τ_I moves steps to the front (in $i^n \cdot a$ we have a at depth n+1, but $\tau_{\{i\}}(i^n \cdot a) = \tau a$ has a at depth 1).

This problem can be explained more carefully as follows: in 5.1.9.2 we found terms t_1, t_2, t_3,... all being different, with the property that for all n: $\pi_1(t_n) = t_n$, that is: every t_n has depth 1. Now consider the following sequence

$$p \equiv (t_1 + i,\ t_1 + i(t_2 + i),\ t_1 + i(t_2 + i(t_3 + i)),\ ...)$$

then it is easy to prove that $\pi_n(p_{n+m}) = p_n$ (m,n≥1) and so p is a projective sequence (see 2.6). Note that the nth term in this sequence has depth n, being the number of occurrences of the atomic action i. We find that $\tau_{\{i\}}(p)$ is equal to

$$q \equiv (t_1 + \tau,\ t_1 + \tau(t_2 + \tau),\ t_1 + \tau(t_2 + \tau(t_3 + \tau)),\ ...)$$

which is *not* a projective sequence. To see this, check that $\mathbb{G}^\infty/\underline{\leftrightarrow}_{rb} \not\models t_n = t_m$ $(n \neq m)$ and $\mathbb{G}^\infty/\underline{\leftrightarrow}_{rb} \not\models \pi_n(q_{n+m}) = q_n$ $(m,n \geq 1)$, e.g. $\pi_1(q_2) = t_1 + \tau \cdot t_2 + \tau$ whereas $q_1 = t_1 + \tau$. Then use the completeness theorem for ACP^τ_ε with respect to $\mathbb{G}^\infty/\underline{\leftrightarrow}_{rb}$ in order to conclude that q is not a projective sequence.

Even more: one easily proves that $\pi_1(\tau_{\{i\}}(p)) = \tau_{\{i\}}(p)$, and since $\tau_{\{i\}}(p)$ contains infinitely many pairwise different subprocesses $t_1, t_2, t_3, \ldots$ it does not bisimulate with any finite graph from $\mathbb{F}$, and so $\pi_1(\tau_{\{i\}}(p))$ cannot be represented by a finite term. Now assume, τ_I *could* be defined on projective sequences, then $\pi_1(\tau_{\{i\}}(p))$ has to be the first component of the projective sequence of $\tau_{\{i\}}(p)$. This is a contradiction.

5.4.31 THE TERM MODEL

Let us adjust the definitions in section 2.5 in order to define the term model for $BPA^\tau_{\delta\varepsilon}$. In paragraph 5.3.2 we already mentioned the action relations defined for $BPA^\tau_{\delta\varepsilon}$-terms: they are not different from the ones for $BPA_{\delta\varepsilon}$, except that this time we also have τ as a label. To construct the term model however, we also need a definition of (bisimulation) equivalence based on these action relations. This will be done in the following.

Let us extend $\mathbb{P}_{\delta\varepsilon}$ by allowing τ to occur in terms as an atomic action.

5.4.32 DEFINITION

A **branching bisimulation** is a binary relation R on $\mathbb{P}_{\delta\varepsilon}$, such that $(a \in A \cup \{\tau\})$:

i. if $p \xrightarrow{a} p'$ and $R(p,q)$ then either $a=\tau$ and $R(p',q)$, or there is v and q' such that $q \Rightarrow v \xrightarrow{a} q'$ and $R(p,v)$ and $R(p',q')$

ii. if $q \xrightarrow{a} q'$ and $R(p,q)$ then either $a=\tau$ and $R(p,q')$, or there is v and p' such that $p \Rightarrow v \xrightarrow{a} p'$ and $R(v,q)$ and $R(p',q')$

iii. if $p\downarrow$ and $R(p,q)$ then there is q' such that $q \Rightarrow q'$ and $q'\downarrow$, with $R(p,q')$

iv. if $q\downarrow$ and $R(p,q)$ then there is p' such that $p \Rightarrow p'$ and $p'\downarrow$, with $R(p',q)$.

We write R: $p \underline{\leftrightarrow}_b q$ if R is a branching bisimulation relating p and q, and just $p \underline{\leftrightarrow}_b q$ in order to express that such a branching bisimulation exists. Using $\underline{\leftrightarrow}_b$ we define the relation $\underline{\leftrightarrow}_{rb}$ as follows.

$p \underline{\leftrightarrow}_{rb} q$ if:

i. if $p \xrightarrow{a} p'$ then for some q': $q \xrightarrow{a} q'$ such that $p' \underline{\leftrightarrow}_b q'$ (for $a \in A \cup \{\tau\}$)

ii. vice versa with p and q interchanged

iii. $p\downarrow$ iff $q\downarrow$.

If $p \underline{\leftrightarrow}_{rb} q$ then we say that p and q are **rooted branching bisimilar**. Obviously, the definition of bisimulation on terms is not much different from the one on graphs. We obtain the model $\mathbb{P}_{\delta\varepsilon}/\underline{\leftrightarrow}_{rb}$.

5.4.33 THEOREM

$\mathbb{G}^\infty/\underline{\leftrightarrow}_{rb}$ and $\mathbb{P}_{\delta\varepsilon}/\underline{\leftrightarrow}_{rb}$ are isomorphic.

PROOF: We already know that term and graph are bijections between $\mathbb{G}^\infty$ and $\mathbb{P}_{\delta\varepsilon}$ (see 2.7.33). Thus, it is left to prove that they respect the equivalence relations $\underline{\leftrightarrow}_{rb}$, that is:

$\mathbb{G}^\infty/\underline{\leftrightarrow}_{rb} \models g=h \Rightarrow \mathbb{P}_{\delta\varepsilon}/\underline{\leftrightarrow}_{rb} \models \text{term}(g)=\text{term}(h)$ and

$\mathbb{P}_{\delta\varepsilon}/\underline{\leftrightarrow}_{rb} \models p=q \Rightarrow \mathbb{G}^\infty/\underline{\leftrightarrow}_{rb} \models \text{graph}(p)=\text{graph}(q)$.

The proof of this fact is left for the exercises.

5.4.34 EXERCISES

1. Prove lemma 5.4.8. That is, let g,h be two graphs, then prove that:
$g \leftrightarrow_{rb} h \Leftrightarrow$ there is an R: $\rho(g) \leftrightarrow_{rb} \rho(h)$ such that R relates root nodes with root nodes only.
2. Draw the process graph of the process p from 5.4.29, and check that in the graph model we have $\pi_1(\tau_{\{i\}}(p)) = \tau_{\{i\}}(p)$.
3. Check that the relations, constructed in 5.4.5.i-vi, are rb-bisimulations. Consider also that we have no rb-bisimulation in 5.4.5.vii , and no branching bisimulation in 5.4.5.viii.
4. Construct a rb-bisimulation between the graphs $a(\tau b + b)$ and ab, and also between $a(\tau(b + c) + b)$ and $a(b + c)$, and between $a\tau(\tau b + \tau\tau b)$ and ab.
5. Let A = {a,b,c} with $\gamma(a,b)=c$ being the only defined communication. Let g be the graph of the process τab, and h the graph of $\tau(\tau a + \tau b)$. Now construct the graphs of $g \| h$, $g \lfloor\!\lfloor h$, $h \lfloor\!\lfloor g$ and $g | h$. The same for $g = a^\omega$ and $h = (\tau b + a)^\omega$.
6. Check that all relations constructed in 5.4.18 are rb-bisimulations.
7. Prove that $\mathbb{G}/\leftrightarrow_{rb} \models$ BE.
8. Find two different solutions for the equation $x = \tau x$.
9. Assume g,h are two process graphs and $g \leftrightarrow_{rb} h$. Show that there exists a layered rb-bisimulation between g and h (see definition 5.4.17).
10. Let us say that two graphs are *weakly* branching bisimilar if there exists a relation R satisfying the conditions of definition 5.4.5, except that part (ii) is replaced by
ii'. if $s \xrightarrow{a} s'$ is an edge in g ($a \in A$, so $a \neq \tau$) and R(s,t), then there exists a path $t \Rightarrow t_1 \xrightarrow{a} t_2 \Rightarrow t'$, such that $R(s,t_1)$, $R(s',t_2)$ and $R(s',t')$.

Prove that two graphs are weakly branching bisimilar iff they are branching bisimilar. Hence, equivalently, we could have used this definition in order to define branching bisimulation.
11. Let R be a branching bisimulation and p,q *divergence free* terms from $\mathbb{P}_{\delta\varepsilon}$, that is without infinite sequences $p \xrightarrow{\tau}\xrightarrow{\tau}\xrightarrow{\tau} \ldots$. Prove that whenever R(p,q), either:

- $p \xrightarrow{\tau} p'$ and R(p',q), or
- $q \xrightarrow{\tau} q'$ and R(p,q'), or
- for all $a \in A \cup \{\tau\}$:
  i. if $p \xrightarrow{a} p'$ then there is q' such that $q \xrightarrow{a} q'$ and R(p',q'), and
  ii. if $q \xrightarrow{a} q'$ then there is p' such that $p \xrightarrow{a} p'$ and R(p',q'), and
  iii. $p{\downarrow}$ iff $q{\downarrow}$.

Furthermore, find a counterexample of this proposition in case p or q is not divergence free. Observe that in the third part, we have exactly the requirements of strong bisimulation.

5.4.35 NOTES AND COMMENTS

The notion of branching bisimulation is introduced in VAN GLABBEEK & WEIJLAND [1989]. This work is extended in VAN GLABBEEK [1990], where most of the results of this section occur. In section 5.8, we will compare the branching bisimulation with the weak bisimulation of MILNER [1989] and BERGSTRA & KLOP [1985]. A graph rewriting system for obtaining normal forms is also presented in BERGSTRA & KLOP [1985].

5.5 RECURSION

In 5.4.34.8 we have seen that the equation $x = \tau x$ cannot be guarded. It turns out that for every process p, τp is a solution for this equation. Because of this, we will define the notion of guardedness in such a way, that only atoms can guard variables, and τ cannot. The use of the abstraction operator τ_I may cause even more problems with respect to recursive specifications, as is shown in the following examples. For the moment, we will consider guardedness only in ACP^τ.

5.5.1 EXAMPLES

1. Consider the recursive equation $x = \tau_{\{i\}}(i \cdot x)$. This equation has infinitely many solutions. For instance $x = \tau a$, $x = \tau aa$, etc. $(a \neq i)$.
2. Consider the recursive equation $x = i \cdot \tau_{\{i\}}(x)$. There are infinitely many solutions, for example $x = ia$, $x = iaa$, etc. $(a \neq i)$.
3. Consider the recursive specification $\{x = i \cdot x,\ y = \tau_{\{i\}}(x)\}$. This specification has a unique solution, as will be shown later.

5.5.2 DEFINITION

The definition of **guardedness** of terms and specifications in ACP^τ that are without the abstraction operator, is precisely as in 2.3.4 and 2.3.6, where 'the axioms' in 2.3.6.ii refer to those of ACP^τ. Note that $\tau \notin A$, so τ cannot guard any variables, it is not an atomic action. We do not allow an occurrence of the abstraction operator in a guarded specification.

A process is **constructible** over ACP^τ if it can be obtained from the atomic actions of A by means of the operators from ACP^τ and guarded recursion (see 2.4.6). Thus, in order to define a process, we can apply the abstraction operator to a process given by a guarded specification (but the abstraction operator does not occur *inside* the specification).

We call a process **specifiable** over ACP^τ if there is a guarded recursive specification over ACP^τ that has this process as a solution. We have that the notions of constructibility and specifiability coincide over ACP, but not over ACP^τ, as the following example shows.

5.5.3 EXAMPLE.

The questions arises here, how to construct a process that can do infinitely many τ-steps. As an example, take the process that can only do τ-steps, i.e. τ^ω. The equation $x=\tau x$ does not provide us with a suitable specification, since it is unguarded, and has infinitely many solutions. It turns out that there is no guarded recursive specification (hence without τ_I) which has τ^ω as a solution in all its models, and thus this process is not specifiable. However, τ^ω *is* constructible: first consider $x=i \cdot x$ $(i \in A)$, a guarded recursive equation. This equation has the unique solution i^ω. Next, define $y=\tau_{\{i\}}(i^\omega)$, then y is the process we were looking for. In general, any process which has the possibility of an infinite repetition of τ-steps can be constructed in this way.

5.5.4 CONSTRUCTIBLE PROCESSES.

As in 2.4.7, we can prove that every constructible process has a head normal form. However, the analogue of 2.4.8 does *not* hold: τ^ω is a constructible process, but, consistently with PR1-PR4, one can define every projection of this process as τ^ω, which is not a finite term. We can only obtain the result for specifiable processes. This still gives us the projection theorem (2.4.9) as a corollary.

5.5.5 LEMMA.
All projections of a specifiable process are equal to a closed term.

PROOF: As in 2.4.8, we prove by induction on k that for all specifiable processes p, $\pi_k(p)$ is equal to a closed term. Let p be specifiable. Take a guarded recursive specification E that specifies p. Obtain a head normal form (5.1.6) which is either τ or $\sum_{i<n} a_i \cdot p_i$. Now $\pi_k(\tau) = \tau$, a closed term. So consider $\pi_k(\sum_{i<n} a_i \cdot p_i)$.

First, $k=1$. Applying π_1 gives us a sum of atomic actions plus $\tau \cdot \pi_1(p_i)$ for those i with $a_i \equiv \tau$. Again find a head normal form for these i from E, and repeat this procedure. Since E is guarded, this must stop after a finite number of expansions, and we have obtained a closed term. The induction step works in the same way.

5.5.6 COROLLARY (projection theorem).
Let E be a guarded recursive specification with solutions p and q. Then for all $n \geq 1$ we have $\pi_n(p) = \pi_n(q)$.

Now we will look at the graph model $\mathbb{G}^\infty/\underline{\leftrightarrow}_{rb}$. As in 2.5, we will show that AIP⁻ holds in this model. Combining this result with the projection theorem, we derive RSP as in 2.4.19. To show AIP⁻, we first have to say what we mean by bounded non-determinism in the present setting.

5.5.7 DEFINITIONS.
Analogously to 2.1.7, we define **generalized action relations**. We will have sequences of atomic actions above the double arrow. Any occurring τ-step will be omitted. Let σ be a sequence of symbols from A ($\sigma \in A^*$), then we use the following notations:

- $t \xrightarrow{\sigma}\!\!\!\!\rightarrow s$: t can evolve into s during a period in which (only) the sequence of actions σ is performed;
- $t \xrightarrow{\sigma}\!\!\!\!\rightarrow \surd$: t can terminate after a period in which (only) the sequence of actions σ is performed.

We use the symbol λ for the empty sequence.
The definition of these generalized action relations is easy to write down:

$$t \xrightarrow{a} s \Rightarrow t \xrightarrow{a}\!\!\!\!\rightarrow s$$
$$t \xrightarrow{\tau} s \Rightarrow t \xrightarrow{\lambda}\!\!\!\!\rightarrow s$$
$$t \xrightarrow{\sigma}\!\!\!\!\rightarrow s \text{ and } s \xrightarrow{\rho}\!\!\!\!\rightarrow r \Rightarrow t \xrightarrow{\sigma\rho}\!\!\!\!\rightarrow r$$
$$t \xrightarrow{a} \surd \Rightarrow t \xrightarrow{a}\!\!\!\!\rightarrow \surd$$
$$t \xrightarrow{\tau} \surd \Rightarrow t \xrightarrow{\lambda}\!\!\!\!\rightarrow \surd$$
$$t \xrightarrow{\sigma}\!\!\!\!\rightarrow s \text{ and } s \xrightarrow{\rho}\!\!\!\!\rightarrow \surd \Rightarrow t \xrightarrow{\sigma\rho}\!\!\!\!\rightarrow \surd$$

TABLE 53. Generalized action relations.

A process p (in a certain model) has **bounded non-determinism** if for each sequence of atomic actions σ, the set of processes q with $p \xrightarrow{\sigma}\!\!\!\rightarrow q$ is finite.

This definition depends on a model, however, and since we have a preference for model-independent reasoning, using the axiomatic approach, we will give an axiomatization of this notion. As an auxiliary notion we need **bounded non-determinism up to depth n**: process p has bounded non-determinism up to depth n, $B_n(p)$, iff for each sequence σ of length less than n, $\{q : p \xrightarrow{\sigma}\!\!\!\rightarrow q\}$ is finite. The predicates B_n are axiomatized in table 54.

$B_0(x)$
$B_n(a)$
$B_n(\tau)$
$B_n(x) \Rightarrow B_{n+1}(ax)$
$B_n(x) \Rightarrow B_n(\tau x)$
$B_n(x)$ and $B_n(y) \Rightarrow B_n(x + y)$

TABLE 54. Bounded non-determinism.

Thus, x has bounded non-determinism iff $B_n(x)$ for all $n \geq 1$.

Now let g be a process graph. We say g is **divergence free** if from no node in g, it is possible to do infinitely many consecutive τ-steps. Note that it follows immediately from the definition of bounded non-determinism that if a process graph is finitely branching and divergence free, then it has bounded non-determinism. If we adapt the proof of 2.4.16 along the lines of 5.5.5, then we obtain the following lemma.

5.5.8 LEMMA.
Any specifiable process has bounded non-determinism.

The following lemma is also easy:

5.5.9 LEMMA.
Let E be a guarded recursive specification. Then E has a solution in the graph model which is finitely branching and divergence free.

5.5.10 THEOREM
$\mathbb{G}^\infty/\underline{\leftrightarrow}_{rb} \models AIP^-$.

PROOF: Let g,h be two process graphs such that $\pi_n(g) \underline{\leftrightarrow}_{rb} \pi_n(h)$ for all n and g has bounded non-determinism. The last condition implies that g has only finitely many nodes at depth n, for all n (depth as defined in 5.4.18). This will be an essential property in the proof.

We have to prove that $g \underline{\leftrightarrow}_{rb} h$. Suppose $n \geq 1$, and let s be a node in g with depth n, and t a node in h with depth n. Now define (for $m \geq 0$):

$s \approx_m t \Leftrightarrow$ there is a relation R between the nodes of g and the nodes of h, such that R is a rb-bisimulation up to the depth n+m between g en h, and a branching bisimulation up to depth m between the subgraphs of s and t.

More formally: if $(g)_s$ is the subgraph of s, and $(h)_t$ is the subgraph of t, then:
$s \approx_m t \Leftrightarrow$ there is a relation R such that R: $\pi_{n+m}(g) \underline{\leftrightarrow}_{rb} \pi_{n+m}(h)$ and
R: $\pi_m((g)_s) \underline{\leftrightarrow}_b \pi_m((h)_t)$ (if $m=0$, the last condition is simply equivalent to $R(s,t)$).
Next we define: $s \approx t \Leftrightarrow$ for all $m \geq 0$, $s \approx_m t$ holds.
We claim that $\approx$ is an rb-bisimulation between g and h. The proof of this claim is exactly like in 2.5.8.

5.5.11 THEOREM
RDP holds in the graph model $\mathbb{G}^\infty/\underline{\leftrightarrow}_{rb}$, i.e: every recursive specification has a solution in $\mathbb{G}^\infty/\underline{\leftrightarrow}_{rb}$.

PROOF: From theorem 2.7.34 we know that $\mathbb{G}^\infty/\underline{\leftrightarrow} \models$ RDP. Allow specifications to have labels τ, considered as atomic actions, then every such specification has a solution in $\mathbb{G}^\infty_\tau/\underline{\leftrightarrow}$, the graph model with τ-labels (compare 5.4.21). Now use the same solution in $\mathbb{G}^\infty/\underline{\leftrightarrow}_{rb}$.

5.5.12 THEOREM.
RSP holds in the graph model $\mathbb{G}^\infty/\underline{\leftrightarrow}_{rb}$, i.e: every guarded recursive specification (without τ_I) has at most one solution in the graph model.

PROOF: Combine 5.5.9 and 5.5.10.

We see that $\mathbb{G}^\infty/\underline{\leftrightarrow}_{rb} \models$ AIP$^-$, RDP, RSP. As in 2.5.9 we see $\mathbb{G}^\infty/\underline{\leftrightarrow}_{rb} \not\models$ AIP. Next we look at the other graph models.

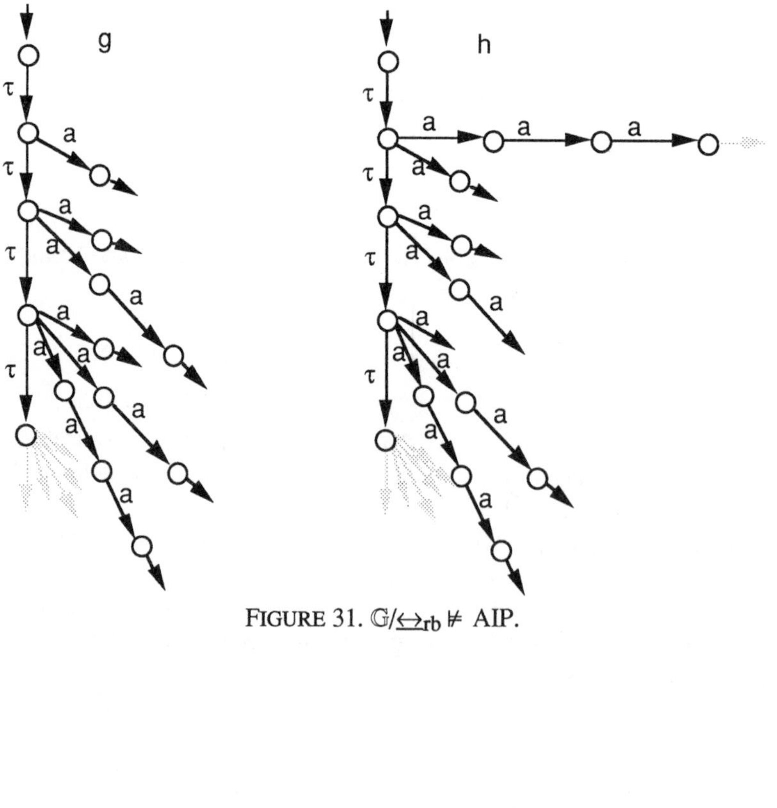

FIGURE 31. $\mathbb{G}/\underline{\leftrightarrow}_{rb} \not\models$ AIP.

5.5.13 THEOREM.

i. $\mathbb{G}/\underline{\leftrightarrow}_{rb} \not\models$ AIP;

ii. $\mathbb{G}/\underline{\leftrightarrow}_{rb} \models$ AIP⁻, RDP⁻, RSP;

iii. $\mathbb{R}/\underline{\leftrightarrow}_{rb} \models$ AIP, RSP;

iv. $\mathbb{F}/\underline{\leftrightarrow}_{rb} \models$ AIP, RSP.

PROOF: Part (i) of this theorem comes somewhat as a surprise. A counterexample is given in fig. 31 above. The remaining parts of the theorem are left to the reader.

5.5.14 EXAMPLE

As an example of a recursive specification that makes use of abstraction in a essential way, we return to the queue of 4.8. The idea behind the following specification is that two queues chained together behave exactly like one single queue, as long as the internal communications are hidden. The idea is illustrated in fig. 32. Here, Q^{ij} stands for the queue with input channel i and output channel j.

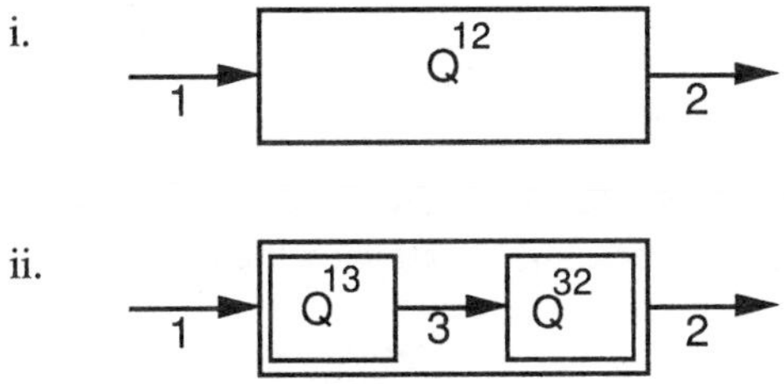

FIGURE 32.

Define $H_3 = \{r_3(d), s_3(d) : d \in D\}$ and $I_3 = \{c_3(d) : d \in D\}$, then table 55 presents a recursive specification of the queue. Note that this is a specification in six variables: Q^{12}, Q^{13}, Q^{32}, Q^{23}, Q^{31} and Q^{21}. The processes Q^{12} and Q^{21} make use of an additional channel 3, Q^{13} and Q^{31} of an extra channel 2, and Q^{23} and Q^{32} of channel 1.

$$Q^{12} = \sum_{d \in D} r_1(d) \cdot \tau_{I_3} \circ \partial_{H_3}(Q^{13} \| s_2(d) \cdot Q^{32})$$

$$Q^{13} = \sum_{d \in D} r_1(d) \cdot \tau_{I_2} \circ \partial_{H_2}(Q^{12} \| s_3(d) \cdot Q^{23})$$

$$Q^{32} = \sum_{d \in D} r_3(d) \cdot \tau_{I_1} \circ \partial_{H_1}(Q^{31} \| s_2(d) \cdot Q^{12})$$

$$Q^{23} = \sum_{d \in D} r_2(d) \cdot \tau_{I_1} \circ \partial_{H_1}(Q^{21} \| s_3(d) \cdot Q^{13})$$

$$Q^{31} = \sum_{d \in D} r_3(d) \cdot \tau_{I_2} \circ \partial_{H_2}(Q^{32} \| s_1(d) \cdot Q^{21})$$

$$Q^{21} = \sum_{d \in D} r_2(d) \cdot \tau_{I_3} \circ \partial_{H_3}(Q^{23} \| s_1(d) \cdot Q^{31})$$

TABLE 55. Queue over D (4th).

Note that this is not a guarded recursive specification. This specification nevertheless has a unique solution in the graph model and its solution is equal to the one from the specifications from 4.8.1, 4.8.3 and 4.8.5.2. The first claim can be proved by showing that the specification from table 55 has a solution with bounded non-determinism. Then it follows from AIP^- that it has a unique solution.

We conclude this section with a result that shows that ACP^τ is a *universal* theory: all computable processes are finitely specifiable in ACP^τ. However, we give no proofs, and assume that the reader is familiar with some notions of recursion theory.

5.5.15 DEFINITION
Let p be a process in one of the models presented in section 5.4. p is said to be **computable** if it is represented by a computable graph (using a certain coding of graphs as natural numbers) or if it is the solution of a computable guarded recursive specification (using a certain coding of ACP^τ-terms as natural numbers). Note that every finite graph and every finite specification determines a computable process.

5.5.16 THEOREM
Let p be a computable process. Then there are a process q and a set $I \subseteq A$, such that q is the solution of a finite guarded recursive specification (without abstraction), and $p = \tau_I(q)$.

5.5.17 REMARK
We see that all computable processes are constructible over ACP^τ. Even more: every partial computable function can be represented by a process, which is the abstraction of a finitely specifiable process. We remark that the equivalent theorem for ACP does not hold: the abstraction operator τ_I in theorem 5.5.16 is essential.

In the presence of ε, the definitions of guardedness is not different from 5.5.2 (except that ACP^τ should be replaced by ACP^τ_ε). All theorems stated in this section hold for ACP^τ_ε as well.

5.5.18 EXERCISES
1. Find out which of the following equations are guarded in ACP^τ: i. $x = \tau | ax$; ii. $x = a | (\tau(x + y) + x)$; iii. $x = a \| b(\tau x + x)$; iv. $x = \tau(\tau x + ax)$; v. $x = \tau \lfloor\!\lfloor x$.
2. Define the relation $\xrightarrow{u}$ as in 2.3.9, and show, that a finite recursive specification E without τ_I is guarded if $\xrightarrow{u}$ is acyclic. Now explain why a guarded recursive specification is divergence free.
3. Prove that the recursive specification $\{x = i \cdot \tau_{\{j\}}(y), y = j \cdot \tau_{\{i\}}(x)\}$ has infinitely many solutions in $\mathbb{G}/\leftrightarrow_{rb}$.
4. Try to define the notion of guardedness for recursive specifications containing τ_I in such a way that every guarded recursive specification has a unique solution. Remember the examples 5.5.1.1-2 and the preceding exercise and consider finite specifications only.
5. Give the proof of 5.5.5 in more detail.
6. Let g be a process graph. Show: if g is finitely branching and divergence free, then g has bounded non-determinism.

7. Prove theorem 5.5.9.
8. Show that the graphs g,h in fig. 31 form a counterexample proving AIP does not hold in $\mathbb{G}^\infty/\underline{\leftrightarrow}_{rb}$.
9. A two-bit buffer with input channel i and output channel j is given by the following equations (see 4.6.1, 4.6.2, 4.6.7.2):

$$B_2^{ij} = \sum_{d\in D} r_i(d)\cdot B_d$$

$$B_d = s_j(d)\cdot B_2^{ij} + \sum_{e\in D} r_i(e)\cdot s_j(d)\cdot B_e.$$

Assuming B^{12} and B^{23} are two one-bit buffers (see 4.6.1), that is:

$$B^{12} = \sum_{d\in D} r_1(d)\cdot s_2(d)\cdot B^{12}$$

$$B^{23} = \sum_{d\in D} r_2(d)\cdot s_3(d)\cdot B^{23},$$

prove that

$$B_2^{13} = \tau_I\circ\partial_H(B^{12}\,\|\,B^{23})$$

(H as in 4.6.1, $I = \{c_2(d): d\in D\}$).
10. Take S, R, H from 4.6.7.3. Define $I = \{c_2(x) : x\in D \text{ or } x\equiv ack\}$ and prove that we have $\tau_I\circ\partial_H(S\,\|\,R) = B^{13}$. This is why we can call this a *correct* communication protocol.

5.5.19 NOTES AND COMMENTS
The main reference for this section is BAETEN, BERGSTRA & KLOP [1987b]. The treatment of bounded non-determinism is from VAN GLABBEEK [1987]. The specification of the queue in 5.5.14 comes from BERGSTRA & KLOP [1986c].

5.6 DIVERGENCE AND FAIRNESS

In this section we will focus on two important issues in process semantics: the issues of divergence and fairness.

5.6.1 EXAMPLE
Suppose a statistician carries out an experiment: he tosses a coin until head comes up. We assume that the probability of tossing heads is between 0 and 1 (so, not equal to 0 or to 1). The process can be described by the following equation:

$$S = toss\cdot tail\cdot S + toss\cdot head.$$

Furthermore, assume this experiment is carried out in a closed room. Standing outside, we cannot observe anything occurring, except if head comes up we can hear the statistician yell: "Head!". So, actions from $I = \{toss, tail\}$ are hidden from us, and we observe the process $\tau_I(S)$. Because the coin is *fair*, after a number of tails (≥0), head will come up. So, our intuition tells us

$$\tau_I(S) = \tau\cdot head$$

saying that after some internal τ-moves we will see head appear. In this section we will present an algebraic rule, to derive this equation formally. In fig. 33 this example is translated into the graph model. As we can see, the definition of rb-bisimulation indeed gives us τ·head.

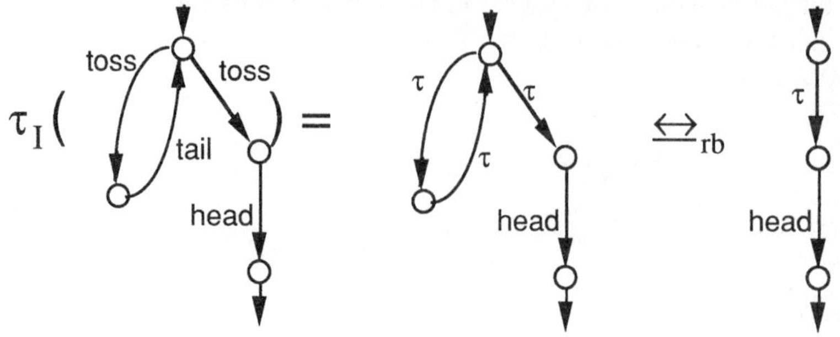

FIGURE 33.

5.6.2 DELAY

Next, we want to consider these matters in a more general, algebraic setting. We see in fig. 33 that the possibility of infinitely many τ-moves is discarded, so the possibility of divergence is discarded.

A very simple process that displays divergence is shown in fig. 34.

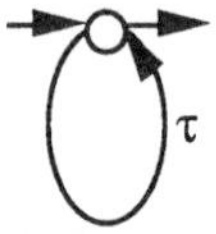

FIGURE 34. Delay.

We call this process **delay** and use the symbol Δ. The process Δ cannot be specified using the equation $X = \tau X + \varepsilon$, since this equation is unguarded. However, defining the process X by $X = iX + \varepsilon$ ($i \in A$), the process can be represented by $\tau_{\{i\}}(X)$. Thus we can define delay as shown in table 56.

$$\frac{X = iX + \varepsilon \quad (i \in A)}{\tau_{\{i\}}(X) = \Delta}$$

TABLE 56. Delay.

As an immediate consequence of this definition we find the following identity:

$$\Delta = \tau{\cdot}\Delta + \varepsilon.$$

In the graph model, this identity corresponds to the root-unwinding of the graph in fig. 34.

5.6.3 BISIMULATION WITH EXPLICIT DIVERGENCE

We can find a model for ACP^{τ}, where divergence is taken into account, by adding to the definition of branching bisimulation on process graphs. We start from the characterization of branching bisimulation given in 5.4.10 in terms of abstract coloured traces.

We call a node in a coloured graph **colour-divergent** if it is the starting point of an infinite path of which all nodes have the same colour. A colouring **preserves colour-divergence** if no colour-divergent node has the same colour as a node that is not colour-divergent.

Now we call two graphs **(rooted) branching bisimilar with explicit divergence**, notation $\underline{\leftrightarrow}_{(r)b\Delta}$, if there exists a (rooted) abstract trace consistent colouring that preserves colour-divergence and for which the root nodes have the same abstract coloured traces.

Note that the extra condition in this definition (as compared to 5.4.10) only makes a difference for nodes that are the starting point of an infinite τ-trace. In other words, we have the following lemma.

5.6.4 LEMMA

Let g,h be two divergence free process graphs. Then $g \underline{\leftrightarrow}_{rb\Delta} h$ iff $g \underline{\leftrightarrow}_{rb} h$.

PROOF: Left for the exercises.

We omit the proof that $\underline{\leftrightarrow}_{rb\Delta}$ is a congruence on the graph domain, and that $\mathbb{G}^{\infty}/\underline{\leftrightarrow}_{rb\Delta}$ is a model of ACP^{τ}. In this model, the delay graph of fig. 34 cannot be simplified any further.

5.6.5 DELAY RULE

Having introduced the additional constant Δ, we have some new axioms. Some of these axioms can be formulated in the so-called **Delay Rule**. The simplest case of this rule occurs when we have an internal loop of length 1. This case is shown in table 57.

$\dfrac{x = ix + y \quad (i \in I)}{\tau_I(x) = \Delta \cdot \tau_I(y)}$	DE_1

TABLE 57. Delay Rule, $n=1$.

More generally, we can formulate a delay rule when we have a cycle of internal steps of length $n \geq 1$.

$x_1 = i_1 \cdot x_2 + y_1$ $x_2 = i_2 \cdot x_3 + y_2$ .... $x_n = i_n \cdot x_1 + y_n$ $\dfrac{i_1, i_2, \ldots, i_n \in I \cup \{\tau\}, \text{ but not all } i_k \equiv \tau}{\tau \cdot \tau_I(x_1) = \tau \cdot \Delta(\tau_I(y_1) + \tau_I(y_2) + \ldots + \tau_I(y_n))}$	DE_n

TABLE 58. Delay Rule, $n \geq 1$, $I \subseteq A$.

Notice that some of the i_k may be equal to τ, but not all of them, since that would make the specification of the x_k unguarded. If we take $n=1$ in table 58, we can recover the rule in table 57 by using the identity in 5.6.2.

5.6.6 CHAOS

Starting from the model in the previous section, there are several ways to proceed. An extreme stand-point is that as soon as divergent behaviour is possible, nothing can be said about the process, no observation is possible. This means that delay is identified with the wholly arbitrary process, called **chaos.** This situation is characterized by the following identity.

$\Delta\delta = \Delta$

TABLE 59. Catastrophic divergence.

With this identity, we can prove the following statements.

5.6.7 LEMMA
i. $\Delta = \varepsilon + \Delta\delta$
ii. $\Delta x = \Delta$
iii. $\Delta + x = \Delta$.

PROOF: i. $\Delta = \varepsilon + \tau\Delta = \varepsilon + \varepsilon + \tau\Delta = \varepsilon + \Delta = \varepsilon + \Delta\delta$;
ii and iii. $\Delta + x = \Delta\delta + x = (\Delta\delta + \varepsilon)\cdot x = \Delta x = \Delta\delta x = \Delta\delta = \Delta$.

The last two parts of this lemma characterize Δ as chaos, that makes any determination of the subsequent or alternative process behaviour impossible.

5.6.8 FAIR ABSTRACTION
In cases as in example 5.6.1, the catastrophic treatment of divergence of 5.6.6 is not satisfactory. Instead, we prefer to abstract away divergence as is done in the graph model $\mathbb{G}^\infty/\underline{\leftrightarrow}_{rb}$. In this case, we have the assumption that the every τ-loop will be exited sooner or later. The fairness principle indicates that the choice in the root of the graph in fig. 33 is **fair,** saying that in the presence of alternative options it is impossible to choose the internal step τ infinitely many times. So, after running through the loop a number of times, the process will terminate.

We can characterize this situation by the following identity.

$\tau\Delta = \tau$

TABLE 60. Fairness principle.

It is simple to see, that this identity holds in the graph model $\mathbb{G}^\infty/\underline{\leftrightarrow}_{rb}$. With this identity, we can prove the following statements.

5.6.9 LEMMA
i. $\Delta = \tau + \varepsilon$
ii. $\Delta\delta = \tau\delta$

PROOF: i. $\Delta = \tau\Delta + \varepsilon = \tau + \varepsilon$; ii. $\Delta\delta = (\tau + \varepsilon)\cdot\delta = \tau\delta + \delta = \tau\delta$.

The last part of this lemma can be phrased as: *deadlock* = *livelock*. We see $\Delta\delta$ is the process that can only do internal moves, and never terminates, so this process can be called **livelock,** and $\tau\delta$ can be called **deadlock** (the process δ is not really deadlock, because it vanishes in a sum context; it would be better to call δ *lock* or *inaction*; we do not do so for historic reasons).

5.6.10 KOOMEN'S FAIR ABSTRACTION RULE

The Delay Rules of 5.6.3 can be rephrased in this setting, as follows.

$$\frac{x = ix + y \quad (i \in I)}{\tau \cdot \tau_I(x) = \tau \cdot \tau_I(y)} \qquad \text{KFAR}_1^b$$

TABLE 61. KFAR_1^b.

$$\begin{array}{l} x_1 = i_1 \cdot x_2 + y_1 \\ x_2 = i_2 \cdot x_3 + y_2 \\ \dots\dots \\ x_n = i_n \cdot x_1 + y_n \\ \underline{\quad i_1, i_2, \dots, i_n \in I \cup \{\tau\}, \text{ but not all } i_k \equiv \tau \quad} \\ \tau \cdot \tau_I(x_1) = \tau \cdot (\tau_I(y_1) + \tau_I(y_2) + \dots + \tau_I(y_n)) \end{array} \qquad \text{KFAR}_n^b$$

TABLE 62. KFAR_n^b, $n \geq 1$, $I \subseteq A$.

In this setting the delay rule is called **Koomen's Fair Abstraction Rule**, abbreviated as $\text{KFAR}^b = \cup_{n\geq 1} \text{KFAR}_n^b$. The b in this name indicates that we have here the formulation that holds in case of branching bisimulation. The original formulation only works in the case of weak bisimulation. KFAR^b says, in abstracting from a set of internal actions, eventually (i.e. after performing a number of τ-steps) an external step will be chosen. We will use KFAR^b in the next section, to verify the Alternating Bit Protocol of section 4.7. From the preceding remarks it follows directly that KFAR^b holds in the graph model.

Now let us apply KFAR^b in the example 5.6.1.

5.6.11 EXAMPLE

We rewrite the definition of S from 5.6.1 in the correct format.

$$\frac{\begin{array}{ll} S = toss \cdot S' + toss \cdot head & \\ S' = tail \cdot S + \delta & I = \{toss, tail\} \end{array}}{\tau \cdot \tau_I(S) = \tau \cdot (\tau_I(toss \cdot head) + \tau_I(\delta)) = \tau \cdot head.}$$

and so: $\tau_I(S) = \tau_I(toss \cdot S' + toss \cdot head) = \tau \cdot \tau_I(S') + \tau \cdot head$ and $\tau \cdot \tau_I(S') = \tau \cdot \tau \cdot \tau_I(S') =$ $= \tau \cdot \tau_I(toss \cdot S') = \tau \cdot \tau_I(S) = \tau \cdot head$, so $\tau_I(S) = \tau \cdot head + \tau \cdot head = \tau \cdot head$ and the desired result is obtained.

5.6.12 THEOREM

KFAR_{n+1}^b is independent from KFAR_n^b. That is, for all n one can construct a model in which KFAR_n^b holds, whereas KFAR_{n+1}^b does not.

PROOF: see exercises.

5.6.13 EXAMPLE

The statistician of example 5.6.1 throws a die until six comes up. We have the process

$$S^* = \text{throw}\cdot\text{one}\cdot S^* + \text{throw}\cdot\text{two}\cdot S^* + \text{throw}\cdot\text{three}\cdot S^* + \\ + \text{throw}\cdot\text{four}\cdot S^* + \text{throw}\cdot\text{five}\cdot S^* + \text{six}.$$

Again, this experiment is carried out in a room, and the observer outside can only hear the yell "Six!". Abstracting from actions I = {throw, one, two, three, four, five}, we want to prove

$$\tau_I(S^*) = \tau\cdot\text{six}.$$

This cannot be done with $KFAR^b$ of 5.6.10 however, since here we are dealing with a more complicated structure. Therefore, it is useful to have a version of $KFAR^b$ that is applicable to arbitrary **clusters** of internal steps. In the following we will present the definition of a cluster, and formulate the Cluster Fair Abstraction Rule $CFAR^b$. It turns out that $CFAR^b$ can be derived from $KFAR^b$ and the other axioms.

5.6.14 DEFINITION

Let $E = \{X = t_X \mid X \in V\}$ be a recursive specification, and let $I \subseteq A$ (the set of actions we want to abstract from). A subset C of the variable set V is called a **cluster of I in E** if the root variable of E is in C and if the following condition holds:

for all $X \in C$ there exist $i_1, ..., i_m \in I \cup \{\tau\}$, $X_1, ..., X_m \in C$, and $Y_1, ..., Y_n \in V\text{-}C$ ($m \geq 1$, $n \geq 0$) such that the equation for X in E is of the form:

$$X = \sum_{1 \leq k \leq m} i_k \cdot X_k + \sum_{1 \leq j \leq n} Y_j .$$

The variables Y_j in this equation are called the **exits** of X, and we write: $U(X) = \{Y_1, ..., Y_n\}$ and $U = \cup_{X \in V} U(X)$ for the exit set of the cluster. Now, the cluster is called **conservative** if every exit $Y \in U$ is accessible from every variable in the cluster (by doing a number of steps from $I \cup \{\tau\}$ in the cluster to a cluster-variable which has exit Y).

5.6.15 DEFINITION

The **Cluster Fair Abstraction Rule $CFAR^b$** is the following rule:

$$\frac{\begin{array}{l} X \text{ the root variable of } E,\ E \text{ guarded},\ I \subseteq A \\ C \text{ a finite conservative cluster of } I \text{ in } E \\ U \text{ the set of exits from the cluster } C \end{array}}{\tau\cdot\tau_I(X) = \tau\cdot\sum_{Y \in U} \tau_I(Y)} \quad CFAR^b$$

TABLE 63. $CFAR^b$.

5.6.16 EXAMPLE

Consider the process S^* of 5.6.13. S^* can be defined by the following guarded recursive specification:

$$\begin{aligned} S^* &= \text{throw}\cdot X_1 + \text{throw}\cdot X_2 + \text{throw}\cdot X_3 + \text{throw}\cdot X_4 + \\ &\quad\ \text{throw}\cdot X_5 + \text{throw}\cdot X_6 + \delta \\ X_1 &= \text{one}\cdot S^* \\ X_2 &= \text{two}\cdot S^* \\ X_3 &= \text{three}\cdot S^* \end{aligned}$$

$X_4 = four \cdot S^*$
$X_5 = five \cdot S^*$
$X_6 = six.$

Then $\{S^*, X_1, ..., X_5\}$ is a finite, conservative cluster of I, so by $CFAR^b$:
$\tau \cdot \tau_I(S^*) = \tau \cdot six$. As before, one can use this result to prove $\tau_I(S^*) = \tau \cdot six$, as desired.

5.6.17 THEOREM
$CFAR^b$ can be derived from BPA_δ^τ, $KFAR^b$, RDP, RSP, RN0-3, RR1,2.

PROOF: Omitted. The axioms RN0-3, RR1,2 are the renaming axioms from 3.6.1.

5.6.18 REGULAR PROCESSES
Using $CFAR^b$ we can prove lemma 2.8.5 for regular processes, in the theory with τ as well. We will use the same definitions as in 2.8. Note that a linear specification now has equations which are either of the form

$$x = \tau$$

or of the form

$$x = \sum_{1 \leq i \leq n} a_i x_i \quad (a_i \in A \cup \{\tau\}).$$

Thus, a linear specification is not necessarily guarded in this setting. We remark that the equation $x = \delta$ is an instance of the second equation with $n=0$.

5.6.19 THEOREM
Let p be a process. For simplicity's sake, we assume we are dealing with one of the models given in section 5.4: the term model or one of the graph models of BPA_δ^τ. Then the following are equivalent:

1. the action graph (see 2.1.11) of p is finite (i.e: $G(p) \in \mathbb{R}$);
2. p is the solution of a finite guarded linear recursive specification.

PROOF: 1 $\Rightarrow$ 2: Suppose $g \in \mathbb{R}$, and replace all τ-labels in g by i-labels (i an atomic action not occurring in g), and find the finite guarded linear specification constructed in 2.8.3. Consider all clusters of $\{i\}$ in this specification, and apply $CFAR^b$. The result is a finite guarded linear specification, which has the graph g as a solution.
2 $\Rightarrow$ 1: easy and left to the reader.

Again, a process which has the properties from 5.6.19 will be called a **regular process.**

5.6.20 EXAMPLE
Let g be the graph on the left-hand side of fig. 35.

Replacing the τ-labels in g by i-labels, we obtain the linear specification $\{x_1 = i \cdot x_2 + a \cdot x_3, x_2 = i \cdot x_1 + i \cdot x_4, x_3 = a \cdot x_5, x_4 = b \cdot x_5, x_5 = \tau \cdot x_5\}$. Now $\{x_1, x_2\}$ and $\{x_5\}$ are clusters of $\{i\}$, and applying $CFAR^b$ (in fact, once $KFAR_2^b$ and once $KFAR_1^b$) we obtain the guarded specification (writing $y_k = \tau_{\{i\}}(x_k)$ for $k=1,2,3,4,5$) $\{y_1 = a \cdot y_3 + \tau \cdot (a \cdot y_3 + \tau \cdot y_4), y_3 = a \cdot y_5,$

$y_4 = b \cdot y_5$, $y_5 = \tau \cdot \delta\}$. This specification can easily be rewritten into a guarded linear specification, with the right-hand graph in fig. 35 as its canonical graph.

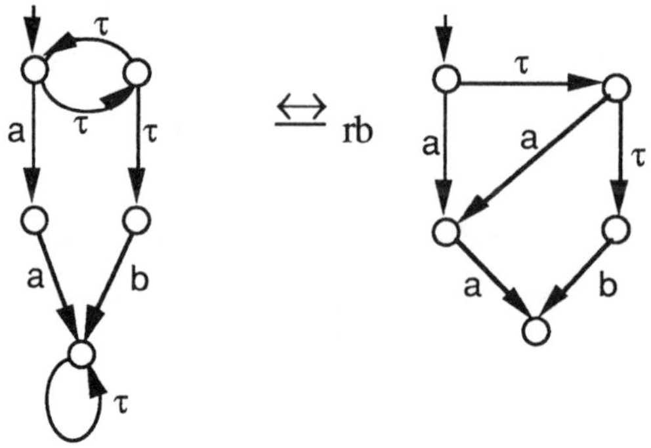

FIGURE 35.

5.6.21 EXERCISES

1. Prove from the definition in table 56 that $\Delta = \tau\Delta + \varepsilon$.
2. Prove lemma 5.6.4.
3. Let g,h be two process graphs. Prove that $g \underline{\leftrightarrow}_{b\Delta} h$ iff there is a branching bisimulation R: $g \underline{\leftrightarrow}_b h$ such that the following extra conditions hold:

- if $R(s,t)$ and $s \xrightarrow{\tau} s_1 \xrightarrow{\tau} s_2 \xrightarrow{\tau} \ldots$ is an infinite τ-path in g starting from s, then there is an infinite τ-path in h that can be presented as $t \Rightarrow t_1 \Rightarrow t_2 \Rightarrow \ldots$ with $R(s_i,t_i)$ for all i.
- vice versa.

4. Consider the graphs in fig. 36. Show that they are branching bisimilar, by a bisimulation relating divergent nodes to divergent nodes only, but that the graphs are nevertheless not branching bisimilar with explicit divergence.

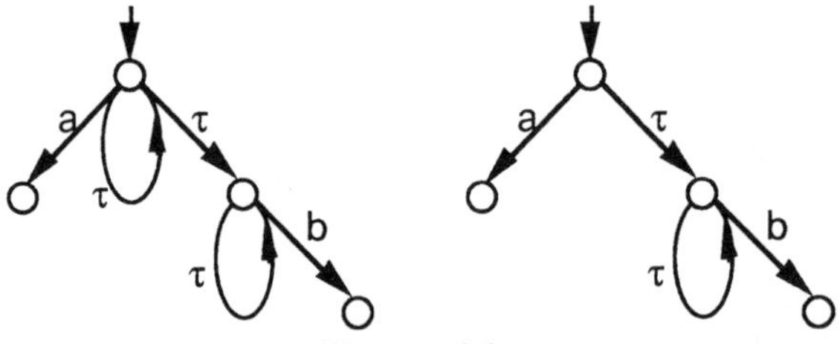

FIGURE 36.

5. Verify that $\underline{\leftrightarrow}_{rb\Delta}$ is a congruence on $\mathbb{G}^\infty$, and that $\mathbb{G}^\infty / \underline{\leftrightarrow}_{rb\Delta}$ is a model of ACP^τ.
6. Show that the equation $\Delta \cdot \Delta = \Delta$ holds in the model $\mathbb{G}^\infty / \underline{\leftrightarrow}_{rb\Delta}$.
7. Give the Delay Rule in the case $n=2$. Also in the case $n=3$.
8. Prove in the theory with catastrophic divergence that $\Delta(x + y) = \Delta x + \Delta y$.
9. Motivate why the equation $\Delta = \varepsilon + \Delta\delta$ can be called *divergence = livelock*.
10. Show that, equivalently, the conclusion of the rule DE_n from table 58 can be formulated as:

$$\tau_I(x_1) = \tau_I(y_1) + \tau \cdot \Delta(\tau_I(y_1) + \tau_I(y_2) + \ldots + \tau_I(y_n))$$

and similarly that the conclusion of the rule $KFAR_n^b$ in table 62 can be rephrased as:

$$\tau_I(x_1) = \tau_I(y_1) + \tau \cdot (\tau_I(y_1) + \tau_I(y_2) + \ldots + \tau_I(y_n)).$$

Prove that DE_1 is derivable from DE_n.

11. A weaker version of the fairness principle is the equation $\Delta \cdot \tau = \tau$ (*abstraction of unstable divergence*). Show that this equation follows from the fairness principle. Using this fairness principle, we can formulate the delay rule of table 57 as follows:

$$\frac{x = ix + jy \quad (i \in I,\ j \in I \cup \{\tau\})}{\tau_I(x) = \tau \cdot \tau_I(y)} \qquad KFAR_1^-.$$

$KFAR^-$ is a weaker version of $KFAR^b$. Formulate $KFAR_2^-$, and use it to verify example 5.6.1.

12. Suppose someone starts a random walk in the lower left-hand corner of the 3×3 grid in figure 37. When arriving in the upper right-hand corner, he stops walking. The resulting process P has atomic actions begin, north, west, south, east, end.

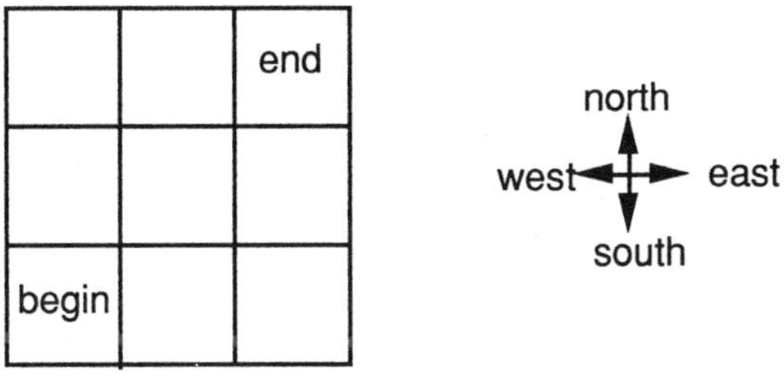

FIGURE 37.

i. Give a recursive specification for P.

ii. Let I = {north, west, south, east}. Calculate $\tau_I(P)$ using $CFAR^b$. Does this result meet with your intuition?

13. Show that, if the processes $y_1, \ldots, y_n$ can be given by a guarded recursive specification, the rules $KFAR_n^b$ are special cases of the rule $CFAR^b$.

14. Prove theorem 5.6.12 by constructing a graph model in which the axioms of BPA_δ^τ and $KFAR_n^b$ hold but $KFAR_{n+1}^b$ does not, thus proving that $KFAR_{n+1}^b$ cannot be derived from $BPA_\delta^\tau + KFAR_n^b$. Use the following definition:

DEFINITION:

1. The set $In_k(s) \subseteq A$ of **k-initial labels** of a node s is defined by:
   $a \in In_k(s)$ iff there is a path $s \Rightarrow s' \xrightarrow{a} s''$ of length $\leq k$.

Intuitively $In_k(s)$ is the set of labels ($\neq\tau$) corresponding to the initial edges from s, provided that the first k-1 τ-edges are 'transparent'.

2. A relation between graphs g and h is called **k-bisimulation**, notation $g \underline{\leftrightarrow}_k h$, if it is a rooted branching bisimulation (see 5.4.4) such that:
if $s \xrightarrow{a} s'$ is an edge in g ($a \in A \cup \{\tau\}$) and R(s,t), then either $a=\tau$ and R(s',t),
or there exists a path $t \Rightarrow t' \xrightarrow{a} t''$ in h, such that R(s,t'), R(s',t") and $In_1(s) \subseteq In_k(t')$;
and vice versa with the roles of g and h interchanged.

So, a k-bisimulation has the extra requirement that the 1-initial labels of the starting node (=s) can all be seen as k-initial labels from the intermediate nodes (such as t'). Now prove that:

i. $\underline{\leftrightarrow}_1$ is a congruence on $\mathbb{G}^\infty$ with respect to + and ·.

ii. $\mathbb{G}^\infty/\underline{\leftrightarrow}_1 \models$ A1-A7 + B1 + B2 (i.e. BPA_δ^τ).

iii. $\mathbb{G}^\infty/\underline{\leftrightarrow}_1 \models \mathrm{KFAR}_1^b$.
iv. Consider the guarded recursive specification $E = \{X = \tau\cdot(a + i\cdot Y),\ Y = b + i\cdot X\}$ with root variable X. Then from E and KFAR_2^b one can derive that $\tau_{\{i\}}(X) = \tau(a + b)$.
v. Draw the graph g_E that is the solution of E, and show that *not* $g_E \underline{\leftrightarrow}_1 \tau(a + b)$, and thus conclude that KFAR_2^b is independent from KFAR_1^b.
vi. Generalize this construction to prove that KFAR_{n+1}^b and KFAR_n^b are independent.

5.6.20 NOTES AND COMMENTS
The material on divergence is based on BERGSTRA, KLOP & OLDEROG [1987], together with unpublished research by Rob van Glabbeek. Definition 5.6.4 is from VAN GLABBEEK [1990]. The idea of the constant chaos is from BROOKES, HOARE & ROSCOE [1984]. Koomen's Fair Abstraction Rule KFAR was first applied by C.J. Koomen in a formula manipulation package based on CCS (see KOOMEN [1985]), and first formulated as a conditional equation in BERGSTRA & KLOP [1986a]. There, the rules KFAR_n are formulated in the setting of weak bisimulation semantics. In the present setting of branching bisimulation semantics, we need to reformulate the KFAR_n rules slightly as KFAR_n^b (just as in BAETEN & VAN GLABBEEK [1987a], where the rule was called HAR). Adding the extra τ-laws easily gives back the original formulation, so KFAR_n^b can be considered a generalization of KFAR_n. We have the same relation between the rule CFAR (first formulated in VAANDRAGER [1986]) and the present CFAR^b. More about fairness in general can be found in FRANCEZ [1986] or PARROW [1985]. For divergence in the setting of CCS, see WALKER [1990] or ACETO & HENNESSY [1989].

The proof of 5.6.17 is from unpublished work of Frits Vaandrager, but similar to a proof in VAANDRAGER [1986]. Vaandrager also suggested exercise 5.6.21.4. Exercise 5.6.21.11 is based on BERGSTRA, KLOP & OLDEROG [1987]. The proof of theorem 5.6.12, as presented in exercise 5.6.21.14, is from unpublished work of Rob van Glabbeek and Jan Friso Groote.

5.7 ALTERNATING BIT PROTOCOL (VERIFICATION)

Let us again consider the alternating bit protocol from section 4.7. In 4.7.6 we already mentioned the introduction of the abstraction operator. Having done so, we will take a closer look at its application in this particular case.

5.7.1 THEOREM
Let S,K,L,R as defined in 4.7.3, H as in 4.7.4 and I as defined in 4.7.6. Then we have:

$$\tau_I\circ\partial_H(S \| K \| L \| R) = B^{14},$$

i.e. the Alternating Bit Protocol is a *correct* communication protocol.

PROOF: We have to prove that

$$\tau_I\circ\partial_H(S \| K \| L \| R) = \Big(\sum_{d\in D} r_1(d)\cdot s_4(d)\cdot\tau_I\circ\partial_H(S \| K \| L \| R)\Big).$$

The proof is easier to follow if we use fig. 22 in 4.7.4, although the proof itself is purely algebraic and independent of fig. 22 or any model. We will use the shorthand notations X, $X1_d$, $X2_d$, Y, $Y1_d$, $Y2_d$ as in 4.7.4. We start with a cluster around $X1$. We have the following guarded recursive specification:

$$X1_d = c_2(d0)\cdot Z_1$$
$$Z_1 = i\cdot Z_2 + i\cdot c_3(d0)\cdot s_4(d)\cdot X2_d$$
$$Z_2 = c_3(\bot)\cdot Z_3$$
$$Z_3 = c_5(1)\cdot Z_4$$
$$Z_4 = i\cdot Z_5 + i\cdot Z_6$$
$$Z_5 = c_6(1)\cdot X1_d$$
$$Z_6 = c_6(\bot)\cdot X1_d,$$

for certain processes $Z_1, ..., Z_6$. Then $\{X1_d, Z_1, Z_2, Z_3, Z_4, Z_5, Z_6\}$ is a conservative cluster of I, and from CFAR^b we find:

$$\tau_I(X1_d) = \tau\cdot\tau_I(i\cdot c_3(d0)\cdot s_4(d)\cdot X2_d) = \tau\cdot s_4(d)\cdot\tau_I(X2_d).$$

So the first cluster has disappeared. We follow the same procedure for the cluster around X2. We have the following guarded recursive specification:

$$X2_d = c_5(0)\cdot Z_1$$
$$Z_1 = i\cdot Z_2 + i\cdot c_6(0)\cdot Y$$
$$Z_2 = c_6(\bot)\cdot Z_3$$
$$Z_3 = c_2(d0)\cdot Z_4$$
$$Z_4 = i\cdot Z_5 + i\cdot Z_6$$
$$Z_5 = c_3(d0)\cdot X2_d$$
$$Z_6 = c_3(\bot)\cdot X2_d,$$

for certain processes $Z_1,...,Z_6$. Again, $\{X2_d, Z_1, Z_2, Z_3, Z_4, Z_5, Z_6\}$ is a conservative cluster of I, thus using CFAR^b we have $\tau_I(X2_d) = \tau\cdot\tau_I(i\cdot c_6(0)\cdot Y) = \tau\cdot\tau_I(Y)$.

Combining the results we find

$$\tau_I(X) = \sum_{d\in D} r_1(d)\cdot\tau_I(X1_d) = \sum_{d\in D} r_1(d)\cdot\tau\cdot s_4(d)\cdot\tau_I(X2_d) = \sum_{d\in D} r_1(d)\cdot s_4(d)\cdot\tau_I(Y).$$

In the same way one can derive $\tau_I(Y) = \sum_{d\in D} r_1(d)\cdot s_4(d)\cdot\tau_I(X)$.

Now consider the guarded recursive specification

$$X_1 = r_1(d)\cdot s_4(d)\cdot X_2$$
$$X_2 = r_1(d)\cdot s_4(d)\cdot X_1.$$

Then $X_1 = \tau_I(X)$, $X_2 = \tau_I(Y)$ is a solution of this specification, but also $X_1 = \tau_I(Y)$, $X_2 = \tau_I(X)$ is a solution. By RSP the solutions are equal, and so $\tau_I(X) = \tau_I(Y)$.

5.7.2 REMARK

The use of CFAR^b in the verification of the Alternating Bit Protocol means in fact that the choice made by the channels is fair. Doing this, we exclude the possibility that any of the channels is completely defective, i.e: that any of the messages is corrupted infinitely many times in a row. After a number of failing attempts, the message must be transmitted correctly.

5.7.3 EXERCISES

1. Let S, K, R be defined as in exercise 4.7.7.1, and define:

$$I = \{c2(x), c3(x) : x\in D\cup\{ack\}\}\cup\{i\}.$$

Now, derive a recursive equation for the process $\tau_I\circ\partial_H(S\,\|\,K\,\|\,R)$. Is this communication protocol correct?

2. Show the correctness of the Alternating Bit Protocol without using the *Cluster* Fair Abstraction Rule, as follows: first rename all internal steps into i, i.e. consider $i_I \circ \delta_H(S \| K \| L \| R)$, and then apply $KFAR_6^b$.

5.7.4 NOTES AND COMMENTS

The verification presented in this section is from BERGSTRA & KLOP [1986a]. Also see BERGSTRA & KLOP [1986c].

5.8 OBSERVATION EQUIVALENCE

The notion of branching bisimulation and its axioms, forms a recent approach to the feature of abstraction in process algebra. The usual approach in ACP, as in many other theories, is that of *observation equivalence* or *τ-bisimulation.* As we will see, a slight change in the definition of branching bisimulation has important consequences for the theory of ACP with τ.

In this section, we work in the theory without constant ε (but with δ). We start off by considering the term model.

5.8.1 DEFINITION

A **τ-bisimulation** is a binary relation R on $\mathbb{P}_\delta$, such that ($a \in A \cup \{\tau\}$):

i. if $p \xrightarrow{a} p'$ and $R(p,q)$ then either $a=\tau$ and $R(p',q)$ or there are v_1, v_2 and q' such that $q \Rightarrow v_1 \xrightarrow{a} v_2 \Rightarrow q'$ and $R(p',q')$;

ii. if $q \xrightarrow{a} q'$ and $R(p,q)$ then either $a=\tau$ and $R(p,q')$ or there are v_1, v_2 and p' such that $p \Rightarrow v_1 \xrightarrow{a} v_2 \Rightarrow p'$ and $R(p',q')$;

iii. if $p \xrightarrow{a} \surd$ and $R(p,q)$ then either $a=\tau$ and $q \Rightarrow \surd$ or there are v_1, v_2 such that $q \Rightarrow v_1 \xrightarrow{a} v_2 \Rightarrow \surd$;

iv. if $q \xrightarrow{a} \surd$ and $R(p,q)$ then either $a=\tau$ and $p \Rightarrow \surd$ or there are v_1, v_2 such that $p \Rightarrow v_1 \xrightarrow{a} v_2 \Rightarrow \surd$.

We write $R: p \underline{\leftrightarrow}_\tau q$, if R is a τ-bisimulation with $R(p,q)$, and just $p \underline{\leftrightarrow}_\tau q$ in order to express that such a τ-bisimulation exists. Processes p and q are **rooted τ-bisimilar**, notation $p \underline{\leftrightarrow}_{r\tau} q$, if there is a τ-bisimulation R that satisfies the following **root condition**:

i. if $p \xrightarrow{\tau} p'$ then for some q',v we have $q \xrightarrow{\tau} v \Rightarrow q'$ and $R(p',q')$;

ii. vice versa, with p and q interchanged.

5.8.2 COMPARISON

Comparing this definition carefully with definition 5.4.31 of branching bisimulation, we find that in all conditions some requirements are omitted. The important difference is that in a corresponding path $q \Rightarrow v_1 \xrightarrow{a} v_2 \Rightarrow q'$ the nodes v_1 and v_2 are no longer required to be related to p and p' respectively (compare to exercise 5.4.34.11). As a consequence, the intermediate nodes in $q \Rightarrow v_1$ may be of a different nature than q, i.e. the intermediate nodes may have different colours.

Now let us consider the theory BPA_δ together with the extra constant τ. Then we obtain:

5.8.3 THEOREM

i. $\underline{\leftrightarrow}_\tau$ is an equivalence on terms from BPA_δ;

ii. $\underline{\leftrightarrow}_{r\tau}$ is a congruence on terms from BPA_δ, with respect to its operators.

The proof of theorem 5.8.3 is straightforward, and omitted here.

From various viewpoints, the definition of τ-bisimulation is very appealing. As an example, let us present the definition of τ-bisimulation again, this time in different notation.

5.8.4 DEFINITION

Let $p,q \in \mathbb{P}_\delta$. In 2.1.7 and 2.3.11 we already defined action relations on $\mathbb{P}_\delta$.

Then, a **generalized a-step** ($a \in A$) from p to q, notation $p \overset{a}{\Rightarrow} q$, is a sequence of the form $p \Rightarrow v_1 \overset{a}{\rightarrow} v_2 \Rightarrow q$. Such generalized steps immediately abstract from all internal steps τ by assuming them to be part of the performance of a.

Similarly, a **generalized termination step** through a, notation $p \overset{a}{\Rightarrow} \surd$, is a sequence $p \Rightarrow v_1 \overset{a}{\rightarrow} v_2 \Rightarrow \surd$.

We will often write $\overset{\tau}{\Rightarrow}$ instead of $\Rightarrow$ (i.e. zero or more τ-steps).

5.8.5 THEOREM

Equivalently, the conditions of τ-bisimulation in definition 5.8.1 can be phrased as follows ($a \in A \cup \{\tau\}$):

i. if $p \overset{a}{\Rightarrow} p'$ and $R(p,q)$ then there is a q' with $q \overset{a}{\Rightarrow} q'$ and $R(p',q')$;

ii. if $q \overset{a}{\Rightarrow} q'$ and $R(p,q)$ then there is a p' with $p \overset{a}{\Rightarrow} p'$ and $R(p',q')$;

iii. if $R(p,q)$ then $p \overset{a}{\Rightarrow} \surd$ iff $q \overset{a}{\Rightarrow} \surd$.

The proof of this theorem is left to the reader. Compare this with the definition of strong bisimulation in 2.5.2.

5.8.6 OBSERVATION EQUIVALENCE

Theorems 5.8.3 and 5.8.5 also motivate the name **observation equivalence**. The name observation refers to the idea that although $\overset{a}{\Rightarrow}$ may consist of a *sequence* of actions, the action a is the only visible part of this sequence. Thus the formulation of theorem 5.8.5 is the straightforward translation of the original definition of bisimulation equivalence.

So the question arises: why don't we define τ in the term model according to 5.8.4 instead of definition 5.4.31? We will motivate our choice algebraically and model-theoretically, and also offer the following intuitive motivation.

We consider a path $a \cdot \tau \cdot b \cdot \tau \cdot c$ with outgoing edges d_1, d_2, d_3, d_4. We see that all three graphs in fig. 38 below are τ-bisimilar (check this by means of definition 5.8.1 or using theorem 5.8.5). Thus, one may add extra b-edges as in (b) and (c) without disturbing bisimilarity. However, in both (b) and (c) a new computation path is introduced, in which the outgoing edge d_2 (or d_3 respectively) is missing, and such a path did not occur in (a). Or – to put it differently – in the path introduced in (b) the options d_1 and d_2 are discarded simultaneously, whereas in (a) it corresponds to a path containing a state where the option d_1 is already discarded but d_2 is still possible. Also, in the path introduced in (c), the choice not to perform d_3 is already made with the execution of the b-step, whereas in (a) it corresponds to a path in which this choice is made only after the b-step. Thus one may argue that τ-bisimulation equivalence observation equivalence does not preserve the branching structure of processes and hence lacks one of the main characteristics of bisimulation semantics.

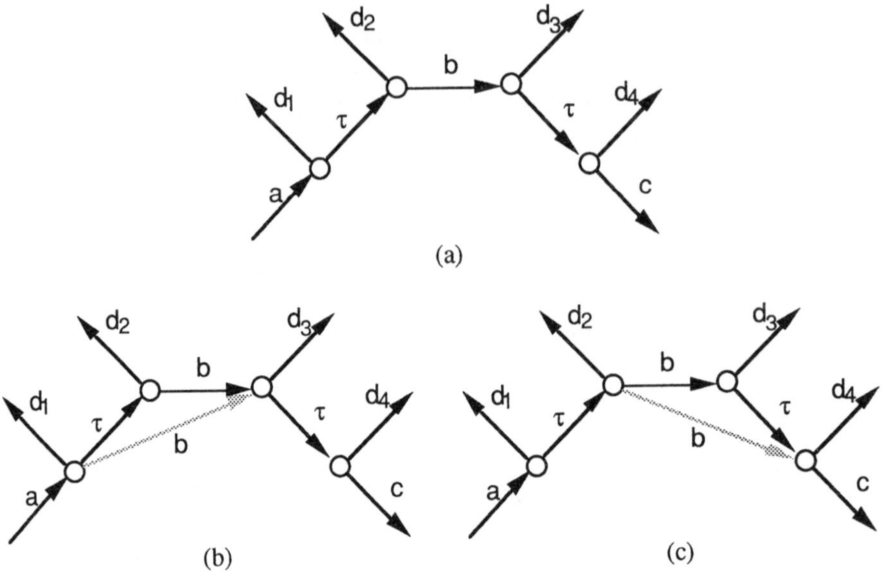

FIGURE 38.

Next, let us take a look at the axioms for τ in the term model $\mathbb{P}_\delta/\underline{\leftrightarrow}_{r\tau}$. From definition 5.8.1 we find immediately that $g \underline{\leftrightarrow}_{rb} h \Rightarrow g \underline{\leftrightarrow}_{r\tau} h$, and so certainly the axioms B1 and B2 of 5.1.3 are valid.

5.8.7 DEFINITION

The theory $BPA_{\delta\tau}$ can be found by adding the axioms from table 64 to the theory BPA_δ.

$x\tau = x$	T1
$\tau x = \tau x + x$	T2
$a(\tau x + y) = a(\tau x + y) + ax$	T3

TABLE 64. Axioms for observation equivalence.

We write $BPA_{\delta\tau}$ for BPA_δ + T1-T3. In order to explain the equations from table 64, one can find the following intuition. The first equation is as before. The second however, says that a silent move τ may consist of *zero* computation steps; therefore the process τx has the possibility of immediately starting to perform x. Finally, the third equation says that when the process $a(\tau x + y)$ is executed, it is possible that we do an a-step and then arrive in a state in which we can do x but the option to do y is no longer present.

5.8.8 THEOREM

$\mathbb{P}_\delta/\underline{\leftrightarrow}_{r\tau} \models$ T1-T3.

PROOF: The axioms T1-T3 are best illustrated by fig. 38. Check that all three graphs pictured there are τ-bisimilar. Furthermore, part (b) can be generalized to the equation T2 and similarly, part (c) can be reformulated as T3.

5.8.9 ACP_τ

Next we would like to extend the theory $BPA_{\delta\tau}$ to ACP_τ by introducing new operators. This involves a few complications however, in particular with respect to the axioms defining $\mathbin{\lfloor\!\lfloor}$ and $\mid$. To give an example, in ACP^τ we can derive

$$a \mid \tau b = (a \mid \tau)\cdot b = \delta$$

since $a \mid \tau = \delta$ and $\delta x = \delta$. However, with observational equivalence, using $\tau x = \tau x + x$ (T2) we obtain

$$a \mid \tau b = a \mid (\tau b + b) = a \mid \tau b + a \mid b.$$

Now if $\gamma(a,b)$ is defined, then $a \mid \tau x$ has a summand $\gamma(a,b)$, so is different from δ. Apparently, with respect to $\mid$, τ no longer behaves as an ordinary atomic action (as it did in ACP^τ), but instead, new laws have to be formulated to describe the interaction between τ and the extension operators. We obtain a new set of axioms, constituting ACP_τ, which is ACP^τ with this different interpretation of τ.

$x + y = y + x$		A1	$x\tau = x$		T1
$x + (y + z) = (x + y) + z$		A2	$\tau x = \tau x + x$		T2
$x + x = x$		A3	$a(\tau x + y) = a(\tau x + y) + ax$		T3
$(x + y)z = xz + yz$		A4			
$(xy)z = x(yz)$		A5			
$x + \delta = x$		A6	$a \mid b = \gamma(a,b)$	if defined	CF1
$\delta x = \delta$		A7	$a \mid b = \delta$	otherwise	CF2
$x \parallel y = x \mathbin{\lfloor\!\lfloor} y + y \mathbin{\lfloor\!\lfloor} x + x \mid y$		CM1	$\tau \mathbin{\lfloor\!\lfloor} x = \tau x$		TM1
$a \mathbin{\lfloor\!\lfloor} x = ax$		CM2	$\tau x \mathbin{\lfloor\!\lfloor} y = \tau(x \parallel y)$		TM2
$ax \mathbin{\lfloor\!\lfloor} y = a(x \parallel y)$		CM3	$\tau \mid x = \delta$		TC1
$(x + y) \mathbin{\lfloor\!\lfloor} z = x \mathbin{\lfloor\!\lfloor} z + y \mathbin{\lfloor\!\lfloor} z$		CM4	$x \mid \tau = \delta$		TC2
$ax \mid b = (a \mid b)x$		CM5	$\tau x \mid y = x \mid y$		TC3
$a \mid bx = (a \mid b)x$		CM6	$x \mid \tau y = x \mid y$		TC4
$ax \mid by = (a \mid b)(x \parallel y)$		CM7			
$(x + y) \mid z = x \mid z + y \mid z$		CM8			
$x \mid (y + z) = x \mid y + x \mid z$		CM9			
$\partial_H(\tau) = \tau$		D0	$\tau_I(\tau) = \tau$		TI0
$\partial_H(a) = a$	if $a \notin H$	D1	$\tau_I(a) = a$	if $a \notin I$	TI1
$\partial_H(a) = \delta$	if $a \in H$	D2	$\tau_I(a) = \tau$	if $a \in I$	TI2
$\partial_H(x + y) = \partial_H(x) + \partial_H(y)$		D3	$\tau_I(x + y) = \tau_I(x) + \tau_I(y)$		TI3
$\partial_H(xy) = \partial_H(x)\cdot\partial_H(y)$		D4	$\tau_I(xy) = \tau_I(x)\cdot\tau_I(y)$		TI4

TABLE 65. ACP_τ.

The axiom system ACP_τ has the same signature as ACP^τ. Again we assume a partial communication function γ is given on A, which is associative and commutative. ACP_τ is presented in table 65. In this table we have $a \in A \cup \{\delta\}$, so $a \not\equiv \tau$.

5.8.10 THEOREMS

We will not go through all the theorems again, but will limit ourselves to a few remarks. A complicating factor is that τ cannot be treated as an atomic action. This makes structural induction proofs much harder. We can prove an elimination theorem, a conservative extension theorem, and we have axioms of standard concurrency. The fifth axiom of standard concurrency of 5.2.4 does not hold in ACP_τ, however (see exercise 5.8.19.4). The expansion theorem still holds, nevertheless, but its proof becomes much more complicated.

5.8.11 COLOURED TRACES

In the following we will present some theorems in order to characterize the difference between τ-bisimulation and branching bisimulation. First of all, notice that it is not possible to characterize τ-bisimulation by means of abstract coloured traces. Check for instance, that the processes $a(\tau b + c) + ab$ and $a(\tau b + c)$ are τ-bisimilar, but they do not have the same set of abstract coloured traces. It is left as an open question whether one can find an alternative notion of abstract coloured traces that coincides with τ-bisimulation.

5.8.12 ACTION RELATIONS

In 5.8.1 we presented the definition of observation equivalence by means of action relations, and thus established the term model $\mathbb{P}_\delta/\underline{\leftrightarrow}_{r\tau}$. Using the same action relations as before, we modified the definition of $\underline{\leftrightarrow}$ and found a new equivalence $\underline{\leftrightarrow}_{r\tau}$. However, it is also possible to obtain the same model by changing the action relations on terms, instead of adjusting the equivalence $\underline{\leftrightarrow}$.

Consider the action relations from 2.1.7 together with the rules from table 66 ($a \in A \cup \{\tau\}$).

$a \xrightarrow{a} \tau$		
$x \xrightarrow{a} x'$ and $x' \xrightarrow{\tau} x''$	$\Rightarrow$	$x \xrightarrow{a} x''$
$x \xrightarrow{\tau} x'$ and $x' \xrightarrow{a} x''$	$\Rightarrow$	$x \xrightarrow{a} x''$
$x \xrightarrow{a} x'$ and $x' \xrightarrow{\tau} \surd$	$\Rightarrow$	$x \xrightarrow{a} \surd$
$x \xrightarrow{\tau} x'$ and $x' \xrightarrow{a} \surd$	$\Rightarrow$	$x \xrightarrow{a} \surd$

TABLE 66. Additional action relations for $BPA_{\delta\tau}$.

The rules from table 66 define a 'closure property' on action relations with τ. In fact they state that τ-steps cannot be separated from the atomic actions that are performed (compare with the generalized steps from definition 5.8.4). Now let us write $\mathbb{P}^*_\delta$ for the set of terms from $BPA_{\delta\tau}$, equipped with these new action relations. Then we obtain the following theorem:

5.8.13 THEOREM

$\mathbb{P}^*_\delta/\underline{\leftrightarrow}$ is isomorphic to $\mathbb{P}_\delta/\underline{\leftrightarrow}_{r\tau}$.

PROOF: omitted.

5.8.14 GRAPH MODEL

The definition of a graph model for ACP_τ is along the same lines as in 5.4.3. What is different here is the definition of the auxiliary operator $\lfloor$. Changes are necessary because of axioms TC3 and TC4. An unfortunate consequence of these changes is, that the set of finitely branching graphs $\mathbb{G}$ is no longer closed under application of $\lfloor$. As a result, we do not have $\mathbb{G}/\underline{\leftrightarrow}_{r\tau}$ as a model of ACP_τ.

5.8.15 NORMAL FORMS

An important difference between branching bisimulation and observation equivalence is the fact that the latter does not allow us to define normal forms as we did in 5.4.13. The point is again illustrated in fig. 38, where three observation equivalent graphs are shown. Observe that it is not possible to contract τ-edges in order to turn all three of these graphs into one unique normal form.

Instead, however, we may define normal forms by adding new edges to the graphs until they are *saturated*. So, all edges of the kind as in part (b) and (c) of fig. 38 are added to the original graph until no edges can be added any more. Observe that adding such edges immediately corresponds to the rules in table 66: consider x, x' and x'' as nodes of a graph, then the rules show precisely how to add new edges. Furthermore, once having a *saturated* graph we find from theorem 5.8.13 that it is unique up to strong bisimulation equivalence. From there we can find unique normal forms as before.

5.8.16 COMPLEXITY

These saturated normal forms are used in algorithms to decide τ-bisimulation equivalence of regular processes. Usually, these algorithms work in two stages: first find the saturated normal forms of the two processes, as in 5.8.15. This algorithm is often referred to as the *transitive closure algorithm*. Finally, it is left to decide strong bisimulation equivalence between the resulting normal forms.

Deciding branching bisimulation can be done much more efficiently, since it does not require saturation. Instead, the normal forms in branching bisimulation can be found by a stepwise reduction process of the regular graph.

5.8.17 CORRESPONDENCE

Let us end this section with a theorem which tells us that in quite a number of cases observation and branching bisimulation equivalence coincide. For instance, consider the practical applications where implementations are verified by abstracting from a set of unobservable actions. In many such cases, the *specification* does not involve any τ-steps at all: in fact all τ-steps that occur in the verification process originate from the abstraction procedure which is carried out on the implementation.

As it turns out, in all such cases there is no difference between observation and branching bisimulation equivalence. For this reason we may expect many of the verification procedures involving observation equivalence will still be valid in the stronger setting of branching bisimulation.

5.8.18 THEOREM

Suppose p and q are two terms from $\mathbb{P}_\delta$, and p is without τ-transitions, that is: there is no sequence $p \xrightarrow{\sigma}\!\!\!\!\to p' \xrightarrow{\tau} p''$ $(k\geq 0)$. Then:

i. $p \underline{\leftrightarrow}_\tau q \quad \Leftrightarrow \quad p \underline{\leftrightarrow}_b q$

ii. $p \underline{\leftrightarrow}_{r\tau} q \quad \Leftrightarrow \quad p \underline{\leftrightarrow}_{rb} q.$

PROOF: We only prove (ii), using the alternative definition of branching bisimulation in 5.4.34.10. Let R be the *maximal* rooted τ-bisimulation between p and q. Note that such a maximal relation is 'transitive', that is:

if $R(p,q)$, $R(p',q)$ and $R(p',q')$ then: $R(p,q')$.

(If R would be commutative, we would have transitivity in the usual sense).

Assume that $R(p,q)$ and $p \xrightarrow{a} p'$, then there is a path $q \Rightarrow q_1 \xrightarrow{a} q_2 \Rightarrow q'$ such that $R(p',q')$. Assume this path has the form $q \xrightarrow{\tau} v_1 \xrightarrow{\tau} \ldots \xrightarrow{\tau} v_k \xrightarrow{\tau} q_1 \xrightarrow{a} q_2 \Rightarrow q'$, then it follows from $q \xrightarrow{\tau} v_1$ and $R(p,q)$ that for some w_1 we have $p \Rightarrow w_1$ and $R(v_1,w_1)$. Since p has no τ-edges we find that $p{\equiv}w_1$. Repeating this argument k times we find that $R(p,v_i)$ and $R(p,q_1)$.

Furthermore, since $R(p,q_1)$ and $q_1 \xrightarrow{a} q_2$ we find that $p \xrightarrow{a} p''$ (p has no τ-steps) such that $R(p'',q_2)$. And since $q_2 \Rightarrow q'$ it follows from the same argument as before that $R(p'',q')$. Thus we find $R(p',q')$, $R(p,q_1)$, $R(p'',q_2)$, $R(p'',q')$ and since R is a maximal (hence 'transitive') rooted τ-bisimulation we have $R(p',q_2)$, as required.

On the other hand, if $q \xrightarrow{a} q'$ then directly $p \xrightarrow{a} p'$ such that $R(p',q')$, since p does not contain any τ-edges.

5.8.19 EXERCISES

1. Check whether the following equations are guarded in ACP_τ:

i. $x = \tau | ax$; ii. $x = a | \tau x$; iii. $x = (a|\tau)x$; iv. $x = \tau(\tau x + ax)$; v. $x = \tau \underline{\|} x$.

2. Prove $ACP_\tau \vdash \tau x \| y = \tau(x \| y)$ but $ACP^\tau \nvdash \tau x \| y = \tau(x \| y)$.

3. Define a constant τ^* on ACP^τ_ε by the equation $\tau^* = \tau + \varepsilon$.

i. Check that $ACP^\tau_\varepsilon \vdash a\tau^* = a,\ \tau^*\tau^* = \tau^*,\ \tau^* + \varepsilon = \tau^*$

ii. Show that $ACP^\tau_\varepsilon \nvdash a(\tau^*x + y) = a(\tau^*x + y) + ax$.

4. Find closed terms x,y,z in ACP_τ such that $(x|y)\underline{\|} z \neq x|(y\underline{\|} z)$. Furthermore show that for all closed terms in ACP_τ we have $(x|ay)\underline{\|} z = x|(ay\underline{\|} z)$, for $a{\in}A$. This shows that the fifth standard concurrency axiom from 5.2.5 does not hold in ACP_τ. Instead, we can replace it by $(x|ay)\underline{\|} z = x|(ay\underline{\|} z)$.

5.8.20 NOTES AND COMMENTS

Most of the material on which this section is based can be found in BERGSTRA & KLOP [1985]; there, ACP_τ was introduced. This paper is in turn based on ideas of MILNER [1980]. The action relations of 5.8.12 are from VAN GLABBEEK [1987]. For 5.8.14, see BAETEN, BERGSTRA & KLOP [1987b]. For an efficient algorithm deciding branching bisimulation (5.8.16) see GROOTE & VAANDRAGER [1990]. The correspondence theorem 5.8.18 is from VAN GLABBEEK & WEIJLAND [1989] or (an earlier version) BAETEN & VAN GLABBEEK [1989]. For a characterization of branching bisimulation in terms of generalized a-steps see DE NICOLA, MONTANARI & VAANDRAGER [1990]. For characterizations in terms of modal logic, see DE NICOLA & VAANDRAGER [1990].

Chapter 6
Features

6.1 PRIORITIES AND INTERRUPTS

In this chapter will develop some additional features to the theory in the former chapters, in order to enlarge the area of its application. Let us start by introducing a mechanism to describe priorities in the system ACP of chapter 4 (see 4.2.1). In ACP with priorities some actions have priority over others in a sum. This mechanism can be used to model interrupts in a distributed system.

6.1.1 REMARK

We will not combine the system ACP with priorities with τ and the abstraction operator of chapter 5. This can be done in several ways, see 6.1.23.

6.1.2 PARTIAL ORDERING

Assume we have a partial ordering on the set of atomic actions A. This means that we have a relation $<$ satisfying, for all $a,b,c \in A$:

1. *at most one* of $a<b$, $b<a$, $a=b$ is the case;
2. $a<b$ and $b<c$ imply $a<c$.

$a<b$ now means that b has priority over a. Special constants like δ, are not included in the ordering, and thus never have priority over other actions (this is forced by axiom A6).

6.1.3 AIM

We want to define an operator θ implementing these priorities, i.e: if $a<b$, $a<c$, and b and c are not related, we want to have:

1. $\theta(a + b) = b$; $\theta(a + c) = c$;
2. $\theta(b + c) = b + c$.

6.1.4 ACTION RELATIONS

It is relatively straightforward to give a definition by action relations of the priority operator. We present such a definition in table 68 below. These rules can be added to the rules of ACP, in table 36 in 4.2.4.

Here, $x \overset{b}{\nrightarrow}$ means that for no expression x' we have $x \xrightarrow{b} x'$, and also we do not have $x \xrightarrow{b} \surd$. There is a problem with this definition, however. Since the rules presented here have negative conditions, we do not have an inductive definition of which action relations actually hold. This causes problems, as the next example shows.

$x \xrightarrow{a} x'$ and for all $b>a$ $x \stackrel{b}{\not\rightarrow}$	$\Rightarrow \theta(x) \xrightarrow{a} \theta(x')$
$x \xrightarrow{a} \surd$ and for all $b>a$ $x \stackrel{b}{\not\rightarrow}$	$\Rightarrow \theta(x) \xrightarrow{a} \surd$

TABLE 68. Action relations for the priority operator.

6.1.5 EXAMPLE

Suppose $\gamma(a,b) = c$ is the only defined communication, and the only priority relation is $c>b$. Consider the following (unguarded) recursive equation:

$$X = a \| \theta \circ \partial_{\{c\}}(b + X).$$

Using the rules of table 68, we can derive that $X \xrightarrow{c} \surd$ iff $X \stackrel{c}{\not\rightarrow}$. This is a contradiction.

There are two solutions to this problem: the first one is to require that we never have $\gamma(a,b)>a$, the second one is to limit ourselves to guarded recursion. We omit proofs that both these solutions solve the problem. Instead, we concentrate on an axiomatization of the priority operator.

6.1.6 AUXILIARY OPERATOR: UNLESS

It turns out that if we want to describe this operator in the system ACP, we will need an extra operator (precisely as we needed $\mathbin{\|\!\!\_}$ and $|$, to describe $\|$). This extra operator is called $\triangleleft$ (**unless**). The idea is: $a \triangleleft b = a$, unless $a<b$ holds in the partial ordering; in that case $a \triangleleft b = \delta$. In general, $x \triangleleft y$ means that all *initial* actions of x smaller than some *initial* action of y, will be eliminated (by replacing them by δ). An example: if $a>b>c$, then

$$(ax + by + cz) \triangleleft (bp + cq) = ax + by + \delta z = ax + by$$

($a,b,c \in A$, and x,y,z,p,q processes).

6.1.7 AXIOM SYSTEM

The signature of the equational specification ACP_θ contains, apart from the elements of the signature of ACP, a binary operator $\triangleleft$ and a unary operator θ. We assume that a partial ordering $<$ on A is given. ACP_θ consists of the axioms from ACP together with the axioms in table 69. Here we have $a,b,c \in A_\delta$, $H \subseteq A$, and x,y,z are arbitrary processes.

$a \triangleleft b = a$	if $\neg(a<b)$	P1
$a \triangleleft b = \delta$	if $a<b$	P2
$x \triangleleft yz = x \triangleleft y$		P3
$x \triangleleft (y + z) = (x \triangleleft y) \triangleleft z$		P4
$xy \triangleleft z = (x \triangleleft z)y$		P5
$(x + y) \triangleleft z = x \triangleleft z + y \triangleleft z$		P6
$\theta(a) = a$		TH1
$\theta(xy) = \theta(x) \cdot \theta(y)$		TH2
$\theta(x + y) = \theta(x) \triangleleft y + \theta(y) \triangleleft x$		TH3

TABLE 69. Additional axioms of ACP_θ.

6.1.8 COMMENTS

The interpretation of the operator as given earlier, may explain the axioms P1-6. For instance P3 follows from the fact that only initial actions of y are relevant, and P5 says that y in $x \triangleleft y$ only works as a 'filter' with respect to initial actions from x. Axiom P4 says that the total effect of y in $x \triangleleft y$ can also be obtained by having all summands of y work on x successively.

Of the axioms TH1-3 only TH3 may need some comment. Clearly, θ does not distribute over +, since in $\theta(x + y)$ there is an interaction between the restrictions concerning the priorities imposed on each other by x and y, while in $\theta(x) + \theta(y)$ we do not have such interaction. Using a 'correction factor' we do have the distributive law TH3.

6.1.9 EXAMPLES

With the partial ordering $b<a$, $c<a$ we have:

1. $\theta(a + b) = \theta(a)\triangleleft b + \theta(b)\triangleleft a = a\triangleleft b + b\triangleleft a = a + \delta = a$.
2. $\theta(b + c) = \theta(b)\triangleleft c + \theta(c)\triangleleft b = b\triangleleft c + c\triangleleft b = b + c$.
3. $\theta(b(a + c)) = \theta(b)\cdot\theta(a + c) = b(\theta(a)\triangleleft c + \theta(c)\triangleleft a) = b(a\triangleleft c + c\triangleleft a) = b(a + \delta) = ba$.
4. $\theta(a + b + c) = \theta(a)\triangleleft(b + c) + \theta(b + c)\triangleleft a = (\theta(a)\triangleleft b)\triangleleft c + (\theta(b)\triangleleft c + \theta(c)\triangleleft b)\triangleleft a =$ $= (a\triangleleft b)\triangleleft c + (b\triangleleft c + c\triangleleft b)\triangleleft a = a\triangleleft c + (b + c)\triangleleft a = a + b\triangleleft a + c\triangleleft a = a + \delta + \delta = a$.
5. $\theta(a + b + c) = \theta(a + b)\triangleleft c + \theta(c)\triangleleft(a + b) = (\theta(a)\triangleleft b + \theta(b)\triangleleft a)\triangleleft c + (\theta(c)\triangleleft a)\triangleleft b =$ $= (a\triangleleft b + b\triangleleft a)\triangleleft c + (c\triangleleft a)\triangleleft b = (a + \delta)\triangleleft c + \delta\triangleleft b = a\triangleleft c + \delta\triangleleft c + \delta = a + \delta + \delta = a$.

6.1.10 LEMMA

The following equations are derivable from ACP_θ:

i. $(x\triangleleft y)\triangleleft z = (x\triangleleft z)\triangleleft y$

ii. $(x\triangleleft y)\triangleleft y = x\triangleleft y$

iii. $\theta(x)\triangleleft x = \theta(x)$

PROOF: 1. $(x\triangleleft y)\triangleleft z = x\triangleleft(y + z)$ (P4) $= x\triangleleft(z + y)$ (A1) $= (x\triangleleft z)\triangleleft y$ (P4).

2. $(x\triangleleft y)\triangleleft y = x\triangleleft(y + y)$ (P4) $= x\triangleleft y$ (A3).

3. $\theta(x)\triangleleft x = \theta(x)\triangleleft x + \theta(x)\triangleleft x$ (A3) $= \theta(x + x)$ (TH3) $= \theta(x)$ (A3).

6.1.11 THEOREM

i. **Elimination**: for all closed ACP_θ-terms t there exists a basic term s (hence without $\theta, \triangleleft, \|, \lfloor\!\lfloor, |, \partial_H$) such that $ACP_\theta \vdash t=s$.

ii. ACP_θ is a **conservative extension** of BPA_δ.

PROOF: As before (see for example 4.3.2). Again, we need a term rewriting system for ACP_θ. We have to work modulo the axioms A1,2 and applications of lemma 6.1.10.i. Consider the term rewriting system consisting of the rules from 4.3.1 together with the ones below. Without proof we claim, that this term rewriting system is confluent and terminating, and so every closed ACP_θ-term has a unique normal form. Lemma 6.1.10 is needed to prove this.

$$a \lhd b \to a \quad \text{if } \neg(a<b)$$
$$a \lhd b \to \delta \quad \text{if } a<b$$
$$x \lhd yz \to x \lhd y$$
$$x \lhd (y + z) \to (x \lhd y)z$$
$$xy \lhd z \to (x \lhd z)y$$
$$(x + y) \lhd z \to x \lhd z + y \lhd z$$
$$(x \lhd y) \lhd y \to x \lhd y$$

$$\theta(a) \to a$$
$$\theta(xy) \to \theta(x) \cdot \theta(y)$$
$$\theta(x+y) \to \theta(x) \lhd y + \theta(y) \lhd x$$
$$\theta(x) \lhd x \to \theta(x).$$

6.1.12 MODELS

Due to the problems with the action relations, we do not have a term model for ACP_θ in the same way we had term models for previous theories. We do get a term model if we allow constants $\langle X \mid E \rangle$ for *guarded* specifications E only.

The definition of the priority operator on the graph models is not difficult (see exercises). This gives us graph models for ACP_θ.

6.1.13 EXAMPLE

In the rest of this section we will present some examples of the way θ can be used. First, we consider an example modeling interrupts.

Suppose we have a printer P that has to print a sequence of data $\langle d_0, d_1, \ldots\ldots \rangle$ ($d_i \in D$, D a finite data set), but can be interrupted by a keyboard K. P and K are interconnected by a communication channel.

6.1.14 SPECIFICATION

The process K has atomic actions k(BR) (key in BREAK), k(SP) (key in START PRINTING) and send actions s(BR), s(SP); the process P has an atomic action p(d) (print d, with $d \in D$) and receive actions r(BR), r(SP).

K is defined by a guarded recursive equation

$$K = (k(BR) \cdot s(BR) + k(SP) \cdot s(SP)) \cdot K$$

and P is given by the following guarded recursive specification:

$$P = W_0$$
$$W_i = r(SP) \cdot P_i + r(BR) \cdot W_i \qquad (i \geq 0)$$
$$P_i = p(d_i) \cdot P_{i+1} + r(BR) \cdot W_i + r(SP) \cdot P_i \qquad (i \geq 0).$$

Here, P_i is the 'printing' state just after $d_0, \ldots, d_{i-1}$ have been printed, and W_i is the 'waiting' state after $d_0, \ldots, d_{i-1}$ have been printed. Communications are defined as usual, and H = {r(BR),s(BR),r(SP),s(SP)}.

6.1.15 PRIORITIES

Next, we define a partial ordering on A. We have c(BR)>p(d) for every d, since a BREAK must interrupt printing, but also c(SP)>p(d) for all d, because s(SP) has to be received by the printer immediately: otherwise K is blocked (between k(SP) and s(SP)) and no BREAK can be sent.

6.1.16 SYSTEM

The intended system now can be described by the process $X = X_0 = \theta \circ \partial_H(K \| P)$. Introducing the abbreviations $X_i = \theta \circ \partial_H(K \| W_i)$ and $Y_i = \theta \circ \partial_H(K \| P_i)$ $(i \geq 0)$, we can derive the following guarded recursive specification $(i \geq 0)$:

$$X_i = k(BR) \cdot c(BR) \cdot X_i + k(SP) \cdot c(SP) \cdot Y_i$$

$$Y_i = p(d_i) \cdot Y_{i+1} + X_i.$$

6.1.17 EXAMPLE

In the following example the priority operator will be used to give lower priority to error messages. In this way we can describe a feature like a *time out*.

Suppose we have a file F containing data $<d_0, d_1, d_2, ...>$ $(d_i \in D$, D a finite data set). These data are sent to a printer P and either will be printed, or a file crash occurs, in which case an error message is generated. F and P are interconnected by a communication channel.

6.1.18 SPECIFICATION

Process F has atomic actions $g(d)$ (get the next element from the file), $s(d)$ (send d to the printer) and cr (crash). Let F_i be the state of F just after $d_0,...,d_{i-1}$ are sent, then F can be given by the following guarded recursive specification:

$$F = F_0$$

$$F_i = g(d_i) \cdot s(d_i) \cdot F_{i+1} + cr \qquad (i \geq 0).$$

Process P has atomic actions $r(d)$ (receive d from the file), $p(d)$ (print d), $o(CR)$ (observe a file crash) and $p(CR)$ (print FILE CRASH). P can be given by the following guarded recursive specification:

$$P = \sum_{d \in D} r(d) \cdot p(d) \cdot P + o(CR) \cdot p(CR).$$

Communication is defined as usual, $H = \{s(d), r(d) : d \in D\}$.

6.1.19 PRIORITIES

The file crash may happen at any moment, but $o(CR)$, the observation of the file crash, may only happen after the file actually has crashed. We can arrange this by giving $o(CR)$ a lower priority then any 'real' action of the process F, thus defining $o(CR) < g(d)$ and $o(CR) < c(d)$ for all $d \in D$. This defines a partial ordering on A.

6.1.20 SYSTEM

The intended system can be described by the process $X = X_0 = \theta \circ \partial_H(F \| P)$. Introducing the abbreviations $X_i = \theta \circ \partial_H(F_i \| P)$ and $Y_i = \theta \circ \partial_H(F_{i+1} \| p(d_i) \cdot P)$ (for $i \geq 0$), one can derive the following guarded recursive specification:

$$X_i = g(d_i) \cdot c(d_i) \cdot Y_i + cr \cdot o(CR) \cdot p(CR)$$

$$Y_i = p(d_i) \cdot X_{i+1} + g(d_{i+1}) \cdot p(d_i) \cdot c(d_{i+1}) \cdot Y_{i+1} + cr \cdot p(d_i) \cdot o(CR) \cdot p(CR).$$

6.1.21 SIMPLIFICATION

We can get a simpler specification by extending the priority relation of 6.1.19: put $g(d) > p(d')$ and $c(d) > p(d')$ for all $d, d' \in D$. This way we express that all 'internal' actions $g(d)$ and $c(d)$ have priority over external actions $p(d)$, because they are executed so much faster. This assumption concerns the so called 'real time' behaviour of the system. Then, we obtain the guarded recursive specification (abbreviations as above):

$$X = g(d_0)\cdot c(d_0)\cdot Y_0 + cr\cdot o(CR)\cdot p(CR)$$
$$Y_i = g(d_{i+1})\cdot p(d_i)\cdot c(d_{i+1})\cdot Y_{i+1} + cr\cdot p(d_i)\cdot o(CR)\cdot p(CR) \quad (i\geq 0).$$

6.1.22 EXERCISES

1. Rewrite the term $\theta(x + y + z)$ into a normal form in two ways, starting by applying TH3 to: i. $\theta(x + (y + z))$, and ii. $\theta((x + y) + z)$. Then show that both normal forms are equal to the term $\theta(x)\triangleleft(y+z) + \theta(y)\triangleleft(x+z) + \theta(z)\triangleleft(x+y)$ (not itself a normal form, but an expression that is symmetric in x, y and z).
2. Prove the following equalities for all processes x,y,z that have a head normal form:
i. $x\triangleleft\delta = x$; ii. $\delta\triangleleft x = \delta$; iii. $a\triangleleft x = a$ or $a\triangleleft x = \delta$;
iv. If $\neg(a<b)$ then $a\triangleleft(x\triangleleft b) = a\triangleleft x$; v. $(x\triangleleft y)\triangleleft a = x\triangleleft y$ if $a\triangleleft y = \delta$;
vi. $(x\triangleleft y)\triangleleft(z\triangleleft y) = (x\triangleleft y)\triangleleft z$; vii. $\theta(x\triangleleft y) = \theta(x)\triangleleft y$.
3. Verify example 6.1.5.
4. Define the priority operator on process graphs (that only have $\downarrow$-labels on endpoints), and show that bisimulation remains a congruence. This establishes a graph model for ACP_θ.
5. Give the derivation of the recursive specification of 6.1.16 and draw the process graph of X. Since this is a specification in ACP, we can calculate $\tau_I(X)$, with $I = \{k(BR),k(SP),c(BR), c(SP)\}$. Derive a specification for $\tau_I(X)$ using KFAR, and interpret your answer.
6. Derive the recursive specification of 6.1.20 and draw the process graph of X. If $I = \{c(d), g(d) : d\in D\} \cup \{cr, o(CR)\}$, calculate $\tau_I(X)$ and interpret of your answer. Do the same for the specification in 6.1.21.
7. Define θ in ACP_ε. P3 and P5 need to be changed.
8. Consider the definition of θ in ACP^τ. There are a couple of possibilities. Identify the problems.

6.1.23 NOTES AND COMMENTS

This section is based on BAETEN, BERGSTRA & KLOP [1986]. The action relations, and example 6.1.5, are given in BAETEN & BERGSTRA [1988b]. The solutions indicated in 6.1.5 can be found in GROOTE [1989]. In VAANDRAGER [1990c], several ways to combine τ and θ are outlined. Unfortunately, there seems to be no canonical and most general integration of both features.

Priority mechanisms are also defined by other authors, see e.g. CLEAVELAND & HENNESSY [1988]. The *disruption operator* of the LOTOS language also gives a way to deal with interrupts, see BRINKSMA [1988].

6.2 ALPHABETS AND CONDITIONAL AXIOMS

In this section we will define the alphabet of a process, and use it to formulate some conditional axioms concerning the distribution of renaming operators over the parallel composition of ACP.

6.2.1 DEFINITION

The **alphabet** of a process x, $\alpha(x)$, is the set of atomic actions that can be executed by x, so $\alpha(x) \subseteq A$. Its axioms are given in table 70. Here we assume that $a \in A$ and $\gamma \in C$, the set of special constants in the signature of the theory in consideration (depending on the theory, C may contain δ, ε or τ). Axiom AB3 is only present when $\tau \in C$. x, y and z are arbitrary processes.

$\alpha(\gamma) = \varnothing$	AB1
$\alpha(a) = \{a\}$	AB2
$\alpha(\tau x) = \alpha(x)$	AB3
$\alpha(ax) = \{a\} \cup \alpha(x)$	AB4
$\alpha(x + y) = \alpha(x) \cup \alpha(y)$	AB5

TABLE 70. Alphabet.

The axioms in table 70 give us an inductive definition on finite terms.

6.2.2 REMARKS

1. To prove that α is well defined, we have to check that for closed terms x,y we have: $x=y \Rightarrow \alpha(x)=\alpha(y)$. This is left as an exercise.
2. $\alpha(\delta)=\varnothing$ is necessary because of axiom A6, $\alpha(\tau)=\varnothing$ because of T1 and $\alpha(\varepsilon)=\varnothing$ by axiom A8.
3. In the rest of this section, we will focus on theory ACP^{τ}. Most results can be adapted for other theories.

6.2.3 RECURSION

So far, α is not yet properly defined for infinite processes. Therefore, we extend the former definition to all constructible processes. Since all finite projections of specifiable processes are equal to closed terms (see 5.5.5), we can use axiom AB6 in table 71 to define the alphabet of specifiable processes. In order to define the alphabet for all constructible processes, we just need an axiom for the abstraction operator. This is axiom AB7.

$\alpha(x) = \bigcup_{n\geq 1} \alpha(\pi_n(x))$	AB6
$\alpha(\tau_I(x)) = \alpha(x) - I$	AB7

TABLE 71. Alphabet for constructible processes.

The first two parts of the following theorem (6.2.4) give a justification for AB6 and AB7.

6.2.4 THEOREM

The following equations are derivable from ACP^{τ} + AB1-5, for all closed terms over ACP^{τ}.

i. $\alpha(x) = \bigcup_{n\geq 1} \alpha(\pi_n(x))$ (AB6)
ii. $\alpha(\tau_I(x)) = \alpha(x) - I$ (AB7)
iii. $\alpha(xy) \subseteq \alpha(x) \cup \alpha(y)$
iv. $\alpha(x \| y) = \alpha(x) \cup \alpha(y) \cup \alpha(x) | \alpha(y)$
(if $B,C \subseteq A$, then we define $B | C = \{a \in A : a=\gamma(b,c)$ for some $b \in B$, $c \in C\}$)
v. $\alpha(x \mathbin{⌊\!⌊} y) \subseteq \alpha(x \| y)$
vi. $\alpha(x | y) \subseteq \alpha(x \| y)$
vii. $\alpha(\partial_H(x)) \subseteq \alpha(x) - H$.

PROOF: The equations i, ii, iii and vii are not difficult to prove by induction on the structure of x. Propositions v and vi directly follow from the axioms CM1 and AB5. So here, we only prove proposition iv.

We use simultaneous induction on the structure of x and y. Note that:

$$\text{either } x=\tau \text{ or } x = \sum_{1\le i\le N} a_i x_i, \text{ and}$$

$$\text{either } y=\tau \text{ or } y = \sum_{1\le k\le K} b_k y_k,$$

for processes x_i, y_k, where $K,N \geq 0$, $a_i, b_k \in A\cup\{\delta,\tau\}$.
Now if either x or y is equal to τ, then $\alpha(x)\,|\,\alpha(y) = \emptyset$, and the theorem becomes trivial. Thus assume neither of them is τ. Then we find:

$$x\|y = \sum_{1\le i\le N} a_i(x_i\|y) + \sum_{1\le k\le K} b_k(x\|y_k) + \sum_{i\le N,k\le K} (a_i|b_k)(x_i\|y_k).$$

And so:

$$\alpha(x\|y) = \bigcup_{i\in N} \{a_i\}\cup\alpha(x_i\|y) \cup \bigcup_{k\in K}\{b_k\}\cup\alpha(x\|y_k) \cup \bigcup_{\text{where defined}} \{\gamma(a_i,b_k)\}\cup\alpha(x_i\|y_k)$$

where the last union is taken over all i,k such that $\gamma(a_i,b_k)$ is defined.
Applying the induction hypothesis, we obtain

$$\begin{aligned}\alpha(x\|y) = {} & \bigcup_{i\in I}\{a_i\} \cup \alpha(x_i) \cup \alpha(y) \cup (\alpha(x_i)|\alpha(y)) \cup \\ & \bigcup_{k\in K}\{b_k\} \cup \alpha(x) \cup \alpha(y_k) \cup (\alpha(x)|\alpha(y_k)) \cup \\ & \bigcup_{\text{where defined}} \{\gamma(a_i,b_k)\} \cup \alpha(x_i) \cup \alpha(y_k) \cup (\alpha(x_i)|\alpha(y_k)) = \\ = {} & \bigcup_{i\in I}\{a_i\} \cup \alpha(x_i) \cup \alpha(x) \cup \\ & \bigcup_{k\in K}\{b_k\} \cup \alpha(y_k) \cup \alpha(y) \cup \\ & \bigcup_{i\in I}\alpha(x_i)|\alpha(y) \cup \bigcup_{k\in K}\alpha(x)|\alpha(y_k) \cup \bigcup_{\text{where defined}} \{\gamma(a_i,b_k)\}\cup(\alpha(x_i)|\alpha(y_k)).\end{aligned}$$

In the last expression, the union of the first line is $\alpha(x)$, of the second $\alpha(y)$, and of the last $\alpha(x)\,|\,\alpha(y)$. This finishes the proof of part iv.

6.2.5 REMARK

In general it is an *undecidable* problem to determine the alphabet of a recursively defined process. A small illustration: if i^ω is given by $x = i\cdot x$, and $i\in I$, then it is not immediately clear that we have $\alpha(\tau_I(i^\omega)\cdot y) = \emptyset$ for all y.

6.2.6 CONDITIONAL ALPHABET AXIOMS

We will use the alphabet to present some rules that can be useful in verifying statements about recursively specified processes. We will prove these **conditional alphabet axioms** for closed terms only. We usually assume that they hold for all processes we consider.

$\alpha(x) \mid (\alpha(y) \cap H) \subseteq H$	$\Rightarrow \partial_H(x \| y) = \partial_H(x \| \partial_H(y))$	CA1
$\alpha(x) \mid (\alpha(y) \cap I) = \emptyset$	$\Rightarrow \tau_I(x \| y) = \tau_I(x \| \tau_I(y))$	CA2
$\alpha(x) \cap H = \emptyset$	$\Rightarrow \partial_H(x) = x$	CA3
$\alpha(x) \cap I = \emptyset$	$\Rightarrow \tau_I(x) = x$	CA4

TABLE 72. Conditional axioms.

6.2.7 THEOREM

The alphabet axioms of 6.2.6 hold for all closed ACP$^\tau$-terms.

PROOF: We will use simultaneous induction on x and y. We can write

$$\text{either } x=\tau \text{ or } x = \sum_{1\le i\le I} a_i x_i, \text{ and}$$

$$\text{either } y=\tau \text{ or } y = \sum_{1\le k\le K} b_k y_k + \sum_{1\le n\le N} h_n y'_n$$

for processes x_i, y_k, y'_n where $I,K,N \ge 0$, $a_i \in A \cup \{\delta,\tau\}$, $b_k \in (A \cup \{\delta,\tau\}) - H$, $h_n \in H$.
We have $a_i \in \alpha(x)$ and $h_n \in \alpha(y) \cap H$, so the assumption says that $\gamma(a_i,h_n) \in H$ (or is not defined) for all i,n. Then we find:

$$\partial_H(x \| y) = \sum_{1\le i\le I} \partial_H(a_i)\cdot\partial_H(x_i \| y) + \sum_{1\le k\le K} b_k\cdot\partial_H(x \| y_k) + \sum_{1\le i\le I, 1\le k\le K} \partial_H(a_i \mid b_k)\cdot\partial_H(x_i \| y_k).$$

Applying the induction hypothesis (this is possible since $\alpha(x_i) \subseteq \alpha(x)$ and $\alpha(y_k) \subseteq \alpha(y)$), we obtain

$$\partial_H(x \| y) = \sum_{1\le i\le I} \partial_H(a_i)\cdot\partial_H(x_i \| \partial_H(y)) + \sum_{1\le k\le K} b_k\cdot\partial_H(x \| \partial_H(y_k)) +$$

$$+ \sum_{1\le i\le I, 1\le k\le K} \partial_H(a_i \mid b_k)\cdot\partial_H(x_i \| \partial_H(y_k)) = \partial_H(x \| \partial_H(y)).$$

The proof of CA2 is analogous to the proof of CA1, and the proofs of CA3 and CA4 are straightforward inductions on the structure of x. Therefore, these proofs are left to the reader.

6.2.8 EXAMPLE

We will prove that two connected bags again form a bag. A bag with input channel i and output channel j is given by the recursive equation

$$B^{ij} = \sum_{d\in D} r_i(d)\cdot(s_j(d) \| B^{ij})$$

(see 3.5.6). It is not difficult to see that $\alpha(B^{ij}) = \{r_i(d), s_j(d) : d \in D\}$ (a full proof of this claim will take some doing and is omitted). We connect B^{12} and B^{23} as in fig. 39.

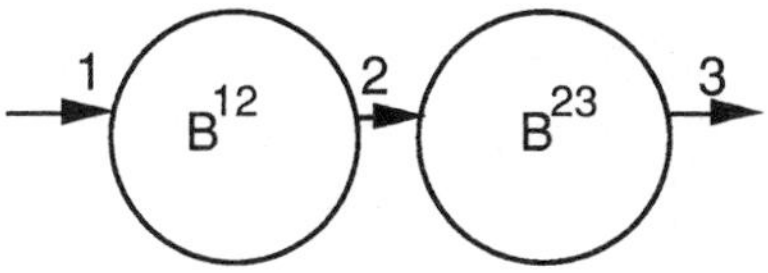

FIGURE 39.

6.2.9 THEOREM

Define $H = \{s_2(d), r_2(d) : d \in D\}$ and $I = \{c_2(d) : d \in D\}$. Then:

$$B^{13} = \tau_I \circ \partial_H(B^{12} \| B^{23}).$$

PROOF: $\partial_H(B^{12} \| B^{23}) = \sum_{d \in D} r_1(d) \cdot \partial_H(s_2(d) \| B^{12} \| B^{23}) =$

$$= \sum_{d \in D} r_1(d) \cdot \partial_H \circ \partial_{\{s2(d)\}}(B^{12} \| (s_2(d) \| B^{23})) =$$

$$= \sum_{d \in D} r_1(d) \cdot \partial_H \circ \partial_{\{s2(d)\}}(B^{12} \| \partial_{\{s2(d)\}}(s_2(d) \| B^{23})) = \qquad (*)$$

$$= \sum_{d \in D} r_1(d) \cdot \partial_H(B^{12} \| (c_2(d) \cdot s_3(d) \| B^{23})) =$$

$$= \sum_{d \in D} r_1(d) \cdot \partial_H(c_2(d) \cdot s_3(d) \| (B^{12} \| B^{23})) =$$

$$= \sum_{d \in D} r_1(d) \cdot \partial_H(c_2(d) \cdot s_3(d) \| \partial_H(B^{12} \| B^{23})) =$$

$$= \sum_{d \in D} r_1(d) \cdot (c_2(d) \cdot s_3(d) \| \partial_H(B^{12} \| B^{23})).$$

Step (*) can be explained from the fact that the process $c_2(d)s_3(d) \| B^{23}$ as well as the process $\partial_{\{s2(d)\}}(s_2(d) \| B^{23})$ satisfies the equation

$$x = c_2(d) \cdot (s_3(d) \| B^{23}) + \sum_{e \in D} r_2(e) \cdot (s_3(e) \| x).$$

Using this result we obtain $\tau_I \circ \partial_H(B^{12} \| B^{23}) =$

$$= \sum_{d \in D} r_1(d) \cdot \tau_I(c_2(d) \cdot s_3(d) \| \partial_H(B^{12} \| B^{23})) =$$

$$= \sum_{d \in D} r_1(d) \cdot \tau_I(\tau_I(c_2(d) \cdot s_3(d)) \| \tau_I \circ \partial_H(B^{12} \| B^{23})) =$$

$$= \sum_{d \in D} r_1(d) \cdot \tau_I(\tau \cdot s_3(d) \| \tau_I \circ \partial_H(B^{12} \| B^{23})) =$$

$$= \sum_{d \in D} r_1(d) \cdot (\tau \cdot s_3(d) \| \tau_I \circ \partial_H(B^{12} \| B^{23})) =$$

$$= \sum_{d \in D} r_1(d) \cdot (s_3(d) \| \tau_I \circ \partial_H(B^{12} \| B^{23})).$$

So the process $\tau_I \circ \partial_H(B^{12} \| B^{23})$ satisfies the equation defining B^{13}. With RSP it then follows that $B^{13} = \tau_I \circ \partial_H(B^{12} \| B^{23})$.

6.2.10 EXAMPLE

n connected bags again yield a bag. For notational reasons we only consider the case $n=3$. We use the same notation as in 6.2.9. Let $H_n = \{s_n(d), r_n(d): d \in D\}$ for $n=2,3$ and $H = H_2 \cup H_3$; furthermore, let $I_n = \{c_n(d) : d \in D\}$ for $n=2,3$ and $I = I_2 \cup I_3$. Then, we have the following theorem.

6.2.11 THEOREM

$B^{14} = \tau_I \circ \partial_H(B^{12} \| B^{23} \| B^{34})$.

PROOF: From 6.2.9 it follows that $B^{24} = \tau_{I3}\circ\partial_{H3}(B^{23} \| B^{34})$ and $B^{14} = \tau_{I2}\circ\partial_{H2}(B^{12} \| B^{24})$. Therefore we have

$$\begin{aligned}
&\tau_I\circ\partial_H(B^{12} \| B^{23} \| B^{34}) = \\
&= \tau_{I2}\circ\tau_{I3}\circ\partial_{H2}\circ\partial_{H3}(B^{12} \| B^{23} \| B^{34}) = \\
&= \tau_{I2}\circ\partial_{H2}\circ\tau_{I3}\circ\partial_{H3}(B^{12} \| B^{23} \| B^{34}) = \\
&= \tau_{I2}\circ\partial_{H2}\circ\tau_{I3}\circ\partial_{H3}(B^{12} \| \partial_{H3}(B^{23} \| B^{34})) = \\
&= \tau_{I2}\circ\partial_{H2}\circ\tau_{I3}(B^{12} \| \partial_{H3}(B^{23} \| B^{34})) = \\
&= \tau_{I2}\circ\partial_{H2}\circ\tau_{I3}(B^{12} \| \tau_{I3}\circ\partial_{H3}(B^{23} \| B^{34})) = \\
&= \tau_{I2}\circ\partial_{H2}\circ\tau_{I3}(B^{12} \| B^{24}) = \tau_{I2}\circ\partial_{H2}(B^{12} \| B^{24}) = \\
&= B^{14}.
\end{aligned}$$

Notice that in the second line of this derivation we used 3.6.3.ii.

6.2.12 EXERCISES

1. Prove 6.2.2.1 assuming x,y are ACP$^\tau$-terms, and find a motivation for 6.2.2.2.
2. Prove the statements i, ii, iii and vii in theorem 6.2.4. Find counterexamples to prove that in general we do not have equalities in iii, v, vi and vii.
3. Why is $\alpha(\tau_I(i^\omega)\cdot y) = \varnothing$ for all y, as noted in 6.2.5? Hint: use KFAR.
4. Prove CA2,3,4 in 6.2.6 for all ACP$^\tau$-terms.
5. Define α on the graph model, and verify axioms AB1-7.
6. Check that the process $c2(d)s3(d) \| B^{23}$ and the process $\partial_{\{s2(d)\}}(s2(d) \| B^{23})$ indeed satisfy the equation
$$x = c2(d)\cdot(s3(d) \| B^{23}) + \sum_{e\in D} r2(e)\cdot(s3(e) \| x).$$
7. Find the steps in the proof of 6.2.9, where the conditional alphabet axioms are used. Verify that the premises of these axioms are satisfied. Do the same for the proof of 6.2.11.
8. Under what conditions do we have $\partial_H(x \| y) = \partial_H(x) \| \partial_H(y)$? (Compare with 3.6.8.10.)

6.2.13 NOTES AND COMMENTS

This section is based on BAETEN, BERGSTRA & KLOP [1987a]. In the literature, the notion of an alphabet of process x usually indicates a superset of what we call $\alpha(x)$ (see e.g. HOARE [1985] or EBERGEN [1988]).

6.3 LOCALIZATION, TRACES AND RESTRICTION

In this section we consider some generalized renaming operators, that are useful in calculations with complex processes. We present some simple examples.

6.3.1 INTUITION

The idea of the **localization operator** is that we want to focus on actions from p that can be executed in a context $\partial_H(\_ \| q)$. For convenience, we assume all communications to be defined as in 4.1.2.

ν_B is the operator, that abstracts from all actions outside of the set B and renames each $c_i(d)$ into its corresponding component (either $s_i(d)$ or $r_i(d)$) which is in B. A precise formulation is given in the following definition.

6.3.2 DEFINITION

Let $B \subseteq A$ such that at most one of $s_i(d)$, $r_i(d)$ is in B (for every data element d and every communication port i). Define $C = \{c_i(d) : \text{one of } s_i(d), r_i(d) \text{ is in } B\}$, and let $f: A \to A$ be the function defined by:

- if $c_i(d) \in C$ then: $f(c_i(d)) = r_i(d)$ if $r_i(d) \in C$, $f(c_i(d)) = s_i(d)$ otherwise;
- if $a \notin C$ then: $f(a) = a$.

Then ν_B is defined by:

$$\nu_B(x) = \rho_f \circ \tau_{A-(B \cup C)}(x).$$

6.3.3 LEMMA

Let $B \subseteq A$ satisfy the condition of 6.3.2, so that ν_B is well defined. Then:

1. $\nu_B(c_i(d)) = s_i(d)$ if $s_i(d) \in B$
2. $\nu_B(c_i(d)) = r_i(d)$ if $r_i(d) \in B$
3. $\nu_B(b) = b$ if $b \in B-C$
4. $\nu_B(a) = \tau$ if $a \in A-(B \cup C)$
5. $\nu_B(x + y) = \nu_B(x) + \nu_B(y)$
6. $\nu_B(xy) = \nu_B(x) \cdot \nu_B(y)$

PROOF: simple.

6.3.4 EXAMPLE

The communication network in fig. 40 has a transmitter S, a receiver R and environment E.

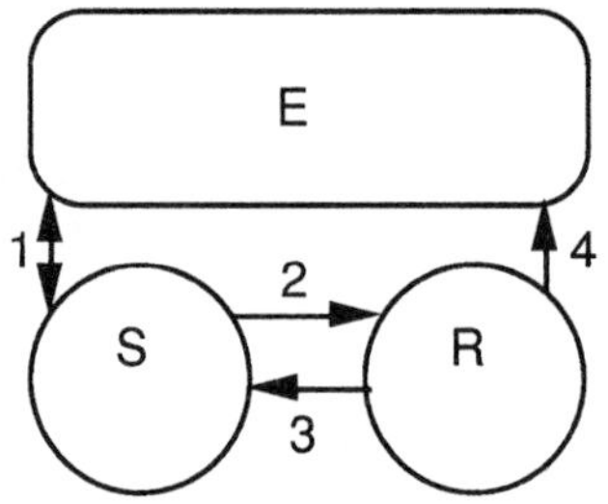

FIGURE 40.

S and R are given by the following recursive equations:

$$S = \sum_{d \in D} r_1(d) \cdot s_2(d) \cdot r_3(ack) \cdot s_1(ack) \cdot S$$

$$R = \sum_{d \in D} r_2(d) \cdot s_4(d) \cdot s_3(ack) \cdot R.$$

In these equations D is a finite data set, and $ack \notin D$ is an acknowledgement. The environment E can send data, and receive an acknowledgement at 1 or receive data at 4. Thus we can specify E using the following recursive equation:

$$E = (\sum_{d \in D} s_1(d) + \sum_{d \in D} r_4(d) + r_1(ack)) \cdot E.$$

However, we have the idea that E should not be able to perform all these actions $s_1(d)$, $r_4(d)$ and $r_1(ack)$ at every moment: first we will have $s_1(d)$, next $r_4(d)$, and then $r_1(ack)$, before the next $s_1(d')$ can be executed. This can be expressed by use of the localization operator. The process $\partial_H(E \| S \| R)$, localized with respect to E, will present the actual order, as is stated in the following theorem.

6.3.5 THEOREM

Let $H = \{s_i(d), r_i(d): d \in D, i=1,2,3,4\}$. Then we have

$$v_{\alpha(E)} \circ \partial_H(E \| S \| R) = \sum_{d \in D} s_1(d) \cdot r_4(d) \cdot r_1(ack) \cdot v_{\alpha(E)} \circ \partial_H(E \| S \| R).$$

PROOF: not difficult.

6.3.6 TRACES

Next we will define the set of traces of a process in ACP^τ. A **trace** of a process is a series of actions, that can performed. In the terminology of 2.1.7 and 5.5.7, σ is a trace of process x if either $x \overset{\sigma}{\twoheadrightarrow} \surd$ or there is a process x' with $x \overset{\sigma}{\twoheadrightarrow} x'$. So, a trace is a sequence of atomic actions, a word in A^* (for some notations see 2.9.2; e.g. λ is the empty word). tr(x) is the set of traces of the process x. We present equations for tr(x) in table 73. We assume $a \in A$ (so $a \neq \delta$).

$$tr(\delta) = tr(\tau) = \{\lambda\}$$
$$tr(a) = \{\lambda, a\}$$
$$tr(\tau x) = tr(x)$$
$$tr(ax) = \{\lambda\} \cup \{a\sigma : \sigma \in tr(x)\}$$
$$tr(x + y) = tr(x) \cup tr(y)$$

TABLE 73. Trace set of a process.

6.3.7 EXAMPLES

1. $tr(a(b + c)) = \{\lambda, a, ab, ac\} = tr(ab + ac)$.
2. $tr(a\delta) = \{\lambda, a\} = tr(a)$.
3. $tr(\tau(\tau a + \tau\delta)) = \{\lambda, a\}$.

We see that the trace set provides us with some information about a process, but also disregards some information, since for instance a(b + c) and ab + ac have the same trace set. Still, for some calculations, the trace set provides sufficient information. This makes some calculations easier. In 6.3.14 we find a theorem in which traces play an important role.

6.3.8 LEMMA

For all closed ACP^τ-terms x we can derive the following equations, using the axioms in table 73:

1. if $\sigma\rho \in tr(x)$ $(\sigma,\rho \in A^*)$, then $\sigma \in tr(x)$ (trace sets are **prefix closed**);
2. $tr(x) = \bigcup_{n \geq 1} tr(\pi_n(x))$;
3. $tr(\tau_I(x)) = \{\lambda_I(\sigma): \sigma \in tr(x)\}$. Here, $\lambda_I(\sigma)$ is the word obtained from σ, by leaving out all elements from I (for σ a word in A^* and $I \subseteq A$).

6.3.9 CONSTRUCTIBLE PROCESSES

Just as in we did in section 6.2, we add two equations, in order to define the trace set for all constructible processes. The following equations are justified by the previous lemma.

$tr(x) = \cup_{n\geq 1} tr(\pi_n(x))$
$tr(\tau_I(x)) = \{\lambda_I(\sigma) : \sigma \in tr(x)\}$

TABLE 74. Trace set of constructible processes.

6.3.10 ALGEBRA OF TRACE SETS

Next, we turn the set of trace sets into an algebra. Let $\mathbb{T}$, the **algebra of trace sets**, be the set of all prefix closed subsets of A^*. Every element of $\mathbb{T}$ is the trace set of a process, except for $\emptyset \in \mathbb{T}$. On $\mathbb{T}$, we define three operators:

1. If $Z \in \mathbb{T}$ and $a \in A$, then $\partial/_{\partial a}(Z) = \{\sigma \in A^* : a\sigma \in Z\}$.
2. If $Z \in \mathbb{T}$, then $first(Z) = \{a \in A : a\sigma \in Z\}$.
3. If $Z \in \mathbb{T}$ and $a \in A$, then $aZ = \{\lambda\} \cup \{a\sigma : \sigma \in Z\}$.

Note that $\partial/_{\partial a}(Z)$ and aZ are again elements of $\mathbb{T}$. We see that $first(Z) \subseteq A$ and $a\emptyset = \{\lambda\}$.

6.3.11 LEMMA

For all $Z \in \mathbb{T}$ with $Z \neq \emptyset$ we have $Z = \cup_{a \in A}\, a\partial/_{\partial a}(Z)$.

PROOF: this follows directly from 6.3.10 (see exercises).

6.3.12 DEFINITION

Now we define the **restriction** of a process to a trace set. If x is a process, and Z is a trace set, then $\nabla_Z(x)$ results from x by disallowing all steps that lead to a trace that is not in Z (the symbol ∇ is pronounced as 'nabla'). ∇_Z can be considered as a generalized renaming operator, and is defined in table 75.

$\nabla_Z(\tau) = \tau$
$\nabla_Z(a) = \partial_{A-first(Z)}(a)$
$\nabla_Z(\tau x) = \tau \cdot \nabla_Z(x)$
$\nabla_Z(ax) = \partial_{A-first(Z)}(a) \cdot \nabla_{\partial/\partial a(Z)}(x)$
$\nabla_Z(x + y) = \nabla_Z(x) + \nabla_Z(y)$

Table 75. Restriction.

In this table we have $Z \in \mathbb{T}$, $a \in A_\delta$, and x,y are arbitrary processes.

6.3.13 LEMMA

Let x be a closed ACP^τ-term and $Z \in \mathbb{T}$. Then:

1. $tr(\nabla_Z(x)) \subseteq Z$
2. if $tr(x) \subseteq Z$, then $\nabla_Z(x) = x$.

PROOF: by induction on the structure of x.

The following theorem allows us to simplify one process in a context with parallel composition. In practical examples, we are dealing with an encapsulated merge of several processes. The transition diagram of the composite process is infinite, or too complicated to calculate. In such cases, it is essential to reduce the components as much as possible, before the merge is tackled. The following theorem gives us a means to do so. We will apply the theorem in example 6.3.4.

6.3.14 THEOREM

Assume p,q are closed ACP$^\tau$-terms.
If $Z \supseteq tr \circ v_{\alpha(p)} \circ \partial_H(p \| q)$, then we have $\partial_H(p \| q) = \partial_H(\nabla_Z(p) \| q)$.

PROOF: By means of a complicated simultaneous induction on the structure of p and q we have to prove the following five equations:

1. $\partial_H(p \| q) = \partial_H(\nabla_Z(p) \| q)$
2. $\partial_H(p \lfloor\!\lfloor q) = \partial_H(\nabla_Z(p) \lfloor\!\lfloor q)$
3. $\partial_H(q \lfloor\!\lfloor p) = \partial_H(q \lfloor\!\lfloor \nabla_Z(p))$
4. $\partial_H(p | q) = \partial_H(\nabla_Z(p) | q)$
5. $\partial_H(p) = \partial_H(\nabla_Z(p))$.

We will spare the reader the details.

6.3.15 EXAMPLE

Let S, R, E as in 6.3.4. Define F by the following recursive equation:

$$F = \sum_{d \in D} s_1(d) \cdot r_4(d) \cdot r_1(ack) \cdot F.$$

Theorem 6.3.5 says that E behaves the same as F in the context $\partial_H(\_ \| S \| R)$. We will prove this by use of the restriction operator. First, we define a trace set Z.

6.3.16 DEFINITION

Inductively we define $Z \in \mathbb{T}$ by:

1. λ, $s_1(d)$, $s_1(d)r_4(d)$, $s_1(d)r_4(d)r_1(ack) \in Z$ for all $d \in D$;
2. if $\sigma \in Z$, then $s_1(d)r_4(d)r_1(ack)\sigma \in Z$ for all $d \in D$.

6.3.17 LEMMA

$Z = tr \circ v_{\alpha(E)} \circ \partial_H(E \| S \| R)$.

PROOF: by 6.3.5 we find $tr \circ v_{\alpha(E)} \circ \partial_H(E \| S \| R) =$

$$= tr\Big(\sum_{d \in D} s_1(d) \cdot r_4(d) \cdot r_1(ack) \cdot v_{\alpha(E)} \circ \partial_H(E \| S \| R)\Big) =$$

$$= \bigcup_{d \in D} s_1(d) tr(r_4(d) \cdot r_1(ack) \cdot v_{\alpha(E)} \circ \partial_H(E \| S \| R)) =$$

$$= \bigcup_{d \in D} s_1(d)(r_4(d)(r_1(ack) tr \circ v_{\alpha(E)} \circ \partial_H(E \| S \| R))).$$

Now it is not difficult to finish the proof.

6.3.18 LEMMA

$\nabla_Z(E) = F$.

PROOF: since $Z = \bigcup_{d \in D} s_1(d)r_4(d)r_1(ack)Z$, we see that for $d \in D$ we have:

$\partial/_{\partial s_1(d)} Z = r_4(d)r_1(ack)Z$, $\partial/_{\partial r_4(d)}(\partial/_{\partial s_1(d)} Z) = r_1(ack)Z$, $\partial/_{\partial r_1(ack)}(\partial/_{\partial r_4(d)}(\partial/_{\partial s_1(d)} Z)) = Z$.

It follows that

$$\nabla_Z(E) = \nabla_Z((\sum_{d\in D} s_1(d) + \sum r_4(d) + r_1(ack))\cdot E) =$$

$$= \sum_{d\in D} \nabla_Z(s_1(d)\cdot E) + \sum_{d\in D} \nabla_Z(r_4(d)\cdot E) + \nabla_Z(r_1(ack)\cdot E) =$$

$$= \sum_{d\in D} s_1(d)\cdot\nabla_{r4(d)(r1(ack)Z)}(E) + \delta + \delta = \sum_{d\in D} s_1(d)\cdot(\delta + r_4(d)\cdot\nabla_{r1(ack)Z}(E) + \delta) =$$

$$= \sum_{d\in D} s_1(d)\cdot r_4(d)\cdot(\delta + \delta + \nabla_Z(E)) = \sum_{d\in D} s_1(d)\cdot r_4(d)\cdot\nabla_Z(E).$$

We see that the process $\nabla_Z(E)$ satisfies the defining equation of F, and so by RSP it follows that $\nabla_Z(E) = F$.

6.3.19 THEOREM

$\partial_H(E\|S\|R) = \partial_H(F\|S\|R)$.

PROOF: 6.3.14, 6.3.17 and 6.3.18.

6.3.20 EXERCISES

1. Let $B \subseteq A$ such that for all i at most one of $s_i(d)$, $r_i(d)$ is in B. Find a function $g: A \to A\cup\{\tau\}$, such that $\nu_B = \rho_g$.
2. Suppose we do not accept 4.1.2 and assume we have an arbitrary communication function, that nonetheless satisfies handshaking. Then what are the conditions on B to make ν_B well-defined?
3. Prove lemma 6.3.3.
4. Prove theorem 6.3.5.
5. Prove 6.3.9.
6. Find the trace sets of the following processes: $\tau\delta$, a^ω, $a^\omega\|b$, $a^\omega\|b^\omega$ (distinguish cases, whether $\gamma(a,b)$ is defined or not).
7. Prove lemma 6.3.11.
8. Define the operator π_n on trace sets and show that $tr\circ\pi_n(x) = \pi_n\circ tr(x)$ for all closed ACP$^\tau$-terms x.
9. Define action relations for the restriction operator.
10. Define the trace set of a process graph and show that the axioms in 6.3.6 and 6.3.8 hold in the model $\mathbb{G}^\infty/\underline{\leftrightarrow}_{rb}$ of ACP$^\tau$.
11. Prove lemma 6.3.13.
12. Complete the proof of lemma 6.3.17.
13. In this exercise, we will consider the **chaining operator** $\gg$. In process $x \gg y$, the output of process x serves as the input of process y. In order to define this operator, we assume we have special atomic actions $\uparrow d$, $\downarrow d$, $s(d)$, $r(d)$, $c(d)$ (for each $d\in D$), with as only defined communication $\gamma(r(d), s(d)) = c(d)$. We consider the renaming functions f and g, with $f(\uparrow d) = s(d)$ and $g(\downarrow d) = r(d)$, and f and g remain fixed on all other actions. Further, $H = \{r(d), s(d) : d\in D\}$ and $I = \{c(d) : d\in D\}$. Now define

$$x \gg y = \tau_I\circ\partial_H(\rho_f(x) \| \rho_g(y)).$$

Notice that this operator indeed can be used for the stated purpose, and show the following useful identity:

$$\alpha(x)\cap H = \alpha(y)\cap H = \alpha(z)\cap H = \emptyset \Rightarrow (x\gg y)\gg z = x\gg(y\gg z).$$

6.3.21 NOTES AND COMMENTS
This section is based on BAETEN, BERGSTRA [1988a]. Exercise 6.3.21.13 on chaining is based on VAANDRAGER [1990a]. More on the use of trace information in process verifications can be found in VAANDRAGER [1990b].

6.4 STATE OPERATOR

In this section we will define a generalized renaming operator, a renaming *with a memory,* in order to describe processes with an independent global state. The **state operator** λ_s is defined such that $\lambda_s(x)$ represents the execution of x in state s. We will show that we can use this operator to translate computer programs (in a higher order language) into process algebra.

6.4.1 INTUITION
Let S be a set, the **state space**. The execution of an atomic action will affect a specific state and so we obtain an equation of the form

$$\lambda_s(ax) = a' \cdot \lambda_{s'}(x),$$

or, in terms of action relations, a rule of the form

$$x \xrightarrow{a} x' \;\Rightarrow\; \lambda_s(x) \xrightarrow{a'} \lambda_{s'}(x').$$

Here, a' is the action which occurs as the result of executing a in state s, and s' is the state which ensues when executing a in state s. Usually, we will talk about the state of a certain *object* (for instance, the value of a variable), and therefore provide the state operator with an index m, where m is an object name. So, λ_s^m means that the object called m is in state s. The execution of a results in an action a', and a state s'. This a' and s' in general depend on a, m and s. Thus, we have two functions **action** and **effect** on such triples.

We write a(m,s) for action(a, m, s);
s(m,a) for effect(a, m, s).

Let us present the following intuition: in $\lambda_s^m(x)$, m represents a computer, s describes the content of its memory, x is the input (the program) and $\lambda_s^m(x)$ describes what happens when x is presented to computer m in state s.

6.4.2 DEFINITION
Let M and S be two given sets, let A be the set of atomic actions, and C the set of special constants. We assume all these sets to be distinct. Now suppose we have two functions **action:** $A \times M \times S \to A \cup C$ and **effect:** $A \times M \times S \to S$.

$\lambda_s^m(\gamma) = \gamma$	SO1
$\lambda_s^m(a) = a(m,s)$	SO2
$\lambda_s^m(\tau x) = \tau \cdot \lambda_s^m(x)$	SO3
$\lambda_s^m(ax) = a(m,s) \cdot \lambda_{s(m,a)}^m(x)$	SO4
$\lambda_s^m(x + y) = \lambda_s^m(x) + \lambda_s^m(y)$	SO5

TABLE 76. State operator.

For $m \in M$ and $s \in S$, we introduce the unary operators λ_s^m, in table 76. There we have $s \in S$, $m \in M$, $\gamma \in C$, $a \in A$, and x,y are arbitrary processes.

6.4.3 REMARK
The state operator introduced just now, is a generalization of the renaming operator of section 3.6. For, if $f: A \to A \cup C$ is given, take $M=\{m\}$ and $S=\{s\}$ and define the action and effect functions as follows:

$a(m,s) = f(a)$ (for all $a \in A$)
$s(m,a) = s$ (for all $a \in A$).

Then we easily find $\lambda_s^m = \rho_f$.

The state operator is a generalization of the restriction operator as well. It is an exercise to prove this.

6.4.4 EXAMPLE
We can draw the following picture of a serial switch (fig. 41).

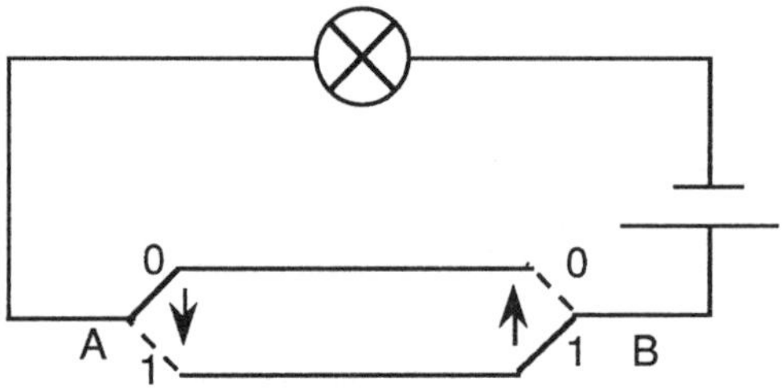

FIGURE 41.

The switches A and B are given by the equations

$A = a \cdot A$
$B = b \cdot B$

(here, the atomic action a stands for switching A, and b for switching B). We have $M=\{m\}$ (in case there is only one object, we will omit m) and $S=\{\langle i,j\rangle : i=0,1, j=0,1\}$. State $\langle i,j\rangle$ stands for the situation in which A is in position i, and B in position j (see fig. 42). We define the action and effect functions by presenting axiom SO4 for all $a \in A$ and $s \in S$ (and $m \in M$) such that $a(m,s) \neq a$ or $s(m,a) \neq s$.

$$\lambda_{\langle i,j\rangle}(ax) = \begin{cases} on(a)\cdot\lambda_{\langle 1-i,j\rangle}(x) & \text{if } i \neq j \\ off(a)\cdot\lambda_{\langle 1-i,j\rangle}(x) & \text{if } i=j \end{cases}$$

$$\lambda_{\langle i,j\rangle}(bx) = \begin{cases} on(b)\cdot\lambda_{\langle i,1-j\rangle}(x) & \text{if } i \neq j \\ off(b)\cdot\lambda_{\langle i,1-j\rangle}(x) & \text{if } i=j \end{cases}$$

Starting in state $\langle 0,1\rangle$ (see figure) we have the process

$P = \lambda_{\langle 0,1\rangle}(A \| B)$.

Now we can prove that

$P = (on(a) + on(b))\cdot(off(a) + off(b))\cdot P$.

6.4.5 EXAMPLE
A random walk.

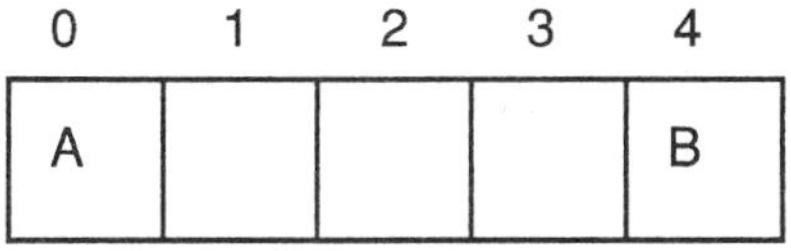

FIGURE 42.

Suppose we have five squares as in figure 42, and suppose the processes A and B each start in a certain square. Then they can start a random walk, so

$A = (la + ra) \cdot A + ha$

$B = (lb + rb) \cdot B + hb$

(we have actions left, right, halt of A and of B). We will describe this process using the state operator. We have $M=\{m\}$ (again omitted) and state space $S=\{\langle i,j\rangle : i,j \in \{0,1,2,3,4\}\}$. The action and effect functions are defined by giving all relevant instantiations of axiom SO4. We obtain:

$$\lambda_{\langle i,j\rangle}(la \cdot x) = \begin{cases} \delta & \text{if } i=0 \text{ or } j=i-1 \\ la \cdot \lambda_{\langle i-1,j\rangle}(x) & \text{otherwise} \end{cases}$$

$$\lambda_{\langle i,j\rangle}(ra \cdot x) = \begin{cases} \delta & \text{if } i=4 \text{ or } j=i+1 \\ ra \cdot \lambda_{\langle i+1,j\rangle}(x) & \text{otherwise} \end{cases}$$

$$\lambda_{\langle i,j\rangle}(ha \cdot x) = ha(i) \cdot \lambda_{\langle i,j\rangle}(x) \qquad \text{(A halts at square i)}$$

and the equations of B are analogous. Then the situation in fig. 42 is described by the process $\lambda_{\langle 0,4\rangle}(A \| B)$.

6.4.6 COMPUTER PROGRAMS

Now we want to use the state operator to translate computer programs into process algebra. The state space S will consist of functions providing every variable in the program with a value. For instance, the state resulting from the execution of the assignment $x:=0$, will be a function $s \in S$ with $s(x)=0$. The set of objects M serve to describe various processors or subroutines with their own variables. However, we get the following problem: translating an instruction read(x) into process algebra, we obtain a process with the possibility of performing $r_1(d)$ for all $d \in D$. We will extend the state operator, in order to deal with this case.

$\Lambda_s^m(\gamma) = \gamma$	GS1
$\Lambda_s^m(a) = \sum_{b \in a(m,s)} b$	GS2
$\Lambda_s^m(\tau x) = \tau \cdot \Lambda_s^m(x)$	GS3
$\Lambda_s^m(ax) = \sum_{b \in a(m,s)} b \cdot \Lambda_{s(m,a,b)}^m(x)$	GS4
$\Lambda_s^m(x + y) = \Lambda_s^m(x) + \Lambda_s^m(y)$	GS5

TABLE 77. Generalized state operator.

6.4.7 DEFINITION

We define the **generalized state operator** as follows. The function action does not necessarily yield one element from $A \cup C$, but a *set* of elements from $A \cup C$, so

$\text{action}: A \times M \times S \to \text{Pow}(A \cup C)$.

Then the effect function will not only depend on the atom, the name and the previous state, but also on the alternative chosen in the action function, so

$\text{effect}: S \times M \times A \times (A \cup C) \to S$.

Things are will probably become clearer in table 77. Here we have $s \in S$, $m \in M$, $\gamma \in C$, $a \in A_\delta$, x,y arbitrary processes. Notice that $\Lambda^m_s(ax) = \delta$ iff $a(m,s) = \varnothing$.

6.4.8 EXAMPLE

We translate a simple computer program into process algebra. In this case we have $M=\{m\}$ (again omitted) and S consists of functions from the set of variables to $\mathbb{N}$ (with some upper bound N, if required). On $\mathbb{N}$ we have functions s (successor) and p (predecessor). If $\sigma \in S$ and x is a variable, then $\sigma\{n/x\}$ is the function which is precisely σ, except that $\sigma(x)=n$, so

$\sigma\{n/x\}(x) = n$, and

$\sigma\{n/x\}(y) = \sigma(y)$ if $x \neq y$.

We have the following program P:

```
read(x)
y:=0
while x≠0 do y:=s(s(y)); x:=p(x)
write(y)
```

(We see that P is a program that doubles the input value.)

Suppose that for all simple instructions v, the translation in process algebra $[\![v]\!]$, is an atomic action. The translation of the program constructs can be found from the following translation of P:

$P = [\![\text{read}(x)]\!] \cdot [\![y:=0]\!] \cdot Z \cdot [\![\text{write}(y)]\!]$

$Z = [\![x \neq 0]\!] \cdot [\![y:=ss(y)]\!] \cdot [\![x:=p(x)]\!] \cdot Z + [\![x=0]\!]$.

Again we define the action and effect functions by giving all relevant instantiations of axiom GS4.

$$\Lambda_\sigma([\![\text{read}(x)]\!] \cdot Q) = \sum_{n<N} r_1(n) \cdot \Lambda_{\sigma\{n/x\}}(Q)$$

$$\Lambda_\sigma([\![y:=0]\!] \cdot Q) = [\![y:=0]\!] \cdot \Lambda_{\sigma\{0/y\}}(Q)$$

$$\Lambda_\sigma([\![\text{write}(y)]\!] \cdot Q) = s_2(\sigma(y)) \cdot \Lambda_\sigma(Q)$$

$$\Lambda_\sigma([\![x \neq 0]\!] \cdot Q) = \begin{cases} \delta & \text{if } \sigma(x)=0 \\ \tau \cdot \Lambda_\sigma(Q) & \text{if } \sigma(x) \neq 0 \end{cases}$$

$$\Lambda_\sigma([\![x=0]\!] \cdot Q) = \begin{cases} \tau \cdot \Lambda_\sigma(Q) & \text{if } \sigma(x)=0 \\ \delta & \text{if } \sigma(x) \neq 0 \end{cases}$$

$$\Lambda_\sigma([\![x=0]\!] \cdot Q) = \delta \qquad \text{if } \sigma(x) \neq 0$$

$$\Lambda_\sigma([\![y:=ss(y)]\!] \cdot Q) = [\![y:=ss(y)]\!] \cdot \Lambda_{\sigma\{\sigma(y)+2/y\}}(Q)$$

$$\Lambda_\sigma([\![x:=p(x)]\!] \cdot Q) = [\![x:=p(x)]\!] \cdot \Lambda_{\sigma\{\sigma(x)-1/x\}}(Q).$$

We see that the actions $[\![x:=0]\!]$ and $[\![x \neq 0]\!]$ act as *guarded commands.* Abstracting from all internal actions we can *prove* that this program indeed doubles any given input value. Putting $I = \{[\![y:=0]\!], [\![y:=ss(y)]\!], [\![x:=p(x)]\!]\}$, we can prove that for all $\sigma \in S$

$$\tau_I \circ \Lambda_\sigma(P) = \sum_{n \in \mathbb{N}} r_1(n) \cdot s_2(2n).$$

6.4.9 EXAMPLE

Again, we consider the queue. In fact, a queue only performs read and write actions, so we may want to write

$$queue = read^\omega \| write^\omega$$

(where $read^\omega$ is defined by the equation $X = read \cdot X$, and $write^\omega$ by $X = write \cdot X$). Again, this view can be implemented by means of the generalized state operator: take $M = \{\langle 1,2 \rangle\}$ (representing the names of the input and output channels; again omitted) and $S = D^*$ (the set of words over the data set D; represents the content of the queue). We define action and effect by the following equations:

$$\Lambda_\sigma(read \cdot Q) = \sum_{d \in D} r_1(d) \cdot \Lambda_{d\sigma}(Q)$$

$$\Lambda_\lambda(write \cdot Q) = \delta$$

$$\Lambda_{\sigma d}(write \cdot Q) = s_2(d) \cdot \Lambda_\sigma(Q).$$

Then it can be proved that $Q = \Lambda_\lambda(read^\omega \| write^\omega)$.

6.4.10 EXERCISES

1. Prove in 6.4.4 that $P = (on(a) + on(b)) \cdot (off(a) + off(b)) \cdot P$.
Hint: first use RSP to show that $\lambda_{\langle 0,1 \rangle}(A \| B) = \lambda_{\langle 1,0 \rangle}(A \| B)$ and $\lambda_{\langle 0,0 \rangle}(A \| B) = \lambda_{\langle 1,1 \rangle}(A \| B)$.
2. In case $I = \{la, ra, lb, rb\}$, prove that for the process in 6.4.5

$$\tau_I \circ \lambda_{\langle 0,4 \rangle}(A \| B) = \tau \cdot \Big(\sum_{0 \le i \le 3} ha(i) \cdot \sum_{i+1 \le j \le 4} hb(j) + \sum_{1 \le j \le 4} hb(j) \cdot \sum_{0 \le i \le j-1} ha(i) \Big).$$

Hint: use CFAR. Thus we have shown that in each possible final state, A is to the left of B.
3. Describe a random walk of A and B on a square plane of nine squares, if the possible actions of each process are left, right, up, down, halt.
4. Define the **alphabet** of an object $m \in M$ as being the set of actions for which action or effect is not fixed, i.e. $\alpha(m) = \{a \in A$: there is $s \in S$ such that $a(m,s) \neq a$ or $s(m,a) \neq s\}$. Prove that for all ACP$^\tau$-terms x,y without any communications: if $\alpha(x) \cap \alpha(m') = \emptyset$ and $\{a(m',s) \in A : a \in \alpha(y), s \in S\} \cap \alpha(m) = \emptyset$, then $\lambda_s^m \circ \lambda_{s'}^{m'}(x \| y) = \lambda_s^m(x) \| \lambda_{s'}^{m'}(y)$.
5. Prove for all closed ACP$^\tau$-terms x: if $H \cap \alpha(m) = \emptyset$, and if $a(m,s) \notin H$ for every $s \in S$ and $a \in A - H$, then $\lambda_s^m \circ \partial_H(x) = \partial_H \circ \lambda_s^m(x)$.
6. Prove for all closed ACP$^\tau$-terms x,y, that if:
- $\alpha(x) \cap \alpha(m) \cap \alpha(m') = \emptyset$,
- for all $s \in S$ and $a \in \alpha(x) \cap \alpha(m)$: $a(m,s) \notin \alpha(m')$,
- for all $s \in S$ and all $a \in \alpha(x) \cap \alpha(m')$: $a(m',s) \notin \alpha(m)$,

then: $\lambda_s^m \circ \lambda_{s'}^{m'}(x) = \lambda_{s'}^{m'} \circ \lambda_s^m(x)$.
7. Prove the equation in the last line of 6.4.8. For sake of simplicity, only consider summands with $n = 0,1,2$.
8. How could one translate an if...then...else...-construct into process algebra? And an instruction $x := y$?
9. Translate some computer program, chosen by yourself, into process algebra.

10. Prove that the processes $\Lambda_\sigma(\text{read}^\omega \| \text{write}^\omega)$ from 6.4.9 satisfy the specification of the queue in table 44 (see 4.8.1).
11. Define action relations for the state operator and the generalized state operator.
12. Define the state operator and the generalized state operator in the model $\mathbb{G}^\infty/\underline{\leftrightarrow}_{rb}$ of ACP^τ. Verify that the axioms hold.

6.4.11 NOTES AND COMMENTS

This section is based on BAETEN & BERGSTRA [1988a]. The state operator has been used in process verifications in VAANDRAGER [1986] and GROENVELD [1987]. In VAANDRAGER [1990a] a formal semantics is given for the parallel object-oriented language POOL, using the ideas of 6.4.8 (for a semantics of POOL in a different setting, see AMERICA, DE BAKKER, KOK & RUTTEN [1989]). Another use of the state operator is given in VERHOEF [1990].

6.5 ASYNCHRONOUS COMMUNICATION

Until now, we have only considered synchronous communication: a communication is the result of the simultaneous execution of two appropriate actions. In this section we describe **asynchronous** communication: after sending a message, it may take some time before it is received. In fact, we will consider two variants: in the first variant, the messages that are on the way are ordered in a queue; in the second, the messages are put in a bag. It will turn out that we are able to describe a cause-and-effect mechanism.

In each case we will use the state operator of the previous section, to describe the mechanisms.

6.5.1 SYNTAX

We define special atomic actions for **mail through a communication channel**. Let D be a finite data set and c a communication channel. Then we have the following atomic actions:

$c\uparrow d$	send d via c: *potential* action;
$c\Uparrow d$	send d via c: *realized* action;
$c\downarrow d$	receive d via c: *potential* action;
$c\Downarrow d$	receive d via c: *realized* action.

$c\uparrow d$ is a potential, an intended action. $c\Uparrow d$ is a realized, real action (note that $c\uparrow d$ and $c\Uparrow d$ appear *simultaneously*). This difference will be made clear later on. With synchronous communication this works similarly: $r_i(d)$ and $s_i(d)$ are potential actions, and $c_i(d)$ is the realized action.

6.5.2 STATE OPERATOR

For every communication channel c we have a state operator λ^c. Now, we distinguish between two cases:

1. The channel behaves like a queue: the data c are kept in an ordered sequence. The state space in this case is D^*. We will deal with this case in 6.5.3. An example is the transmission of a radio message to a space satellite.
2. The channel behaves like a bag: the data in c are kept in a multi-set. A **multi-set** is not the same thing as an ordinary set, since it can contain the same element more times: for every $d \in D$

we keep track of how many there are in the channel (see 3.5). The state space is the set of multi-sets over D. This case is considered in 6.5.4. An example is sending letters by ordinary mail.

6.5.3 MAIL THROUGH A QUEUE-LIKE CHANNEL

We describe the action and effect functions by listing all relevant instantiations of axiom SO4. If $\sigma \in D^*$ and $\sigma \neq \lambda$ (the empty word), then $last(\sigma)$ is the last element of σ. We have the following axioms:

$$\lambda^{c}_{\sigma}(c{\uparrow}d \cdot x) = c{\Uparrow}d \cdot \lambda^{c}_{d\sigma}(x)$$
$$\lambda^{c}_{\sigma d}(c{\downarrow}d \cdot x) = c{\Downarrow}d \cdot \lambda^{c}_{\sigma}(x)$$
$$\lambda^{c}_{\sigma}(c{\downarrow}d \cdot x) = \delta \text{ if } last(\sigma) \neq d \text{ or } \sigma = \lambda.$$

6.5.4 MAIL THROUGH A BAG-LIKE CHANNEL

Again, we give all relevant instantiations of SO4. Let c be a channel, and M a multi-set over D.

$$\lambda^{c}_{M}(c{\uparrow}d \cdot x) = c{\Uparrow}d \cdot \lambda^{c}_{M \cup \{d\}}(x)$$
$$\lambda^{c}_{M \cup \{d\}}(c{\downarrow}d \cdot x) = c{\Downarrow}d \cdot \lambda^{c}_{M}(x)$$
$$\lambda^{c}_{M}(c{\downarrow}d \cdot x) = \delta \qquad \text{if } d \notin M.$$

6.5.5 EXAMPLE

Suppose we have a communication network as in fig. 43. Here 1 and 2 are ordinary ports, and c and c' are queue-like channels.

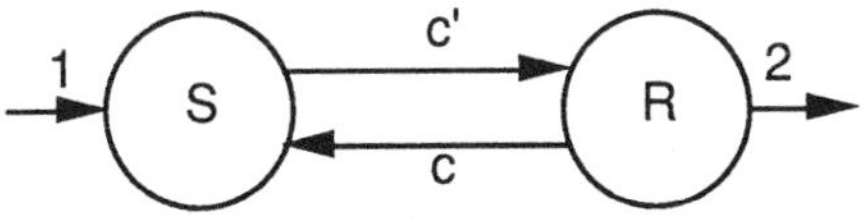

FIGURE 43.

Define $S = \sum_{d \in D} r1(d) \cdot c{\uparrow}d \cdot c'{\downarrow}ack \cdot S$ and $R = \sum_{d \in D} c{\downarrow}d \cdot s2(d) \cdot c'{\uparrow}ack \cdot R$,

then: $\lambda^{c}_{\lambda} \circ \lambda^{c'}_{\lambda}(S \| R) = \sum_{d \in D} r1(d) \cdot c{\Uparrow}d \cdot c{\Downarrow}d \cdot s2(d) \cdot c'{\Uparrow}ack \cdot c'{\Downarrow}ack \cdot \lambda^{c}_{\lambda} \circ \lambda^{c'}_{\lambda}(S \| R)$.

This is not difficult. An undesirable feature is the double use of the symbol λ: on the line it is the state operator, and as a subscript it stands for the empty word in D^*.

6.5.6 CAUSALITY

One could say that $c{\Uparrow}d$ is the realized form of $c{\uparrow}d$, and in an analogous way $c{\Downarrow}d$ is the action $c{\downarrow}d$ after execution or realization. There also is a causal effect: $c{\uparrow}d$ causes $c{\downarrow}d$. These concepts will be made clear in the following.

6.5.7 REALIZATION

Suppose the set of atomic actions is partitioned into two parts: we have the potential actions in P, and the realized actions in R; $A = P \cup R$. For every element $a \in P$ there is a corresponding element $\mathrm{a} \in R$; we say a is the **realization** of a. On the set P we have a binary relation $\Vdash$;

$a \Vdash b$ means a **causes** b. If $a \Vdash b$ for certain a and b, then a is a **cause** or **stimulus**, and b an **effect** or **response**. Let $R(a)$ be the set of effects from a. Note that an action can be a cause and an effect at the same time.

The execution of an a now has two consequences: a changes into a, and all $b \in R(a)$ become **operational**: they can be executed from now on. We describe this by use of the state operator. The state space now consists of subsets of P: the set of operational actions. Again, we present all relevant instantiations of axiom SO4:

$$\lambda_S(a \cdot x) = a \cdot \lambda_{S \cup R(a)}(x) \qquad \text{if } a \text{ is not an effect;}$$
$$\lambda_S(a \cdot x) = a \cdot \lambda_{(S-\{a\}) \cup R(a)}(x) \qquad \text{if } a \in S \text{ and } a \text{ is an effect;}$$
$$\lambda_S(a \cdot x) = \delta \qquad \text{if } a \notin S \text{ and } a \text{ is an effect.}$$

6.5.8 EXAMPLES

1. Suppose $a \Vdash d$ and $c \Vdash b$. Then we have $\lambda_\emptyset(ab \parallel cd) = (a \| c)(b \| d)$.
2. If $d \Vdash a$ and $b \Vdash c$, then $\lambda_\emptyset(ab \parallel cd) = \delta$.
3. Suppose $a \Vdash c$ and $d \Vdash b$. Then $\lambda_\emptyset((ab)^\omega \| (cd)^\omega) = (acdb)^\omega$.

6.5.9 NOTE

Once an action has been executed, it is non-operational, no matter how often it was made operational. For instance we have $\lambda_\emptyset(bbcc) = bbc\delta$, if $b \Vdash c$. Replacing sets by multi-sets in definition 6.5.7, we obtain a variant which sets counters.

6.5.10 EXERCISES

1. Assume we have asynchronous communication and a bag-like channel, then calculate:

i. $\lambda^c_\emptyset(c{\uparrow}d \cdot c{\downarrow}d)$; ii. $\lambda^c_\emptyset(c{\uparrow}d \cdot \sum_{e \in D} c{\downarrow}e)$; iii. $\lambda^c_\emptyset(c{\uparrow}d \cdot c{\uparrow}e \cdot \sum_{f \in D} c{\downarrow}f \cdot \sum_{g \in D} c{\downarrow}g)$;

iv. $\lambda^c_\emptyset(c{\uparrow}d \| c{\downarrow}d)$.

2. Verify the formula for the process $\lambda^c_\lambda \circ \lambda^{c'}_\lambda(S \| R)$ in 6.5.5.
3. Verify the examples 6.5.8.
4. Define a causality mechanism with more then one cause for each effect.
5. Assume we have a network with components CM (Command Module), P (Printer) and D (Display). CM can turn on the printer, the printer will stop by itself. When the paper runs out, this message is put on the screen. After new paper is supplied, the printing will continue. When P is ready, this is reported to CM. The components are given by the following recursive equations:

$$CM = PC \cdot RP \cdot CM$$
$$P = STP \cdot PAD \cdot P'$$
$$P' = STOP \cdot P + POP \cdot NP \cdot P'$$
$$D = START \cdot D'$$
$$D' = DSTOP \cdot D + DPOP \cdot OK \cdot D'.$$

Here, we have the following atomic actions: *PC* = printing command; *RP* = reply from printer; *STP* = start printer; *PAD* = printer asks for data; *STOP* = printer stops; *NOP* = no paper; *NP* = new paper; *START* = display 'start'; *DSTOP* = display 'stop'; *DNOP* = display 'nop'; *OK* = display 'ok'. Assume we have the following causality relations: $PC \Vdash STP$; $STP \Vdash START$; $STOP \Vdash DSTOP$; $DSTOP \Vdash RP$; $POP \Vdash DPOP$; $DPOP \Vdash NP$; $NP \Vdash OK$.

Now derive a recursive specification for the system $\lambda_\emptyset(CM \| P \| D)$.

6.5.11 NOTES AND COMMENTS

This section is based on BERGSTRA, KLOP & TUCKER [1985]. The presentation here however, using the state operator, comes from BAETEN [1986].

6.6 ASYMMETRIC COMMUNICATION

In this section we will again consider synchronous communication. We will describe two asymmetric (and synchronous) communication mechanisms. In this description we will make use of the θ operator from section 6.1.

We start with two processes S and R, connected by a communication port j. We describe three ways in which S and R may communicate: **handshaking, put** and **get**.

6.6.1. HANDSHAKING

This is the situation we are used to, illustrated in fig. 44.

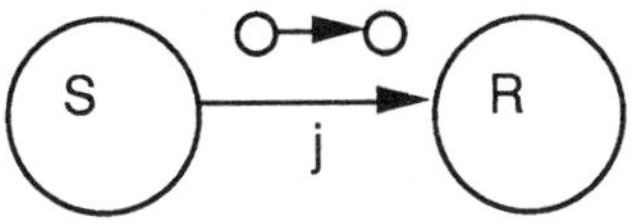

FIGURE 44. Handshaking.

We define $r_j(D) = \{r_j(d) : d \in D\}$, and $s_j(D)$, $c_j(D)$ similarly. Then we find the following properties:

$$s_j(D) \subseteq \alpha(S),\ r_j(D) \cap \alpha(S) = \emptyset$$
$$r_j(D) \subseteq \alpha(R),\ s_j(D) \cap \alpha(R) = \emptyset.$$

Communication: $\gamma(s_j(d), r_j(d)) = c_j(d)$.

The composition of S and R as parallel processes, is given by $\partial_{s_j(D)} \circ \partial_{r_j(D)}(S \| R)$, or $\partial_{H_j}(S \| R)$ for short ($H_j = s_j(D) \cup r_j(D)$).

6.6.2. PUT

S puts a message at the port, no matter whether R is able to receive it or not. S will do $put_j(d)$, and if R can do $r_j(d)$, then we obtain the communication $c_j(d)$. Otherwise we just have $put_j(d)$, and the message will be lost. This is illustrated in fig. 45.

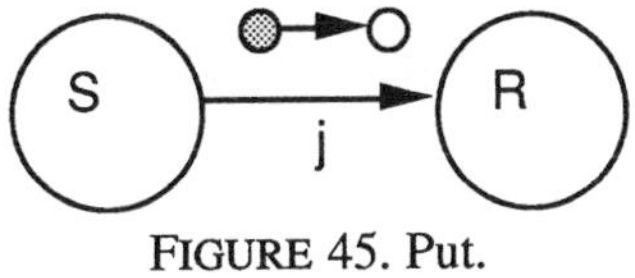

FIGURE 45. Put.

In this case we have the properties:

$$put_j(D) \subseteq \alpha(S),\ r_j(D) \cap \alpha(S) = \emptyset$$
$$r_j(D) \subseteq \alpha(R),\ put_j(D) \cap \alpha(R) = \emptyset,$$

but moreover we must assume

$$c_j(D) \cap \alpha(S) = \emptyset,\ c_j(D) \cap \alpha(R) = \emptyset.$$

Communication: $\gamma(put_j(d), r_j(d)) = c_j(d)$.

Priorities: we define an ordering by putting $put_j(d) < c_j(d)$ for all d. Let θ_{put_j} be the operator corresponding to this ordering. Then the parallel composition of R and S is given by

$$\partial_{r_j(D)} \circ \theta_{put_j}(S \| R).$$

Applying the operator $\partial_{put_j(D)}$ gives back handshaking.

6.6.3. GET

R tries to read a message from channel j. If S can send d, we have a resulting communication $c_j(d)$. Otherwise, R will do $get_j(\perp)$. A typical appearance of get is as follows:

$$R = \sum_{d \in D} get_j(d) \cdot X_d + get_j(\perp) \cdot X_\perp .$$

This is illustrated in fig. 46.

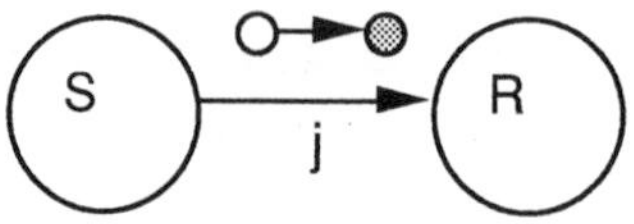

FIGURE 46. Get.

We define $D_\perp = D \cup \{\perp\}$, and have the following properties:

$$s_j(D) \subseteq \alpha(S),\ get_j(D_\perp) \cap \alpha(S) = \emptyset$$
$$get_j(D_\perp) \subseteq \alpha(R),\ s_j(D) \cap \alpha(R) = \emptyset$$
$$c_j(D) \cap \alpha(S) = \emptyset,\ c_j(D) \cap \alpha(R) = \emptyset.$$

Communication: $\gamma(s_j(d), get_j(d)) = c_j(d)$.

Priorities: we define an ordering by putting $get_j(\perp) < c_j(d)$ for all d. Let θ_{get_j} be the operator corresponding to this ordering. Then the parallel composition of S and R is:

$$\partial_{get_j(D)} \circ \partial_{s_j(D)} \circ \theta_{get_j}(S \| R),$$

or, if $H_j = get_j(D) \cup s_j(D)$, by

$$\partial_{H_j} \circ \theta_{get_j}(S \| R).$$

Again, applying $\partial_{get_j(\perp)}$, we have handshaking.

6.6.4 MOTIVATION

One can think of put, as of the transmission of a radiographic message, which is sent no matter whether it is received or not. The get mechanism is of course the counterpart of put. One can think of a machine, which regularly reads data from a queue. When the queue is empty, an error message will be read.

6.6.5 BROADCASTING

Without much effort, we can generalize the put mechanism to a **broadcast** mechanism, in which case a message is sent to a large number of receivers at the same time (think of a radio or television broadcast). We have the following atomic actions:

$brc_j(d)$ = broadcast d through j

$r_j(d)$ = receive d through j

$r_j^m(d)$ = d is received m times through j   ($m \geq 1$, $r_1^m(d) \equiv r_j(d)$)

$c_j^m(d)$ = d is communicated m times through j ($m \geq 1$).

We will also write $c_j^0(d)$ instead of $brc_j(d)$.

Communications: $\gamma(r_j^m(d), r_j^k(d)) = r_j^{m+k}(d)$, $\gamma(c_j^p(d), r_j^k(d)) = c_j^{p+k}(d)$, if $m,k \geq 1$, $p \geq 0$ (so we have in particular that $\gamma(brc_j(d), r_j(d)) = c_j^1(d)$).

Priorities: we define an ordering by putting $c_j^m(d) < c_j^{m+1}(d)$ for all d (we want to maximize the number of communications). Let θ_{brc_j} be the operator corresponding to this ordering, and define $r_j^{\leq N}(D) = \cup_{m \leq N} r_j^m(D)$, then the system with N listeners is given by:

$$\partial_{r_j^{\leq N}(D)} \circ \theta_{brc_j}(S \| R_1 \| R_2 \| \ldots \| R_N).$$

The architecture for N=3 is illustrated in fig. 47.

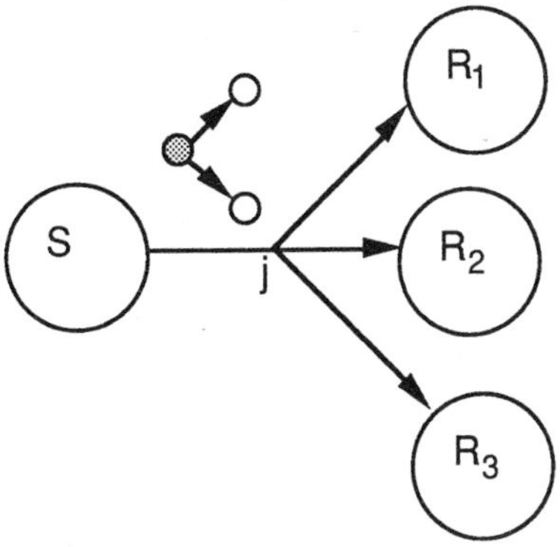

FIGURE 47. Broadcast.

6.6.6 EXAMPLE

Let D be a finite data set, and define $D' = D \cup \{reset\}$. Suppose we have a network as in fig. 48, and the processes are given by the following equations.

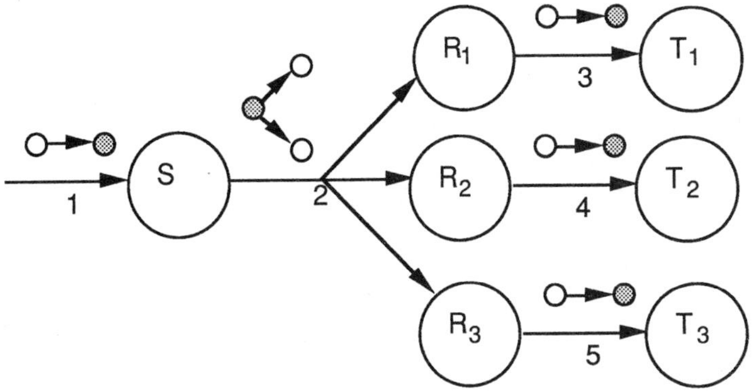

FIGURE 48.

$$S = \sum_{d \in D} get_1(d) \cdot brc_2(d) \cdot i \cdot brc_2(reset) \cdot S + get_1(\perp) \cdot S$$

$$R_n = \sum_{d \in D} r_2(d) \cdot (s_{n+2}(d) + r_2(reset)) \cdot R_n \qquad (n=1,2,3)$$

$$T_n = \sum_{d \in D} get_{n+2}(d) \cdot print(d) \cdot T_n + get_{n+2}(\perp) \cdot T_n \qquad (n=1,2,3).$$

Then the process is given by:

$$\partial^3_{r_2(D')} \circ \partial_{s_3(D)} \circ \partial_{s_4(D)} \circ \partial_{s_5(D)} \circ \theta_{brc_2} \circ \theta_{get_3} \circ \theta_{get_4} \circ \theta_{get_5}(S \| R_1 \| R_2 \| R_3 \| T_1 \| T_2 \| T_3).$$

6.6.7 EXERCISES

1. Describe the behaviour of the process in 6.3.6 (no calculations, but an informal description will do).

2. Check that the Alternating Bit Protocol with all occurrences of $s_j(d)$ replaced by $put_j(d)$, is a correct protocol.

3. To show that replacing asymmetric by symmetric communication does not always give the same result, consider the following pathological communication protocol.

Suppose we have the architecture of fig. 49.

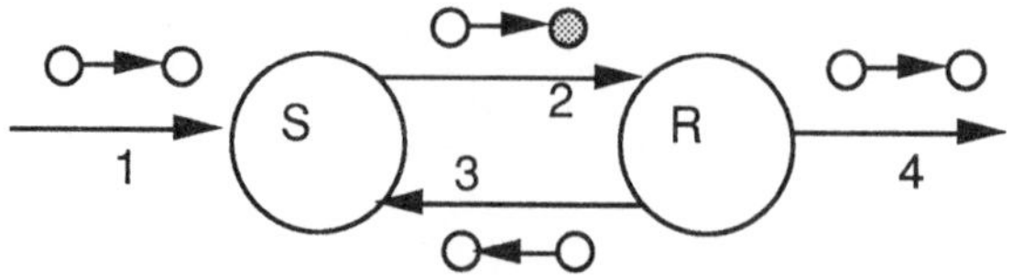

FIGURE 49.

The processes S and R are given by the following specifications:

$$S = \sum_{d \in D} r_1(d) \cdot S_d$$

$$S_d = s_2(d) \cdot i \cdot S_d + r_3(ack) \cdot S \qquad \text{for } d \in D$$

$$R = \sum_{d \in D} get_2(d) \cdot s_4(d) \cdot s_3(ack) \cdot R' + get_2(\bot) \cdot R$$

$$R' = \sum_{d \in D} get_2(d) \cdot R' + get_2(\bot) \cdot R.$$

Now let $P = \partial_{H_3} \circ \partial_{H_2} \circ \theta_{get_2}(S \| R)$, and define $I = \{get_2(\bot), i, c_3(ack)\} \cup c_2(D)$. Now prove with KFAR that

$$\tau_I(P) = \tau \cdot \sum_{d \in D} r_1(d) \cdot s_4(d) \cdot \tau_I(P),$$

so P is a correct communication protocol. Prove, however, that P^*, obtained by replacing all $get_2(d)$ by $r_2(d)$, and all $get_2(\bot)$ by δ, contains a deadlock. So we see that the behaviour of P has deteriorated, by increasing the level of synchronization. Explain this, and consider the special role of KFAR in the verification.

6.6.8 NOTES AND COMMENTS

This section is based on unpublished work of Jan Bergstra (1985), and the presentation is taken from BAETEN [1986].

6.7 PROCESS CREATION

In this section we will describe a mechanism for process creation. We work in the system ACP or an extension of ACP. We will show that process creation is definable in ACP^τ.

6.7.1 DEFINITION

Let D be a finite data set. For every $d \in D$ we have an atomic action $cr(d)$. $cr(d)$ means that a process is created starting from information d. An action $cr(d)$ does not communicate and is not the result of any communication. Let $cr(D) = \{cr(d) : d \in D\}$.

$E_\phi(\tau) = \tau$	
$E_\phi(a) = a$	if $a \notin cr(D)$
$E_\phi(cr(d)) = \overline{cr}(d) \cdot E_\phi(\phi(d))$	for $d \in D$
$E_\phi(\tau x) = \tau \cdot E_\phi(x)$	
$E_\phi(ax) = a \cdot E_\phi(x)$ if $a \notin cr(D)$	
$E_\phi(cr(d) \cdot x) = \overline{cr}(d) \cdot E_\phi(\phi(d) \parallel x)$	for $d \in D$
$E_\phi(x + y) = E_\phi(x) + E_\phi(y)$	

TABLE 78. Process creation.

Let ϕ be a function, assigning a process $\phi(d)$ to every $d \in D$. Now we define the **process creation operator** E_ϕ by the equations of table 78. In table 78 we have $a \in A$, $\gamma \in C$, the set of special constants, and x,y are arbitrary processes. $\overline{cr}(d)$ is an atomic action (for all $d \in D$), to mark that a process creation has taken place ($\phi(d)$ is 'born').

6.7.2 LEMMA

Suppose there is no communication, then we have for all closed ACP$^\tau$-terms x,y:

$$E_\phi(x \parallel y) = E_\phi(x) \parallel E_\phi(y).$$

PROOF: by induction on the structure of x and y.

In the following we will make use of this lemma for recursively defined processes.

6.7.3 EXAMPLES

1. Let $D = \{d\}$, $\phi(d) = cr(d)$. Let $P = E_\phi(cr(d))$, then $P = \overline{cr}(d) \cdot P$. So we see that even the simplest examples give rise to recursive equations.

2. Let $D = \{d\}$, $\phi(d) = a \cdot cr(d) \parallel b \cdot cr(d)$. Let $\gamma(a,b)$ be undefined, then it follows by lemma 6.7.2 that for $P = E_\phi(cr(d))$ the recursive equation $P = \overline{cr}(d) \cdot (aP \parallel bP)$ holds.

3. Let $D = \{d\}$, $\phi(d) = a \cdot (cr(d) \parallel cr(d)) + b$. Let $\gamma(a,b)$ be undefined, then, again by 6.7.2, assuming $P = E_\phi(cr(d))$ we have $P = \overline{cr}(d) \cdot a(P \parallel P) + b\delta$, so the number of P's may decrease or increase.

6.7.4 EXAMPLE: A GROUP OF ANIMALS.

Let D be a finite set of genetic codes, with a mixing operation $*: D \times D \to D$ and a predicate $F \subseteq D$ (F stands for female). For all $a \in D$ define the following processes:

$$P_a = (hunt(a) + sleep(a) + eat(a) + rest(a)) \cdot P_a + end(a)$$

for $a \notin F$: $\quad Q_a = \sum_{b \in D} mate(a,b) \cdot Q_a + end(a)$

for $a \in F$: $\quad Q_a = \sum_{b \in D} mate(a,b) \cdot Q_a + end(a) + \sum_{b \notin F} mate(a,b) \cdot (create(a*b) \cdot Q_a + end(a))$

The defined communications are

$\gamma(end(a),end(a)) = \overline{end}(a)$, and $\gamma(mate(a,b),mate(b,a)) = \overline{mate}$.

Let $H = \{end(a): a \in D\}$ and $H' = \{mate(a,b): a,b \in D\}$. Define $\phi(a) = \partial_H(P_a \parallel Q_a)$, for $a \in D$. Let $S = \partial_{H'}(E_\phi(\phi(a_0) \parallel \phi(a_1)))$, for some a_0, $a_1 \in D$. S describes a group of animals, starting from two individuals. Every animal is able to hunt, sleep, eat, rest, mate, create (if female) and end (its life). The group can develop in several ways.

6.7.5 BAG

Let $C = \sum_{d \in D} r_1(d) \cdot cr(d) \cdot C$, $\phi(d) = s_2(d)$ and $I = \overline{cr}(D)$. Then we can derive the following recursive equation, assuming $B = \tau_I \circ E_\phi(C)$:

$B = \sum_{d \in D} r_1(d) \cdot (s_2(d) \| B)$ (again use 6.7.2). Therefore B is a bag (see 3.5).

This can be motivated as follows: the input action $r_1(d)$ creates the possibility of doing the output action $s_2(d)$.

6.7.6 EXERCISES

1. Prove lemma 6.7.2.
2. Derive the recursive equations in 6.7.3.
3. Derive the recursive equation in 6.7.5.
4. The operator E_ϕ can be defined in ACP$^\tau$. Indeed, define new actions $cr^*(d)$ (for all $d \in D$), and $stop$, $stop^*$, $\overline{stop}$, with defined communications $\gamma(cr(d), cr^*(d)) = \overline{cr}(d)$ ($d \in D$) and $\gamma(stop, stop^*) = \overline{stop}$. Then define K_ϕ as follows:

$$K_\phi = \sum_{d \in D} cr^*(d) \cdot (K_\phi \| \phi(d)) + stop^*.$$

Let $H = \{cr(d), cr^*(d) : d \in D\} \cup \{stop, stop^*\}$, and let $I = \{\overline{stop}\}$. Assume p is a process in which E_ϕ does not occur. Now prove

$$E_\phi(p) = \tau_I \circ \partial_H(K_\phi \| p),$$

by showing that the operator $\tau_I \circ \partial_H(K_\phi \| \_)$ satisfies all laws of table 78.

5. (A sieve of Eratosthenes) We write a program Z generating all prime numbers in $N^* = \{1,2,...,N\}$ as follows. We have the following atomic actions:

$s_0(i)$	output i ($i \in N^*$)
$r_i(j)$, $s_i(j)$, $c_i(j)$	communication via internal channels ($i,j \in N^*$)
$cr(i,j)$, $\overline{cr}(i,j)$	actions of process creation ($i,j \in N^*$)

Moreover we use the following expressions:

$$t(i=0 \bmod j) = \begin{cases} \tau & \text{if } i=0 \bmod j \ (i,j \in N^*) \\ \delta & \text{otherwise} \end{cases}$$

$$t(i \neq 0 \bmod j) = \begin{cases} \tau & \text{if } i \neq 0 \bmod j \ (i,j \in N^*) \\ \delta & \text{otherwise} \end{cases}$$

The encapsulation set H is defined as $H = \{r_i(j), s_i(j) : i,j \in N^*\}$, and the abstraction set I by $I = \{c_i(j), \overline{cr}(i,j) : i,j \in N^*\}$.

Then $Z = \tau_I \circ \partial_H \circ E_\phi(S_1)$, with $S_1 = cr(1,2) \cdot s_1(3) \cdot s_1(4) \cdot .... \cdot s_1(N)$. S_1 creates a process for the first prime number 2, and next it sends all numbers 3,4,...,N through channel 1 ($\phi(1,2)$ will receive these numbers). Finally we have to define a function ϕ:

$$\phi(i,j) = S_{i,j} = s_0(j) \cdot \sum_{k \in N^*} r_i(k) \cdot [t(k=0 \bmod j) \cdot S_{i,j} + t(k \neq 0 \bmod j) \cdot cr(j,k) \cdot R_{i,j}]$$

$$R_{i,j} = \sum_{k \in N^*} r_i(k) \cdot [t(k=0 \bmod j) \cdot R_{i,j} + t(k \neq 0 \bmod j) \cdot s_j(k) \cdot R_{i,j}].$$

$\phi(i,j)$ is explained as follows: $S_{i,j}$ will be created as soon as $S_{h,i}$ finds a new prime number j (h,i,j are successive prime numbers). First, $S_{i,j}$ will output the prime number j, and next it will receive new numbers. All incoming numbers are tested to find out if they are equal to 0 modulo j. The first $k \neq 0 \bmod j$ must be a prime number (it has survived the whole pipeline from S_1 to $S_{1,2}$ to $S_{2,3}$ to $S_{3,5}$ ... until $S_{i,j}$). For this k a new process $S_{j,k}$ is created. Then $S_{i,j}$ only needs to filter numbers from the pipeline, that are divisible by j. All other numbers are sent to $S_{j,k}$.

Take $N=10$. Prove that $Z = s_0(2) \cdot s_0(3) \cdot s_0(5) \cdot s_0(7) \cdot \delta$. First draw the communication network of the processes that are involved, and a process graph of the process before and after abstraction.

6.7.7 NOTES AND COMMENTS

This section is based on BERGSTRA [1990]. For another approach to process creation, see AMERICA & DE BAKKER [1988].

6.8 SYNCHRONOUS COOPERATION

In chapter 4 we presented ACP, in which parallelism is described by interleaving and so in ACP we implicitly have *asynchronous* cooperation of parallel processes. In many cases however, it turns out that a process can be described much easier in a clocked network instead. Therefore in this section we will present a variant of ACP, called the *Algebra of Synchronous Processes* (ASP), in which *synchronous* cooperation can be modeled.

We will not extensively present all results that can be obtained in ASP. As throughout this chapter, we leave it to the reader to construct models and prove the axiom system complete. Nevertheless, the results that *are* given here may give the reader a good impression of the possibilities and possible applications.

6.8.1. SYNCHRONOUS COMPOSITION

The theory ASP embodies a different extension of BPA_δ from chapter 2. That is, instead of defining the extension operator $\|$ we will introduce a different operator $|$ as follows.

Suppose that – as before – we have a partial binary communication function γ on A which is commutative and associative. Furthermore, assume there exists a unit element $1 \in A$ such that $\gamma(1,a) = \gamma(a,1) = a$ for all $a \in A$. This unit element represents an idle action during which a process is still running but not performing any significant step. The idle action 1 can serve to abstract from atomic actions in the context of a communication. For this reason we will consider the renaming operator 1_I, renaming actions from $I \subseteq A$ into 1.

Now, just as in the case of ACP, the extension operator $|$ will be a proper extension of the communication function, only this time we do not need any additional operators other than $|$ to model parallel composition. Assume two processes $a \cdot b$ and $c \cdot d$ are performed in parallel, then $|$ is the *synchronous communication merge* on processes, that is: $a \cdot b | c \cdot d = (a|c) \cdot (b|d)$. So from two BPA_δ-processes we construct a new BPA_δ-process by 'stepwise communication'. This intuition can be formally described by adding the following axioms to our algebra for all $a,b \in A$ (see table 79).

6.8.2. ASP

The equational specification ASP has in its signature:

- a set of constants A, a constant $1 \in A$ and a constant $\delta \notin A$. On A a partial communication function γ is given satisfying the requirements of 4.1.1, and such that $\gamma(1,a) = a$ for all $a \in A$.
- binary operators $+$ alternative composition
  $\cdot$ sequential composition
  $|$ synchronous communication merge
- unary operators ∂_H encapsulation, for $H \subseteq A-\{1\}$
  1_I abstraction, for $I \subseteq A$.

The equations of ASP are those given in table 79, together with A1-A7 from BPA_δ. The symbols a,b,c range over $A \cup \{\delta\}$, and we assume $H \subseteq A-\{1\}$ and $I \subseteq A$. Since the set of atomic actions A is a parameter of ASP, we will sometimes write ASP(A). However, if A is some fixed set then we will write ASP for short.

Observe that we do not need to include $1|a = a$ or $\delta|a = \delta$ as axioms in ASP, since they are instances of CF1 and CF2, respectively.

$a\|b = \gamma(a,b)$	if $\gamma(a,b)$ is defined	CF1
$a\|b = \delta$	otherwise	CF2
$ax\|b = (a\|b)x$		SC1
$a\|by = (a\|b)y$		SC2
$ax\|by = (a\|b)(x\|y)$		SC3
$(x + y)\|z = x\|z + y\|z$		SC4
$x\|(y + z) = x\|y + x\|z$		SC5
$\partial_H(a) = a$	if $a \notin H$	D1
$\partial_H(a) = \delta$	if $a \in H$	D2
$\partial_H(x + y) = \partial_H(x) + \partial_H(y)$		D3
$\partial_H(xy) = \partial_H(x) \cdot \partial_H(y)$		D4
$1_I(a) = a$	if $a \notin I$	U1
$1_I(a) = 1$	if $a \in I$	U2
$1_I(x + y) = 1_I(x) + 1_I(y)$		U3
$1_I(xy) = 1_I(x) \cdot 1_I(y)$		U4

TABLE 79. ASP(A).

6.8.3 MULTI-SETS OF ATOMS

Another way to look at $|$ is as follows: from the properties of γ (see 4.1.1) it follows that in expressions with only $|$, we may leave out the brackets; thus we can write $a|a|b|c$ instead of $((a|(a|b))|c)$. Therefore, we may consider such expressions as ***multi-sets*** of atomic actions, which are all performed simultaneously. Note that, in case one of the two processes terminates in one step (e.g. in $a|(b \cdot y)$), after the communication action $a|b$ the process continues with y, which fits into the idea of a multi-set representation of actions.

6.8.4 THEOREM

i. **Elimination**: for every closed ASP-term s, there exists a closed BPA_δ-term t such that ASP ⊢ s=t.

ii. ASP is a **conservative extension** of BPA_δ, that is: for every two BPA_δ-terms s and t we have: ASP ⊢ s=t ⇔ BPA_δ ⊢ s=t.

PROOF: as before.

6.8.5 THEOREM

For all closed ASP-terms x, y, z we have that:

i. ASP ⊢ $x|y = y|x$

ii. ASP ⊢ $(x|y)|z = x|(y|z)$.

PROOF: by induction on the structure of the ASP-terms.

The equations in theorem 6.8.5 are the axioms of **standard concurrency** for ASP. Note that in ACP we had six such axioms, because of the presence of three parallel operators.

Since all atomic actions of the form $a|b$ are considered as a communication instead of the parallel execution of two atoms, the question arises how parallel composition can be represented in the theory ASP. We have to find a new construct in our theory.

6.8.6 DEFINITION

Let $\mathcal{P}$ be a set of *ports* and assume A to be a fixed set of atomic actions. Then $A^{\mathcal{P}}$ is defined as the set of all functions from $\mathcal{P}$ into A.

Functions $\mathbf{v} \in A^{\mathcal{P}}$ are called (atomic) *vectors* and represent the simultaneous execution of the atomic actions $\mathbf{v}(P)$ at all ports $P \in \mathcal{P}$. Vectors are considered to be the new atomic actions in our algebra ASP($A^{\mathcal{P}}$).

6.8.7 EXAMPLE

Suppose a *buffer* B consists of two ports 'left' and 'right'. Assume A contains actions r(x), s(x) (for $x \in \{a,b\}$), where r(x) stands for receiving the value x, and s(x) stands for sending x. A possible definition of B could read as follows:

$$B = \begin{pmatrix} r(a) \\ 1 \end{pmatrix} \cdot \begin{pmatrix} 1 \\ s(a) \end{pmatrix} + \begin{pmatrix} r(b) \\ 1 \end{pmatrix} \cdot \begin{pmatrix} 1 \\ s(b) \end{pmatrix}.$$

So, B can receive a value (either a or b) at the left port and then send it away at the right port.

6.8.8 CONSTANTS

Note that in the signature of both ASP(A) and ASP($A^{\mathcal{P}}$), there exist constants δ and 1. Although it is not necessary to identify these constants with atomic vectors (they both can exist in their own right) we often choose to interpret δ as the vector with only δ's at all its components, and 1 as the vector with all 1's. The *vectors* δ and 1 are denoted by **δ** and **1** respectively. So **δ** = (δ δ ... δ) and **1** = (1 1 ... 1).

Starting from a fixed algebra ASP(A), we have to define a new communication function between the atomic vectors (apart from the restrictions on a communication function). From the definition of the communication function on A, we often choose to define | on atomic vectors from $A^{\mathcal{P}}$ as follows.

6.8.9 DEFINITION

Suppose γ is a communication function on A, then the **natural extension** of γ is defined as follows.

If **v** and **w** are two functions from $A^{\mathcal{P}}$ then for all $P \in \mathcal{P}$:

$$\gamma(\mathbf{v},\mathbf{w})(P) = \begin{cases} \text{not defined, if for some } P \in \mathcal{P} \ \gamma(\mathbf{v}(P),\mathbf{w}(P)) \text{ is not defined} \\ \gamma(\mathbf{v}(P),\mathbf{w}(P)) \ \text{otherwise.} \end{cases}$$

So the natural extension of a communication function results from applying the communication function at all ports separately but with the restriction that it is defined at all ports. Otherwise the whole communication fails, i.e. is not defined. In the same way we define a natural extension of the renaming operators. Although ASP($A^{\mathcal{P}}$) permits us to define different renamings, it turns out to be useful to define a natural extension of renamings from ASP(A).

6.8.10 DEFINITION

1. Let f: A $\rightarrow$ A be an atomic renaming on A. Then for all $\mathbf{v} \in A^{\mathcal{P}}$ the **natural extension** $\mathbf{f}^{\mathcal{P}}$ of f is defined by: $\mathbf{f}^{\mathcal{P}}(\mathbf{v})(P) = f(\mathbf{v}(P))$.
2. The natural extension $\rho_f^{\mathcal{P}}$ of ρ_f (see 3.6.1) is defined as: $\rho_f^{\mathcal{P}} := \rho_{f^{\mathcal{P}}}$, often denoted by ρ_f if no confusion arises. Similarly, the natural extension of a simple renaming r_H is denoted by $\mathbf{r}_H^{\mathcal{P}}$ or $\mathbf{r}_H$ (see 3.6.2).

Note that the natural extension of a simple renaming need not be simple.

6.8.11 EXAMPLE

In the next four paragraphs we will present a small example of an application of ASP, in order to show how to work with it. Consider the configuration in fig. 50.

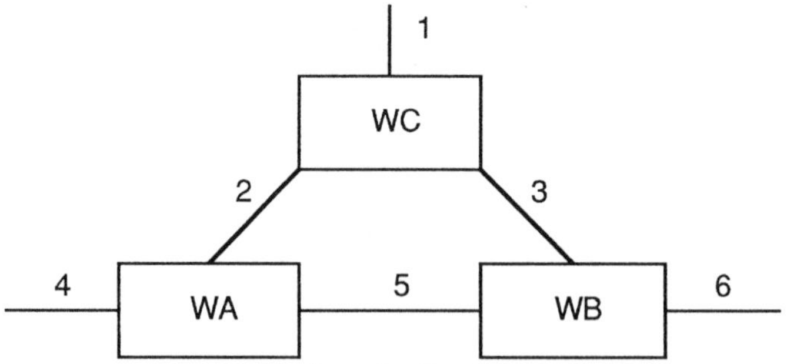

FIGURE 50. A workcell configuration.

Imagine a factory in which unfinished semi-products p have to be turned into commercial products prod(p). Now, the configuration works as follows: from port 1, WC receives a message to generate n products of the form prod(p). So, WC will send the instruction to WA to pick up n products at port 4 and pass it through to WB. Moreover, WC will send the instruction to WB to pick up n products from port 5 and produce n products of the form prod(p).

The configuration of fig. 50 consists of three components and six ports. So we set $\mathcal{P} = \{1,2,...,6\}$. Ports 1, 2 and 3 are for the transmission of positive integers n as well as a 'ready' message r. We will assume that $n \leq N$ for some fixed N. Ports 4, 5 and 6 are for transmitting products of the form p or prod(p). So we have

$D = \{n : 1 \leq n \leq N\} \cup \{r\} \cup \{p, prod(p)\}$,

$A = \{r(x), s(x), c(x) : x \in D\} \cup \{1\}$.

On A the function γ is defined by

$\gamma(r(x),s(x)) = \gamma(s(x),r(x)) = c(x)$ and $\gamma(1,a) = \gamma(a,1) = a$ $(a \in A)$,

and all other communications on A are undefined.

We will work in the algebra ASP($A^{\mathcal{P}}$) with the natural extensions of the communication function $|$ (see 6.8.9) and the renaming operators (see 6.8.10). The constants of ASP($A^{\mathcal{P}}$) are all 6-dimensional vectors $(a_1\ a_2\ ...\ a_6)$ with $a_i \in A$. At this point we will introduce some shorthand notations that are very useful to avoid the elaborate vector notations.

6.8.12 DEFINITION

Assume we have a set of ports $\mathcal{P}$ and let $a \in A$ be some atomic action from ASP then for all $Q \in \mathcal{P}$ we define $a_Q \in A^{\mathcal{P}}$ by:

$$a_Q(P) = \begin{cases} a & \text{if } P=Q \\ 1 & \text{if } P \neq Q. \end{cases}$$

So we have that $r(p)_2 = (1\ r(p)\ 1\ 1\ 1\ 1)$ and $s(r)_5 = (1\ 1\ 1\ 1\ s(r)\ 1)$. Because of a strong tradition in process algebra we will write $r_2(p)$ instead of $r(p)_2$ and $s_5(p)$ instead of $s(p)_5$. This way we obtain a notation which is very similar to that in ACP.

6.8.13 SPECIFICATION

In table 80 we find a specification of the three separate components.

$$WA = \mathbf{1} \cdot \sum_{1 \leq n \leq N} r_2(n) \cdot WA(n)$$
$$WA(0) = s_2(r)$$
$$WA(n+1) = r_4(p) \cdot s_5(p) \cdot WA(n)$$

$$WB = \mathbf{1} \cdot \sum_{1 \leq n \leq N} r_3(n) \cdot \mathbf{1} \cdot WB(n)$$
$$WB(0) = s_3(r)$$
$$WB(n+1) = r_5(p) \cdot s_6(prod(p)) \cdot WB(n)$$

$$WC = \sum_{1 \leq n \leq N} r_1(n) \cdot WC(n)$$
$$WC(n) = (s_2(n) | s_3(n)) \cdot \mathbf{2n} \cdot r_2(r) \cdot r_3(r) \cdot s_1(r)$$

TABLE 80. A specification of the workcell.

In the equation for WC(n) we have used the abbreviation $\mathbf{n}$ for $\mathbf{1}^n$, which is defined by use of an inductive definition ($\mathbf{1}^1 = \mathbf{1}$, $\mathbf{1}^{n+1} = \mathbf{1} \cdot \mathbf{1}^n$). In the same way we define t^n for ASP-terms t and $n \geq 1$. Now define:

$I = \{r(p), c(x) : x \in D\}$

WORKCELL = $\mathbf{1}_I$(WA|WB|WC).

We abstract from actions like r(p) and thus assume that there is an unlimited supply of goods available at port 4. Then we can prove the following theorem:

6.8.14 THEOREM

$$ASP(A^{\mathcal{P}}) + RSP \models \text{WORKCELL} = \sum_{1\le n\le N} r_1(n)\cdot\mathbf{3}\cdot\{s_6(prod(p))\cdot\mathbf{1}\}^n\cdot s_1(r).$$

PROOF: left for the exercises.

6.8.15 EXERCISES

1. In order to find a graph model for ASP, consider the following definition:

DEFINITION: If g and h are two process graphs, then g|h is defined as follows. Let a, b ∈ A. First, consider the smallest graph (g|h)* with nodes consisting of pairs of nodes and single nodes of g and h, such that:

i. The root of (g|h)* is the pair of root nodes from g and h.
ii. A node (r,s) has label √ iff both r and s do; a single node r has label √ iff it did so before, i.e. if it already had a label √ in g or in h.
iii. If g has an edge $r \xrightarrow{a} r'$ and h has an edge $s \xrightarrow{b} s'$ such that γ(a,b) = c, then (g|h)* has an edge of the form $(r,s) \xrightarrow{c} (r',s')$. We have the same condition with g and h interchanged.
iv. If g has an edge $r \xrightarrow{a} r'$ and h has a node s↓ then g|h has an edge $(r,s) \xrightarrow{a} r'$. We have the same condition with g and h interchanged.
v. If either g or h has an edge $r \xrightarrow{a} r'$ then so has (g|h)*.

Then g|h can be found from (g|h)* by deleting all edges and nodes that are inaccessible from the root node.

Now prove the following statements:

i. The equivalence relation $\underline{\leftrightarrow}$ is a congruence with respect to |;
ii. $\mathbb{G}^\infty/\underline{\leftrightarrow} \models$ ASP, where $\mathbb{G}$ has operators +, · as before, and | as above.
iii. Extend ASP with ε to ASP_ε, in such a way that $\mathbb{G}^\infty/\underline{\leftrightarrow} \models ASP_\varepsilon$.

2. Formulate an expansion theorem for ASP and prove that it holds for all closed terms. Observe that the name *expansion* does not apply to ASP because we do not have an numerical 'explosion' of the number of summands.
3. Prove theorem 6.8.14, using induction on n.

6.8.16 NOTES AND COMMENTS

This section is based on WEIJLAND [1989], but the definition of the theory ASP already appears in BERGSTRA & KLOP [1984b]. Weijland took the example of the workcell from MAUW [1990] and BIEMANS & BLONK [1986]. Synchronous cooperation also occurs in other process algebras, notably in SCCS, see MILNER [1983].

6.9 SIGNALS AND OBSERVATION

A mechanism that is not described in the regular theory of ACP is the presence of visible aspects of the state of a process. Usually, the state of a process can only be understood (or observed) via the actions that can be performed from that state. In this section, we describe *signals*, that persist in time for some extended duration. Then, we define a *signal insertion* operator, that can put a signal as a label at a node in the graph of a process. The addition of an *observation* mechanism allows one process to be influenced by a signal of another. This can be considered as another communication mechanism.

6.9.1 SIGNAL ALGEBRA

We start from a given finite set of **atomic signals** ATS. Then, the set of **signals** S is the power set of ATS, with empty set $\varnothing$, set union $\cup$ and set intersection $\cap$. We will identify the singleton sets with the atomic signal in it, so we write $s_1 \cup s_2 \cup ... \cup s_n$ for $\{s_1, s_2, ..., s_n\}$.

6.9.2 SIGNAL INSERTION

The **(root) signal insertion** operator [.,.] takes a signal and a process, and places the signal at the root node of the process. In the setting of BPA, axioms for this operator are easily given. See table 81, where $u \in S$, and x,y are arbitrary processes.

$[u, x] \cdot y = [u, x \cdot y]$	RS1
$[u, x] + y = [u, x + y]$	RS2
$[u, [v, x]] = [u \cup v, x]$	RS3
$[\varnothing, x] = x$	RS4

TABLE 81. Signal insertion.

In the theory BPA_δ, we need no extra equations. An interesting consequence is

$$[u, x] = [u, \delta] + x,$$

allowing one to separate signal and process. Notice that in BPA or BPA_δ, this operator does not allow the insertion of a signal at a terminal node of a process. For this purpose, we need a separate *terminal* signal insertion operator. On the other hand, the problem does not occur in BPA_ε or $BPA_{\delta\varepsilon}$, as the term $x \cdot [\varepsilon, u]$ describes process x with terminal signal u.

6.9.3 EXAMPLE

A traffic light TL with signals red, yellow, green and action change may be described by the following equation:

$$TL = [green, change] \cdot [yellow, change] \cdot [red, change] \cdot TL.$$

6.9.4 ROOT SIGNAL

It is useful to have an additional operator, the **root signal** operator, that determines the root signal of a process. The equations in table 82 are straightforward. Here $a \in A_\delta$.

$S(a) = \varnothing$	S1
$S(x + y) = S(x) \cup S(y)$	S2
$S(x \cdot y) = S(x)$	S3
$S([u, x]) = u \cup S(x)$	S4

TABLE 82. Root signal operator.

6.9.5 PARALLEL COMPOSITION

An extension of signal insertion to PA or ACP is straightforward: one adds equations MSI1,2,3 below. It becomes more interesting if we allow for **observation**, i.e. if in a parallel composition, one process may be influenced by observing a signal of another process. In order to describe observation, we assume that we have given a partial **observation function** obs: $A \times ATS \to A$, satisfying the requirement that

1. obs(obs(a, s), s') is never defined

(compare the introduction of the communication function in 4.1).

If obs(a, s) is defined for some $s \in ATS$, we call a an **observation action**. The following axioms list some requirements that ensure the observation function and communication function do not have unwanted interactions.

2. For no $a \in A$ we have that obs(a, s) and $\gamma(a,b)$ are both defined (for some $b \in A$);
3. obs(γ(a, b), s) is never defined;
4. γ(obs(a, s), b) is never defined.

Now the observation function on atomic actions and atomic signals is the starting point for the definition of the **(signal) observation operator** /. This operator describes the inspection of a signal by a process (compare the introduction of the communication merge in 4.2).

We sum things up in table 83, where $a \in A_\delta$, $s \in ATS$, $u,v \in S$. The equations MSI1, OCM without the last summand, and O1-7 together with the axioms of PA (see 3.1) form the theory PAS; all axioms of table 83 combined with ACP (see 4.2) form the theory ACPS. We can add the constant ε to these theories by simply adding the axiom $\varepsilon/s = \delta$ to the regular ε-axioms.

$a/s = obs(a,s)$	if obs(a,s) defined	O1
$a/s = \delta$	otherwise	O2
$a/\emptyset = \delta$		O3
$a/(u \cup v) = a/u + a/v$		O4
$(x + y)/u = x/u + y/u$		O5
$(x \cdot y)/u = (x/u) \cdot y$		O6
$[u, x]/v = [u, x/v]$		O7
$x \parallel y = x \mathbin{⌊\!⌊} y + (x/S(y)) \mathbin{⌊\!⌊} y + y \mathbin{⌊\!⌊} x + (y/S(x)) \mathbin{⌊\!⌊} x + x \mid y$		OCM
$[u, x] \mathbin{⌊\!⌊} y = [u, x \mathbin{⌊\!⌊} y]$		MSI1
$[u,x] \mid y = [u, x \mid y]$		MSI2
$x \mid [u,y] = [u, x \mid y]$		MSI3

TABLE 83. ACPS.

6.9.6 STANDARD OBSERVATION FUNCTION

It is useful to have a standard observation function (cf. the standard communication function introduced in 4.1). Let us define the following atomic actions, for each $s \in ATS$:

- t(s) attempt to observe (test for) atomic signal s;
- cf(s) confirmation of successful observation of atomic signal s.

The standard signal observation function then has obs(t(s), s) = cf(s) for all $s \in ATS$, and is undefined in all other cases.

6.9.7 EXAMPLE

A stack with atomic signals empty and non-empty can be described as follows:

$$S_\lambda = [\text{empty}, \sum_{d\in D} r_1(d)\cdot S_d]$$

$$S_{d\sigma} = [\text{non-empty}, \sum_{e\in D} r_1(d)\cdot S_{ed\sigma}] + s_2(d)\cdot S_\sigma$$

(conventions as in 2.9.2). We can compose this stack with a reader as follows:

$$R = t(\text{non-empty})\cdot \sum_{d\in D} r_2(d)\cdot R_d + t(\text{empty})\cdot \text{idle}\cdot R$$

$$H = \{r2(d), s2(d) : d\in D\} \cup \{t(\text{empty}), t(\text{non-empty})\}$$

$$X = \partial_H(S_\lambda \| R).$$

The composite process X describes the way a stack is read in most implementations.

6.9.8 EXERCISES

1. Describe a system of a traffic light and a passing car, using the standard observation function.
2. Prove that all operators except +, $\cdot$, [.,.], γ, obs can be eliminated from closed ACPS-terms.
3. Prove the merge is commutative and associative for all closed ACPS-terms.
4. Give an operational semantics for ACPS in terms of action relations.
5. Describe a graph model for ACPS, and define an appropriate notion of bisimulation. In this graph model, each node is labeled with a signal, an element of S, and two nodes can be in a bisimulation relation only if they have the same signal.
6. Give axioms for a terminal signal insertion operator $\langle .,. \rangle$, that allows to put signals at terminal states in the theories BPA, BPA_δ, PA, PA_δ and ACP.
7. Give axioms for a global insertion operator &, that takes a signal and a process, and inserts the signal at every state of the process.

6.9.9 NOTES AND COMMENTS

This section is based on BERGSTRA [1988]. Further development of the theory ACPS can be found in BROUWER [1990].

Chapter 7

Semantics

7.1 BISIMULATION AND TRACE SEMANTICS

So far, we only considered models having the property of containing a submodel which is isomorphic to the initial algebra of the current theory (for instance see 2.7.35). In other words we may say that if two finite processes in a model are equal, this equality must be derivable from the theory.

Models that with respect to finite processes correspond to the graph model or the term model are said to be models in **bisimulation semantics**. Because for every one of our theories, its initial model is a model in bisimulation semantics, our axiom systems are said to be a **complete axiomatization** of bisimulation semantics. In this chapter we will consider other semantics than bisimulation semantics, and we will present complete axiomatizations of these alternative semantics as well.

Because all operators except for + and · can be eliminated from closed terms, we will mainly restrict ourselves to the theory BPA, with special constant δ. The addition of the special constant τ leads to many interesting observations, and a vastly increased complexity. We do not include it here, in order to focus on a few key issues.

We will discuss semantics that identify more processes than bisimulation semantics does. The advantage of this is clear: calculations become easier, and more simplifications can be made. On the other hand, some differences between processes are disregarded, and as a consequence, in some cases some operators cannot be defined any more. Thus, we will see that deadlock behaviour cannot be determined in trace semantics, and that the priority operator is not definable in failure semantics.

We start with the repetition of an earlier result.

7.1.1 THEOREM

The theory BPA_δ (displayed once more in table 84) is a complete axiomatization of bisimulation semantics, as given by the model $\mathbb{G}^\infty/\underline{\leftrightarrow}$ (with the signature of BPA_δ). Thus:

for all closed BPA_δ-terms t,s we have: $BPA_\delta \vdash s=t \iff \mathbb{G}^\infty/\underline{\leftrightarrow} \models s = t.$

PROOF: Immediate from 2.5.10 and 2.7.33.

$x + y = y + x$	A1
$(x + y) + z = x + (y + z)$	A2
$x + x = x$	A3
$(x + y)z = xz + yz$	A4
$(xy)z = x(yz)$	A5
$x + \delta = x$	A6
$\delta x = \delta$	A7

TABLE 84. BPA_δ.

Completeness theorems such as 7.1.1 can also be found for the extended theories as ACP (see 4.5.13). The proof of this is as follows.

7.1.2 THEOREM

The theory ACP (see table 35 in 4.2.1) is a complete axiomatization of bisimulation semantics, as given by the model $\mathbb{G}^\infty/\underline{\leftrightarrow}$ (over the signature of ACP). That is:

for all closed ACP-terms t,s we have: $\quad ACP \vdash s=t \;\Leftrightarrow\; \mathbb{G}^\infty/\underline{\leftrightarrow} \models s = t.$

PROOF: We use graph(s) (see 2.7.30) also for ACP-terms, since by theorem 4.3.1 every ACP-term s can be rewritten into a unique basic term s' over BPA_δ. Thus we have $ACP \vdash s{=}s'$ and $graph(s) \equiv graph(s')$ and we obtain:

$graph(s) \underline{\leftrightarrow} graph(t) \;\Leftrightarrow\; graph(s') \underline{\leftrightarrow} graph(t') \;\Leftrightarrow\; BPA_\delta \vdash s'{=}t'$ (by 7.1.1)

and of course $BPA_\delta \vdash s'{=}t' \Rightarrow ACP \vdash s'{=}t'$ and $ACP \vdash s'{=}t' \Rightarrow BPA_\delta \vdash s'{=}t'$ since ACP is a conservative extension of BPA_δ (see 4.3.1.ii). Thus we find:

$graph(s) \underline{\leftrightarrow} graph(t) \;\Leftrightarrow\; ACP \vdash s'{=}t' \Leftrightarrow ACP \vdash s{=}t$ (by definition).

So basically, all we need to prove completeness of an extension of BPA is (1) completeness of the basic theory, (2) an elimination theorem and (3) conservativity. It is for this reason that we considered these theorems over and over again, when introducing new extensions. The completeness theorems for the theory BPA extended with δ, ε, and τ are thus sufficient for completeness of their extensions.

7.1.3 TRACE SEMANTICS

Another semantics, that indirectly has been mentioned earlier, is **trace semantics**. In trace semantics two processes are equal if they have the same traces.

It is interesting to note that trace sets, as defined in 6.3.6, do not contain enough information to provide us with a new model of BPA_δ. In particular, the behaviour of δ cannot be modeled. Using the obvious definition of $\cdot$ on trace sets, we obtain

$\{\lambda\} = tr(\delta) = tr(\delta x) = tr(\delta)\cdot tr(x) = \{\lambda\}\cdot tr(x) = tr(x)$

so all trace sets are proved equal (this is an inconsistency). This is why, in the following, we will introduce extended traces, carrying extra information about termination.

7.1.4 DEFINITION

An **extended trace** is defined as follows:

i. any ordinary trace (i.e. a word in A^*) is an extended trace;
ii. if σ is a trace in A^*, then $\sigma\!\downarrow$ is an extended trace.

An **extended trace set** Z, is a set of extended traces with the property:

if $\sigma\rho \in Z$, then $\sigma \in Z$

(we say: Z is **prefix closed**).

Let $\mathbb{T}^*$ be the family of extended trace sets. Next, we turn $\mathbb{T}^*$ into a model of BPA_δ.

7.1.5 DEFINITION

We define the constants and operators of BPA_δ on $\mathbb{T}^*$. $tr^*(t)$ will be the interpretation of the term t.

i. $tr^*(\delta) = \{\lambda\}$

ii. $tr^*(a) = \{\lambda, a, a{\downarrow}\}$, for all $a \in A$

iii. if $Z,W \in \mathbb{T}^*$, then $Z+W = Z \cup W$

iv.if $Z,W \in \mathbb{T}^*$, then $Z \cdot W = \{\sigma \in Z: \sigma \text{ without } {\downarrow}\} \cup \{\sigma\rho: \sigma{\downarrow} \in Z \text{ and } \rho \in W\}$.

Note that for all $Z,W \in \mathbb{T}^*$ we have $Z+W, Z \cdot W \in \mathbb{T}^*$.

7.1.6 THEOREM

The theory BPA_δ + TR (where the axiom TR is given in table 85) is a complete axiomatization of the trace semantics of $\mathbb{T}^*$.

$z(x + y) = zx + zy$	TR

TABLE 85. The trace axiom TR.

PROOF: First we prove that $\mathbb{T}^*$ is a model BPA_δ + TR. Let x,y BPA_δ-terms, then:

- A1: $tr^*(x + y) = tr^*(x) \cup tr^*(y) = tr^*(y) \cup tr^*(x) = tr^*(y + x)$;
- A2, A3: are equally simple;
- A4: let σ be a trace in $tr^*((x + y)z)$. We have two possibilities. The first posibility is $\sigma \in tr^*(x + y)$, and σ does not end in $\downarrow$. Then we find $\sigma \in tr^*(x) \cup tr^*(y)$, so $\sigma \in tr^*(x)$ or $\sigma \in tr^*(y)$. Then it follows that $\sigma \in tr^*(xz)$ or $\sigma \in tr^*(yz)$, so $\sigma \in tr^*(xz + yz)$.

    Secondly, there may be a $\rho{\downarrow}$ in $tr^*(x + y)$, and a trace π in $tr^*(z)$, such that $\sigma = \rho\pi$. Now, $\rho{\downarrow}$ is in $tr^*(x + y) = tr^*(x) \cup tr^*(y)$, hence in $tr^*(x)$ or in $tr^*(y)$. If $\rho{\downarrow} \in tr^*(x)$, then $\sigma \in tr^*(xz)$, and if $\rho{\downarrow} \in tr^*(y)$, then $\sigma \in tr^*(yz)$. In both cases $\sigma \in tr^*(xz) \cup tr^*(yz) = tr^*(xz + yz)$. So we proved $tr^*((x + y)z) \subseteq tr^*(xz + yz)$. It is just as easy to prove the converse inclusion.
- A5: is simple and
- A6, A7 follow from $tr^*(\delta) = \{\lambda\}$;
- TR follows just like A4.

We conclude that $\mathbb{T}^*$ is a model of BPA_δ + TR.

Conversely, we have to prove that if two BPA_δ-terms have the same extended trace set, they can be proved equal in BPA_δ + TR. Let s,t be two BPA_δ-terms. Using A4 and TR (and A5) we can eliminate all brackets. By A3 all double summands can be removed. Using these operations, s and t can be reduced to normal forms s',t' from which the extended trace sets can immediately be read off. We find that s', t' are identical (except for the order of the summands, i.e. modulo A1 and A2), precisely when the extended trace sets are equal.

7.1.7 REMARK

We have turned $\mathbb{T}^*$ into a model of BPA_δ, but still, trace semantics is not suitable for describing deadlock behaviour since $\mathbb{T}^* \models ab = a(b + \delta) = ab + a\delta$, and so in trace semantics processes without deadlock always are identified with ones that *do* contain a possibility of deadlock. Or – to put it differently – trace identity does not preserve deadlock behavior and so trace semantics cannot be used in applications in which we are interested in the deadlock behaviour of a process. For this reason, other semantics were suggested, identifying more processes than bisimulation semantics, but fewer than trace semantics, such that deadlock behaviour could be modelled. In the next sections we will consider some of these semantics.

7.1.8 EXERCISES

1. Find the extended trace sets of the following processes:
i. a^{ω}; ii. $\tau\delta$; iii. the solution of $x = ax + a$.

2. A process p is called **deterministic** if for all $q \in Sub(p)$ (the set of subprocesses, defined in 2.8) we have that $q \xrightarrow{a} x$ and $q \xrightarrow{a} y$ imply $x = y$. Show that, in the case of deterministic processes, we can conclude the deadlock behaviour from the extended trace sets.

3. Extend the definition of tr in 7.1.5 with the equation: $tr(\varepsilon) = \{\lambda, \downarrow\}$. Prove that $BPA_{\delta\varepsilon} + TR$ is a complete axiomatization of $\mathbb{T}^*$.

4. Observe that the only plausible definition of τ in $\mathbb{T}^*$ would be to put $tr(\tau) = \{\lambda, \downarrow\} = tr(\varepsilon)$, in order to obtain a model for $BPA^{\tau}_{\delta\varepsilon}$. Hence in trace semantics, ε and τ cannot be distinguished.

5. Define the operators $\|, \lfloor\!\lfloor, |, \partial_H$ on $\mathbb{T}^*$. Show that ACP + TR is a complete axiomatization of trace semantics with these extra operators.

Note that $\mathbb{T}^* \models (x + y) \| z = x \| z + y \| z$, so trace semantics allows a much simpler axiomatization of the merge.

7.1.9 NOTES AND COMMENTS

Bisimulation semantics was defined by PARK [1981]. It is the standard semantics of process algebra as treated in this book, in sections 2.5, 2.7 or BERGSTRA & KLOP [1984b], and also of CCS (see MILNER [1989]), and coincides in the present setting with the semantics of the theory of DE BAKKER & ZUCKER [1982]. For trace theory, see e.g. HOARE [1980], REM [1983] or KALDEWAIJ [1986]. The issue of trace semantics vs. branching semantics is discussed in DE BAKKER, BERGSTRA, KLOP & MEYER [1984].

7.2 FAILURE AND READY SEMANTICS

We have seen that deadlock behaviour is not preserved in trace semantics. In this section, we will define a semantics, failure semantics, that adds extra information about deadlock behaviour to the extended trace set of a process. In the explanation of failure semantics we will also consider a variant, called ready semantics. Failure semantics as well as ready semantics are often used in concurrency. In our explanations we will start from the graph model, but we will discuss a more direct representation as well.

7.2.1 DEFINITION

Let g be a process graph (not containing τ-labels) and s a node in g. Let σ be the word in A^*, obtained from a path from the root to s (so σ is a trace of g). Let $M(s)$ be the set of labels from $A \cup \{\downarrow\}$ of outgoing edges from s (with $\downarrow \in M(s)$ iff $s\downarrow$). Then $(\sigma, M(s))$ is called a **ready pair** of g, and for all $X \subseteq (A \cup \{\downarrow\}) - M(s)$, $[\sigma, X]$ is called a **failure pair** of g. Thus, for *each subset* of the complement of a ready pair, we get a failure pair.

A more intuitive explanation: $(\sigma, M(s))$ represents the information that after executing trace σ, the process can be in the position of doing actions from $M(s)$ (after executing σ we see a *menu* M(s); ↓ denotes the possibility of termination), and a failure pair [σ, X] represents the information that after executing σ the process can deadlock if actions from X are tried.

Note that from the set of ready pairs of a process graph, the set of failure pairs can be deduced, but not the other way around; we will see examples of this in the sequel.

7.2.2 DEFINITION

Let g be a process graph.

The **ready set** of g is the set all ready pairs of g. The **failure set** of g consists of all failure pairs of g.

Two graphs g,h are **ready equivalent**, $g \equiv_R h$, if they have the same ready sets, and **failure equivalent**, $g \equiv_F h$, if they have the same failure sets.

7.2.3 EXAMPLES

i. The graph corresponding to the constant a ($a \in A$) has ready set $\{(\lambda,\{a\}), (a,\{\downarrow\})\}$, and failure set $\{[\lambda,X] : X \subseteq (A \cup \{\downarrow\})-\{a\}\} \cup \{[a,Y] : Y \subseteq A\}$.

ii. The one-node graph representing δ has ready set $\{(\lambda,\emptyset)\}$, and failure set $\{[\lambda,X] : X \subseteq A \cup \{\downarrow\}\}$.

iii. The terms ab and ab + aδ from 7.1.7 are distinguished by the ready pair $(a,\emptyset)$ and the failure pairs $[\lambda,X]$ (for $X \subseteq A \cup \{\downarrow\}$). We see that in ready and failure semantics, deadlock behaviour is recorded.

7.2.4 THEOREM

Let g,h be two graphs. Then:

i. if $g \leftrightarrow h$, then $g \equiv_R h$;

ii. if $g \equiv_R h$, then $g \equiv_F h$;

iii. if $g \equiv_F h$, then $tr^*(g) = tr^*(h)$.

PROOF: simple (see exercises).

7.2.5 REMARK

In 7.2.4 we have none of the reverse implications. This is proved by the following counterexamples.

i. The two graphs in fig. 51 have the same ready set but do not bisimulate.

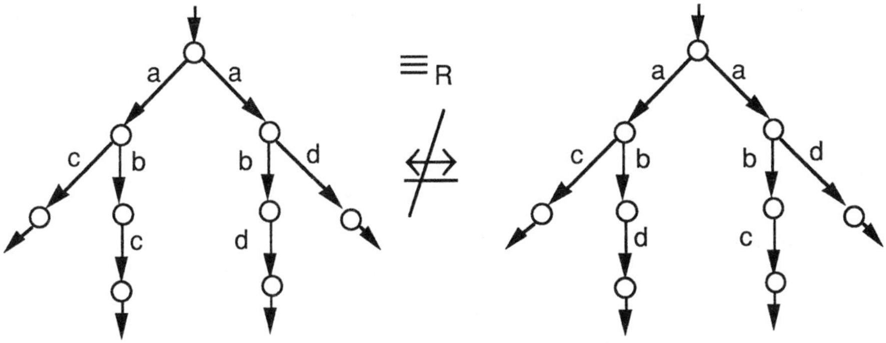

FIGURE 51.

ii. The two graphs in fig. 52 have the same failure set but not the same ready set (the distinguishing ready pair is (a,{b,c}); any failure pair of the added node is also a failure pair of the other two nodes reached by an a-step).

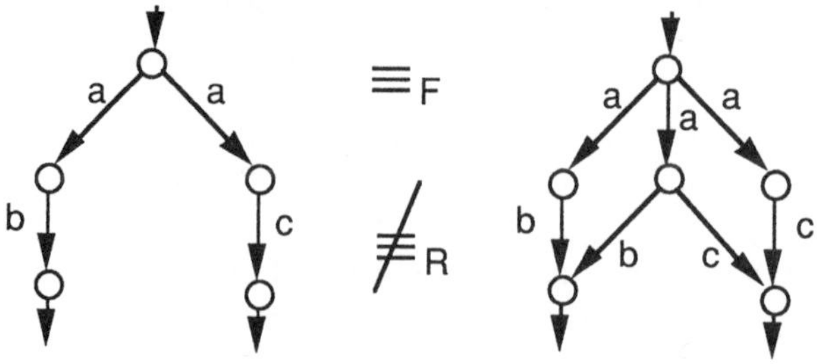

FIGURE 52.

iii. The two graphs in fig. 53 have the same extended trace set but not the same failure set (a distinguishing failure pair is [a,{b}]).

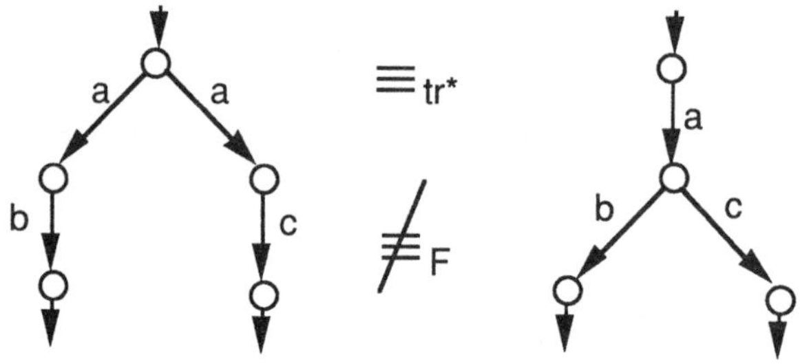

FIGURE 53.

Note that all three examples concern BPA-terms (hence without δ), and so do not depend on special behaviour of δ.

7.2.6 THEOREM

$\equiv_R$ and $\equiv_F$ are congruence relations on $\mathbb{G}^\infty$.

PROOF: omitted.

7.2.7 THEOREM

The theory BPA_δ + RE1-RE2 (with RE1 and RE2 given in table 86) is a complete axiomatization of ready semantics, as in the model $\mathbb{G}^\infty/\equiv_R$.

$a(bx + u) + a(by + v) = a(bx + by + u) + a(bx + by + v)$	RE1
$a(b + u) + a(by + v) = a(b + by + u) + a(b + by + v)$	RE2

TABLE 86. Ready axioms RE1 and RE2.

PROOF: We will show that $\mathbb{G}^\infty/\equiv_R$ is a model for BPA_δ + RE1-RE2. The proof that the submodel $\mathbb{F}/\equiv_R$ is isomorphic with the initial model of this axiom scheme, is again omitted.

By 7.2.4.i, all axioms of BPA_δ hold in $\mathbb{G}^\infty/\equiv_R$. The 'cross' axiom RE1 is illustrated in fig. 54. The rest of the proof is left for the exercises.

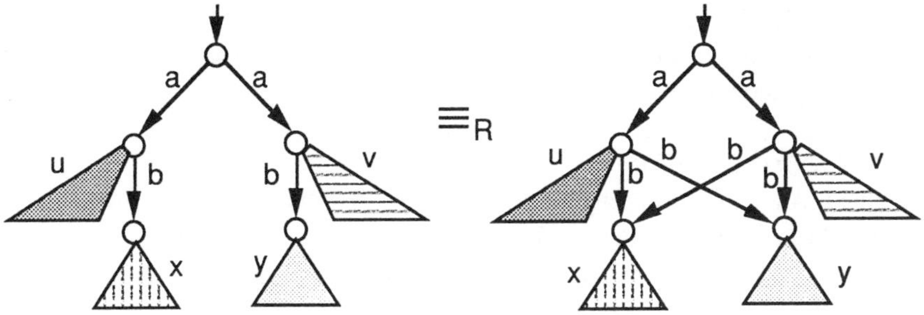

FIGURE 54.

7.2.8 THEOREM

The theory BPA_δ + RE-RE2 + FA1 (with FA1 as given in table 87) is a complete axiomatization of failure semantics, as in the model $\mathbb{G}^\infty/\equiv_F$.

$ax + a(y + z) = ax + a(x + y) + a(y + z)$	FA1

TABLE 81. Failure axiom FA1.

PROOF: omitted. One example of the 'fork' axiom FA1 is given in fig. 52 (in 7.2.5).

To conclude this section, we give an explicit presentation of a ready model, without referring to graphs.

7.2.9 DEFINITION

A set R is a **ready set** if R consists of a set of ready pairs (σ,X), with $\sigma \in A^*$ and $X \subseteq A \cup \{\downarrow\}$, satisfying the following conditions:

i. There is exactly one ready pair $(\lambda,X) \in R$. This set X is the menu of the root node of the process. We will refer to this set as M_R.

ii. there is an X with $(\sigma a, X) \in R$ iff there is Y with $(\sigma, Y \cup \{a\}) \in R$ (for each $a \in A$).

Next we turn the set of ready sets into a model of BPA_δ + RE1-RE2, by the following definitions:

i. The ready set of δ is $\{(\lambda,\emptyset)\}$.

ii. The ready set of $a \in A$ is $\{(\lambda,\{a\}), (a,\{\downarrow\})\}$.

iii. If R, S are two ready sets, then we define:

- $R + S = (R - \{(\lambda, M_R)\}) \cup (S - \{(\lambda, M_S)\}) \cup \{(\lambda, M_R \cup M_S)\}$
- $R \cdot S = \{(\sigma, X \cup M_S) : (\sigma, X \cup \{\downarrow\}) \in R \text{ with } \downarrow \notin X\} \cup$
  $\{(\sigma\rho, Y) : \rho \neq \lambda \text{ and there is } X \text{ with } (\sigma, X \cup \{\downarrow\}) \in R \text{ and } (\rho, Y) \in S\}$.

7.2.10 REMARK

The proof that this indeed gives us a model for BPA_δ + RE1-2, and a similar presentation of an explicit failure model are omitted.

7.2.11 EXERCISES

1. Determine the failure sets and the ready sets of the graphs corresponding to the following terms: i. $ab + a\delta$; ii. $ab + a$; iii. $a(b\delta + c\delta)$; iv. $a(b + c)$; v. $ab + ac$; vi. $ab + ac + a(b + c)$.
2. Prove theorem 7.2.4.
3. Prove that RE1-RE2 from table 86 are valid in $\mathbb{G}^\infty/\equiv_R$.

4. Prove that FA from table 87 is valid in $\mathbb{G}^{\infty}/{\equiv_F}$.
5. Give an explicit presentation of a failure model, similar to the presentation in 7.2.9.
6. Give the ready and failure semantics for the theory BPA_ε.

7.2.12 NOTES AND COMMENTS

Failure semantics is introduced in BROOKES, HOARE & ROSCOE [1984], ready or readiness semantics in OLDEROG & HOARE [1983]. The testing equivalence of DE NICOLA & HENNESSY [1984] coincides with failure equivalence in the present setting, as do the equivalences of KENNAWAY [1981] and DARONDEAU [1982]. Here, we follow the treatment of BERGSTRA, KLOP & OLDEROG [1988].

7.3 FAILURE TRACE AND READY TRACE SEMANTICS

Failure and ready semantics, as discussed in the former section, lie in between bisimulation and trace semantics. For a number of purposes, however, failure and ready semantics identify too many processes. In this section two semantics are discussed, that identify fewer processes than failure or ready semantics, but still more than bisimulation semantics (which can simplify verifications significantly).

First we remark that failure and ready semantics identify too many processes to define the priority operator of 6.1.

7.3.1 THEOREM

The priority operator θ cannot be added to failure or ready semantics.

PROOF: suppose a,b,c,d,e,f are atoms with partial ordering $f<b<d$. Consider the processes $p \equiv a(bc + d) + a(be + f)$ and $q \equiv a(be + d) + a(bc + f)$. Clearly we have $p \equiv_R q$ (and so $p \equiv_F q$). We see however $\theta(p) = ad + abe$ and $\theta(q) = ad + abc$, so we do *not* have $\theta(p) \equiv_F \theta(q)$ (not even $tr(\theta(p)) = tr(\theta(q))$).

We now want to have a semantics, to which θ can be added without problem, and that still identifies as many processes as possible. Again we start from process graphs.

7.3.2 DEFINITION

Let g be a process graph, and π a path in g, starting from the root. A **ready trace** for π is the trace σ of π, together with for every node s, its menu $M(s) \subseteq A \cup \{\downarrow\}$ (see 7.2.1). We have seen that a ready pair carries M(s) only at the last node in the trace, and a trace carries no menus at all. A ready trace is denoted by placing the menus in the right places in the trace σ.

7.3.3 EXAMPLE

Let the graph in fig. 55 be given.

This graph has ready traces {a} a {a} a {↓}, {a} a {b,c} b {↓}, {a} a {b,c} c {↓}, and further all ready traces obtained by leaving out parts of these ready traces.

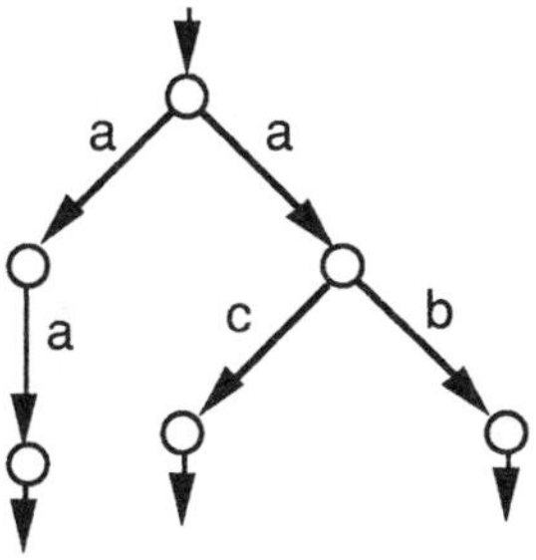

FIGURE 55.

7.3.4 DEFINITION

Let g be a process graph. The **ready trace set** of g is the set of all ready traces of g. Two graphs g,h are **ready trace equivalent**, $g \equiv_{RT} h$, if their ready trace sets are equal.

7.3.5 DEFINITION

In the same way we present the definitions of the failure case. Again, let π be a path from the root node. A **failure trace** for π is the trace σ of π, together with for every node s, a set X disjoint from its menu $M(s) \subseteq A \cup \{\downarrow\}$ (see 7.2.1); the **failure trace set** of a graph g contains all failure traces, and two graphs g,h are **failure trace equivalent**, $g \equiv_{FT} h$, if their failure trace sets are equal.

7.3.6 THEOREM

Let g,h be two process graphs. Then we have:

i. if $g \underline{\leftrightarrow} h$, then $g \equiv_{RT} h$;
ii. if $g \equiv_{RT} h$, then $g \equiv_{FT} h$;
iii. if $g \equiv_{RT} h$, then $g \equiv_{R} h$;
iv. if $g \equiv_{FT} h$, then $g \equiv_{F} h$.

PROOF: simple (see exercises).

7.3.7 COUNTEREXAMPLES

Again we do not have any of the inverse implications in 7.3.6. Counterexamples can easily be constructed after we have presented the axiom schemes for these semantics.

7.3.8 THEOREM

$\equiv_{RT}$ and $\equiv_{FT}$ are congruence relations on $\mathbb{G}^{\infty}$.

PROOF: omitted.

7.3.9 THEOREM

The theory BPA_{δ} + PR1-PR4 + RTR (with RTR is given in table 88, and the projection axioms in 2.4.1) is a complete axiomatization of ready trace semantics, as in the model $\mathbb{G}^{\infty}/\equiv_{RT}$.

$\pi_1(x) = \pi_1(y) \quad \Rightarrow \quad z(x + y) = zx + zy$	RTR

TABLE 88. Ready Trace Rule RTR.

7.3.10 COMMENT

We will not prove theorem 7.3.9 but only give some comment on the Ready Trace Rule RTR. To be able to formulate this rule one needs the projection axioms PR of 2.4.1. The rule states that the 'wrong' distributivity $z(x + y) = zx + zy$ holds, as long as the first projections of x and y are equal, i.e. as long as the set of initial steps, the menu of x is equal to the set of initial steps, the menu of y. It is not hard to see that the ready trace sets of both processes are equal. We give a typical example of the effect of the 'narrowing' axiom RTR in fig. 56.

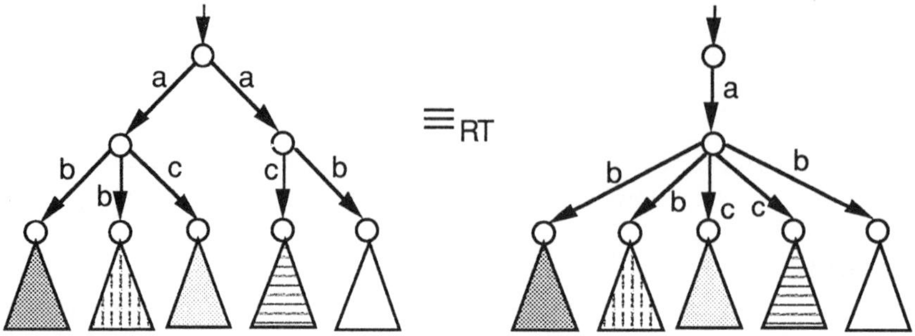

FIGURE 56.

Without any further comment or proof, we now present the complete axiom system of failure trace theory.

7.3.11 THEOREM

The theory $BPA_{\delta\tau}$ + FA2 + PR1-PR4 + RTR (with the axiom FA2, a weaker variant of FA1 given in table 89) is a complete axiomatization of failure trace semantics, as in the model $\mathbb{G}^{\infty}/\equiv_{FT}$.

$ax + ay = ax + a(x + y) + ay$	FA2

TABLE 83. Failure Trace Rule.

7.3.12 OVERVIEW

We will end this section with an overview of the semantics that have been discussed so far.

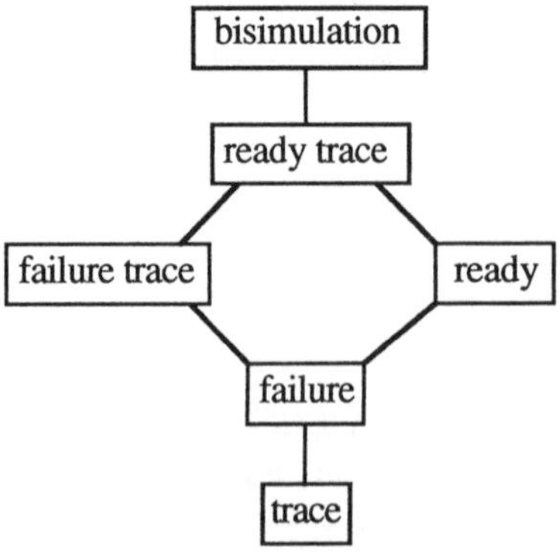

FIGURE 57.

In fig. 57 the semantics are put in a picture we can call the ***linear time – branching time spectrum*** (linear time being represented by trace semantics, branching time by bisimulation semantics). In the downward direction, more and more processes are identified. There is no inclusion relation between ready and failure trace semantics.

7.3.13 EXERCISES

1. Show that the processes p and q from the proof of theorem 7.3.1 do not have the same ready trace sets.
2. Prove theorem 7.3.6.
3. a. Find graphs g,h such that $g \equiv_{RT} h$ but not $g \underline{\leftrightarrow} h$
   b. Find graphs g,h such that $g \equiv_{FT} h$ but not $g \equiv_{RT} h$
   c. Find graphs g,h such that $g \equiv_{R} h$ but not $g \equiv_{RT} h$
   d. Find graphs g,h such that $g \equiv_{F} h$ but not $g \equiv_{FT} h$
   e. Find graphs g,h such that $g \equiv_{FT} h$ but not $g \equiv_{R} h$
   f. Find graphs g,h such that $g \equiv_{R} h$ but not $g \equiv_{FT} h$.
4. Prove RTR from the axioms BPA_δ + PR1-PR4 + RE1-RE2, thus proving algebraically that ready trace equivalence implies ready equivalence.
5. Show that the relations $\equiv_{RT}$ and $\equiv_{FT}$ on graphs are also congruences with respect to the operators $\|$, $⫫$, $|$, ∂_H, θ, $\triangleleft$. Thus, we see that we can define the priority operator in ready trace and failure trace semantics.
6. Define an explicit model for ready trace semantics (as we did in 7.2.11 for ready semantics). Do the same for failure trace semantics.
7. Give the ready trace and failure trace semantics for the theory BPA_ε.
8. Let g,h be process graphs. A relation R between nodes of g and h is called a **ready simulation** if, whenever R(s,t), then M(s) = M(t) (the menus are equal) and whenever $s \xrightarrow{a} s'$, there is a node t' with $t \xrightarrow{a} t'$ and R(s', t'). g and h are called **ready similar** if there is a ready simulation between g and h and a ready simulation between h and g.

i. Show that processes a(bc + bd) and abc + a(bc + bd) + abd are ready similar but not bisimilar.

ii. Show that ready similarity is a process equivalence strictly between bisimulation and ready trace equivalence in fig. 57.

7.3.14 NOTES AND COMMENTS

Ready trace semantics is introduced in PNUELI [1985] (there called 'barbed semantics') and also occurs in BAETEN, BERGSTRA & KLOP [1987c], including theorem 7.3.1, theorem 7.3.9 and the Ready Trace Rule. Failure trace semanticsis given in PHILLIPS [1987] under the name 'refusal trace semantics'. There, also axiom FA2 and theorem 7.3.11 occur. The semantic lattice in fig. 57 is from VAN GLABBEEK [1990]. Ready similarity occurs under different names in BLOOM, ISTRAIL & MEYER [1988] and LARSEN & SKOU [1989].

Chapter 8
Sources and related work

8.1 HISTORICAL REMARKS

Process algebra, as described in this book, has for the most part been the work of people at the Centre of Mathematics and Computer Science in Amsterdam. There, J.A. Bergstra and J.W. Klop started with the theory PA in 1982, motivated by a question of J.W. de Bakker (see [BERGSTRA & KLOP [1982]). As a general reference to their work, see BERGSTRA & KLOP [1984b], in which a fairly detailed discussion of related work can be found as well. The most extensive treatment of their work can be found in the Dutch book BAETEN [1986], which was the starting point for this book.

Compared to other concurrency theories, this work is closely related to the work on CCS. The theory of CCS is briefly discussed in the following section 8.2. The seminal work of MILNER [1980] in which CCS was introduced, clearly sets out the goals of algebraic concurrency theory. We may see the theory of ACP^{τ} as a remodularization of CCS. CCS has been worked out and extended in the work of HENNESSY & PLOTKIN [1980] and HENNESSY [1983]. See also HENNESSY & MILNER [1985], GRAF & SIFAKIS [1984] and BROOKES & ROUNDS [1981]. MILNE [1982] has the so-called 'dot calculus', with $\cdot$ as parallel composition, prefix multiplication, two operators for alternative composition (internal and external choice) and, in contrast with Milner, n-ary communication. This group of process theories differs in an important respect from process algebra as treated in this book, and that is that they all start from one specific model and try to find laws that hold in this model, whereas we start from a set of laws and try to find models for them.

Also very important in concurrency theory has been the work of HOARE [1978] on CSP. This theory was based on trace semantics (see 7.1). CSP was later augmented with TCSP in order to facilitate theoretical analysis (see BROOKES, HOARE & ROSCOE [1984], HOARE [1985]). TCSP is based on failure semantics (see 7.2). TCSP later was called CSP again. This second CSP is briefly discussed in section 8.3. Related to the CSP approach is the work of OLDEROG & HOARE [1983], BACK & MANNILA [1982] and PRATT [1982].

Of course, both Hoare and Milner were inspired by earlier work, like for instance DIJKSTRA [1968] and BEKIC [1984] (containing work of Bekic dating back to 1960). After CCS, Milner also developed the calculus SCCS, which has synchronous cooperation (see MILNER [1983]), and cooperated with Milne, who named his calculus CIRCAL (see MILNE [1983]).

The work of Bergstra and Klop was influenced by the topological process theory of DE BAKKER & ZUCKER [1982], who consider process domains as solutions of domain equations, and use topological techniques, as indicated in 2.4.7 (this work was later continued in DE BAKKER & MEYER [1987, 1988] and AMERICA & RUTTEN [1989]). Also CCS had an influence, through the work of KOOMEN [1982], as had TCSP. Other related concurrency theories we can mention are MEIJE (inspired by SCCS), see AUSTRY & BOUDOL [1984], and invariants calculus of APT, FRANCEZ & DE ROEVER [1980].

One of the theories of concurrency that is not directly related is the theory of Petri nets, see REISIG [1985] or PETRI [1980]. Petri nets give a graphical presentation of parallel processes; in Petri net semantics even less processes are identified than in bisimulation semantics, for instance, the axiom CM1 is rejected. Other concurrency theories we can mention are temporal logic (predicate logic enriched with operators to be able to speak about points of time and time periods; there is a lot of literature about this subject, in GRAF & SIFAKIS [1984] we find a relation with CCS) and trace theory (the theory in which only traces of a process are considered, see 7.1), see e.g. MAZURKIEWICZ [1984], MEYER [1985] and the Dutch group of REM [1983], VAN DE SNEPSCHEUT [1985], TIJMEN UDDING [1984], KALDEWAIJ [1986] and others.

A number of issues that are directly related to the process algebra theory as treated in this book have been left out. We do not even provide references to more advanced topics such as probabilistic processes, mobility, real time, real space, algebraic approaches to true concurrency, topics that are the subject of current research. Furthermore, we do not consider relations between process algebra and logic, as in HENNESSY & MILNER [1985], STIRLING [1990] or DE NICOLA & VAANDRAGER [1990]. Also, formulation of process semantics in terms of testing is not considered, see DE NICOLA & HENNESSY [1984], ABRAMSKY [1987], HENNESSY [1988b], KUURMAN [1990]. To conclude, we mention a number of other issues that are not treated, in no particular order:

- the relation of process algebra with Hoare's logic, see PONSE [1989], PONSE & DE VRIES [1989];
- more advanced protocol verification, see GROENVELD [1987], VAANDRAGER [1990c], MULDER [1990a], MULDER [1990b], VAN RENESSE [1989];
- verification of systolic algorithms, see KOSSEN & WEIJLAND [1990], WEIJLAND [1987], MULDER & WEIJLAND [1990], KOSSEN & WEIJLAND [1987], VERHOEF [1990];
- research concerning machine readable forms of process algebra, such as the specification languages PSF (see MAUW & VELTINK [1988], MAUW & VELTINK [1989a], MAUW & VELTINK [1989b], MAUW & WIEDIJK [1989]), CRL (see SPECS [1989]), LOTOS (see ISO [1987]);
- a constructive version of AIP, see MAUW [1987];
- a POOL implementation of ACP, see VRANCKEN [1988];
- connections of process algebra with database modelling, see WIERINGA [1990].

8.2 CCS

CCS is short for **Calculus of Communicating Systems**, and is mainly the work of Milner. The original reference is MILNER [1980], now superseded by MILNER [1989].

8.2.1 ATOMIC ACTIONS

In CCS we have for every atomic action precisely one other atomic action with which it communicates. Therefore we have a set **names** Δ, and a set of **co-names** $\overline{\Delta} = \{\bar{a} : a \in \Delta\}$. a communicates with $\bar{a}$ only, however the result is not some atomic action, but τ (the silent step). $A = \Delta \cup \overline{\Delta}$, $A_\tau = A \cup \{\tau\}$.
Further, CCS has **renamings**: every function $R: \Delta \to \Delta$ yields a renaming since R can be extended to A_τ by putting $R(\tau) = \tau$ and $R(\bar{a}) = \overline{R(a)}$.

8.2.2 ALTERNATIVE COMPOSITION

As in ACP (+).

8.2.3 SEQUENTIAL COMPOSITION

CCS does not have the general multiplication $\cdot$, but only **prefix multiplication**: if $a \in A_\tau$ and x is a process then ax is a new process. The starting process is NIL (**inaction**), later called 0 in MILNER [1989]. NIL is as δ, however CCS does not have successful termination: in ACP we both have a and $a\delta$, but in CCS we only have aNIL.

8.2.4 PARALLEL COMPOSITION

The operator $|$ in CCS is like our $\|$, only with a restricted communication format, as indicated in 8.2.1. There are no auxiliary operators like our left-merge or communication merge.

8.2.5 RESTRICTION

This operator can be compared to encapsulation in process algebra: if x is a process, and $a \in A$, then $x \backslash a$ is Milner's notation for $\partial_{\{a,\bar{a}\}}(x)$.

8.2.6 ABSTRACTION

There is no abstraction operator in CCS, as it is included in the definition of communication (see 8.2.1). However, we can express abstraction by means of $\backslash$, $|$ and μ (see 8.2.7): $\tau_{\{a\}}(x)$ is represented in CCS by the process $(x \,|\, \mu y.\bar{a}y)\backslash a$.

8.2.7 RECURSION

If $x = t(x)$ is a recursive equation, then $\mu x.t(x)$ is a process satisfying this equation. If the equation is guarded then this is its unique solution. If the equation has more than one solution, Milner has a method to pick out one of them, which will be $\mu x.t(x)$.

8.2.8 SEMANTICS

The semantics of CCS is bisimulation semantics (see section 7.1). CCS is not an axiomatic theory, but instead has a fixed model, a transition model with as a congruence relation **observational congruence**, discussed in section 5.8.

8.2.9 EXERCISES

1. Give an axiom system for CCS.
2. Give action relations for the operators of CCS.

8.2.10 NOTES AND COMMENTS

This section is based on VAN GLABBEEK [1986]. Another reference is BROOKES [1983].

8.3 CSP

CSP is short for **Communicating Sequential Processes**, and is mainly the work of Hoare. In HOARE [1978] the term CSP is used for a certain concurrency theory, based on trace semantics. Later on, however, it was replaced by TCSP ('Theoretical CSP') that was based on failure semantics. Unfortunately, the theory TCSP now is very often referred to as CSP, as in HOARE [1985]. This second CSP is discussed in this section.

8.3.1 ATOMIC ACTIONS

An alphabet A is given. In CSP an $a \in A$ only communicates with itself, and the result is a again (in terms of process algebra: $\gamma(a,a) = a$). CSP does not have τ.

8.3.2 ALTERNATIVE COMPOSITION

CSP has two choice operators: external choice $\Box$ and internal choice $\sqcap$. $\Box$ is deterministic: the choice depends on the environment, so it can be manipulated; $\sqcap$ is non-deterministic, and cannot be influenced by the environment. A non-deterministic choice can occur when actions that determine the choice are hidden. $\Box$ and $\sqcap$ are both commutative, associative and idempotent (see axioms), so the possibilities of choice form a *set*. We can see the difference between $\Box$ and $\sqcap$ in combination with deadlock: $x \Box \delta = x$, however $x \sqcap \delta \neq x$. A choice $x \sqcap y$ can be represented in process algebra (and CCS) by $\tau x + \tau y$. $\Box$ cannot directly be translated in process algebra; it is not the same as +, since $\Box$ removes all possible non-determinism. $\Box$ however, can be axiomatized in terms of +, $\cdot$ and δ.

8.3.3 SEQUENTIAL COMPOSITION

Like CCS, CSP has prefix multiplication: if $a \in A$ and x is a process, then $a \rightarrow x$ is the CSP notation for $a \cdot x$. The starting process is STOP (**inaction**, **deadlock**). CSP has only one kind of termination, just like CCS.

8.3.4 PARALLEL COMPOSITION

CSP has two operators for parallel composition: $|||$ stands for interleaving without communication (like $\|$ in PA) and $\|$ stands for communication without interleaving (so it only permits communications). For example:

$(a \to STOP \,\square\, b \to STOP) \; ||| \; a \to STOP =$
$\quad a \to (a \to STOP) \,\square\, b \to (a \to STOP) \,\square\, a \to (a \to STOP \,\square\, b \to STOP)$, whereas
$(a \to STOP \,\square\, b \to STOP) \; \| \; a \to STOP = a \to STOP$.

(Using BPA notation, we can use the terms $(a + b) \; ||| \; a = aa + ba + a(a + b)$ and $(a + b) \, \| \, a = a$.)

8.3.5 RESTRICTION, ENCAPSULATION

This operator does not exist in CSP, however, it can be expressed using $\|$, if the alphabet A is finite. For example if $A = \{a,b,c\}$, then $\partial_{\{a\}}(x)$ is represented by the process $x \, \| \, \mu x.(bx \,\square\, cx)$ (with μ as in CCS).

8.3.6 ABSTRACTION

CSP has the **concealment** operator $/a$ (often denoted as $\backslash a$), for $a \in A$: x/a is precisely $\tau_{\{a\}}(x)$. Because CSP has two choice operators, and more processes are identified than in bisimulation semantics, the constant τ is not needed, silent steps can always be eliminated.

8.3.7 RECURSION

Recursion is treated as in CCS. The method of chosing a solution, in case there is more than one, is different in CSP from that in CCS; in CCS, $\mu x.x$ denotes a different process than it does in CSP.

8.3.8 SEMANTICS

CSP works with failure semantics (see section 7.2).

8.3.9 AXIOMS

We present an axiom scheme for CSP, which is complete for finite processes.

In it, we use $P = a_1 \to P_1 \,\square\, a_2 \to P_2 \,\square\, \ldots \,\square\, a_n \to P_n = \mathop{\square}_{i=1}^{n} a_i \to P_i$ and $Q = \mathop{\square}_{j=1}^{m} b_j \to Q_j$.

Also, we define $\mathop{\square}_{i=1}^{0} a_i P_i = STOP$.

External choice:	$x \,\square\, y = y \,\square\, x$
	$x \,\square\, (y \,\square\, z) = (x \,\square\, y) \,\square\, z$
	$x \,\square\, x = x$
	$x \,\square\, STOP = x$
Internal choice:	$x \sqcap y = y \sqcap x$
	$x \sqcap (y \sqcap z) = (x \sqcap y) \sqcap z$
	$x \sqcap x = x$
Distributive laws:	$x \,\square\, (y \sqcap z) = (x \,\square\, y) \sqcap (x \,\square\, z)$
	$x \sqcap (y \,\square\, z) = (x \sqcap y) \,\square\, (x \sqcap z)$
	$a \rightarrow x \sqcap a \rightarrow y = a \rightarrow (x \sqcap y)$
	$a \rightarrow x \,\square\, a \rightarrow y = a \rightarrow (x \sqcap y)$
Communication:	$x \parallel y = y \parallel x$
	$(x \sqcap y) \parallel z = x \parallel z \sqcap y \parallel z$
	$P \parallel Q = \underset{a_i = b_j}{\square}\, a_i \rightarrow (P_i \parallel Q_j)$
Interleaving:	$x \,\vert\vert\vert\, y = y \,\vert\vert\vert\, x$
	$(x \sqcap y) \,\vert\vert\vert\, z = x \,\vert\vert\vert\, z \sqcap y \,\vert\vert\vert\, z$
	$P \,\vert\vert\vert\, Q = \underset{i}{\square}\, a_i \rightarrow (P_i \,\vert\vert\vert\, Q) \,\square\, \underset{i}{\square}\, b_j \rightarrow (P \,\vert\vert\vert\, Q_j)$
Concealment:	$(x \sqcap y)/a = x/a \sqcap y/a$
	$(a \rightarrow x \,\square\, y)/a = x/a \sqcap (x \,\square\, y)/a$
	$(\underset{i}{\square}\, a_i \rightarrow P_i)/a = \underset{i}{\square}\, a_i \rightarrow (P_i/a)$ if all $a_i \neq a$
Recursion:	$\mu x.P = P[x:=\mu x.P]$
	(this is P with $\mu x.P$ substituted for x).

TABLE 90. CSP.

8.3.10 EXERCISES

1. Give an axiomatization of the CSP operators $\square$, $\sqcap$, $\vert\vert\vert$, $\parallel$ in process algebra.
2. Translate the axiom system of 8.3.9 into process algebra, and check that CSP works with failure semantics.

8.3.11 NOTES AND COMMENTS

This section is based on VAN GLABBEEK [1986]. Another reference is BROOKES [1983].

Bibliography

S. ABRAMSKY [1987], *Observation equivalence as a testing equivalence,* Theor. Comp. Sci. 53, pp. 225-241.

L. ACETO & M. HENNESSY [1989], *Termination, deadlock and divergence,* report 6/88, Dept. of Comp. Sci., University of Sussex.

G.J. AKKERMAN [1987], *Knuth-Bendix completions of process algebra axiomatizations,* report IR-135, Dept. of Math. & Comp. Sci., Free University of Amsterdam.

P. AMERICA & J.W. DE BAKKER [1988], *Designing equivalent semantic models for process creation,* Theor. Comp. Sci. 60, pp. 109-176.

P. AMERICA, J.W. DE BAKKER, J.N. KOK & J.J.M.M. RUTTEN [1989], *Denotational semantics of a parallel object-oriented language,* Inf. & Comp. 83, pp. 152-205.

P. AMERICA & J.J.M.M. RUTTEN [1989], *Solving reflexive domain equations in a category of complete metric spaces,* Journal of Comp. & System Sci. 39, pp. 343-375.

K.R. APT, N. FRANCEZ & W.P. DE ROEVER [1980], *A proof system for communicating sequential processes,* TOPLAS 2, pp. 359-385.

D. AUSTRY & G. BOUDOL [1984], *Algèbre de processus et synchronisation,* Theor. Comp. Sci. 30, pp. 91-131.

R.J.R. BACK & H. MANNILA [1982], *On the suitability of trace semantics for modular proofs of communicating processes,* Dept. of Comp. Sci., Univ. of Helsinki.

J.C.M. BAETEN [1986], *Procesalgebra,* Kluwer Programmatuurkunde, Deventer 1986 (in Dutch). Second printing, 1988.

J.C.M. BAETEN & J.A. BERGSTRA [1988a], *Global renaming operators in concrete process algebra,* Inf. & Comp. 78, pp. 205-245.

J.C.M. BAETEN & J.A. BERGSTRA [1988b], *Processen en procesexpressies,* Informatie 30, pp. 214-222 (in Dutch).

J.C.M. BAETEN, J.A. BERGSTRA & J.W. KLOP [1986], *Syntax and defining equations for an interrupt mechanism in process algebra,* Fund. Inf. IX, pp. 127-168.

J.C.M. BAETEN, J.A. BERGSTRA & J.W. KLOP [1987a], *Conditional axioms and α/β–calculus in process algebra,* in: Proc. IFIP Conf. on Formal Description of Programming Concepts III, Ebberup 1986 (M. Wirsing, ed.), North-Holland, Amsterdam, pp. 77-103.

J.C.M. BAETEN, J.A. BERGSTRA & J.W. KLOP [1987b], *On the consistency of Koomen's Fair Abstraction Rule,* Theor. Comp. Sci. 51, pp. 129-176.

J.C.M. BAETEN, J.A. BERGSTRA & J.W. KLOP [1987c], *Ready trace semantics for concrete process algebra with the priority operator,* British Comp. Journal 30, pp. 498-506.

J.C.M. BAETEN & R.J. VAN GLABBEEK [1987a], *Another look at abstraction in process algebra,* in: Proc. 14th ICALP, Karlsruhe 1987 (Th. Ottmann, ed.), LNCS 267, Springer Verlag, pp. 84-94.

J.C.M. BAETEN & R.J. VAN GLABBEEK [1987b], *Merge and termination in process algebra,* in: Proc. FST&TCS 7, Pune 1987 (K.V. Nori, ed.), LNCS 287, Springer Verlag, pp. 153-172.

J.C.M. BAETEN & R.J. VAN GLABBEEK [1989], *Abstraction and empty process in process algebra,* Fund. Inf. XII, pp. 221-241.

J.W. DE BAKKER, J.A. BERGSTRA, J.W. KLOP & J.-J. CH. MEYER [1984], *Linear time and branching time semantics for recursion with merge,* Theor. Comp. Sci. 34, pp. 135-156.

J.W. DE BAKKER & J.-J. CH. MEYER [1987], *Order and metric in the stream semantics of elemental concurrency,* Acta Inf. 24, pp. 491-511.

J.W. DE BAKKER & J.-J. CH. MEYER [1988], *Metric semantics for concurrency,* BIT 28, pp. 504-529.

J.W. DE BAKKER & J.I. ZUCKER [1982], *Processes and the denotational semantics of concurrency,* Inf. & Control 54, pp. 70-120.

K.A. BARTLETT, R.A. SCANTLEBURY & P.T. WILKINSON [1969], *A note on reliable full-duplex transmission over half-duplex lines,* Comm. of the ACM 12, pp. 260-261.

H. BEKIC [1984], *Programming languages and their definition,* (C.B.Jones, ed.), LNCS 177, Springer Verlag.

J.A. BERGSTRA [1988], *ACP with signals,* in: Algebraic and Logic Programming (J. Grabowski, P. Lescanne & W. Wechler, eds.), LNCS 343, Springer Verlag, pp. 11-20.

J.A. BERGSTRA [1990], *A process creation mechanism in process algebra,* in: Applications of Process Algebra (J.C.M. Baeten, ed.), Cambridge University Press, pp. 81-88.

J.A. BERGSTRA & J.W. KLOP [1982], *Fixed point semantics in process algebras,* report IW 206, Math. Centre, Amsterdam. Submitted for publication in Inf. & Control.

J.A. BERGSTRA & J.W. KLOP [1984a], *The algebra of recursively defined processes and the algebra of regular processes,* in: Proc. 11th ICALP, Antwerpen 1984 (ed. J. Paredaens), LNCS 172, Springer Verlag, pp. 82-95.

J.A. BERGSTRA & J.W. KLOP [1984b], *Process algebra for synchronous communication,* Inf. & Control 60, pp. 109-137.

J.A. BERGSTRA & J.W. KLOP [1985], *Algebra of communicating processes with abstraction,* Theor. Comp. Sci. 37, pp. 77-121.

J.A. BERGSTRA & J.W. KLOP [1986a], *Verification of an alternating bit protocol by means of process algebra,* in: Math. Methods of Spec. and Synthesis of Software Systems '85 (eds. W. Bibel & K.P. Jantke), Math. Research 31, Akademie-Verlag Berlin, pp. 9-23. (Also LNCS 215, Springer Verlag, pp. 9-23.)

J.A. BERGSTRA & J.W. KLOP [1986b], *Algebra of communicating processes,* in: Math. & Comp. Sci. I (J.W. de Bakker, M. Hazewinkel & J.K. Lenstra, eds.), CWI Monograph 1, North-Holland, Amsterdam, pp. 89-138.

J.A. BERGSTRA & J.W. KLOP [1986c], *Process algebra: specification and verification in bisimulation semantics,* in: Math. & Comp. Sci. II (M. Hazewinkel, J.K. Lenstra & L.G.L.T. Meertens, eds.), CWI Monograph 4, North-Holland, Amsterdam, pp. 61-94.

J.A. BERGSTRA & J.W. KLOP [1988], *A complete inference system for regular processes with silent moves,* in: Proc. Logic Colloquium, Hull 1986 (F.R. Drake & J.K. Truss, eds.), North-Holland, Amsterdam, pp. 21-81.

J.A. BERGSTRA & J.W. KLOP [1989], *Process theory based on bisimulation semantics,* in: Linear Time, Branching Time and Partial Order in Logics and Models for Concurrency (J.W. de Bakker, W.P. de Roever & G. Rozenberg, eds.), LNCS 354, Springer Verlag, pp. 50-122.

J.A. BERGSTRA, J.W. KLOP & E.-R. OLDEROG [1987], *Failures without chaos: a new process semantics for fair abstraction,* in: Proc. IFIP Conf. on Formal Description of Programming Concepts III, Ebberup 1986 (M. Wirsing, ed.), North-Holland, Amsterdam, pp. 77-103.

J.A. BERGSTRA, J.W. KLOP & E.-R. OLDEROG [1988], *Readies and failures in the algebra of communicating processes,* SIAM Journal on Comp. 17, pp. 1134-1177.

J.A. BERGSTRA, J.W. KLOP & J.V. TUCKER [1985], *Process algebra with asynchronous communication mechanisms,* in: Proc. Seminar on Concurrency (S.D. Brookes, A.W. Roscoe & G. Winskel, eds.), LNCS 197, Springer Verlag, pp. 76-95.

J.A. BERGSTRA & J. TIURYN [1987], *Process algebra semantics for queues,* Fund. Inf. X, pp. 213-224.

J.A. BERGSTRA & J.V. TUCKER [1984], *Top down design and the algebra of communicating processes,* Sci. Comp. Progr. 5, pp. 171-199.

F. BIEMANS & P. BLONK [1986], *On the formal specification and verification of CIM architectures using LOTOS,* Computers in Industry 7, pp. 491-504.

B. BLOOM, S. ISTRAIL & A.R. MEYER [1988], *Bisimulation can't be traced: preliminary report,* in: Proc. 15th POPL, San Diego, Ca., ACM, pp. 229-239.

E. BRINKSMA [1988], *On the design of extended LOTOS – a specification language for open distributed systems,* Ph.D. thesis, University of Twente.

S.D. BROOKES [1983], *On the relationship of CCS and CSP,* in: Proc. 10th ICALP, Barcelona (J.Díaz, ed.), LNCS 154, Springer Verlag, pp. 83-96.

S.D. BROOKES, C.A.R. HOARE & W. ROSCOE [1984], *A theory of communicating sequential processes,* Journal of the ACM 31, pp. 560-599.

S.D. BROOKES & W.C. ROUNDS [1981], *Possible futures, acceptances, refusals and communicating processes,* in: Proc. 22nd Found. of Comp. Sci. Symp., IEEE, New York.

W.S. BROUWER [1990], *Stable signals and observation in a process specification formalism,* M.Sc. Thesis, University of Amsterdam.

M. BROY [1988], *Views on queues,* Sci. Comp. Progr. 11, pp. 65-86.

R. CLEAVELAND & M. HENNESSY [1988], *Priorities in process algebra,* in: Proc. 3rd LICS, Edinburgh, Comp. Society Press, Washington D.C., pp. 193-202.

PH. DARONDEAU [1982], *An enlarged definition and complete axiomatisation of observational congruence of finite processes,* in: Proc. 5th Int'l Symp. on Progr., Aarhus (M. Dezani-Ciancaglini & U. Montanari, eds.), LNCS 137, Springer Verlag, pp. 47-62.

R. DE NICOLA & M. HENNESSY [1984], *Testing equivalences for processes,* Theor. Comp. Sci. 34, pp. 83-133.

R. DE NICOLA, U. MONTANARI & F.W. VAANDRAGER [1990], *Back and forth bisimulations,* report CS-R9021, Centre for Math. & Comp. Sci., Amsterdam. To appear in Proc. CONCUR'90, Amsterdam (J.C.M. Baeten & J.W. Klop , eds.), LNCS, Springer Verlag.

R. DE NICOLA & F.W. VAANDRAGER [1990], *Three logics for branching bisimulation,* in: Proc. 5th Logic in Comp. Sci., Philadelphia, Computer Society Press, Washington D.C., pp. 118-129.

T. DENVIR, W. HARWOOD, M. JACKSON & M. RAY [1985], *The analysis of concurrent systems, Proc. of a Tutorial and Workshop, Cambridge Univ. 1983,* LNCS 207, Springer Verlag.

E.W. DIJKSTRA [1968], *Cooperating sequential processes,* in: Programming Languages (F. Genuys, ed.), Academic Press, New York, pp. 43-112.

J.C. EBERGEN [1988], *A technique to design delay-insensitive VLSI circuits,* Ph.D. Thesis, Eindhoven University of Technology.

N. FRANCEZ [1986], *Fairness,* Springer Verlag.

R.J. VAN GLABBEEK [1986], *Notes on the methodology of CCS and CSP,* report CS-R8624, Centre for Math. & Comp. Sci., Amsterdam.

R.J. VAN GLABBEEK [1987], *Bounded nondeterminism and the approximation induction principle in process algebra,* in: Proc. STACS 1987 (F.J. Brandenburg, G. Vidal-Naquet & M. Wirsing, eds.), LNCS 247, Springer Verlag, pp. 336-347.

R.J. VAN GLABBEEK [1990], *Comparative concurrency semantics, with refinement of actions,* Ph.D. Thesis, Free University, Amsterdam.

R.J. VAN GLABBEEK & F.W. VAANDRAGER [1987], *Petri net models for algebraic theories of concurrency,* in: Proc. PARLE 87, Vol II, Eindhoven (J.W. de Bakker, A.J. Nijman & P.C. Treleaven, eds.), LNCS 259, Springer Verlag, pp. 224-242.

R.J. VAN GLABBEEK & F.W. VAANDRAGER [1989], *Modular specifications in process algebra – with curious queues,* in: Algebraic Methods: Theory, Tools and Applications (M. Wirsing & J.A. Bergstra, eds.), LNCS 394, Springer Verlag, pp. 465-506.

R.J. VAN GLABBEEK & W.P. WEIJLAND [1989], *Branching time and abstraction in bisimulation semantics (extended abstract),* in: Information Processing 89 (G.X. Ritter, ed.), North-Holland, Amsterdam, pp. 613-618.

S. GRAF & J. SIFAKIS [1984], *A modal characterization of observational congruence on finite terms of CCS,* in: Proc. 11th ICALP, Antwerpen (J. Paredaens, ed.), LNCS 172, Springer Verlag, pp. 222-234.

S.A. GREIBACH [1965], *A new normal form theorem for context-free phrase structure grammars,* Journal of the ACM 12, pp. 42-52.

R.A. GROENVELD [1987], *Verification of a sliding window protocol by means of process algebra,* report P8701, Programming Research Group, University of Amsterdam.

J.F. GROOTE [1989], *Transition system specifications with negative premises,* report CS-R8950, Centre for Math. & Comp. Sci., Amsterdam. To appear in Proc. CONCUR'90, Amsterdam (J.C.M. Baeten & J.W. Klop , eds.), LNCS, Springer Verlag.

J.F. GROOTE & F.W. VAANDRAGER [1989], *Structured operational semantics and bisimulation as a congruence (extended abstract),* in: Proc. ICALP 89, Stresa (G. Ausiello, M. Dezani-Ciancaglini & S. Ronchi Della Rocca, eds.), LNCS 352, Springer Verlag, pp. 423-438.

J.F. GROOTE & F.W. VAANDRAGER [1990], *An efficient algorithm for branching bisimulation and stuttering equivalence,* report CS-R9001, Centre for Math. & Comp. Sci., Amsterdam. To appear in: Proc. ICALP, Warwick 1990, LNCS, Springer Verlag.

J.Y. HALPERN & L.D. ZUCK [1987], *A little knowledge goes a long way: simple knowledge-based derivations and correctness proofs for a family of protocols (extended abstract),* in: Proc. 6th Principles of Dist. Comp., Vancouver, ACM, pp. 269-280.

M. HENNESSY [1981], *A term model for synchronous processes,* Inf. & Control 51, pp. 58-75.

M. HENNESSY [1983], *Synchronous and asynchronous experiments on processes,* Inf. & Control 59, pp. 36-83.

M. HENNESSY [1988a], *Axiomatising finite concurrent processes,* SIAM Journal on Comp. 17, pp. 997-1017.

M. HENNESSY [1988b], *Algebraic theory of processes,* MIT Press, Cambridge Ma.

M. HENNESSY & R. MILNER [1985], *Algebraic laws for nondeterminism and concurrency,* Journal of the ACM 32, pp. 137-161.

M. HENNESSY & G. PLOTKIN [1980], *A term model for CCS,* in: Proc. 9th MFCS (P.Dembinski, ed.), LNCS 88, Springer Verlag, pp. 261-274.

C.A.R. HOARE [1978], *Communicating sequential processes,* Comm. of the ACM 21, pp. 666-677.

C.A.R. HOARE [1980], *A model for communicating sequential processes,* in: On the construction of Programs (R. McKeag & A. McNaghton, eds.), Cambridge University Press, pp. 229-243.

C.A.R. HOARE [1985], *Communicating sequential processes,* Prentice Hall International.

ISO [1987], *Information processing systems – open systems interconnection – LOTOS – a formal description technique based on the temporal ordering of observational behaviour,* ISO/TC97/SC21 (E. Brinksma, ed.).

A. KALDEWAIJ [1986], *A formalism for concurrent processes,* Ph.D. Thesis, Eindhoven University of Technology.

J.K. KENNAWAY [1981], *Formal semantics of nondeterminism and parallelism,* Ph.D. Thesis, University of Oxford.

C.J. KOOMEN [1982], *A structure theory for communication network control,* Ph.D. Thesis, Technical University Delft.

L. KOSSEN & W.P. WEIJLAND [1987], *Verification of a systolic algorithm for string comparison,* report CS-R8734, Centre for Math. & Comp. Sci., Amsterdam.

L. KOSSEN & W.P. WEIJLAND [1990], *Correctness proofs for systolic algorithms: palindromes and sorting,* in: Applications of Process Algebra (J.C.M. Baeten, ed.), Cambridge University Press, pp. 89-125.

C.P.J. KOYMANS & J.C. MULDER [1990], *A modular approach to protocol verification using process algebra,* in: Applications of Process Algebra (J.C.M. Baeten, ed.), Cambridge University Press, pp. 261-306.

C.P.J. KOYMANS & J.L.M. VRANCKEN [1985], *Extending process algebra with the empty process ε,* report LGPS 1, Dept. of Phil., State University of Utrecht.

E. KRANAKIS [1987], *Fixed point equations with parameters in the projective model,* Inf. & Comp. 75, pp. 264-288.

L.W. KUURMAN [1990], *The jungle of process semantics,* report P9001, Programming Research Group, University of Amsterdam.

K.G. LARSEN & R. MILNER [1987], *A complete protocol verification using relativized bisimulation,* in: Proc. ICALP 87, Karlsruhe (Th. Ottmann, ed.), LNCS 267, Springer Verlag, pp. 126-135.

K.G. LARSEN & A. SKOU [1989], *Bisimulation through probabilistic testing,* in: Proc. Principles of Progr. Lang. 89, Austin, Tx., ACM, pp. 344-352.

S. MAUW [1987], *A constructive version of the approximation induction principle,* in: Proc. SION Conf. CSN 87, CWI, Amsterdam, pp. 235-252.

S. MAUW [1990], *Process algebra as a tool for the specification and verification of CIM-architectures,* in: Applications of Process Algebra (J.C.M. Baeten, ed.), Cambridge University Press, pp. 53-80.

S. MAUW & G.J. VELTINK [1988], *A process specification formalism,* report P8814, Programming Research Group, University of Amsterdam. To appear in Fund. Inf.

S. MAUW & G.J. VELTINK [1989a], *An introduction to PSF_d,* in: Proc. TAPSOFT 89, Vol. II (J. Díaz & F. Orejas, eds.), LNCS 352, Springer Verlag, pp. 272-285.

S. MAUW & G.J. VELTINK [1989b], *A tool interface language for PSF,* report P8912, Programming Research Group, University of Amsterdam.

S. MAUW & F. WIEDIJK [1989], *Specification of the transit node in PSF_d,* report P8908, Programming Research Group, University of Amsterdam. To appear in Proc. METEOR Workshop Methods based on Formal Specifications, Mierlo 89 (L. Feijs & J.A. Bergstra, eds.), LNCS, Springer Verlag.

A. MAZURKIEWICZ [1984], *Traces, histories, graphs: instances of a process monoid,* in: Proc. Math. Found. Comp. Sci. (M.P. Chytil & V. Koubek, eds.), LNCS 176, Springer Verlag, pp. 115-133.

J.-J.CH. MEYER [1985], *Merging regular processes by means of fixed point theory,* Theor. Comp. Sci. 45, pp. 193-260.

G.J. MILNE [1982], *Abstraction and nondeterminism in concurrent systems,* 3rd Int'l Conference on Distr. Systems, IEEE, pp. 358-364.

G.J. MILNE [1983], *CIRCAL: a calculus for circuit description,* Integration 1, pp. 121-160.

R. MILNER [1980], *A calculus of communicating systems,* LNCS 92, Springer Verlag.

R. MILNER [1983], *Calculi for synchrony and asynchrony,* Theor. Comp. Sci. 25, pp. 267-310.

R. MILNER [1984], *A complete inference system for a class of regular behaviours,* Journal of Comp. & Systems Sci. 28, pp. 439-466.

R. MILNER [1989], *Communication and concurrency,* Prentice Hall International.

F. MOLLER [1989], *Axioms for concurrency,* Ph.D. Thesis, report CST-59-89, Dept. of Comp. Sci., Univ. of Edinburgh.

J.C. MULDER [1990a], *On the Amoeba protocol,* in: Applications of Process Algebra (J.C.M. Baeten, ed.), Cambridge University Press, pp. 147-171.

J.C. MULDER [1990b], *Case studies in process specification and verification,* Ph.D. Thesis, University of Amsterdam.

J.C. MULDER & W.P. WEIJLAND [1990], *Verification of an algorithm for log-time sorting by square comparison,* in: Applications of Process Algebra (J.C.M. Baeten, ed.), Cambridge University Press, pp. 127-145.

E.R. NIEUWLAND [1990], *Proving mutual exclusion with process algebra,* in: Applications of Process Algebra (J.C.M. Baeten, ed.), Cambridge University Press, pp. 45-51.

H.M. OGUZTUZUN [1989], *A game characterization of the observational equivalence of processes,* in: Proc. AMAST Conf., Iowa City Ia., pp. 195-196.

E.-R. OLDEROG & C.A.R. HOARE [1983], *Specification-oriented semantics for communicating processes,* in: Proc. 10th ICALP, Barcelona (J.Díaz, ed.), LNCS 154, Springer Verlag, pp. 561-572.

D.M.R. PARK [1981], *Concurrency and automata on infinite sequences,* in: Proc. 5th GI Conference (P. Deussen, ed.), LNCS 104, Springer Verlag, pp. 167-183.

J. PARROW [1985], *Fairness properties in process algebra – with applications in communication protocol verification,* Ph.D.Thesis, DoCS 85/03, Dept. of Computer Systems, Uppsala University.

G.E. PETERSON & M.E. STICKEL [1981], *Complete sets of reductions for some equational theories,* Journal of the ACM 28, pp. 233-264.

C. PETRI [1980], *Introduction to general net theory,* in: Net Theory and Applications (W. Brauer, ed.), LNCS 84, Springer Verlag, pp. 1-19.

I.C.C. PHILLIPS [1987], *Refusal testing,* Theor. Comp. Sci. 50, pp. 241-284.

G.D. PLOTKIN [1983], *An operational semantics for CSP,* in: Proc. Conf. Formal Description of Progr. Concepts II, Garmisch 1982 (D. Bjørner, ed.), North-Holland, Amsterdam, pp. 199-225.

A. PNUELI [1985], *Linear and branching structures in the semantic and logics of reactive systems,* in: Proc. 12th ICALP, Nafplion (W. Brauer, ed.), LNCS 194, Springer Verlag, pp. 15-32.

A. PONSE [1989], *Process expressions and Hoare's logic,* report CS-R8905, Centre for Math. & Comp. Sci., Amsterdam. To appear in Inf. & Comp.

A. PONSE & F.-J. DE VRIES [1989], *Strong completeness for Hoare logics of recursive processes: an infinitary approach,* report CS-R8957, Centre for Math. & Comp. Sci., Amsterdam.

V.R. PRATT [1982], *On the composition of processes,* in: Proc. 9th POPL, ACM, pp. 213-223.

W. REISIG [1985], *Petri nets,* EATCS monograph on TCS, Springer Verlag.

M. REM [1983], *Partially ordered computations, with applications to VLSI design,* in: Proc. Found. of Comp. Sci. IV.2 (J.W. de Bakker & J. van Leeuwen, eds.), MC Tract 159, Math. Centre, Amsterdam, pp 1-44.

M. REM [1987], *Trace theory and systolic computations,* in: Proc. PARLE Vol. I (J.W. de Bakker, A.J. Nijman & P.C. Treleaven, eds.), LNCS 258, Springer Verlag, pp. 14-33.

R. VAN RENESSE [1989], *The functional processing model,* Ph.D. Thesis, Free University, Amsterdam.

J.L.A. VAN DE SNEPSCHEUT [1985], *Trace theory and VLSI design,* LNCS 200, Springer Verlag, 1985.

SPECS [1989], *Definition of MR and CRL Version 2.0,* Deliverable WP5.4, RACE project 1046, SPECS.

C. STIRLING [1990], *Modal and temporal logics,* in: Handbook of Logic in Computer Science (S. Abramsky, ed.), to appear.

J. TIJMEN UDDING [1984], *Classification and composition of delay-insensitive circuits,* Ph.D. Thesis, Eindhoven University of Technology.

F.W. VAANDRAGER [1986], *Verification of two communication protocols by means of process algebra,* report CS-R8608, Centre for Math. & Comp. Sci., Amsterdam.

F.W. VAANDRAGER [1990a], *Process algebra semantics of POOL,* in: Applications of Process Algebra (J.C.M. Baeten, ed.), Cambridge University Press, pp. 173-236.

F.W. VAANDRAGER [1990b], *Some observations on redundancy in a context,* in: Applications of Process Algebra (J.C.M. Baeten, ed.), Cambridge University Press, pp. 237-260.

F.W. VAANDRAGER [1990c], *Algebraic techniques for concurrency and their application,* Ph.D. Thesis, University of Amsterdam.

C. VERHOEF [1990], *On the register operator,* report P9003, Programming Research Group, University of Amsterdam.

J.L.M. VRANCKEN [1986], *The algebra of communicating processes with empty process,* report FVI 86-01, Dept. of Comp. Sci., Univ. of Amsterdam.

J.L.M. VRANCKEN [1988], *The implementation of process algebra specifications in POOL-T,* report P8807, Programming Research Group, University of Amsterdam.

D.J. WALKER [1990], *Bisimulation and divergence,* Inf. & Comp. 85, 1990, pp. 202-241.

W.P. WEIJLAND [1987], *A systolic algorithm for matrix-vector multiplication,* in: Proc. SION Conf. CSN 87, CWI, Amsterdam, pp. 143-160.

W.P. WEIJLAND [1989a], *The algebra of synchronous processes,* Fund. Inf. XII, pp. 139-162.

W.P. WEIJLAND [1989b], *Synchrony and asynchrony in process algebra,* Ph.D. Thesis, University of Amsterdam.

R. WIERINGA [1990], *Algebraic foundations for dynamic conceptual models,* Ph.D. Thesis, Free University, Amsterdam.

G. WINSKEL [1982], *Event structure semantics for CCS and related languages,* in: Proc. 9th ICALP, Aarhus (M. Nielsen & E.M. Schmidt, eds.), LNCS 140, Springer Verlag, pp. 561-576.

Glossary

abstract datatype 10
abstraction 113
action graph 20
action relations 18
- for BPA 18, 24
- for PA 69, 79
- for ACP 95, 101
- generalized 19, 146
- with recursion 28
- for renaming 89
- and observation congruence 166
- with priority operator 169
algebra 6
- Σ-algebra 7
- $\mathbb{A}$ is an algebra for ... 8
- initial 8, 19, 24
Alternating Bit Protocol 108, 160
alphabet 175
Approximation Induction Principle 33
- Restricted 35
arity 3
associativity 6
atomic actions (steps) 16
axioms 3
- conditional 6, 177
- of standard concurrency 71, 97, 125, 128, 202
axiomatization
- sound 142
- complete 8, 209
bag 84, 85, 179, 198
Basic Process Algebra 15
binary function 3
bisimulation
- autobisimulation 51
- k-bisimulation 159
- rooted branching (rb-) 130, 143
- semi-branching 132
- strong 130
- τ-bisimulation 162
- maximal 48, 50
- on $\mathbb{P}$ 38
- on $\mathbb{G}^\infty$ 47
- semantics 209
branching structure 16
broadcast 195
cause 192
channel 92
- internal 92
- external 92
chaining operator 185
chaos 154
cluster 156
Cluster Fair Abstraction Rule 156
colouring (of a graph) 49
- consistent 49, 134
- canonical 50, 135

communication 91
- asymmetric 193
- asynchronous 190
- function 91
- merge 93
commutativity 16
complete algebra 8
completeness theorem 41
complexity of equivalences 167
composition
- alternative 16
- sequential 16
computable process 150
concatenation (of strings) 62
concealment 225
confluence 12
congruence 8
conservative
- extension 30, 70, 96, 124, 128, 201
- cluster 156
constructible process 145, 182
context 4
contraction (of edges) 140
cooperation
- synchronous 199
counter 64, 85
critical pairs 12
cycle (in a graph) 45
deadlock 21, 154, 224
- having deadlock 25, 79, 126
delay 152
Delay Rule 153
depth (of a node) 54, 137
derivability 4
(right) distributivity 16
divergence 151
- catastrophic 154
- divergence free (process graph) 147
- explicit divergence 152
- colour-divergent 153
domain (of an algebra) 6
edge (in a graph) 45
effect 192
elimination theorem 70, 96, 124, 128, 201
encapsulation 88
- operator 88
equations
- conditional 6
- derived 4
- recursive 25
equivalence relation 4
exit 156
expansion theorem 71, 98, 125, 128
failure
- axiom 215
- equivalent 213
- pair 212
- set 213
- trace 217
- trace rule 218
- trace set 217
- trace equivalent 217
fairness 151
- fair abstraction 154

- fairness principle 154
- Koomen's Fair Abstraction Rule 155
get 194
graph 45
- acyclic, cyclic 45
- canonical 60
- countably branching 45
- finite 45
- finitely branching 45
- regular 45
- subgraph 45
- trivial 45
- process graph 45
guarded 27, 145
- completely guarded 27
handshaking 92, 98, 193
idempotency 16
identity
- syntactical 5
inaction 223, 224
interleaving (arbitrary) 67
interpretation 7
isomorphic 8, 46

Limit Rule 44
localization 180
location operator 92
label (of an edge) 45
layered (bisimulation) 54, 137
livelock 154
mail through a communication channel 191
merge 68, 80, 103
- left-merge 68
- n-merge 73
multiplication 16
- prefix multiplication 17, 223
multi-set 191
model 6
- 𝔸 is a model for ... 8
- term model 10, 39
- projective limit model 42, 142
- graph model 45, 55, 57, 129
name 223
- co-name 223
natural extension 202, 203
node (in a graph) 45
- endnode 45
- internal 45
- termination node 45
- double 139
- manifestly inert 139
non-determinism 16, 17
- bounded 34, 147
- bounded up to depth n 34, 147
norm (of a node) 139
normal form 11
- abstract 135
- being in normal form 11
- having a normal form 11
- head normal form 31
- of a graph 50
- head normal form with silent step 122
normalization
- strong 12
- ground 12
observation equivalence 162, 224
observation 206
- function 206
- action 206
- operator 207
occurrence (of a term) 5
one-bit buffer 105
operator symbol 3
path (in a graph) 45
port 92, 202
prefix closed trace set 211
priority operator 169
process 16
- creation 197
- deterministic 212
- empty 23
- finite 31
- (finitely) definable 32
- subprocess 60
- regular 60
projection 29, 55
- projection theorem 33, 146
- with termination 35
- with silent step 121
projective
- sequence 42
- limit 43
put 194
queue 114, 117, 149
realization 192
recursion 26, 88, 145
Recursive Definition Principle 33
- Restricted 35
Recursive Specification Principle 34
reduction 11
- one step reduction 11
- reduction relation 11
ready
- axioms 214
- equivalent 213
- pair 212
- set 213, 215
- similar 219
- simulation 219
- trace 216
- trace rule 217
- trace set 217

- trace equivalent 217
reflexivity 4
renaming 87, 223
- operator 87
- simple 87
response 192
restriction operator 182
rewrite rule 11
root (of a graph) 45
- unwinding 51
- condition 130, 162
satisfaction 7
saturated graph 167
semantics 6
- operational 18
sharing (edges) 140
signal 205
- atomic 205
- insertion 206
- observation operator 207
- root signal operator 206
sieve of Eratosthenes 199
signature 3
solution (of a recursive equation) 26
sound axiomatization 8
specification
- algebraic 6
- conditional 6
- equational 3
- recursive 26
- linear 60
specifiable process 145
stack 62, 207
- terminating 64
state (of a process) 60
- state space 185
- state operator 186
- generalized state operator 188
step (atomic action) 16
- silent 119, 164
- generalized 163
- communication step 91
stimulus 192
stuttering lemma 132
substitution 4
summand 19
- BPA-summand 19
symbols
- constant 4
- function 4
symmetry 4
synchronous
- communication 91
- composition 200
- cooperation 199
syntax 6
termination 21
- operator 76
terms
- basic 17, 22, 23, 121, 127
- ground, closed 4
- open 4
- subterms 5
term rewriting system 11
theory 6
tick 18
trace 18, 181
- axiom 211
- coloured 50
- abstract coloured 50
- extended 210
- extended trace set 210
- semantics 210
- set 182
- prefix closed trace set 211
transitivity 5
tree 45
two-bit buffer 151
unary function 3
unless operator 170
universe (of an algebra) 6
universal quantification 7
variable
- bound variable 4
- root variable 26
vector 202
well-founded 28
workcell 203

Index of names

S. Abramsky	222
L. Aceto	160
G.J. Akkerman	99
P. America	190, 199, 222
K.R. Apt	222
D. Austry	222
R.J.R. Back	221
J.W. de Bakker	21, 29, 38, 45, 190, 199, 212, 221, 222
J.C.M. Baeten	25, 29, 38, 43, 45, 61, 79, 90, 101, 117, 126, 129, 151, 160, 168, 174, 179, 185, 190, 197, 219, 221
K.A. Bartlett	114
H. Bekic	70, 221
J.A. Bergstra	21, 25, 29, 38, 43, 45, 61, 63, 66, 69, 70, 75, 83, 87, 90, 93, 96, 99, 105, 108, 114, 117, 122, 126, 144, 151, 160, 162, 168, 174, 179, 185, 190, 197, 199, 205, 208, 212, 221, 222
F. Biemans	205
P. Blonk	205
B. Bloom	219
G. Boudol	222
E. Brinksma	174
S.D. Brookes	160, 216, 221, 224, 225
W.S. Brouwer	208
M. Broy	117
R. Cleaveland	174
Ph. Darondeau	216
R. De Nicola	168, 216, 222
T. Denvir	117

E.W. Dijkstra 221
J.C. Ebergen 179
N. Francez 160, 222
R.J. van Glabbeek 21, 25, 29, 38, 43, 45, 61, 70, 79, 96, 101, 114, 117, 122, 126, 129, 144, 151, 160, 168, 219, 224, 225
S. Graf 221, 222
S.A. Greibach 29
R.A. Groenveld 190, 222
J.F. Groote 168, 174
J.Y. Halpern 114
W. Harwood 117
M. Hennessy 92, 96, 160, 174, 216, 221, 222
C.A.R. Hoare 21, 25, 29, 90, 117, 160, 179, 212, 216, 221, 224
S. Istrail 219
M. Jackson 117
A. Kaldewaij 212, 222
J.K. Kennaway 216
J.W. Klop 21, 25, 29, 38, 43, 45, 61, 63, 66, 69, 70, 75, 83, 87, 93, 96, 99, 105, 108, 114, 126, 144, 151, 160, 162, 168, 174, 179, 205, 212, 216, 219, 221, 222
J.N. Kok 190
C.J. Koomen 160, 222
L. Kossen 222
C.P.J. Koymans 25, 66, 79, 114
E. Kranakis 29, 45,
L.W. Kuurman 222
K.G. Larsen 114, 219
H. Mannila 221
S. Mauw 205, 222
A. Mazurkiewicz 222
A.R. Meyer 219
J.-J.Ch. Meyer 212, 222
G.J. Milne 29, 221, 222
R. Milner 21, 25, 29, 61, 63, 90, 114, 122, 144, 166, 205, 212, 221, 222, 223
F. Moller 70
U. Montanari 168
J.C. Mulder 114, 222
H.M. Oguztuzun 43
E.-R. Olderog 160, 216, 221
D.M.R. Park 61, 212
J. Parrow 160
G.E. Peterson 99
C. Petri 222

I.C.C. Phillips 219
G.D. Plotkin 21, 221
A. Pnueli 219
A. Ponse 222
V.R. Pratt 117, 221
M. Ray 117
W. Reisig 222
M. Rem 108, 212, 222
R. van Renesse 222
W.P. de Roever 222
W. Roscoe 160, 216, 221
W.C. Rounds 221
J.J.M.M. Rutten 190, 222
R.A. Scantlebury 114
J. Sifakis 221, 222
A. Skou 219
J.L.A. van de Snepscheut 222
M.E. Stickel 99
C. Stirling 222
J. Tiuryn 117
J.V. Tucker 75, 99
J. Tijmen Udding 222
F.W. Vaandrager 25, 90, 114, 117, 160, 168, 174, 185, 190, 222
G.J. Veltink 222
C. Verhoef 190, 222
J.L.M. Vrancken 25, 66, 79, 101, 222
F.-J. de Vries 222
D.J. Walker 160
W.P. Weijland 61, 122, 144, 168, 205, 222
F. Wiedijk 222
R. Wieringa 222
P.T. Wilkinson 114
G. Winskel 93
L.D. Zuck 114
J.I. Zucker 21, 29, 38, 45, 212, 222

Index of symbols and notation

ALGEBRA

(Σ,E)	equational specification	3
Σ	signature	3
$\vdash$	derivability	4
$\models$	satisfiability	7
C[ ]	context	4
$\equiv$	syntactical identity	5
$G \Rightarrow s=t$	conditional equation	6
$\frac{G}{s=t}$	conditional equation	6
$\mathbb{A}$	algebra	6
$\mathbb{A}/R$	algebra modulo a congruence relation	9
$Alg(\Sigma,E)$	set of Σ-algebras that satisfy E	8
$I(\Sigma,E)$	initial algebra	8
$I(\Sigma)$	set of closed terms over signature Σ	10
(Σ,R)	term rewriting system	3
$\rightarrow$	one step reduction	11
$\rightarrow$	reduction relation	11
$\mathbb{N}$	natural numbers	6

CONSTANTS, PROCESSES

A	set of atomic actions	15
$A^{\mathcal{P}}$	set of atomic vectors	201
ATS	set of atomic signals	205
C	set of special constants	87
S	set of signals	205
δ	deadlock, lock, inaction	22
$\boldsymbol{\delta}$	vector of δ's	201

ε	empty process	23
τ	silent step	119
1	idle action	199
1	vector of 1's	201
Δ	delay	152
a^{ω}	solution of $X = a \cdot X$	26, 43
$brc_j(d)$	broadcast message d at port j	194
$c_j(d)$	communicate message d at port j	92
$get_j(d)$	get message d at port j	194
$put_j(d)$	put message d at port j	193
$r_j(d)$	receive message d at port j	92
$s_j(d)$	send message d at port j	92
a(m,s)	action function	185
s(m,a)	effect function	185
$c\uparrow d$	potential send message d at port j	190
$c\Uparrow d$	realized send message d at port j	190
$c\downarrow d$	potential receive message d at port j	190
$c\Downarrow d$	realized receive message d at port j	190

OPERATORS

$+$	alternative composition	15
$\sum_i x_i$	alternative composition, sum notation	22
$\cdot$	sequential composition	15
$\prod_i x_i$	sequential composition, product notation	78
$\parallel$	parallel composition, merge	67
$\lfloor\!\lfloor$	left-merge	67
$\mid$	communication merge	93
$\mid$	synchronous merge	199
$x^{\underline{n}}$	n-merge	73
$\surd$	termination operator	76
$\circ$	composition of functions or operators	87
$\lhd$	unless operator	170
∇_Z	restriction operator	182
$\gg$	chaining operator	184
1_I	abstraction operator	200
[.,.]	(root) signal insertion operator	205
/	(signal) observation operator	206
α	alphabet operator	175
δ_H	encapsulation operator	88
∂_H	encapsulation operator	88
γ	communication function	91
θ	priority operator	169
λ_s^m	state operator	185
Λ_s^m	generalized state operator	187

ν_B	localization operator	179
π_n	projection operator	29, 35
$\tilde{\pi}_n$	alternative projection operator	37
ρ	root unwinding	51
ρ_f	renaming operator	87
τ_I	abstraction operator	121
ϕ	process creation function	197
B_n	bounded non-determinism	34, 147
E_ϕ	process creation operator	197
graph	turning a term into a graph	56
id	identity function	87
G	canonical graph	60
obs	observation function	206
S	root signal operator	205
term	turning a graph into a term	55
tr	trace operator	181
tr*	turning a term into an extended trace set	211
tree	turning a graph into a tree	53

MODELS AND EQUIVALENCES

$\mathbb{A}$	initial algebra	19
$\mathbb{A}^n$	finite model	43
$\mathbb{A}^\infty$	projective limit model	42
$\mathbb{F}$	set of finite acyclic process graphs	46
$\mathbb{G}$	set of finitely branching process graphs	46
$\mathbb{G}^\infty$	set of countably branching process graphs	46
$\mathbb{P}$	set of process expressions	38
$\mathbb{P}_\delta$	set of process expressions with deadlock	41
$\mathbb{P}_\varepsilon$	set of process expressions with empty process	41
$\mathbb{R}$	set of regular process graphs	46
$\mathbb{T}$	algebra of trace sets	182
$\mathbb{T}^*$	set of extended trace sets	211
$\mathbb{0}$	trivial process graph	45
$(g)_s$	subgraph of g from node s	45
N(g)	normal form of a process graph	50
$N_a(g)$	abstract normal form of a process graph	135
$\underline{\leftrightarrow}$	(strong) bisimulation	38, 47
$\underline{\leftrightarrow}_b$	branching bisimulation	130, 143
$\underline{\leftrightarrow}_{rb}$	rooted branching bisimulation	130, 143
$\underline{\leftrightarrow}_\tau$	τ-bisimulation	162
$\underline{\leftrightarrow}_{r\tau}$	rooted τ-bisimulation	162
$\equiv_F$	failure equivalence	213
$\equiv_{FT}$	failure trace equivalence	217
$\equiv_R$	ready equivalence	213

$\equiv_{RT}$	ready trace equivalence	217

AXIOMS, PROOF RULES AND AXIOM SYSTEMS

A1-5	axioms of BPA	16
A6-7	deadlock axioms	22
A8-9	empty process axioms	23
AB1-7	alphabet axioms	175
ACP	Algebra of Communicating Processes	93
ACP_ε	ACP with empty process	100
ACP_θ	ACP with priorities	170
ACP_τ	ACP for observation equivalence	165
ACP^τ	ACP with silent step	122
ACP^τ_ε	ACP with empty process and silent step	126
ACPS	ACP with signals and observation	206
AIP	Approximation Induction Principle	33
AIP^-	Restricted AIP	34, 35
ASP	Algebra of Synchronous Processes	199
B1,2	axioms for silent step	121
BE	axiom for silent step in the presence of the empty process	127
BPA	Basic Process Algebra	16
BPA_δ	BPA with deadlock	22
BPA_ε	BPA with empty process	23
$BPA_{\delta\varepsilon}$	BPA with deadlock and empty process	23
$BPA_{\delta\tau}$	BPA with deadlock for observation equivalence	164
BPA^τ_δ	BPA with deadlock and silent step	121
$BPA^\tau_{\delta\varepsilon}$	BPA with deadlock, empty process and silent step	127
CA1-4	conditional alphabet axioms	177
CF1,2	axioms of ACP	94
CM1-9	axioms of ACP	94
CTM1	axiom of ACP_ε	100
D0	axiom of ACP_ε	100
D0	axiom of ACP_τ	165
D1-4	encapsulation axioms	88
DE_n	Delay Rule	153
FA1	failure axiom	215
FA2	failure trace rule	217
GS1-5	axioms for generalized state operator	187
$KFAR^b_n$	Koomen's Fair Abstraction Rule	155
$KFAR^b$	Koomen's Fair Abstraction Rule	155
$KFAR^-$	abstraction of unstable divergence	159
$CFAR^b$	Cluster Fair Abstraction Rule	156
LR	Limit Rule	44
M1-4	axioms of PA	68
MSI1-3	axioms of ACPS	206

O1-7	axioms of ACPS	206
OCM	axiom of ACPS	206
P1-6	priority axioms	170
PA	Process Algebra	68
PA_δ	PA with deadlock	75
PA_ε	PA with empty process	76
PR1-4	projection axioms	29
PRE1-4	projection axioms with empty process	35
PRT1,2	projection axioms for silent step	121
RDP	Recursive Definition Principle	33
RDP^-	Restricted RDP	34, 35
RE1,2	ready axioms	214
RN0-3	renaming axioms	87
RR1,2	renaming axioms	87
RS1-4	signal insertion axioms	205
RSP	Recursive Specification Principle	34
RTR	ready trace rule	217
S1-4	axioms of root signal operator	205
SC1-5	axioms of ASP	200
SO1-5	axioms for state operator	185
T1-3	axioms for observation equivalence	164
TC1-4	axioms of ACP_τ	165
TE1-4	axioms of PA_ε	77
TH1-3	priority axioms	170
TI0	axiom of ACP^τ	127
TI0	axiom of ACP_τ^ε	165
TI1-4	abstraction axioms	121
TM1-4	axioms of PA_ε	77
TM1,2	axioms of ACP_τ	165
TM5,6	axioms of ACP_ε	100
TR	trace axiom	211
U1-4	axioms of ASP	200

OTHERS

$\xrightarrow{a}$	action relation	18, 24, 46
$\xrightarrow{a}\surd$	action relation	18
$\stackrel{\sigma}{\twoheadrightarrow}$	sequence of action relations	18, 46
$\Rightarrow$	generalized τ-step	129
$\stackrel{a}{\Rightarrow}$	generalized a-step	163
$\rightarrow_F$	graph rewriting	140
$\downarrow$	successful termination	24, 45
$\Downarrow$	generalized termination	134
$\leq$	summand inclusion	19, 21
$<$	priority ordering on atomic actions	169

$\xrightarrow{u}$	occurs unguarded in	28
$\langle X \mid E \rangle$	solution of a recursive specification	28
$a \Vdash b$	*a* causes *b*	192
$\mathcal{P}$	set of ports	201
(σ, X)	ready pair	212
$[\sigma, X]$	failure pair	212